CU00547213

Social
Development

REVIEW OF PERSONALITY AND SOCIAL PSYCHOLOGY

Editor

Nancy Eisenberg, *Arizona State University*

Social Development

Editor
NANCY EISENBERG

15

REVIEW of PERSONALITY and SOCIAL PSYCHOLOGY

Published in cooperation with the Society for Personality and Social Psychology, Inc.

SAGE Publications
International Educational and Professional Publisher
Thousand Oaks   London   New Delhi

For information address:

 Sage Publications, Inc.
2455 Teller Road
Thousand Oaks, California 91320

SAGE Publications Ltd.
6 Bonhill Street
London EC2A 4PU
United Kingdom

SAGE Publications India Pvt. Ltd.
M-32 Market
Greater Kailash I
New Delhi 110 048 India

Printed in the United States of America

Library of Congress Cataloging-in-Publication Data

ISBN 0-8039-5684-3 — ISBN 0-8039-5685-1 (pbk.)
Review of Personality and Social Psychology ISSN 0270-1987
Library of Congress Card Number 80-649712

95 96 97 98 99 10 9 8 7 6 5 4 3 2 1

Sage Production Editor: Yvonne Könneker

CONTENTS

Editor's Introduction

NANCY EISENBERG

Nancy Eisenberg is Regents' Professor of Psychology at Arizona State University. Her research interests are in social development, including the development of prosocial behavior, empathy, emotionality, and regulation skills. She is author of *The Caring Child* and *Altruistic Emotion, Cognition, and Behavior.*

In discussions of the state of the field of psychology, it is almost a cliche to assert that there is a need for work bridging the subdisciplines (as well as bridging disciplines). Yet even today social psychologists and developmental psychologists study the same or similar processes and behaviors and have no awareness of the overlap. Findings in social psychology frequently raise important questions for developmentalists, or vice versa—questions that often are not recognized by investigators due to their lack of knowledge of work and ideas outside of their own perspectives. This book is an attempt to foster an awareness of the interesting research on the interface of social and developmental psychology.

A social psychologist friend of mine once mentioned that social psychologists tend to start reading and writing books after the first few chapters. What he meant is that the origins of most social psychological phenomena are ignored by social psychologists. But it is difficult to understand a behavior or process without knowledge of its origins and development. In a complementary fashion, developmentalists often are not interested in the outcome of a developmental process in adulthood, factors in adulthood that influence the expression of a behavior or predisposition, or additional development past adolescence (or sometimes even past infancy).

As a developmental psychologist investigating social development, I have had to become a social psychologist, and I urge my developmental students to do the same. I find not only that social psychologists are studying most of

AUTHOR'S NOTE: This book was sponsored by the Society for Personality and Social Psychology. I also thank Margaret Clark, editor of the series, and all the members of the editorial board who helped evaluate the original chapter proposals and provided critiques of the chapters. My participation in this project also was supported by grants from the National Institute of Mental Health (K02 MH00903) and the National Science Foundation (DBS-9208375); I am grateful for their support.

the same topics that I am examining (e.g., empathy, prosocial behavior, emotion, regulation, self-attributions), but also that differences in the theoretical perspectives of the two fields help me think about an issue in a more differentiated and multilevel manner. Indeed, totally new issues can emerge from an awareness and synthesis of developmental and social psychological perspectives. Although the methods typically used by developmentalists and experimental social psychologists differ to some degree, each offers unique possibilities by which to explore questions of interest. On the practical side, some methods are much easier to use with children (e.g., naturalistic observations), whereas some procedures are more feasible with adults (e.g., exposing individuals to relatively distressing stimuli).

Most of the contributors to this volume are interface people with dual identities; the rest are primarily social psychologists or developmental psychologists whose work has been mostly in one subdiscipline but is relevant to research in the other. The unifying thread in this book is not in regard to content; in fact, the authors deal with a broad array of topics. Rather, the unifying theme is the relevance of the issues discussed to both subdisciplines.

Some broad themes do underlie a number of chapters. The first is an emphasis on attributions and related inferential processes. Roberta Corrigan, in "How Infants and Young Children Understand the Causes of Events" (Chapter 1), examines the development of children's understanding of the causes of events, including human behavior. She draws on perspectives from social psychology, cognitive psychology (including cognitive development), and philosophy in considering various conceptual frameworks and integrating empirical findings. Her review of the research suggests that mechanisms that are not central to social psychological theories of causal attributions are basic in the early development of inferences about causality. In addition, she reviews research on the development of event representations in young children, preschoolers' theory of mind, and the role of language in causal understanding.

Rachel Karniol (Chapter 2, "Developmental and Individual Differences in Predicting Others' Thoughts and Feelings: Applying the Transformation Rule Model") presents a model of individuals' inferences about others' internal states, and tests developmental predictions derived from her model (see Karniol, 1990). This model is relevant to an understanding of adults' as well as children's social cognition. Karniol also presents new data from two studies that she is working on. In the first, she is examining developmental differences in children's use of transformational rules. In the second, she is testing hypotheses about a dispositional characteristic (i.e., perspective taking) that appears to be relevant to individual differences in predicting others' thoughts and feelings.

Although considering a quite different issue—parenting—Joan E. Grusec and Norma Mammone (Chapter 3, "Features and Sources of Parents' Attributions About Themselves and Their Children") also draw heavily on attribution theories, as well as work on self-efficacy, cognitive structures, and an understanding of dispositional characteristics. Using these constructs, they grapple with issues related to the development of parents' conceptions of their own children and of themselves as participants in parenting interactions (also see Bugental, 1991; Dix & Grusec, 1985). A particularly interesting aspect of this chapter, and one that is highly relevant to social psychologists studying relationships and adult attachment styles, is the focus on early relationships as a model for adults' cognitive representations of relationships and, consequently, for their parenting-related affect and behavior.

Attributional processes also play a role in some of the topics of other chapters. Lee Jussim and Jacquelynne Eccles (Chapter 4, "Naturally Occurring Interpersonal Expectancies") review the literature on interpersonal expectancies and critically evaluate the hypothesis that people become what significant others such as friends, parents, teachers, and employers expect them to become (Jussim, 1991). Implicit in the notion of self-fulfilling prophecies is the possibility that others' perceptions influence individuals' self-perceptions as well as behaviors. Jussim and Eccles examine whether perceivers' expectancies sometimes create self-fulfilling prophecies in natural settings, or if the apparent effects are due to reality or to perceptual biases on the part of perceivers. It appears that perceivers' naturally developed expectations do sometimes create self-fulfilling prophecies and perceptual biases. These effects are modest, but the real-life consequences of expectancy effects can be costly to individuals and to society.

Diane N. Ruble and Carol S. Dweck (Chapter 5, "Self-Conceptions, Person Conceptions, and Their Development") also discuss inferential processes in a thoughtful and in-depth analysis of self-conceptions and person conceptions (e.g., conceptions of stable personalities). They grapple with the difficult problem of interpreting data that have been viewed as demonstrating that young children have an understanding of traits and personality. Ruble and Dweck conclude that what appears to be an understanding of dispositions often may reflect global evaluations of liking or categorization of individuals as good or bad based on initial descriptions of behavior. They also discuss the motivational and behavioral implications of the more domain-specific, differentiated dispositional conceptions of older children, versus the more global, undifferentiated evaluative concepts of younger children. Further, Ruble and Dweck consider the relevance of findings in the developmental literature to recent social psychological work on trait inference processes among adults; they speculate about the role of affectively charged evaluations in the process of representing others. Because self-conceptions and person conceptions have broad motivational and behavioral consequences, these topics are central to phenomena of interest to both social psychologists and developmentalists.

Other contributors to this volume focus on aspects of cognition other than inferences and attributions. Nancy G. Guerra, L. Rowell Huesmann, and Laura Hanish (Chapter 6, "The Role of Normative Beliefs in Children's Social Behavior") explore the role of cognition in the regulation of social behavior, particularly aggression. Unlike most developmentalists studying aggression from a cognitive orientation, they do not emphasize information-processing skills (see Dodge, 1986); rather, they consider cognitive schemata called normative beliefs. Normative beliefs are defined as an individual's cognitions about the acceptability or unacceptability of behaviors that regulate the corresponding behaviors for himself or herself. Normative beliefs represent abstracted general knowledge that may be linked to internalized self-evaluative responses or external sanctions (or both). These authors deal with the difficult task of conceptually differentiating their construct of normative beliefs from related constructs (e.g., personal beliefs, internalized standards, social norms), present a model of the role of normative beliefs in social behavior, and report preliminary data from research on normative beliefs.

Daphne Blunt Bugental, Eta K. Lin, and Joshua E. Susskind (Chapter 7, "Influences of Affect on Cognitive Processes at Different Ages: Why the Change?") deal with the interesting issue of how affect influences cognition and whether such effects change with age. They summarize the major mechanisms that have been used to account for the relation between affect and cognition (e.g., association networks, motivational processes) and then consider the possible moderating role of development. Based in part on Bugental's research, they argue that age-related differences in dealing with negative affect are partly due to greater autonomic arousal among younger children, which is associated with deficits in cognitive processing. In contrast, negative arousal seems to enhance the processing of older children. The theme of attributions reemerges in this chapter; individual differences in self-attributions of control appear to moderate older children's processing of information.

The topic of emotion is central in two other chapters. In Chapter 8, ("The Development of Emotional Self-Regulation in Infancy and Early Childhood"), Lisa J. Bridges and Wendy S. Grolnick present their conceptualization of emotional self-regulation and its development. They argue that emotional self-regulation is a primary goal of individuals from early infancy on, and that this goal is obtained with social and nonsocial (e.g., orientation of attention) processes. In addition, Bridges and Grolnick discuss developmental trends and individual differences in emotional self-regulation in the early years and beyond, and explore temperamental and relational (e.g., parent-child interaction and attachment) factors that may influence its development.

Stephanie A. Shields approaches the general theme of emotion from a very different perspective (Chapter 9, "The Role of Emotion Beliefs and Values in Gender Development"). Drawing on a social-psychological model of gender in context (e.g., Deaux & Major, 1987) and work on the development of emotion and gender-related beliefs, knowledge, and behavior, Shields argues that societal stereotypes about emotion are central to the acquisition and practice of gender-coded behavior and to our basic concepts of femininity and masculinity. She also develops support for the notion that beliefs about emotion frequently are gender coded (i.e., emotions are expected to be more typical, natural, or appropriate for one sex than the other). A review of relevant social and developmental research is used to garner support for her arguments.

An obvious but underutilized arena for the interface of social and developmental psychology is individual differences in significant psychological constructs across the life span. For example, although temperament in childhood and adult personality are obviously related constructs, there is little contact between these two bodies of literature. Focusing on a different construct, but one that might be related to temperament (e.g., emotion regulation processes, sociability, and shyness), William G. Graziano and Stefanie B. Waschull examine self-monitoring from a developmental perspective (Chapter 10, "Social Development and Self-Monitoring"). They first discuss self-monitoring from the perspective of Lewin's (1935) theory; then they consider self-monitoring in relation to the development of emotion and motivational systems and examine socialization and personality correlates. Finally, they consider self-monitoring in light of the idea that social-cognitive representations may be modularized. Throughout, they bring developmental ideas and research, as well as social psychological theory, to bear on a topic that has been neglected in developmental psychology.

William J. Froming, Richard P. Moser, Paula Mychack, and William Nasby (Chapter 11, "A Control Theory Approach to Social Development") present a piece that is unique in this volume. Their goal is to take a theory used primarily in social psychology—Carver and Scheier's (1981) control theory model of self-regulation—and modify it to deal with an issue of central importance in developmental psychology. Specifically, they use Carver and Scheier's framework to consider the issue of the regulation of *others'* behavior rather than self-regulation, particularly in the parent-child dyad. Within this framework, they analyze the process of the transmission of standards from adult to child, and how the parent as an external regulatory mechanism influences the development of the child's self-regulation. They draw on literature from social and developmental psychology to illustrate and support their arguments and suggest issues for further consideration from a control theory approach.

The chapters in this volume can be viewed as examples of exciting areas of overlap between developmental and social psychology. However, many important areas of interface are not discussed in any detail (if at all) by the contributors to this volume. These include issues such as continuity and change in dispositional characteristics over the life span; the role of socialization in a host of adult characteristics and behaviors including moral behaviors, sympathy, and social and relationship competence; links between early perceptions of the self as an active learner and accomplishments in adulthood; the development of, and individual differences in, stereotyping; and the efficacy of various coping behaviors at different ages and across the life span. Clearly, developmentalists and social psychologists have much to talk about and learn from one another.

REFERENCES

Bugental, D. B. (1991). Affective and cognitive processes within threat-oriented family systems. In I. Sigel, A. V. McGillicuddy-DeLisi, & J. J. Goodnow (Eds.), *Parental belief systems: The psychological consequences for children* (2nd ed., pp. 219-248). Hillsdale, NJ: Erlbaum.

Carver, C. S., & Scheier, M. F. (1981). *Attention and self-regulation: A control-theory approach to human behavior.* New York: Springer-Verlag.

Deaux, K., & Major, B. (1987). Putting gender into context: An interactive model of gender-related behavior. *Psychological Review, 94,* 369-389.

Dix, T. H., & Grusec, J. E. (1985). Parent attribution processes in child socialization. In I. Sigel (Ed.), *Parent belief systems: Their psychological consequences for children* (pp. 201-233). Hillsdale, NJ: Erlbaum.

Dodge, K. A. (1986). A social information processing model of social competence in children. In M. Perlmutter (Ed.), *Minnesota symposium on child psychology* (pp. 77-125). Hillsdale, NJ: Erlbaum.

Karniol, R. (1990). Reading people's minds: A transformation rule model for predicting others' thoughts and feelings. In M. P. Zanna (Ed.), *Advances in experimental social psychology: Vol. 23* (pp. 211-248). San Diego, CA: Academic Press.

Jussim, L. (1991). Social perception and social reality: A reflection-construction model. *Psychological Review, 98,* 54-73.

Lewin, K. (1935). *A dynamic theory of personality* (D. K. Adams & K. E. Zener, Trans.). New York: McGraw-Hill.

How Infants and Young Children Understand the Causes of Events

ROBERTA CORRIGAN

Roberta Corrigan is a Professor of Educational Psychology in the Learning and Development Program at the University of Wisconsin–Milwaukee. She received a Ph.D. in developmental psychology from the University of Denver. She has been examining the relations between language and cognition in her research with both adults and children for the last two decades. She has published more than 25 articles in a variety of cognitive, developmental, and social psychology journals and books. Most recently, she has been investigating how differences in people's causal schemas influence their comprehension and production of language. She is the coeditor of two books, *Linguistic Categorization* and *The Reality of Linguistic Rules*.

The nature of people's causal attributions has been a major topic of interest in social psychology for at least three decades. Most everyday processing involves extracting information from temporally related sequences of social events (e.g., Trafimow & Wyer, 1993). Causal reasoning is a critical component of understanding events.

Attribution theory is concerned with people's social judgments about causes. Kelley's (1967, 1972) model of causal logic, which details how individuals make attributions when presented with multiple sources of information, was a major impetus for social psychology research on adults during the 1970s and 1980s. Mainly within the Piagetian framework, many developmental researchers also attempted to examine the onset of attribution-relevant logic in children (see Kassin, 1981; Ruble & Rholes, 1981, for reviews). Recently, Kelley's view that individuals use scientific methods to understand everyday events has been challenged and Piagetian theory has been criticized for its emphasis on the "child-as-scientist." In addition, researchers have found that infants and young children are much more competent than Piaget had presumed.

The major thesis put forward in this chapter is that causal understanding is a critical, central component of children's and adults' naive theories about

---

AUTHOR'S NOTE: The preparation of this chapter was supported by a University of Wisconsin System sabbatical leave. I would like to thank John Surber and Peggy Denton for their helpful comments on the manuscript.

their physical and social worlds and the concepts embedded within their theories. By the time they are in preschool, children assume that all social behaviors are caused and that most behaviors have psychological causes. Causal reasoning is thus seen as a primary building block for subsequent developments.

In this chapter, I examine the causal understanding of events in the first 6 years of life within the context of current theoretical approaches to adult competence. Young children have had relatively less time than adults to develop sophisticated knowledge bases, therefore their inference processes are simpler. As a result, they exhibit only the most essential social cognitive processing. Kassin and Baron (1986) argue that the most basic determinants of adult social cognition develop early in life and show little variability as a function of age, education, culture, or IQ. In adults, the most basic processes (i.e., those that were the earliest to develop) show less effects of distraction, competing task demands, culture, or individual differences. Thus it is important to examine children's development in order to identify processes that are most likely to be basic for adults.

I begin by contrasting two theoretical frameworks that cite alternative sources of information as basic in making causal attributions. I describe Kelley's (1967, 1972) theory and modifications within the regularity framework and discuss distinctions between automatic and controlled processing and social and nonsocial causality in the context of generative frameworks. I conclude that generative information is more basic than regularity information and consider the possibility that causal reasoning arises from basic perceptual abilities in very early infancy.

In the second section of the chapter, I introduce another group of social psychological models, knowledge-structure approaches, which have been used to describe adults' schemas and scripts. According to these models, adults use world knowledge to make attributions by filling in missing parts of an event. I also review the common-sense theories that underlie adults' schemas and scripts and that they use to explain events. In the final part of the second section, I describe quantitative changes in preschoolers' event representations and qualitative changes in their explanatory theories and demonstrate the critical importance of causal reasoning for both.

In the third section of the chapter, I focus on relations between language and social cognition in the causal reasoning of both children and adults. I argue that, because children lack certain sophisticated linguistic knowledge that is not transparent in the input, the interpretation of events described by language is most likely due to basic social cognitive processing rather than to language itself. I present several examples both of the influence of causal schemas on language and of the influence of social interactions on children's causal explanations. Due to space limitations, I cannot examine all topics relevant to the development of children's attributions. In particular, I do not review research on achievement-related attributions such as that deriving from the work of Weiner. I also do not review the literature on moral judgments, attributions of responsibility, or self-attributions.

The first question I raise concerns the type of information most basic for making causal attributions. White (1989, 1990, 1992) contrasts two types of theories of causality: According to regularity theories, people judge cause and effect on the basis of regularity information such as probabilistic information, abnormal conditions, or covariation; and according to generative theories, causation involves observation of actual events in which an effect is generated (Harre & Madden, 1975) and causal mechanisms are perceived.

REGULARITY INFORMATION
OR GENERATIVE TRANSMISSION?

Judging Causality on the
Basis of Regularity Information

The best-known regularity theory in philosophy is that of Hume, who argues that inferential processes produce causal attributions. Cues such as the spatial and temporal contiguity of two events, their repeated co-occurrence, and the similarity between their characteristics lead people to construct a notion of causality (Shultz & Kestenbaum, 1985). In psychology, White (1990, 1992) includes among regularity theories those of Hewstone and Jaspars (1987), Hilton and Slugoski (1986), and Kelley (1967, 1972).

The social psychological literature stemming from Kelley's (1967, 1972) work has focused on one form of regularity information, covariation, as the primary cue to causality. Kelley believes that people make observations across interpersonal events about covariations over actors (consensus), targets (distinctiveness), and time (consistency) and calculate an intuitive ANOVA independent of content to derive their attributions. Some criticisms of Kelley's theory are as follows:

1. Subjects in typical experiments have information about only half of the cells necessary to calculate the intuitive ANOVA; nevertheless, they generate attributions (Hewstone & Jaspars, 1987).

2. People often show biases not predicted by the covariational model, such as attributing effects to a person rather than to a stimulus or to circumstances (see Cheng & Novick, 1990, for a review).

3. The underlying logic that a person uses to calculate the ANOVA is not specified and is unnecessarily complex (Schneider, 1991; but see Cheng & Novick, 1990).

4. The individual's knowledge about particular situations is ignored (Schneider, 1991).

Recent work on causal attributions has retained the emphasis on regularity information, while modifying Kelley's covariational model in various ways. One set of models emphasizes counterfactual reasoning. When deciding on the cause of an event, people compare the world with alternative states or to their knowledge of likely worlds (Dunning & Parpal, 1989). The attributer asks if it is true that if X had not happened, then Y would not have occurred (see Lipe, 1991, for a review of research on counterfactual reasoning).

Another set of regularity models involves contrastive reasoning, which emphasizes the sufficiency rather than the necessity of a factor. Is it the case that if X occurs and events are allowed to follow their natural course, then Y will occur? Unusual or abnormal events are often those that evoke causal interest. For example, in the abnormal conditions focus model, causality is attributed to an abnormal condition, that is, one that occurs improbably (Hilton & Slugoski, 1986) and is therefore a special case of covariation in which the target effect is abnormal (Cheng & Novick, 1990).

In sum, most social psychological models of causal attribution assert that people make judgments of causality through use of some sort of regularity information such as covariation.

Developmental Insights on Regularity Theories

During the mid-1970s through mid-1980s, researchers investigated developmental changes in the use of rules to generate causal attributions (see Shultz & Kestenbaum, 1985, for a review). Results suggested that preschool children may be able to use covariation information under optimal circumstances (Shultz & Mendolson, 1975), but that more sophisticated use of covariational reasoning may not be available until adolescence or later (Shaklee & Elek, 1988). In particular, covariation is difficult to use when more than one cause-effect instance is present, when the information is presented in summary form, or when there is a temporal delay between the cause and effect (Bar-Tal, 1990). Other causal cues such as temporal priority, similarity, temporal contiguity, and spatial contiguity are more often used by young children, particularly when their understanding is measured via some behavioral indicator rather than verbally (Shultz & Kestenbaum, 1985). Thus work with children is consistent with the view that something other than regularity information must be underlying children's earliest understanding of causality. Following Kassin and Baron's (1986) argument, if regularity information is not developmentally basic, then it is also unlikely to be basic for adult social cognitive processing.

Causality as Generative

Researchers adopting an alternative theoretical approach, deriving from the philosophical tradition of Kant, argue that causal relations are generative (White, 1989, 1990, 1992). Generation means that "causes must literally do something to bring about their effects, either directly or through some intermediary chain of events" (Bullock, 1985, p. 172). Shultz (1982a) argues convincingly that reasoning about social and physical causation is fundamentally similar because in both realms people believe that causes actually generate their effects. However, generation involves mechanisms of energy transmission from a causal entity to an effected entity in physical events and the enactment of intentions to perform a behavior in social events. Thus particular inference rules may be restricted to one domain or the other.

Whether or not an entity has the power to produce causal changes is defined by its chemical, physical, or genetic structure. For example, only animate agents have the power to enact intentions, plans, or purposes. Three-year-olds can sometimes determine whether or not a substance is a causal power. They appear to understand that humans have intentions but may also view involuntary acts (such as sneezes) as intentional (Miller & Aloise, 1989). Kalish and Gelman (1992) asked children to predict whether an object would break based on its substance rather than on its object identity. For example, would a glass frying pan break when dropped? Children who maintained that frying pans of unspecified substance would not break when dropped insisted that a glass frying pan would break. By the age of 3, they had learned the causal implications of some material properties.

White (1989) suggests that covariation information will be preferred over other causal cues if causal relations are basically covariational. Instead, both children and adults prefer information about generative transmission (Shultz & Kestenbaum, 1985; White, 1992). Shultz (1982b) gave children between 3 and 15 years of age conflicting information from generative and covariation cues. In condition 1, they saw the following sequence of events:

1. A flashlight (A) pointing at a spot of light on a wall
2. A second light (B) pointing at the same location without the spot
3. Both lights pointed at the same spot on the wall
4. Both flashlights turned to face the child with flashlight B, but not A, emitting light

In condition 2, the generative transmission information (4) was presented first and the covariation information (1-3) was presented second. Children were questioned about what caused the spot on the wall after both the generative and the covariation information. Children changed their causal attributions to conform with generative cues that conflicted with earlier covariation information (condition 1) more often than they shifted from generative to covariation information (condition 2). Shultz and Kestenbaum (1985) suggest that the cues to causality order from more to less basic as follows: generative cues, temporal priority, spatial contiguity, temporal contiguity, covariation, and similarity.

In the social realm, Miller and Aloise (1989) document that, contrary to commonly accepted conclusions, preschoolers assume that behaviors have psychological causes and prefer internal over external causes. They are aware of intentionality as a generative mechanism and use a matching rule first to figure out another's intention from objectively available evidence and then to check whether the intention matches the behavioral outcome in order to distinguish between intentional outcomes, mistakes, and accidents (Shultz & Wells, 1985). Miller and Aloise (1989) assert that preschoolers tend to overattribute intentions, believing that human behaviors (and some physical events) are intended even when they are not. This overattribution is due, in part, to preferences for generative cues to causality. Preschoolers who lack knowledge of specific causal mechanisms because they have a limited knowledge base may fall back on intention as a reasonable choice. Miller and Aloise argue that a child's main developmental task is to figure out which phenomena are not caused by intentions.

Evidence that the most basic causal reasoning is generative bears on a controversial issue in social psychology, the question of whether attributions are made automatically (Schneider, 1991). White (1989) maintains that counterfactual and contrastive criteria for assessing causality involve controlled processing, which occurs only for events that are not automatically, causally processed. Only after adults decide whether a causal candidate is generative do they use covariation information. Automatic processing is used for familiar, normal, or expected events, whereas controlled processing may be used for events that are abnormal or unfamiliar, or that violate expectations.

Evidence for the automatic-controlled distinction comes from an investigation of adults' attributions in launching-effect tasks (Schlottman & Shanks, 1992). The launching effect occurs when one object appears to cause another to move even though the first object has not actually touched the second object (Michotte, 1963). Over trials, Schlottman and Shanks (1992) varied whether movement of object B was contingent on or independent of an apparent impact by object A. Subjects rated perceived causality in single launch events and judged the necessity of collisions for movement in the overall set of events. The subjects always perceived launching when object A appeared to hit object B, even if movements of the two objects were independent. The degree of contiguity influenced perceptions, but contingency did not. However, when asked to judge whether it was necessary for object A to hit object B in order for object B to move, subjects showed an effect of the contingency manipulation. Schlottman and Shanks argue for a distinction between judged and perceived causality.

Because of the importance of generative mechanisms in understanding both physical and social causality and the possibility that causal processing may be automatic and involve direct perception, researchers have turned to research on infants for clues to the origins of causal reasoning.

Understanding Generative Mechanisms in Infancy

Contrary to the Piagetian view that dominated research in the 1960s and 1970s, recent researchers have found infants to be remarkably competent in many domains. White (1988) theorizes that the time constraints associated with visual sensory (iconic) memory are the basis for infants' concepts of causality. In several studies, Leslie and his colleagues (Leslie, 1982; Leslie & Keeble, 1987) used a habituation-dishabituation technique to explore infants' perceptions of causality regarding the launching effect documented by Michotte (1963). Infants were repeatedly shown a stimulus or event until they habituated (the response to the stimulus or event dropped off). A different stimulus or event was then presented. If infants viewed the second event to be the same as the first, then they remained habituated. If they viewed the second stimulus or event to be novel, they dishabituated (their response increased). Leslie (1982) found that infants distinguished between direct-launching and nonlaunching events. Leslie and Keeble (1987) found evidence suggesting that infants as young as 6 months perceive causal rather than only spatio-temporal properties of an event. They argue that causal percepts arise from lower-level visual processes of perception of the movement of non-self-propelled objects.

White (1988) argues that an understanding of intended or personally caused action develops when infants generalize their perceptual experiences to relations between internal events and behavior. In contrast, Premack (1990) speculates that infants perceive movement in self-propelled objects as intentional. The infant's concept is automatic, is more primitive than the adult's, and does not involve making judgments about or interpreting the perception. Although Premack maps out a number of experiments to test the direct perception of intention, none has been carried out with infants.

Summary

Two theoretical positions have been delineated regarding the type of information that is most basic for making causal attributions. Although most social psychological theories emphasize the role of regularity information such as covariation, developmental research suggests that generative mechanisms may be more basic. It appears that causality can be directly perceived under some circumstances, even by young infants, and is processed automatically rather than in a controlled fashion. Looking for causal mechanisms and attending to causal structure is basic to social cognition. Even preschoolers assume that behaviors have psychological causes and that intentionality is a generative mechanism.

When regularity information is used in more conscious processing, covariation patterns of antecedent and consequent information such as those described by Kelley (1967) are only a part of the multiple cues that individuals may use in assessing causality (Einhorn & Hogarth, 1986). Use of complex covariation information is an advanced developmental skill, yet there is evidence that even very young children make causal attributions. Cues to causality do not always lead to causal judgments. When presented with an event, people use world knowledge in addition to that which is presented to make attributions about the target behavior. Children generally have less world knowledge than adults and must acquire knowledge about specific causal mechanisms through experience. The next section of this chapter describes the role of knowledge structures in the causal reasoning of both adults and preschoolers.

KNOWLEDGE-STRUCTURE APPROACHES

Knowledge-structure-based approaches describe the knowledge that people use to explain everyday social events (e.g., Abelson & Black, 1986; Hilton & Knibbs, 1988), either as they observe them or as they read about them (Read, 1987; Trabasso & van den Broek, 1985). Knowledge structures have been labeled in various ways, including "schemas" and "scripts."

Event Schemas in Adults

Knowledge structures allow previous conceptions of events to interact with current causal cues (Einhorn & Hogarth, 1986). Initial processing of the causal structure of events is probably automatic; if the individual is faced with incongruous information, then the probability increases that the individual will engage in additional conscious processing to discover an explanation (Hansen, 1985). A major tenet of the knowledge-structure position is that cognitive structures allow people to infer what is most likely to happen in a given situation, even if they are provided with only a small amount of situational information (Abelson & Black, 1986).

Event schemas include temporal and causal information. Adults find it easier to recall causally connected events rather than those connected only temporally, and they recall aspects of events containing causal relations more readily than aspects lacking such relations (Bower, Black, & Turner, 1979). Likewise, causal dependencies are critical for comprehension of narrative text. Readers construct causal chains to maintain causal coherence, thus facilitating memory (Trabasso & van den Broek, 1985).

Naive Theories in Adults

It has been proposed that a deeper level of causal analysis, labeled "naive theories" (Wellman, 1990), is essential to our schemas for specific events. People use these common-sense theories about the world to explain events and define component concepts. It should be noted that the term *schema* or *script* is sometimes used in the literature in a broader sense to include the level of explanation described here as a theory. For example, Murphy and Medin (1985) state that "theory refers to any host of 'mental explanations' [including scripts, rules, and book-learned scientific knowledge], rather than a complete organized scientific account" (p. 290). For a discussion of the issues involved in defining a naive theory and how these theories differ from scientific theories, refer to Murphy and Medin (1985) or Wellman (1990).

Adults' naive theory of psychology (also labeled "theory of mind") causes them to assume that people's behaviors are caused by mental states such as their beliefs, desires, intentions, or feelings. An example of a causal relation between behavior and desires or beliefs is that after hearing Jane utter a sentence, listeners decide whether it is a lie based on whether Jane intends to deceive and whether she believes the sentence to be false (Rips & Conrad, 1989). Our naive theory allows us to distinguish between truth and deception, intended and accidental behaviors, and plans and outcomes. According to Wellman (1990), our everyday theory of mind is the "causal glue" of schemas.

Do children's representations of the world depend critically on causal structure? To what extend are children's explanations of human behavior determined by a theory of mind?

The Development of Event Representations in Preschoolers

Researchers claim that event representations are the building blocks for all other forms of representation (e.g., Farrar & Goodman, 1990; Nelson, 1986). If so, event representations must be present at a very early age. An important technique for investigating event representations in toddlers with limited verbal skills is elicited imitation. In this method, a model performs a set of actions using props and the toddler is prompted to imitate. The amount of imitation produced is a measure of recall, either immediate or delayed. Research using imitation tasks indicates that children as young as 11 to 24 months have generalized expectations about what usually happens during an event (e.g., Hertsgaard & Bauer, 1990). The causal-enabling structure of an event is critical for its representation. Enabling relations (which include those often labeled as causal or logical) exist when "for a given end-state or goal, one action in an event is both temporally prior to and necessary for a subsequent action" (Bauer, 1993, p. 1). Few developmental differences have been reported regarding children's use of causal structure in representing events. In fact, it has been suggested that "causal relations provide an invariant core around which a new representation can be organized" (Bauer & Thal, 1990, p. 299). Before well-integrated scenes emerge within an event representation, understanding the causal connections among the actions may help to organize the event (Ratner, Smith, & Padgett, 1990).

In a typical study of children's event structures, temporal order can be controlled and causal-enabling structure can be manipulated by comparing events in which order is not necessary with events in which order is fixed (act A enables act B, which would not occur without it). An example of an arbitrary sequence from Hertsgaard and Bauer (1990) is "put Big Bird in truck/load blocks in truck." Changes in the order of the sequence would not substantively change the overall event. An example of a causal-enabling sequence is "make a ramp/push car down ramp." In this sequence, the order is critical because the car cannot roll down the ramp if the ramp has not been built. As evidenced by their imitation, children recall aspects of an event containing causal relations more frequently, more accurately, and at younger ages than aspects lacking causal relations, even after only one exposure to an event and after a delay (Bauer, 1993; Bauer & Fivush, 1992; Hertsgaard & Bauer, 1990). Bauer and Thal (1990) found that 21- to 24-month-old children correctly reproduced novel sequences, indicating that familiarity with a sequence is not a necessary condition for correct reproduction of it. Because the recall of novel sequences containing causal relations is superior to recall for familiar events lacking such relations, Bauer and Thal suggest that temporal organization is not imposed on existing unordered event representations but is part of representations from inception (but see O'Connell & Gerard, 1985).

Causal relations do not appear to enhance recall of an event by allowing children to infer the acts rather than to remember their order explicitly;

instead, facilitation occurs because children organize the material into "chunks" (Bauer, 1992). Components of a sequence joined by enabling relations are more tightly linked than components lacking such relations; children who were asked to imitate an event sequence that had irrelevant acts inserted between two acts joined by an enabling relation were likely to omit the irrelevant act (Bauer, 1992). Children who were asked to sort pictures of the actions involved in a complicated event sequence (making clay) were most likely to identify categories that contained actions most causally central to the event, suggesting that causal connections between the actions formed the basis for the organization of these categories.

Preschoolers' Theory of Mind

A growing area of developmental research concerns children's theory of mind (Astington, Harris, & Olson, 1988; Frye & Moore, 1991). Children's knowledge of the mind is basic to their understanding of the social world because they come to realize that people's behaviors are caused by internal mental states such as beliefs and desires (Wellman, 1990). Theory-of-mind research is similar to earlier Piagetian work that conceived of the child as actively seeking and constructing knowledge. However, "newer work recontextualizes the solitary thinker in a social world composed of enculturated and communicating human adults" (Feldman, 1992, p. 107).

Children's theory of mind changes qualitatively with development. Infants do not have a theory of mind; however, in late infancy they begin to engage in pretend play that indicates their ability to distinguish reality from the counterfactual world, though they cannot yet relate these beliefs causally to situations in the world (Au, 1992; Leslie, 1988). Two-year-olds understand that people behave because of their desires, but they do not understand that they are also influenced by beliefs.

Between 3 and 4 years of age, children begin to understand that people act because of both beliefs and desires. They realize that beliefs, desires, and goals are causally related to emotions such as surprise or curiosity and that the same situations can produce diverging emotions (Wellman & Benarjee, 1988). However, they do not understand that beliefs may not faithfully represent reality. Sometime after the age of 4, children begin to understand that people can behave on the basis of false beliefs. Wimmer and Perner (1983) constructed a scenario where a child's beliefs about where an object was located were in conflict with the beliefs of a character in a scenario. When asked where the character would search for the object, 4- and 5-year-olds said that he would look where he believed it to be. On the other hand, 3-year-olds said that the character would look in the place where the object was actually located. More research is necessary to determine the extent to which social experience and interaction may influence theory-of-mind developments. For example, children may have fewer experiences with false beliefs than other areas where there is lack of correspondence between mental states and the world, thus leading to the later development of this understanding (Moses, 1993).

Older children come to view the mind as having executive, mediating, and interpretive functions. Intention comes to be more than simple purpose, it becomes a plan of action. Young children understand that people may go to the store because of their beliefs and desires, but older children understand that they may do so because of a committed plan (Wellman, 1990). Additionally, the use of stable personality traits to explain behaviors, a traditional concern of attribution researchers, increases dramatically after the age of 8. In fact, adults from Western cultures tend to overattribute dispositions and to expect more cross-situational stability than actually exists; in contrast, young children from both Eastern and Western cultures rarely attribute causality to stable dispositions and treat disposition labels as descriptions of current behaviors (e.g., Miller, 1986). However, there is some recent evidence that 5- and 6-year-olds may be able to infer future behavior from instances of past behavior, suggesting some understanding of stable personal dispositions (Gnepp & Chilamkurti, 1988; Ruble, Newman, Rholes, & Altshuler, 1988).

Wellman (1990) notes that person-perception researchers have often concluded that preschoolers' attributions are based on concrete behavioral and situational factors rather than on psychological factors. Preschoolers' lack of trait attributions is used to support this perspective. Wellman (1990) argues that theory-of-mind research suggests that "young children's appreciation of persons . . . and their actions is generally mentalistic although not trait-dependent" (p. 300). One factor that deserves further attention is whether different kinds of traits that have been identified (e.g., Chaplin, John, & Goldberg, 1988; Yuill, 1992) differ developmentally.

Although the general sequence of developmental changes in children's theory of mind is agreed on by most researchers, they disagree about the exact age at which the belief-desire theory of mind emerges, with some theorists placing it closer to age 4 than age 3 (e.g., Perner, 1991). There is also disagreement about whether these changes actually constitute "theories." Researchers such as Wellman (1990) who argue that children have coherent naive theories use as evidence general structural changes and reorganizations in the child's view of the mind that affect many areas of psychological knowledge. Flavell (1988) reviews evidence for concurrent changes in many domains at the age of 3 or 4 years, including the understanding of false beliefs, of appearance-reality (e.g., a sponge that looks like a rock is still a sponge), that a message can refer to more than one thing, and that an individual can simultaneously occupy more than one social role.

Several authors (Bullock, 1985; Sophian & Huber, 1984) argue that causal reasoning itself may undergo qualitative changes at around 4 years of age. Prior to this age, children can identify generative mechanisms when they are obviously available and familiar to them. For example, Keil (1979) found that children between 18 and 30 months were surprised when a small brick did not fall after removal of its single spatial support but were not as surprised when one of two supports was removed and the brick remained suspended in a balance position that an adult would view as impossible. However, before the age of about 4, children may not be surprised by the apparent lack of a causal mechanism in an event that they are viewing. For example, Bullock (1984) led children to believe that two objects moved together because of a hidden string. They were then allowed to inspect the part of the apparatus that supposedly contained the string connection but found it empty. Whereas many 4-year-olds and most 5-year-olds and adults accused the experimenter of trickery or began to search for another connection, 3-year-olds rarely did so. After the age of 4, children understand that mechanisms are necessary for causal relations and they will search for a mechanism where none is obvious (Bullock, 1985). That is, causal judgment becomes more controlled. To my knowledge, there has been no research that relates these changes in causality to other changes that appear to occur around the same time as a result of changes in children's theory of mind.

Preschoolers generally assume that all events are caused, and they interpret random physical events, noncausal negative consequences to a wrongdoer, and nonintentional events as causal (Gelman & Kalish, 1993). They tend to assume that every object is a member of some natural-kind category, that is, categories that share theoretically important properties (e.g., bird). Concepts are embedded in theories and are coherent when they fit with people's theories of the world (Gelman & Coley, 1991). This tendency to view objects as natural-kinds can lead to assumptions that all categories, including arbitrary artifact categories or social categories, are discovered rather than invented, and that membership in a category cannot be altered (see Rothbart & Taylor, 1992, for similar arguments regarding the power of social category labels). This tendency also leads children to overgeneralize their inferences about category members. For example, preschoolers correctly infer that different dogs have the same "kind of insides"; however, they incorrectly infer that different chairs (e.g., kitchen chairs and living room chairs) also do (Gelman & Coley, 1991). Overattribution of causality can also lead to the view that beliefs are accurate reflections of the true state of the world (Gelman & Kalish, 1993). In addition, because of other reasoning biases of preschoolers, such as the assumption that good things go together, the overattribution of intent may be further amplified when there are positive outcomes to an event (Miller & Aloise, 1990).

Changes in the theory of mind may influence other developments in causal understanding. Kelley's (1972) discounting principle suggests that individuals will discount the role of a given cause if there are other plausible causes present. Most discounting research with young children requires them to judge that characters' behaviors may not accurately reflect their motives or emotions. Theory-of-mind research suggests that children are unlikely to show discounting until after the age of 3 or 4 (Miller & Aloise, 1990). More research is needed to determine the precise relationship between causal biases such as discounting and other theory-of-mind developments.

Summary

Recently researchers have made advances toward more precise specification of a theory of everyday life. They have found that individuals' knowledge structures for everyday events include both causal and temporal information. Initial processing of schematic information is probably automatic rather than controlled. New schemas for events appear to be organized around causal information; event schemas are not unordered sequences to which order is later imposed. Differences in organization and recall of event schemas for toddlers compared to adults appear to be more quantitative than qualitative.

However, not all development during the preschool years is quantitative in nature. Sometime around the age of 3 to 4, children's naive psychology undergoes a qualitative change from a theory that explains the actions of themselves and other people on the basis of desire to a more adultlike theory based on beliefs and desires. Children's theory of mind has wide-ranging implications for their understanding of the social world. A belief that the world is causally structured is central to the preschooler's theory of mind, as it is to the toddler's processing of events, and to the infant's more primitive perceptual understandings. In fact, a belief that the world is structured in terms of causality may be developmentally basic in the sense described by Kassin and Baron (1985).

At the same time that infants and toddlers are forming event representations and older preschoolers are undergoing qualitative changes in their theory of mind, they are also learning language. Language is another domain in which causal understanding plays a key role. In the next section of this chapter, relations between language and social cognition in causal understanding are examined.

THE ROLE OF LANGUAGE IN CAUSAL UNDERSTANDING

Although the role of language in social psychology was largely ignored between 1920 and 1980, there has been a resurgence of interest in the topic during the last decade (Giles & Coupland, 1991; Semin & Fiedler, 1992). The social psychology of language investigates "how cognitive factors mediate language reception and production, how language functions as a dependent as well as an independent variable in social contexts, both reflecting and determining our social reality" (Giles & Coupland, 1991, p. xi). In this section of the chapter, I examine the relations between language and social cognition from two perspectives suggested by Nelson (1991): Conceptual representations derived from social experiences may provide support for acquired language forms; and language highlights relations that were not previously apparent in the child's nonlinguistic social cognitive representations.

Language Reflects Children's Social Understandings

Language provides a mirror of children's understanding of the world. Social psychologists are interested in how social knowledge is mapped onto different language categories (Semin & Fiedler, 1992). The first example of this concerns a large body of social psychology research that now suggests that different interpersonal verbs elicit different causal attributions: Causality is implicit in the verb.

Imagine, for example, situations described by sentences such as "Sue criticized Jane" or "Sue admired Jane." When the task is to judge why these events occurred, people reliably attribute the cause of the event to Sue in the first sentence (because Sue is critical) and to Jane in the second sentence (because Jane is admirable).

Brown and Fish (1983a, 1983b) suggest that there are two basic causal schemas governing interpersonal interactions: one for experiencers (the individual who experiences a mental or emotional state as a result of another) and one for agents (the individual who acts upon another). They speculate that causal schemas are universals of human thought, and support this contention with data from Chinese and Japanese speakers whose languages are structured very differently from English, but whose speakers show similar patterns of attributions. When individuals are asked to describe why an interpersonal event occurs, causal attributions depend on the type of verb used to describe the event. For experiencer verbs, such as "admire" or "embarrass," greater causal weight is given to the stimulus (the person or thing in the sentence that does not experience the feeling or state; see also Au, 1986; Corrigan, 1988, 1992, 1993; Fiedler & Semin, 1988). For action verbs, such as "criticize" or "help," greater causal weight is usually given to the agent. However, factors such as the social status relationship between the sentence participants can shift attributions away from the agent (Corrigan, 1988, 1992, 1993; Garvey, Caramazza, & Yates, 1976), suggesting that people's underlying schemas are broader than the basic causal schemas proposed by Brown and Fish.

Brown and Fish (1983a, 1983b) also note an interesting fact about English derivational morphology. Derivatives of verbs (e.g., adjectives such as "admirable" from "admire") frequently refer to the same sentence participant to which people attribute causality. That is, in the sentence "John admires Ted," people usually attribute causality to Ted; the derived adjective "admirable" also refers to Ted. Experiencer verbs generally have derived forms that refer to the sentence participant who is not the experiencer, regardless of the verb's position in the sentence; similarly, causality is attributed to that sentence participant. Attribution of causality and verb derivatives seem to match for most verbs with derived forms.

Brown and Fish (1983a, 1983b) argue that this phenomenon arises because underlying social cognitive schemas about events produce both the attribution patterns and the derived morphology. Alternatively, the derived morphology of the language could lead to the social cognitive schemas (Hoffman & Tchir, 1990). That is, because English speakers know that "admirable" refers to Ted, they attribute causality to Ted when they hear the verb "admire."

Developmental research may help resolve the controversy over this relationship between language and social cognition. If children too young to have many derived forms as part of their vocabulary show the same pattern of attributions as adults, it cannot be due to the influence of the derivational morphology (Au, 1986). Corrigan and Stevenson (1994) found that 3- and 4-year-olds produced the same pattern of attributions to a set of verbs as did adults in a previous study (Corrigan, 1993). It is highly unlikely that children of this age know the forms derived from the verbs in the study—for example, that "memorable" derives from "remember." Therefore, it is plausible that the cognitive schemas of the children precede their language.

A second example where social cognitions relevant to causality may influence language comes from work described by Au (1992). She addresses the issue of whether languages that differ in their encoding of counterfactual reasoning are associated with speakers who differ in their counterfactual thinking.

In English, counterfactual reasoning is expressed with a subjunctive construction such as "If I were you, I would choose the red one" or tense "If I had been there, she wouldn't have misunderstood." In Chinese, there are no tense markers for verbs, making it more difficult to keep track of premises and implications. Bloom (1981) claims that English speakers answering questions about a counterfactual story were able to appreciate that the implications of the story were contrary to fact 98% of the time, whereas native Chinese speakers only did so 6% of the time. He views this finding as support for the notion that language influences thought.

However, Au (1992) argues that the counterfactual in the Chinese version of Bloom's story was not expressed properly. After correcting this error, she found that native Chinese speakers had no difficulty with counterfactual thinking. Furthermore, Au argues that counterfactual reasoning is fundamental to many universal human activities such as frustration, regret, or resentment, thus supporting the notion that speakers of all languages should be able to reason counterfactually regardless of their language.

Developmental studies of English-speaking children indicate that they can think and talk about counterfactual possibilities before they can use the English subjunctive, at around age 6 (Au, 1992). The ability to distinguish explicitly between pretense and reality, which arises as part of a child's developing theory of mind at around age 3, seems to relate to the child's ability to reason counterfactually. Au notes that preschoolers also comment on their wrong ideas and talk about desires for contrary-to-the-fact situations, both of which require counterfactual reasoning. In sum, counterfactual reasoning is an integral part of everyday life for both children and adults, regardless of whether it is formally expressed in a given language.

Linguistic Influences on the Child's Theory of Mind

Although children's social cognition often affects their language, language may also influence their cognitions. Nelson (1992) argues that major performance changes that occur between the ages of 3 and 4 on many theory-of-mind tasks may result from changes in language. For younger children, language is simply a way to tell people what they think and remember; for 4-year-olds, language becomes a means of representing what others know and of comparing that representation with their own representations of the world.

Children may use linguistic labels to guide inferences about important underlying (causal) properties. Gelman and Coley (1991) propose that children use language to help set up categories that function like adults' natural-kind categories, even before the children have a complete theory in a given domain. These labels may sometimes, but not always, guide inferences about important underlying causal properties of objects; for example, calling a pterodactyl a "dinosaur" led children to infer that it did not live in a nest, whereas without the name, children assumed that it did (Gelman & Coley, 1990). Children as young as 2 years base inferences about objects on the similarity of the words used to label them. Parental naming strategies such as the context in which a word is used or the range of examples labeled may have important effects on which labels children view as important to their theories (Gelman & Coley, 1991).

Other effects of parental language have been found in naturalistic conversations about causality and mental states. Dunn and Brown (1993) found changes between the contexts in which 33- and 40-month-old children discussed causality with their mothers. The earliest discussions occurred in the context of satisfying the children's own needs or wishes. Later, they discussed causality in relation to reflecting on the causes of internal states and the causes of social practices. Brown and Dunn (1991) suggest that the 1-year lag they found between children's use of feeling/desire terms (at 24 months) and their use of terms to refer to mental states (at 36 months) resulted, at least partially, from differences in language environments. They found that mothers were more likely to describe the causes and consequences of desires than of mental states.

Young children's experiences with language may influence their social cognition at later ages. Three-year-olds who listen to and engage in discussion of a wide range of feelings with their families are more likely to discuss the causes and consequences of those feelings; differences in discourse patterns are related to children's ability to recognize emotions in a perspective-taking task when they are 6 years of age (Dunn, Brown, & Beardsall, 1991). Dunn, Brown, Slomkowki, Tesla, and Youngblade (1991) examined children who had participated in family discourse about feelings and causality at 33 months. The children were tested at 40 months on a false-belief task designed by Bartsch and Wellman (1990) that asks children to explain actions taken by someone who holds false beliefs. Differences in performance on the task were related to earlier differences in family discourse. Discourse may allow children to distance themselves from others, to reflect on their emotional experiences, and to negotiate shared meanings about experience.

CONCLUSIONS

The notion that the comprehension of causal relations is the key to understanding our physical and social world is rapidly gaining empirical support. This understanding begins in early infancy, perhaps based on perceptual abilities, when infants show in rudimentary form many of the skills, including causal understanding, that emerge later in childhood.

Causal processing is initially automatic and perceptual, perhaps for both physical and psychological causes. Research with infants and preschoolers has shown that the most basic source of causal attributions is the understanding of generative mechanisms that are either perceivable or discoverable (energy transmission for physical events and intentions for social events). However, young children and adults may make use of regularity information such as covariation once they have made an initial judgment about whether a potential cause is a causal power (White, 1989).

In understanding events, individuals use schemas that contain causal information. Again, the causal information appears to be processed automatically. Generative mechanisms and other cues to causality constrain the construction of causal schemas in particular ways. Causal information is critical to young children as they form new schemas for events, guiding both encoding and recall. Evidence from young children's imitation of event sequences suggests that toddlers as young as 11 months of age can recall event sequences that contain causal-enabling relations. Differences in the organization and recall of event schemas for toddlers compared to adults appear to be more quantitative than qualitative in nature, with causal structure playing a central role for all age groups.

On the other hand, there are qualitative changes during the preschool years in children's understanding that their actions and those of other people are caused by internal mental states such as beliefs and desires. This developing theory of mind has a major impact on children's causal attributions. Although traits are part of the adult theory of mind, it is unclear to what extent preschoolers are capable of using these theory-of-mind concepts.

Another qualitative change in thinking that occurs at the onset of the preschool years is the acquisition of language. The child may use language to express social cognitive understanding of different types of events or counterfactual thinking. However, language in social interactions is also an important influence in shaping the young child's social and causal understanding.

The ability to perceive and infer causal connections is a fundamental human "cement to the universe" (Mackie, 1980). Developmental research highlights the importance of causal understanding for the infant and young child and allows us to trace the changes in that understanding from their origins in perception to the full-blown attribution abilities of the adult so well documented in the social psychology literature.

REFERENCES

Abelson, R., & Black, J. (1986). Introduction. In J. Galambos, R. Abelson, & J. Black (Eds.), *Knowledge structures* (pp. 1-18). Hillsdale, NJ: Erlbaum.

Astington, J., Harris, P., & Olson, D. (1988). *Developing theories of mind.* Cambridge, UK: Cambridge University Press.

Au, T. K. (1986). A verb is worth a thousand words: The causes and consequences of interpersonal events implicit in language. *Journal of Memory and Language, 25,* 104-122.

Au, T. K. (1992). Counterfactual reasoning. In G. Semin & K. Fiedler (Eds.), *Language, interaction and social cognition* (pp. 194-213). London: Sage.

Bar-Tal, D. (1990). Attribution theory of human development. In R. M. Thomas (Ed.), *The encyclopedia of human development and education* (pp. 112-118). Oxford: Pergamon Press.

Bartsch, K., & Wellman, H. (1989). Young children's attribution of action to beliefs and desires. *Child Development, 69,* 946-964.

Bauer, P. (1992). Holding it all together: How enabling relations facilitate young children's event recall. *Cognitive Development, 7,* 1-28.

Bauer, P. (1993, March). *Application of world knowledge: Examples from research on event memory.* Paper presented as part of the symposium "Can Infants Really Think? How Infants Use Their Knowledge About the World to Think Through Problems and Plan Solutions" at the Society for Research in Child Development, New Orleans, LA.

Bauer, P., & Fivush, R. (1992). Constructing event representations: Building on a foundation of variation and enabling relations. *Cognitive Development, 7,* 381-401.

Bauer, P., & Thal, D. (1990). Scripts or scraps: Reconsidering the development of sequential understanding. *Journal of Experimental Child Psychology, 50,* 287-304.

Bloom, A. (1981). *The linguistic shaping of thought: A study in the impact of language on thinking in China and the west.* Hillsdale, NJ: Erlbaum.

Bower, G., Black, J., & Turner T. (1979). Scripts in memory for text. *Cognitive Psychology, 11,* 177-220.

Brown, J., & Dunn, J. (1991). "You can cry, mum": The social and developmental implications of talk about internal states. *British Journal of Developmental Psychology, 9,* 237-256.

Brown, R., & Fish, D. (1983a). The psychological causality implicit in language. *Cognition, 14,* 237-273.

Brown, R., & Fish, D. (1983b). Are there universal schemas of psychological causality. *Archives de Psychologie, 51,* 145-153.

Bullock, M. (1984). Preschoolers' understanding of causal connections. *British Journal of Developmental Psychology, 2,* 139-148.

Bullock, M. (1985). Causal reasoning and developmental change over the preschool years. *Human Development, 28,* 169-191.

Chaplin, W., John, O., & Goldberg, L. (1988). Conceptions of states and traits: Dimensional attributes with ideals as prototypes. *Journal of Personality and Social Psychology, 54,* 541-557.

Cheng, P., & Novick, L. (1990). A probabilistic contrast model of causal induction. *Journal of Personality and Social Psychology, 58,* 545-567.

Corrigan, R. (1988). Who dun it? The influence of actor-patient animacy and type of verb in the making of causal attributions. *Journal of Memory and Language, 27,* 447-465.

Corrigan, R. (1992). The relationship between causal attributions and judgements of the typicality of events described by sentences. *British Journal of Social Psychology, 31,* 351-368.

Corrigan, R. (1993). Causal attributions to states and events described by different classes of verbs. *British Journal of Social Psychology, 32,* 335-348.

Corrigan, R., & Stevenson, C. (1994). Children's causal attributions to states and events described by different classes of verbs. *Cognitive Development, 9,* 235-256.

Dunn, J., & Brown, J. (1993). Early conversations about causality: Content, pragmatics and developmental change. *British Journal of Developmental Psychology, 11,* 107-123.

Roberta Corrigan   **23**

Dunn, J., Brown, J., & Beardsall, L. (1991). Family talk about feeling states and children's later understanding of others' emotions. *Developmental Psychology, 27,* 448-455.

Dunn, J., Brown, J., Slomkowki, C., Tesla, C., & Youngblade, L. (1991). Young children's understanding of other people's feelings and beliefs: Individual differences and their antecedents. *Child Development, 62,* 1352-1366.

Dunning, D., & Parpal, M. (1989). Mental addition versus subtraction in counterfactual reasoning: On assessing the impact of personal actions and life events. *Journal of Personality and Social Psychology, 57,* 5-15.

Einhorn, H., & Hogarth, R. (1986). Judging probable cause. *Psychological Bulletin, 99,* 3-19.

Farrar, J., & Goodman, G. (1990). Developmental changes in event memory. *Child Development, 63,* 174-187.

Feldman, C. (1992). The new theory of theory of mind. *Human Development, 35,* 107-117.

Fiedler, K., & Semin, G. (1988). On the causal information conveyed by different interpersonal verbs: The role of implicit sentence context. *Social Cognition, 6,* 21-39.

Flavell, J. (1988). The development of children's knowledge about the mind: From cognitive connections to mental representations. In J. Astington, P. Harris, & D. Olson (Eds.), *Developing theories of mind* (pp. 244-271). Cambridge, UK: Cambridge University Press.

Frye, D., & Moore, C. (1991). *Children's theories of mind.* Hillsdale, NJ: Erlbaum.

Garvey, C., Caramazza, A., & Yates, J. (1976). Factors influencing assignment of pronoun antecedents, *Cognition, 3,* 227-243.

Gelman, S., & Coley, J. (1991). The acquisition of natural kind terms. In S. Gelman & J. Byrnes (Eds.), *Perspectives on language and thought* (pp. 146-196). Cambridge, UK: Cambridge University Press.

Gelman, S., & Kalish, C. (1993). Categories and causality. In R. Pasnak & M. Howe (Eds.), *Emerging themes in cognitive development: Vol. II. Competencies* (pp. 3-32). New York: Springer-Verlag.

Giles, H., & Coupland, N. (1991). *Language: Contexts and consequences.* Buckingham, UK: Open University Press.

Gnepp, J., & Chilamkurti, C. (1988). Children's use of personality attributions to predict other people's emotional and behavioral reactions. *Child Development, 59,* 743-754.

Hansen, R. (1985). Cognitive economy and commonsense attribution processing. In J. Harvey & G. Weary (Eds.), *Attribution basic issues and applications* (pp. 65-85). New York: Academic Press.

Harre, R., & Madden, E. (1975). *Causal powers: A theory of natural necessity.* Oxford: Blackwell.

Hertsgaard, L., & Bauer, P. (1990). *Thirteen- and sixteen-month olds' long-term recall of event sequences.* Poster presented at the Society for Research in Child Development, Seattle, WA.

Hewstone, M., & Jaspers, J. (1987). Covariation and causal attribution: A logical model of the intuitive analysis of variance. *Journal of Personality and Social Psychology, 53,* 663-672.

Hilton, D., & Knibbs, C. (1988). The knowledge-structure and inductivist strategies in causal attribution: A direct comparison. *European Journal of Social Psychology, 18,* 79-92.

Hilton, D., & Slugoski, B. (1986). Knowledge-based causal attribution: The abnormal conditions focus model. *Psychological Review, 93,* 75-88.

Hoffman, C., & Tchir, M. (1990). Interpersonal verbs and dispositional adjectives: The psychology of causality embodied in language. *Journal of Personality and Social Psychology, 58,* 765-778.

Kalish, C., & Gelman, S. (1992). On wooden pillows: Multiple classification and children's category based inductions. *Child Development, 63,* 1536-1557.

Kassin, S. (1981). From laychild to "layman": Developmental causal attribution. In S. Brehm, S. Kassin, & F. Gibbons (Eds.), *Developmental social psychology* (pp. 169-190). New York: Oxford University Press.

Kassin, S., & Baron, R. (1986). On the basicity of social perception cues: Developmental evidence for adult processes? *Social Cognition, 4,* 180-200.

Keil, F. (1979). The development of the young child's ability to anticipate the outcomes of simple causal events. *Child Development, 50,* 455-462.

Kelley, H. (1967). Attribution in social psychology. *Nebraska Symposium on Motivation, 15,* 192-238.

Kelley, H. (1972). Causal schemata and the attribution process. In E. Jones, D. Kanouse, H. Kelley, R. Nisbett, S. Valins, & B. Weiner (Eds.), *Attribution: Perceiving the causes of behavior.* Morristown, NJ: General Learning Press.

Leslie, A. (1982). The perception of causality in infants. *Perception, 11,* 173-186.

Leslie, A. (1988). Some implications of pretense for mechanisms underlying the child's theory of mind. In J. Astington, P. Harris, & D. Olson (Eds.), *Developing theories of mind* (pp. 19-46). Cambridge, UK: Cambridge University Press.

Leslie, A., & Keeble, S. (1987). Do six month old infants perceive causality? *Cognition, 25,* 265-288.

Lipe, M. (1991). Counterfactual reasoning as a framework for attribution theories. *Psychological Bulletin, 109,* 456-471.

Mackie, J. (1980). *The cement of the universe.* Oxford: Clarendon Press.

Michotte, A. (1963). *The perception of causation.* New York: Basic Books.

Miller, J. (1986). Early cross-cultural commonalities in social explanation. *Developmental Psychology, 22,* 514-520.

Miller, P., & Aloise, P. (1989). Young children's understanding of the psychological causes of behavior: A review. *Child Development, 60,* 257-285.

Miller, P., & Aloise, P. (1990). Discounting in children: The role of social knowledge. *Developmental Review, 10,* 266-298.

Moses, L. (1993). Young children's understanding of belief constraints on intention. *Cognitive Development, 8,* 1-25.

Murphy, G., & Medin, D. (1985). The role of theories in conceptual coherence. *Psychological Review, 92,* 289-316.

Nelson, K. (1986). *Event knowledge: Structure and function in development.* Hillsdale, NJ: Erlbaum.

Nelson, K. (1991). The matter of time: Interdependencies between language and thought in development. In S. Gelman & J. Byrnes (Eds.), *Perspectives on language and thought* (pp. 278-318). Cambridge, UK: Cambridge University Press.

Nelson, K. (1992). Emergence of autobiographical memory at age 4. *Human Development, 35,* 172-177.

O'Connell, B., & Gerard, A. (1985). Scripts and scraps: The development of sequential understanding. *Child Development, 56,* 671-681.

Perner, J. (1991). *Understanding the representational mind.* Cambridge: MIT Press.

Premack, D. (1990). The infant's theory of self-propelled objects. *Cognition, 6,* 1-16.

Ratner, H., Smith, B., & Padgett, R. (1990). Children's organization of events and event memories. In R. Fivush & J. Hudson (Eds.), *Knowing and remembering in young children* (pp. 65-93). New York: Cambridge University Press.

Read, S. (1987). Constructing causal scenarios: A knowledge structure approach to causal reasoning. *Journal of Personality and Social Psychology, 52,* 288-302.

Rips, L., & Conrad, F. (1989). Folk psychology of mental activities. *Psychological Review, 96,* 187-207.

Rothbart, M., & Taylor, M. (1992). Category labels and social reality: Do we view social categories as natural kinds? In G. Semin & K. Fiedler (Eds.), *Language, interaction and social cognition* (pp. 11-36). London: Sage.

Ruble, D., Newman, L., Rholes, W., & Altshuler, J. (1988). Children's "naive psychology": The use of behavioral and situational information for the prediction of behavior. *Cognitive Development, 3,* 89-112.

Ruble, D., & Rholes, W. (1981). The development of children's perceptions and attributions about their social world. In J. Harvey, W. Ickes, & R. Kidd (Eds.), *New directions in attribution research: Vol. 3* (pp. 3-36). Hillsdale, NJ: Erlbaum.

Schlottman, A., & Shanks, D. (1992). Evidence for a distinction between judged and perceived causality. *The Quarterly Journal of Experimental Psychology, 44A,* 321-342.

Schneider, D. (1991). Social cognition. *Annual Review of Psychology, 42,* 527-561.

Semin, G., & Fielder, K. (1992). The inferential properties of interpersonal verbs. In G. Semin & K. Fiedler (Eds.), *Language, interaction and social cognition* (pp. 58-78). London: Sage.

Shaklee, H., & Elek, M. (1988). Cause and covariate: Development of two related concepts. *Cognitive Development, 3,* 1-14.

Shultz, T. (1982a). Causal reasoning in the social and nonsocial realms. *Canadian Journal of Behavioural Science, 14,* 307-322.

Shultz, T. (1982b). Rules of causal attribution. *Monographs of the Society for Research in Child Development, 47,* 1-51.

Shultz, T., & Kestenbaum, M. (1985). Causal reasoning in children. *Annals of Child Development, 2,* 195-249.

Shultz, T., & Mendolson, R. (1975). The use of covariation as a principle of causal analysis. *Child Development, 46,* 394-399.

Shultz, T., & Wells, D. (1985). Judging the intentionality of action-outcomes. *Developmental Psychology, 21,* 83-89.

Sophian, C., & Huber, A. (1984). Early developments in children's causal judgments. *Child Development, 55,* 512-526.

Trabasso, T., & van den Broek, P. (1985). Causal thinking and the representation of narrative events. *Journal of Memory and Language, 24,* 612-630.

Trafimow, D., & Wyer, R. (1993). Cognitive representation of mundane social events. *Journal of Personality and Social Psychology, 64,* 365-376.

Wellman, H. (1990). *The child's theory of mind.* Cambridge: MIT Press.

Wellman, H., & Benarjee, M. (1988). Mind and emotion: Children's understanding of the emotional consequences of beliefs and desires. *British Journal of Developmental Psychology, 9,* 191-214.

White, P. (1988). Causal processing: Origins and development. *Psychological Bulletin, 104,* 36-52.

White, P. (1989). A theory of causal processing. *British Journal of Psychology, 80,* 431-454.

White, P. (1990). Ideas about causation in philosophy. *Psychological Bulletin, 108,* 3-18.

White, P. (1992). Causal powers, causal questions, and the place of regularity information in causal attribution. *British Journal of Psychology, 83,* 161-188.

Wimmer, H., & Perner, J. (1983). Beliefs about beliefs: Representation and constraining function of wrong beliefs in young children's understanding of deception. *Cognition, 13,* 103-128

Yuill, N. (1992). Children's conception of personality traits. *Human Development, 35,* 265-279.

2

Developmental and Individual Differences in Predicting Others' Thoughts and Feelings: Applying the Transformation Rule Model

RACHEL KARNIOL

Rachel Karniol is in the Department of Psychology at Tel Aviv University, Ramat Aviv, Israel.

This chapter focuses on the process by which we gain access to and predict other people's likely psychological experiences. This process lies at the heart of both social and developmental psychology because, as Heider (1958) notes, we react to what we think other people are thinking and feeling. To do so, however, we must learn to think of others as psychological entities whose experiences we can never be privy to; yet we must develop ways of "reading their minds" despite this obstacle.

In this context, developmental psychologists have recently begun to examine children's acquisition of a theory of mind (e.g., Astington, Harris, & Olson, 1988; Perner, 1991), focusing on the growing understanding of other people's and their own psychological processes, including thoughts and feelings. One of the many fascinating questions that investigations of a theory of mind must address is how children, and later adults, gain access to other people's thoughts and feelings. That is, children may know that others have thoughts and feelings (e.g., Flavell, 1974; Selman, 1980; Shantz, 1975), but how do they understand what specific thoughts and feelings others may have?

Attempts to answer this question usually refer to the ability to adopt another person's role or perspective. Although perspective taking is presumed to provide entry to other minds, how such entry is gained remains elusive (e.g., Chandler, 1976, 1988; Strayer, 1987). Despite the recognition that stored knowledge structures are implicated in the process (e.g., Flavell, 1974; Higgins, 1981), cognitive psychological principles have not been explicitly incorporated in models of role taking.

AUTHOR'S NOTE: I would like to thank four anonymous reviewers for their helpful comments on an earlier version of this chapter.

Social psychologists have explicitly adopted both the models and methods of cognitive psychology in studying social cognition (e.g., Smith & Zarate, 1992; Wyer & Srull, 1980); however, the term *perspective taking* is rarely mentioned within the context of social cognition as a means of gaining access to other people's psychological processes (but see Higgins, 1981). Social psychologists working in the area of helping (e.g., Batson et al., 1989; Cialdini et al., 1987; Davis, 1983; Dovidio, Allen, & Schroeder, 1990) have incorporated the concept of empathy, which is viewed either as a trait or as a state induced by manipulations of the observer's perspective. But these discussions do not focus on perspective taking as a process of cognitively gaining access to others' points of view, despite the critical role assigned to it.

The transformation rule model (Karniol, 1986, 1990) was developed to provide a cognitive account of the underpinnings of this process; it represents an attempt to delineate the *knowledge structures* that are implicated and the *cognitive procedures* that are executed when individuals "put themselves in other people's shoes." In this chapter, I outline the transformation rule model and discuss two new studies with the aim of showing that a developmental variable (grade) and an individual difference variable (perspective taking) have analogous effects on the use of transformation rules for making predictions about other people's likely thoughts and feelings. Thus I illustrate how developmental and social research can be used jointly to further our understanding of the social cognitive processes involved in role taking. Such a demonstration is important for social psychologists and developmental psychologists, both of whom are relatively insulated in their own fields and tend not to use the same language when discussing similar phenomena. It is important to recognize that the interface between these fields is demanded by their respective interest in similar processes.

THE TRANSFORMATION RULE MODEL

The transformation rule model is similar to models of question answering (Graesser, Byrne, & Behrens, 1992; Kolodner, 1984; Lehnert, 1981) in assuming that the *procedures* for using knowledge must be differentiated from the *knowledge structures* to which the procedures are applied. To give a mathematical example, the rules of addition and subtraction are independent procedural knowledge structures; specific numbers representing declarative knowledge are "plugged in" to solve a problem of addition or subtraction. Similarly, procedural knowledge about how to answer questions, draw inferences, or make predictions is independent from the declarative knowledge structures about objects, people, and situations. Such independence implies that the same procedures can be applied to various declarative knowledge structures, and the same content can be used to make a variety of inferences or predictions (e.g., Vorauer & Ross, 1993). Yet declarative knowledge and procedural knowledge must work in concert with each other to make predictions.

For this joint enterprise, relevant input needs to activate both procedural and declarative knowledge. The activation of declarative knowledge structures always proceeds the same way, with multiple nodes being directly activated by the relevant input. Procedures perform a transformation on relevant input (Bargh, 1989). Declarative knowledge structures that are activated by the input provide the *content* with which predictions based on these transformations are made. Procedural knowledge narrows the search of declarative knowledge by looking for intersections between nodes and determining which particular ones represent plausible answers.

For instance, questions about how something will be done versus why it will be done (e.g., "How will he kill his wife?" versus "Why will he kill his wife?") may both activate the same declarative memory structures (i.e., murder scripts); but in one case, only structures that relate to "means" provide good answers whereas in the other case, only structures that relate to "goals" provide good answers. Declarative knowledge cannot determine the appropriate answer to a given question. The procedural knowledge that directs the search must include specifications of the kinds of responses that are "legal," as well as decision criteria for choosing among alternative responses.

One function of procedural knowledge, then, is to apply a criterion of "legality" and to eliminate responses that, though possible, are highly unlikely to be correct. I assume that in the context of making predictions about others' thoughts and feelings, a *hierarchy of transformation rules* provides the criterion for determining "legality." This hierarchy is a heuristic device that directs the search process by indicating *possible directions* in which others' thoughts and feelings may be channelled. For such a device to be applied, observers must assume that targets' psychological reactions are rule governed (see Berlyne, 1965) and that transformation rules connect targets' psychological reactions to their prior perceptions.

The crux of the problem is that even though observers assume the existence of such transformation rules, the transformation rules that account for targets' reactions are unknown to them. Because they have no direct knowledge of targets' transformation rules, observers assume that the transformation rules they themselves know account for the link between targets' perceptions and their psychological reactions. For example, someone who does not know of the existence of a power function cannot assume its use by others to solve a problem. Similarly, observers can only use the transformation rules they know for making predictions about others' likely psychological reactions.

What are the transformation rules? Each transformation rule represents knowledge about one possible relation between contexts and psychological reactions to them. In deriving the rules, I was guided by models of directed thinking specifying the types of transformations that can link perceptions with stored knowledge.

Some of the transformation rules are based on Schank's (1982) analysis of the types of transformations that account for how reminding occurs. First, any stimulus may lead to dictionary-based reminding. Concepts exist in a "mental dictionary" that includes standard dictionary-type entries that are culturally shared. Such a transformation rule, which I call *category instantiation,* allows stimuli to lead to psychological experiences by focusing on other category members or superordinates (e.g., "When she sees the book she will think that it's a science fiction book because of its strange title").

Second, visually based reminding represents a transformation that uses perceptual similarity between external stimuli and internal representations (Smith & Zarate, 1992). I derived two transformation rules involving perceptual analogues. *Category-based similarity shift* represents culturally shared perceptual analogues in which others are assumed to have psychological experiences that relate stimuli to other stimuli in the same category (e.g., "When he sees the book he will think about other books written by the same author"). *Target-relevant similarity shift* accounts for idiosyncratically determined perceptual analogues (e.g., "When she sees the book she will remember that her grandfather has the same book").

An additional transformation rule is based on the notion of the script (Schank & Abelson, 1977), a coherent sequence of events expected by the individual involving him or her either as participant or as observer. Stimuli may be expected to evoke culturally shared scripts that are connected to them, where such scripts are not unique to the individual in whose memory they are stored. This gives rise to a transformation rule I call *scripted connections* (e.g., "When he see the book he will think they probably got me a birthday present because it's my birthday").

Individuals' understanding of human goal systems (Schank & Wilensky, 1978) enables them to generate desires, plans, and expectations that targets may have in response to stimuli. Thus I derived a transformation rule called *stimulus-directed desires/plans/expectations,* in which common knowledge about others' plans and goals is used to relate stimuli to likely psychological experiences (e.g., "When she sees the book she will think about whether she should read it").

Based on Tulving's (1972) definition of episodic memory as memory for temporally dated events that are autobiographically referenced, I derived two transformation rules that build on episodic knowledge that is unique to the target. For instance, if a stimulus has featured in some episode in the target's past and is expected to elicit recall of this episode, this represents *stimulus-containing reminiscences* (e.g., "When he sees the book he will feel very good because he had looked for it everywhere"). *Stimulus-associated reminiscences* are implicated if the stimulus leads to the recall of a stimulus-related episode in the target's past (e.g., "When she sees the book she will be reminded of the movie (based on the book) that she saw").

Building on the notion of recursive thought (Laing, Phillipson, & Lee, 1966; Miller, Kessel, & Flavell, 1970), I also derived two transformation rules that allow targets to think about themselves. In *stimulus-contingent state of target,* the stimulus is assumed to produce a psychological state in the target, who is then assumed to focus on this state of self (e.g., "When he sees the book he will feel great because he has been wanting to read it for a long time"). In *stimulus-reminded state of target,* the stimulus is assumed to remind, rather than to be a cause of, some state of the self (e.g., "When she sees the book she will think how great it is to read because she likes to read").

In the final transformation rule, *state/characteristic of stimulus,* the target is assumed to have a psychological experience in direct response to an external or internal feature of the stimulus (e.g., "When he sees the book he will think the book is interesting because of its cover").

Hierarchy of Transformation Rules

The 10 transformation rules are further classified in reference to Whorf's (1956) distinction between associations and social connections (for examples and discussion, see Karniol, 1986). Associations relate to an individual's personal experiences and cannot be understood without knowing these personal experiences. In the associative mode, the way A is transformed into B can only be understood via an associative chain that may be unique to the individual in question. On the other hand, connections are intelligible without reference to a specific target's personal experience and represent shared social knowledge; anyone within a given culture would be expected to understand how connections can transform A into B. Based on this distinction, five rules can be classified as associations.

- Stimulus-containing reminiscences
- Stimulus-associated reminiscences
- Target-relevant similarity shift
- Stimulus-contingent state of target
- Stimulus-reminded state of target

Five rules were classified as social connections.

- State/characteristic of stimulus
- Stimulus-directed desires/plans/expectations
- Category-based similarity shift
- Category instantiation
- Scripted connections

The transformation rules are a heuristic device that channels the memory search observers conduct and narrows the range of possible predictions. This device also guides observers in selecting one of the available transformation rules to make a prediction. The way rule selection occurs is critical for formulating explicit hypotheses about how individuals make predictions. For instance, if the selection process is random, one would expect rule repetition to occur at a rate no different than chance. I have shown in previous research (Karniol, 1986, Study 1 & 2) that rule repetition is significantly more frequent than chance would dictate. A second possibility is that the rules are stored as in a storage bin (Wyer & Srull, 1980), with the most recently used rule being placed at the top of the bin. This would imply that the last rule selected would have a greater chance of being reselected than other rules. In my research (Karniol, 1986, Study 1 & 2), a recently used rule had no greater chance of being reused than other rules.

The storage system and selection process that my data seem to support is a hierarchical storage system in which the rules observers know are organized in a fixed order. Such a hierarchy functions like a *metarule* so that the entire hierarchy is accessed each time. Individuals engage in sequential examination of the rules and terminate the search as soon as they find the first transformation rule that appears adequate given the context. Such a fixed hierarchical system has far-reaching implications, some of which are addressed later in this chapter.

Let me illustrate how the hierarchy of transformation rules works. Take an example of a target child who is looking at a book and an observing child who wants to predict the target child's thoughts and feelings. If the observing child has the following three rules sequentially ordered in his or her hierarchy—stimulus-directed desires/plans/expectations, stimulus-containing reminiscences, and state/characteristic of stimulus—after accessing the hierarchy, he or she would first try to link the stimulus with possible desires and goals. If the search in this direction proves fruitful (e.g., the book is a desirable children's book), the search would stop; the observer would make a prediction that the target wants to buy the book or expects to get it as a gift. If the search in this direction is not fruitful (e.g., the book is an advanced text in statistics), the next rule in the hierarchy would be attempted. If recalling an occasion on which similar books played some special role (e.g., the child's mother is a professor who has statistics books), the observer searches for some event in the target's past that matches this specification. If such an event is found, a prediction is made (e.g., "She'll think how she saw the book on her mom's desk last week"). Otherwise, the next rule is attempted until all the rules in the observer's hierarchy are exhausted.

As this example illustrates, the transformation rule hierarchy is accessed whenever the need arises to predict what another person is likely to experience. At the same time, declarative knowledge is searched so that the transformation rules can be examined in light of the input context and the target of prediction. Declarative knowledge structures imbue the transformation rules with content when predictions are made.

The way declarative knowledge is organized is therefore critical for understanding how the content of predictions varies with the targets of prediction and the predictive context. In my model, declarative knowledge structures are assumed to be of two types: prototypical knowledge structures and idiosyncratic knowledge structures. Prototypical knowledge represents generalized knowledge about people and situations (Cantor & Mischel, 1979; Cantor, Mischel, & Schwartz, 1982; Schank & Abelson, 1977). Idiosyncratic knowledge represents knowledge regarding deviations of self, social categories, and known others from prototypical others in behavior, past history, and reactions (Bond & Brockett, 1987; Bond & Sedikides, 1988; Kolodner, 1984). Knowledge structures about social targets and categories are assumed to be created only to the extent that they are known to differ from prototypic individuals in their behavior or reactions. Prototypic knowledge serves as the anchor of comparison for knowledge about other people (Carbonell, 1980; Kolodner, 1984; Schank, 1982). When the target is a stranger[1] unaffiliated with any social category, default values are assigned and the target is assumed to function like a prototypic individual.

Because prototypic knowledge is the default value used to make predictions about others, the rules in the hierarchy are arranged to allow for optimal predictability about the prototypic person. In general, rules representing social connections tend to be higher up in the hierarchy than associations because they are more likely to provide adequate predictions about prototypic others. This has important implications both for the development of transformation rules and for making predictions about nonprototypic others.

Once a transformation rule is selected, declarative knowledge must be used to "fill in" the content of the prediction. To do so, the observer needs to decide whether the target is likely to have an affective or cognitive reaction. That is, each transformation rule can, in principle, be associated with affective or cognitive reactions.[2] Although both developmental and individual differences may determine the citation of affective versus cognitive reactions, such citation reflects the impact of the declarative knowledge activated by the input, rather than the impact of procedural knowledge.

To summarize, each prediction represents the integration of both procedural and declarative knowledge. Procedural knowledge is reflected in the transformation rule the prediction exemplifies; declarative knowledge about individuals and social categories is reflected in variations in transformation rule use for different targets (e.g., young/old, male/female, friend/stranger); individual and developmental differences in declarative knowledge are reflected in the content of predictions (e.g., the citation of affective versus cognitive reactions).

STUDY 1: DEVELOPMENTAL DIFFERENCES IN TRANSFORMATION RULE USE

In the model, the development of three types of knowledge is a prerequisite for making predictions about others' thoughts and feelings:

1. A hierarchy of transformation rules that encodes the kinds of psychological reactions that people can have
2. Prototypical knowledge structures that encode how the prototypical person behaves and reacts in different settings
3. Idiosyncratic knowledge structures that encode how self, social categories, and known others deviate from prototypical others

Developmental differences in making predictions may reflect procedural knowledge, declarative knowledge, or their integration in the predictive context. With respect to procedural knowledge, the distinction between associations and connections is an important one developmentally. Because rules representing associations involve a more personalized and sophisticated understanding of others' likely thoughts and feelings, such rules are likely to emerge later in development. If this is the case, younger children should evidence a restricted variety of transformation rules, whereas older children should evidence a greater variety of transformation rules. The specific rules that should emerge with development are those representing associations.

With respect to declarative knowledge, the distinction between others' thoughts versus their feelings is important developmentally. Because making predictions about others' feelings requires an understanding of how situations relate to affective experiences (Karniol & Ben-Moshé, 1991; Roseman, 1984), one might expect that it would be more difficult to make predictions about how different contexts relate to affective states. Hence younger children should be less likely to make predictions about affective states and would be expected to make more predictions about others' "state of mind" or cognitive experiences.

These hypotheses were tested (Karniol & Ziv, 1994) with children in the third grade, the fifth and sixth grade, and the seventh and eighth grade, who made predictions about others' likely thoughts or likely feelings in 10 contexts (e.g., "When he saw the airplane taking off"). Subjects selected an affective or a cognitive experience by crossing off the other alternative (he thought/felt . . . because . . .) and indicated why that cognition or affect would be experienced.

The answers were coded into one of the ten transformation rules by two independent raters. Agreement between raters was 86%. Subjects had a score of 0 to 10, reflecting the number of times they used each transformation rule. From these data, three scores were derived for each subject.

1. The variety of transformation rules used
2. The number of times rules that represent associations were used
3. The number of times affective reactions were cited

Analyses of variance with grade as the only variable were conducted to examine for developmental differences on all three measures. Linear trends

TABLE 2.1 Variety of Rules, Number of Associations, and Affective Predictions, by Children of Three Grade Levels, Study 1

	Grade			Grade Effect	Linear Trend
	3	5 & 6	7 & 8	(2, 72)	(1, 72)
Variety of rules	3.73	4.13	4.31	2.76*	16.27**
Associations	.92	1.78	2.62	9.31**	17.61**
Affective predictions	1.15	3.75	4.54	10.39**	20.18**

$*p < .10; **p < .01.$

were examined using a procedure recommended by Kirk (1968). The means and associated F values for these analyses are shown in Table 2.1

The first analysis was conducted to test the hypothesis that with grade, a greater variety of transformation rules would be used. This analysis indicates a trend for differences between the three grade groups: Older children tended to use a greater variety of transformation rules in making their predictions than younger children (see Table 2.1). A test of the linear trend was significant.

The next analysis was conducted to test the hypothesis that the use of those rules that represent associations increases with grade. The number of times subjects used each of the transformation rules classified as associations was examined. This analysis indicated significant differences between groups: Older children used rules representing associations significantly more than younger ones. The linear trend was also significant.

As the data in Table 2.1 indicate, the youngest children hardly used rules that represent associations whereas older children used them frequently. This pattern indicates that the use of transformation rules that represent associations, which require a more sophisticated understanding of others' psychological processes, emerges later in development.

The final hypothesis addressed in this study concerns the citation of affective reactions. To test whether such citations increase with grade, the number of times subjects cited affective reactions was examined. Significant differences between groups were found: Older children cited more affective reactions than younger children. The linear trend was also significant. It is interesting to note this trend in light of arguments that children of preschool age can identify emotional reactions that are context appropriate (Shantz, 1975; Strayer, 1987).

To summarize, the data from this study indicate that developmental differences in predictions about other people's thoughts and feelings reflect age-related differences in both procedural and declarative knowledge structures. The variety of rules children use increases linearly with grade. This linear increase occurs primarily because transformation rules that indicate a more sophisticated understanding of other people's psychological processes are used more often with increasing age. Similarly, older children make more predictions about others' likely affective reactions than do younger children. Thus this study illustrates that development entails changes both in children's procedural knowledge, as evident in the variety and types of transformation rules, and in their declarative knowledge, as evident in the content of predictions.

STUDY 2: INDIVIDUAL DIFFERENCES IN ADOLESCENTS' USE OF TRANSFORMATION RULES FOR PROTOTYPIC AND NONPROTOTYPIC TARGETS

The transformation rule hierarchy is constructed so that rules applicable to the prototypic person are at the top of the hierarchy. There is generally little need to examine rules low in the hierarchy for making predictions about prototypic targets. Consequently, the variety of rules used for making predictions about prototypic targets is limited.

For nonprototypic targets, the variety of transformation rules used depends on what being nonprototypic implies. For instance, social category membership (e.g., age, sex, political affiliation) is not always relevant for making predictions about how group members will think or feel (e.g., being "thick-skinned" versus being tall). When the relevant declarative knowledge structure carries no implications about how the target should react, predictions about that target can be made with rules that are also appropriate for prototypic targets.

When knowledge about social category membership is relevant, it may lead to the selection of transformation rules that would not be used for making predictions about the prototypic person, with these selected rules being lower in the transformation rule hierarchy. If transformation rules that are appropriate for nonprototypic targets are lower in the transformation rule hierarchy and the hierarchy is always accessed from the top down, over a series of predictions, a greater variety of transformation rules would be used for making predictions about individuals in social categories that are considered nonprototypic than for prototypic individuals.[3]

Take the example of a teenager who must make predictions about what either a young target or an old target would think or feel in a given setting. There is some evidence that the prototype of the "average person" held by young people of both sexes is of a male (Martin, 1987) who is close to their own age (Brewer, Dull, & Lui, 1981). Eagly and Kite (1987) argue that the default value in contexts where no information is provided is that of a young male. Insofar as individuals know how old people differ from young ones, such knowledge about the elderly should guide and constrain rule selection. If the rules at the top of the hierarchy are those most appropriate for making predictions about prototypic others, some of them may be inappropriate for old people; observers may need to descend further down the hierarchy of transformation rules to find rules for the elderly. Consequently, one would expect a greater variety of transformation rules to be used by young people for making predictions about old targets than about young targets.

The hypothesis that young people will use a greater variety of transformation rules for making predictions about old targets than about young ones appears to run counter to the finding that categories in which individuals are members are represented in a more complex way (Linville, 1982). Note, however, that the hypothesis of greater variety is not based on young people's having greater complexity of knowledge about the elderly; rather, knowledge about how the elderly differ from young people leads to the use of a greater variety of transformation rules in making predictions about older people. Referring to the transformation rule hierarchy, one would expect predictions about the elderly to be made primarily with transformation rules that seem more applicable to older than younger people (e.g., involving reminiscences). Similarly, if the prototypic person is viewed as male, one would expect a greater variety of transformation rules to be used by both sexes for making predictions about female targets than for male targets.

The above hypotheses are based on the assumption that making predictions about others' thoughts and feelings requires two parallel processes to occur. Individuals must access procedural knowledge in order to channel their search of declarative memory. In turn, declarative knowledge determines rule selection because knowledge about targets must be integrated with the context of the prediction. The integration of different knowledge structures and the feeding back of this knowledge to influence rule selection represents an effortful process. If the process is effortful, there may be individual differences in the tendency to engage in it.

In particular, differences in perspective-taking ability may be expected to be manifest in individual differences in transformation rule use. Specifically, individuals who indicate that they habitually try to understand other people's perspectives are likely to be individuals with a greater variety of transformation rules in their hierarchies. They should also be more willing to make the effort to search through the hierarchy of transformation rules and to integrate procedural knowledge with declarative knowledge. Thus individuals high in perspective taking would be expected to evidence greater differentiation between targets in different social categories.[4] Such people should have a less homogeneous and more differentiated perception of others than those who are low on this dimension. They would be expected to evidence a greater variety of rules for making predictions about nonprototypic targets, but would not be expected to differ from those low in perspective taking in making predictions about prototypic targets.

This hypothesis appears to contradict the finding that categorical thinking is highly correlated with authoritarianism and negatively correlated with empathy (Greif & Hogan, 1973). I am not arguing that perspective taking leads to categorical thinking, but that being high in perspective taking increases the likelihood that individuals will utilize knowledge about social categories to make differential predictions about category members.

The associative transformations, which represent transformation rules that are cognitively more sophisticated, would be expected to be used more by individuals high in perspective taking than by other people. In Study 1, such rules were found to be developmentally more advanced, and one would therefore expect their use to be more prevalent in individuals high in perspective taking. Finally, given that developmentally more advanced children provided more predictions that focused on feelings rather than cognitions, one might expect individuals high in perspective taking to make more predictions citing others' likely affective reactions. Study 2 (Karniol & Shomroni, 1993) was conducted to examine these hypotheses. The subjects were 132 urban, Israeli eleventh and twelfth graders (59 boys and 73 girls) who were tested in their classes without their teacher present. Subjects were told that the study was concerned with "understanding other people" and that their responses would remain anonymous. There was no time limit. Subjects first completed the Davis (1983) Interpersonal Reactivity Index (IRI), a 28-item self-report scale, with 7 items that assess perspective taking.[5] This was followed by the sentence completion task (Karniol, 1986), with 12 sentence stems in which a target person saw or heard a given stimulus (e.g., the airplane taking off, the school). Subjects had to complete half the sentence stems by indicating what the target would think and why; for the other half, subjects indicated what the target would feel and why. Targets varied on two dimensions, sex and age (young/old); each subject responded to only one target combination. The responses were coded into one of the ten transformation rules by two independent raters who were unaware of subjects' perspective-taking scores. Agreement between raters was 89%.

Analyses Excluding Individual Differences

The first analyses were conducted to examine the impact of targets' social category membership. Analyses of variance with sex of subject, sex of target, and age of target between subject variables were conducted on the variety of transformation rules, the number of predictions made with rules that represent associations, and the number of predictions citing affective reactions.

The analysis of the variety of rules showed only a significant age-of-target effect, $F(1, 124) = 7.10, p < .009$. Consistent with the hypothesis that rules are examined in sequence from the top down, a greater variety of rules was used for old targets ($M = 5.73$) than for young targets ($M = 5.17$). However, the variety of rules used for female targets did not differ from that used for male targets. It appears that the declarative knowledge structures that are involved in selecting transformation rules are a prototypic knowledge structure about young targets of both sexes and a nonprototypic knowledge structure about old people of both sexes.

These two knowledge structures are similarly implicated in the analysis of the number of predictions made with those rules that represent associations. In this analysis, the age-of-target effect was also significant, $F(1, 124) = 19.06, p < .001$; more associations were used for making predictions about old targets ($M = 5.27$) than about young targets ($M = 3.75$).

But there was also a significant interaction of sex of target with age of target in the use of associations, $F(1, 124) = 3.97, p < .05$. This interaction was due to the fact that predictions with rules representing associations were made equally often, $F(1, 124) = 1.78, n.s.,$ for male targets of both ages ($M = 3.91$ and $M = 4.65$, for young males and old males) but were made significantly more often, $F(1, 124) = 19.89, p < .001$, for old female targets ($M = 5.61$) than for young female targets ($M = 3.61$). The declarative knowledge structure that appears to be relevant in this context is that of "a grandmother type" (Brewer et al., 1981) who is apparently considered by adolescents to have her own ways of reacting to situations. But young males, old males, and young females are all expected to have analogous ways of having their thoughts and feelings channelled. Note, though, that even if the same channelling routes are assumed to be taken, this does not mean that the content of predictions in such cases needs to be identical.

This last point is underscored by the analysis of the number of predictions citing affective reactions rather than cognitions. In this analysis, only a main effect for sex of target emerged, $F(1, 124) = 9.14$, $p < .005$, with more predictions citing affective reactions for female than for male targets ($Ms = 4.94$ and 4.09).

This indicates that, in terms of psychological functioning, knowledge about females is differentiated from knowledge about males, regardless of age. But knowledge about "how females react" does not impact on the selection of specific transformation rules; instead such knowledge influences the content of predictions about female targets, with females being expected to evidence affective reactions in the very same contexts that males are expected to have cognitions that are largely devoid of affect. This pattern seems to be based on the stereotype of females as more emotional than males (Ashmore, 1981; Eagly & Steffen, 1984). Yet, even though "grandmother types" were expected to have their psychological reactions channelled in different ways than young females, "grandmothers" were not expected to differ from young females in the likelihood of evidencing affective reactions to these grandmotherly ways of transforming stimuli into psychological experiences.

The general pattern that emerges indicates that declarative knowledge structures relating to targets' social category are not isomorphic in terms of when they impact prediction making. Recall that the variety of rules showed a significant age-of-target effect but no sex-of-target effect; yet both associations and predictions citing affective reactions evidenced sex-of-target effects. This suggests that declarative knowledge about targets' sex most likely comes into play at a rather late stage of the process, whereas age-of-target knowledge influences the prediction-making process at earlier stages. It is not clear why this is the case. One possibility is that high school students are especially concerned with age-based distinctions and that this particular pattern would not be manifest with adults. In fact, in research with adults (Karniol & Bresler, 1989) significant sex-of-target effects emerged when no other social category information was provided. For adolescents, information about age may dominate information about sex; alternatively, adolescents may not have well-embellished knowledge structures about how females and males differ from each other in psychological processes.

It is interesting to note that sex of subject had no effect on any of the measures even though females are generally considered more socially perceptive (Maccoby & Jacklin, 1974; but see Eisenberg & Lennon, 1983). Moreover, sex of subject did not interact with sex of target even though it may have been expected that male and female adolescents would use the transformation rules differently and would have different declarative knowledge structures about their own sex than about the opposite sex.

Analyses Including Individual Differences

To examine the remaining hypotheses, subjects' perspective-taking scores were computed and the analyses of variance were rerun, with perspective-taking scores covaried. On the variety of rules, the impact of perspective taking was significant, $F(1, 120) = 5.25, p < .05$; individuals high in perspective taking used a greater variety of rules. Interestingly, though, the age-of-target effect remained significant after covarying perspective-taking scores, $F(1, 120) = 6.88, p < .01$. The analyses of the number of associations and the number of affective predictions indicate that perspective taking did not influence these measures, all $Fs < 1$. Moreover, all the significant effects remained significant after covarying perspective taking.

Two interesting results then need to be accounted for: first, the fact that perspective taking contributed significantly to the variety of rules used, and second, the fact that covarying perspective-taking scores did not eliminate the effect of social category membership on any of the dependent measures. The finding that perspective taking was associated with a greater variety of transformation rules is consistent with the hypotheses. On the other hand, perspective taking was expected to influence the tendency to integrate declarative knowledge with procedural knowledge; hence covarying perspective taking was expected to eliminate the impact of social category membership on all three dependent measures. The data do not support this hypothesized link between perspective taking and declarative knowledge.

This pattern suggests that in adolescents, the availability of procedures, not declarative knowledge, differentiates good perspective takers from poor ones. This is especially interesting given that in the first study, in which younger children served as subjects, developmental differences were found on measures that reflect declarative knowledge as well as measures that reflect procedural knowledge. Presumably, this divergence between adolescents and younger children is due to the fact that, by late adolescence, declarative knowledge structures are fully embellished and await the application of relevant procedures for making predictions about others' thoughts and feelings.

CONCLUSIONS

In the two studies presented in this chapter, developmental and individual differences were shown to have some analogous effects on the use of transformation rules for making predictions about other people's likely thoughts and feelings.

Study 1, which examined developmental differences, indicated that some of the procedures used to make predictions about others' thoughts and feelings are available to children as young as third grade. But young children's procedural knowledge is not well developed. Their knowledge of the possible routes that others' thoughts and feelings can take is restricted; they have fewer transformation rules in their hierarchy and tend to use rules that can be "read off" the situation, rather than rules that require knowledge about the target to be integrated with procedural knowledge. This pattern dovetails with some of the conclusions reached by Higgins (1981) in his distinction between "situational role taking" and "personal role taking," with the latter requiring an integration among various knowledge sources.

Young children's declarative knowledge base in this realm is not well developed either; they appear to be less knowledgeable about the affective reactions that situations elicit (Schwartz & Trabasso, 1984), as they avoid making predictions about others' likely affective reactions. Yet because information about targets' social category membership was not provided in this study, it cannot be used to draw conclusions about children's declarative knowledge structures relating to social targets and the possible role such structures may play in determining transformation rule use.

Study 2 does allow one to draw some conclusions about the role of declarative knowledge relating to social targets, as well as the impact of individual differences in perspective taking on the use of both procedural and declarative knowledge. Individual differences in perspective taking are apparently only related to the use of procedural knowledge and contribute directly to the variety of rules used. On the other hand, individual differences in perspective taking do not influence which particular rules are selected or the nature of the psychological experience cited (i.e., cognitive versus affective reactions). Moreover, covarying the influence of perspective taking did not eliminate the impact of declarative knowledge about targets' age and sex category. Thus individual differences in perspective taking appear to be independent of the declarative knowledge structures that were relevant in this study (i.e., situation knowledge and knowledge about prototypic targets varying in age and sex). But individual differences in perspective taking do influence the procedures individuals have available for making predictions. The possibility that there are individual differences in the nature of declarative knowledge representations in other contexts must be examined in future research.

In general, in these studies, individuals who were developmentally less advanced and less socially perceptive evidenced a narrower range of transformation rules, reflecting a deficiency in their procedural knowledge. In addition, developmentally less advanced individuals used cognitively less advanced transformation rules and focused primarily on cognitive aspects of others' psychological experiences, reflecting less elaborate declarative knowledge structures about situations.

The two studies illustrate that developmental differences and individual differences both need to be incorporated within the same model, and that variations in them can be used to empirically test hypotheses based on the model. Research that examines both developmental and social-personality variables is necessary to further our understanding of social cognitive processes. Such a combined endeavor will yield a more accurate picture of the underlying psychological processes than research based on either research tradition alone. Because the transformation rule model generates explicit hypotheses about the way individuals who vary in developmental level or in social-personality variables make predictions about others' likely thoughts and feelings—hypotheses that cannot be derived from other extant models— the transformation rule model is heuristically valuable in attempts to gain a more adequate understanding of the processes involved in role taking.

NOTES

1. Predictions about known others may implicate different rules than predictions about prototypic others (Karniol, Ayalon, & Rish, in preparation).

2. In previous research, certain rules were found to be used more often with affective reactions, whereas other rules were used more often with cognitions. Space limitations preclude a detailed discussion of this issue.

3. Another way of accessing transformation rules lower in the hierarchy is to bypass rules inappropriate for nonprototypic categories. This should result in a complete lack of overlap between the rules used for prototypic targets versus those used for nonprototypic targets. The pattern of transformation rule use, in which all rules are occasionally used for making predictions about all social targets, does not support such a possibility.

4. Note that if one assumes that such people are cognitively more complex (Linville, 1982), one can derive a similar hypothesis about their use of a greater variety of rules. But the complexity hypothesis leads to the opposite prediction about the number of rules that should be used in making predictions about old versus young targets.

5. Although all four subscales of the IRI were examined, in this chapter I report only the analyses for perspective taking (PT). Because of the high correlation ($r = .53$) between the Perspective Taking and Empathic Concern scales of the IRI, covariance was conducted using the SPSS hierarchical covariance program, entering the four dimensions of the IRI with PT covaried first, thus eliminating the contribution of empathic concern to the PT scores.

REFERENCES

Ashmore, R. D. (1981). Sex stereotypes and implicit personality theory. In D. L. Hamilton (Ed.), *Cognitive processes in stereotyping and intergroup behavior* (pp. 37-81). Hillsdale, NJ: Erlbaum.

Astington, J. W., Harris, P. L., & Olson, D. R. (1988). *Developing theories of mind.* Cambridge, UK: Cambridge University Press.

Bargh, J. A. (1989). Conditional automaticity: Varieties of automatic influence in social perception and cognition. In J. S. Uleman & J. A. Bargh (Eds.), *Unintended thought* (pp. 3-51). New York: Guilford.

Batson, C. D., Batson, J. G., Griffitt, C. A., Barrientos, S., Brandt, J. R., Sprengelmeyer, P., & Bayly, M. J. (1989). Negative-state relief and the empathy-altruism hypothesis. *Journal of Personality and Social Psychology, 56,* 922-933.

Berlyne, D. E. (1965). *Structure and direction in thinking.* New York: John Wiley.

Bond, C. F., Jr., & Brockett, D. R. (1987). A social context-personality index theory of memory for acquaintances. *Journal of Personality and Social Psychology, 52,* 1110-1121.

Bond, C. F., Jr., & Sedikides, C. (1988). The recapitulation hypothesis in person retrieval. *Journal of Experimental Social Psychology, 24,* 195-221.

Brewer, M. B., Dull, V., & Lui, L. (1981). Perceptions of the elderly: Stereotypes as prototypes. *Journal of Personality and Social Psychology, 41,* 656-670.

Cantor, N., & Mischel, W. (1979). Prototypes in person perception. In L. Berkowitz (Ed.), *Advances in experimental social psychology: Vol. 12* (pp. 3-52). New York: Academic Press.

Cantor, N., Mischel, W., & Schwartz, J. C. (1982). A prototypic analysis of psychological situations. *Cognitive Psychology, 19,* 45-77.

Carbonell, J. G. (1980). Towards a process model of human personality traits. *Artificial Intelligence, 15,* 49-74.

Chandler, M. J. (1976). Social cognition: A selective review of current research. In W. F. Overton & J. M. Gallagher (Eds.), *Knowledge and development: Vol. 1* (pp. 93-147). New York: Plenum.

Chandler, M. J. (1988). Doubt and developing theories of mind. In J. W. Astington, P. L. Harris, & D. R. Olson (Eds.), *Developing theories of mind* (pp. 387-413). Cambridge, UK: Cambridge University Press.

Cialdini, R. B., Schaller, M., Houlihan, D., Arps, K., Fultz, J., & Beaman, A. L. (1987). Empathy-based helping: Is it selflessly or selfishly motivated? *Journal of Personality and Social Psychology, 52,* 749-758.

Davis, M. H. (1983). Measuring individual differences in empathy: Evidence for a multidimensional approach. *Journal of Personality and Social Psychology, 44,* 113-126.

Dovidio, J. F., Allen, J. L., & Schroeder, D. A. (1990). Specificity of empathy-induced helping: Evidence for altruistic motivation. *Journal of Personality and Social Psychology, 59,* 249-260.

Eagly, A. H., & Kite, M. E. (1987). Are stereotypes of nationalities applied to both men and women? *Journal of Personality and Social Psychology, 53,* 451-462.

Eagly, A. H., & Steffen, V. J. (1984). Gender stereotypes stem from the distribution of men and women into social roles. *Journal of Personality and Social Psychology, 46,* 735-754.

Eisenberg, N., & Lennon, R. (1983). Sex differences in empathy and related capacities. *Psychological Bulletin, 94,* 100-131.

Flavell, J. H. (1974). The development of inferences about others. In T. Mischel (Ed.), *Understanding other persons* (pp. 66-116). Oxford, UK: Blackwell.

Graesser, A. C., Byrne, P. J., & Behrens, M. L. (1992). Answering questions about information in databases. In T. W. Laver, E. Peacock, & A. C. Graesser (Eds.), *Questions and information systems* (pp. 229-252). Hillsdale, NJ: Erlbaum.

Greif, E. B., & Hogan, R. (1973). The theory and measurement of empathy. *Journal of Counselling Psychology, 20,* 280-284.

Heider, F. (1958). *The psychology of interpersonal relations.* New York: John Wiley.

Higgins, E. T. (1981). Role taking and social judgment: Alternative developmental perspectives and processes. In J. H. Flavell & L. Ross (Eds.), *Social cognitive development* (pp. 119-153). New York: Cambridge University Press.

Karniol, R. (1986). What will they think of next? Transformation rules used to predict other people's thoughts and feelings. *Journal of Personality and Social Psychology, 51,* 932-944.

Karniol, R. (1990). Reading people's minds: A transformation rule model for predicting others' thoughts and feelings. In M. P. Zanna (Ed.), *Advances in experimental social psychology: Vol. 23* (pp. 211-248). San Diego, CA: Academic Press.

Karniol, R., & Ben-Moshé, R. (1991). Drawing inferences about others' cognitions and affective reactions: A test of two models for representing affect. *Cognition and Emotion, 5,* 241-253.

Karniol, R., & Bresler, O. (1989). *Transformation rule use for making predictions about same and opposite sex targets.* Unpublished manuscript.

Karniol, R., & Shomroni, D. (1993). *Individual differences in adolescents' use of transformation rules for prototypic and nonprototypic targets.* Unpublished manuscript.

Karniol, R., & Ziv, L. (1994). *Developmental differences in transformation rule use: Becoming efficient at making predictions about others' thoughts and feelings.* Unpublished manuscript.

Kirk, R. E. (1968). *Experimental design: Procedures for the behavioral sciences.* Belmont, CA: Brooks/Cole.

Kolodner, J. L. (1984). *Retrieval and organization strategies in conceptual memory: A computer model.* Hillsdale, NJ: Erlbaum.

Laing, R. D., Phillipson, H., & Lee, A. R. (1966). *Interpersonal perception.* New York: Harper & Row.

Lehnert, W. G. (1981). Plot units and narrative summarization. *Cognitive Science, 5,* 293-331.

Linville, P. A. (1982). The complexity-extremity effect and age based stereotyping. *Journal of Personality and Social Psychology, 42,* 193-211.

Maccoby, E. E., & Jacklin, C. N. (1974). *The psychology of sex differences.* Stanford, CA: Stanford University Press.

Martin, C. L. (1987). A ratio measure of sex stereotyping. *Journal of Personality and Social Psychology, 52,* 489-499.

Miller, P. H., Kessel, F. S., & Flavell, J. H. (1970). Thinking about people thinking about people thinking about . . . : A study of social cognitive development. *Child Development, 41,* 613-623.

Perner, J. *Understanding the representational mind.* Cambridge: MIT Press.

Roseman, I. J. (1984). Cognitive determinants of emotion: A structural theory. In P. Shaver (Ed.), *Review of personality and social psychology: Vol. 5* (pp. 11-36). Beverly Hills, CA: Sage.

Schank, R. (1982). *Dynamic memory: A theory of learning in computers and people.* London: Cambridge University Press.

Schank, R., & Abelson, R. (1977). *Scripts, plans, goals and understanding.* Hillsdale, NJ: Erlbaum.

Schank, R., & Wilensky, R. (1978). A goal-directed production system for story understanding. In D. A. Waterman & F. Hayes-Roth (Eds.), *Pattern-directed inference systems.* New York: Academic Press.

Schwartz, R. M., & Trabasso, T. (1984). Children's understanding of emotions. In C. E. Izard, J. Kagan, & R. B. Zajonc (Eds.), *Emotions, cognition, and behavior* (pp. 409-437). Cambridge, UK: Cambridge University Press.

Selman, R. L. (1980). *The growth of interpersonal understanding.* New York: Academic Press.

Shantz, C. U. (1975). The development of social cognition. In E. M. Hetherington (Ed.), *Review of child development research: Vol. 5* (pp. 257-323). Chicago: University of Chicago Press.

Smith, E. R., & Zarate, M. A. (1992). Exemplar-based model of social judgment. *Psychological Review, 99,* 3-21.

Strayer, J. (1987). Affective and cognitive perspectives on empathy. In N. Eisenberg & J. Strayer (Eds.), *Empathy and its development* (pp. 218-244). Cambridge, UK: Cambridge University Press.

Tulving, E. (1972). Episodic and semantic memory. In E. Tulving & W. Donaldson (Eds.), *Organization of memory* (pp. 382-403). New York: Academic Press.

Vorauer, J. D., & Ross, M. (1993). Making mountains out of molehills: An informational goals analysis of self and social perception. *Personality and Social Psychology Bulletin, 19,* 620-632.

Whorf, B. L. (1956). On the connection of ideas. In J. B. Carroll (Ed.), *Language, thought, and reality: Selected writings of Benjamin Lee Whorf* (pp. 35-39). Cambridge: MIT Press. (Original work published 1927)

Wyer, R. S., & Srull, T. K. (1980). The processing of social stimulus information: A conceptual integration. In R. Hastie, T. M. Ostrom, E. B. Ebbesen, R. S. Wyer, Jr., D. L. Hamilton, & D. E. Carlston (Eds.), *Person memory* (pp. 227-300). Hillsdale, NJ: Erlbaum.

3

Features and Sources of Parents' Attributions About Themselves and Their Children

JOAN E. GRUSEC
NORMA MAMMONE

Joan E. Grusec is Professor of Psychology at the University of Toronto. She received a Ph.D. from Stanford University and taught at Wesleyan University and the University of Waterloo before moving to her present position. Her research interests include the origins of parenting beliefs and their relation to parenting behavior, the effects of discipline on socialization outcomes, and the development of altruism. She is the coauthor of *Social Development: History, Theory, and Research* and *Punishment* and coeditor of *Foundations of Psychology*.

Norma Mammone is a graduate student at the University of Toronto, enrolled in the Applied Developmental Psychology program. Her research interests have included attachment history, parenting cognitions, and parenting behavior in families where there is child maltreatment. She is presently extending her research to include family dynamics, parenting behaviors, and children's subsequent social and emotional development.

Developmental psychologists have had a long-standing interest in predicting parenting behavior and child outcomes from parents' general attitudes about child rearing. By and large, however, their results have been disappointing (Holden & Edwards, 1989). In the last few years, a reoriented interest in parent cognition has renewed optimism that links between parents' thoughts and their behavior might be demonstrable (e.g., Goodnow & Collins, 1990; Sigel, McGillicuddy-DeLisi, & Goodnow, 1991). The new approach differs from the old in a fundamentally important way. Instead of focusing on overriding attitudes and beliefs about child rearing, the new approach considers specific thoughts or beliefs that pertain to a particular interaction between parent and child. Rather than assessing relations among parental attitudes (e.g., acceptance or rejection of dependency), parent behavior, and behavior shown by a child, interest is in thoughts the parent has while the child is behaving in a particular manner (e.g., "She's clinging to me because she's tired and frustrated"; "I simply don't know how to stop this behavior"). These cognitions are seen as mediators between or moderators of a child's specific behavior and the parent's specific response.

A number of different beliefs or cognitions have been the subject of study. In this chapter we focus on two that have received the most attention: those having to do with how effectively parents believe they can control the behavior of their child and those having to do with why they believe their children are behaving as they are. In both cases, researchers, in addition to drawing on leads from mainstream developmental psychology, have availed themselves of concepts developed by social psychologists. We begin by reviewing some of the research that has attempted to relate cognitions about parenting self-efficacy, as well as cognitions involving causal attributions for children's behavior, to parental affect and behavior. We then consider how these cognitions develop.

PARENTING COGNITIONS

Parenting Self-Efficacy

Studies of parenting self-efficacy have taken their theoretical impetus from several sources. Attribution theory (e.g., Weiner, 1980) provides one set of leads in its suggestion that causes of behavior can be located at the intersection of factors on the dimensions of internality/externality, stability/instability, and controllability/uncontrollability. Self-efficacious individuals are those who attribute positive parenting outcomes to factors that are dispositional or internal, that are unchanging, and over which they have control. These include features of the situation such as their own parenting ability, amount of effort expended, and ease of the parenting task. Conversely, parents who attribute positive outcomes to external, unstable, and uncontrollable events such as a fleeting good mood, chance, or luck are likely to be low in self-efficacy or to have what Abramson, Seligman, and Teasdale (1978) label a "depression-prone attributional style." With respect to unsuccessful parenting outcomes, attributions of internality, instability, and controllability are more likely to be associated with high levels of self-efficacy, and attributions of internality, stability, and uncontrollability are more likely to be associated with low self-efficacy.

Another dimension of causal attributions (Abramson et al., 1978) has to do with the degree to which factors are seen as global (affecting a wide variety of outcomes) or specific (having a narrower focus): Highly self-efficacious individuals make global attributions for successful outcomes and specific ones for unsuccessful outcomes. These attributional dimensions are assumed to have an impact on behavior primarily because they influence affect as well as expectations about future behavior. For example, individuals who make stable internal attributions for outcomes are more likely to experience guilt after failure, and competence, pride, and confidence after success. People who attribute failure to stable internal factors experience depression and give up, whereas those who attribute it to controllable events such as lack of effort initiate mastery-oriented responses (Abramson et al., 1978).

Bandura's (1977) self-efficacy theory provides another way of viewing beliefs about one's ability to parent effectively. According to this theory, people develop domain-specific beliefs about their own abilities and characteristics that guide their behavior by determining what they try to achieve and how much effort they put into their performance in a particular situation or domain. These self-percepts provide a framework or structure against which information is judged: They determine how or whether individuals put into action the knowledge they have. Bandura suggests that when people have negative self-percepts about a situation, believing they are ineffective and lack the ability to perform well, they become preoccupied with themselves as well as emotionally aroused, two conditions that distract from performing effectively. Efficacy beliefs are self-confirming. Individuals with strong ones are more likely to persist at tasks with eventual success, thereby confirming their view of their own ability, whereas those with weak efficacy beliefs do not persist, experience more failure, and thereby have their negative self-perceptions confirmed. Although performance outcomes are seen to be the strongest determinants of self-efficacy beliefs, other sources of information such as vicarious experience, social persuasion, social comparison, and emotional arousal can also be influential.

Attribution and self-efficacy theory have been used as springboards to understanding self-efficacy in the parenting domain. We turn to a review of work in the area.

Parenting Efficacy as Perceptions of Relative
Control of Adult and Child Over the Interaction

A major program of research on parenting self-efficacy is currently being undertaken by Bugental and her colleagues. Bugental (e.g., Bugental, 1991; Bugental & Shennum, 1984) describes parents in terms of the amount of power they perceive themselves to have in interactions with a child relative to the amount of power they ascribe to the child. To measure relative power,

Bugental developed the Parent Attribution Test (PAT), which was originally derived from Weiner's (1980) taxonomy of causal attributions. Adults responding to the PAT are asked to assign importance to a variety of factors in determining hypothesized successful or unsuccessful outcomes in interacting with children. Half of the items refer to characteristics of the adult, whereas the other half pertain to characteristics of the child, with causes being either internal (due to ability or effort) or external (due to luck or other people) and either stable (ability, other people) or unstable (effort, luck). The causal factors were drawn from free responses of parents to open-ended questions about the causes of their own caregiving success and failure, with these responses analyzed by multidimensional scaling methods to determine the structure that adults impose on their analyses of caregiving outcomes. Two dimensions of locus were identified: adult versus child, and controllability (e.g., problems due to lack of effort versus being sick). The measure ultimately yields two scores in particular that Bugental has used in most of her research, one yielding an assessment of the adult's perceived control over caregiving failure (ACF) and the other an assessment of the child's perceived control over caregiving failure (CCF).

Bugental (1991) proposes that beliefs about this relative control in relationships form a cognitive structure or schema operating at the preconscious level that is triggered by the presence of a difficult child in an ambiguous or threatening situation. When faced with difficult children, adults with high control are prepared to engage in solution-oriented thinking that allows them to react to the child in ways that are successful in encouraging the behavior they want. Adults with low control schemas, on the other hand, experience negative affective reactions as well as threat-focused and pessimistic conscious ideation. This maladaptive reaction to threat leads to behavior, some that occurs with little conscious control and some that is more deliberately managed, that is ineffective in eliciting responsivity from the difficult child. Thus the child's difficult behavior is maintained and the validity of the adult's low control schema is supported. Because individuals with low control beliefs function well when confronted with easy children, Bugental treats self-efficacy as a variable that moderates, rather than mediates, parenting behavior; that is, that operates only in situations involving difficult children rather than across all situations involving children.

Bugental's model is supported by the results of a series of studies in which mothers are assessed in interaction with their own children as well as with unrelated children with whom they have no history of interaction. In this way, Bugental has been able to demonstrate that adult reactions are a function of control schemas and not just of expectations related to a particular child.

At the behavioral level, low control mothers have been observed to generate affectively confusing or inconsistent messages when interacting with difficult children, for example, negative messages delivered in a kidding, sarcastic, or condescending fashion, neutral statements with inappropriately high voice assertion, statements of approval or positive affect with relatively low voice assertion, and smiles with an accompanying frown (Bugental, Mantyla, & Lewis, 1989). These patterns of behavior are described as a reflection of "leakage of feelings of powerlessness" that are confusing to the child because they send conflicting messages—reassurance on the one hand and a suggestion of displeasure on the other. Thus difficult children's lack of responsiveness and noncompliance is maintained by the slowing of responses, increasing avoidant behavior, and further noncompliance that are reactions to confusing parenting behavior. Low control mothers also are more likely to use abusive discipline such as kicking, biting, and beating, as well as coercive discipline such as spanking, pushing, and slapping (Bugental, Blue, & Cruzcosa, 1989). These strong power assertive practices also promote negative and noncompliant behavior.

At the affective level, low control mothers differ from high control mothers in their increased facial and vocal evidence of sadness over the course of interaction with difficult children, as well as increased negative thoughts, with this pattern most pronounced for mothers who see themselves as low in power and the child as high in power (Bugental, Blue, & Lewis, 1990; Bugental et al., 1993). Moreover, when exposed to unresponsive children, low control mothers show increases in defensive arousal (increased heart rate and skin conductance) relative to high control mothers (Bugental et al., 1993). Finally, Bugental et al. (1993) report that perceptions of self-efficacy also have an impact on information-processing patterns in that low control adults have difficulty acquiring new information, as well as performing effectively on a cognitively demanding task, when they are involved in difficult interactions. In contrast, high control adults show enhancements in information processing. Thus it appears that individuals with low efficacy perceptions reallocate attention to their heightened state of emotional arousal at the expense of resources that could be used to acquire new information. On the other hand, high control individuals use cognitive resources to meet new challenges.

It should be noted that in all of Bugental's research, low control mothers showed maladaptive responses only in their interactions with difficult children, not with easy children. This is important because it suggests that parental control attributions do not have main effects, but only produce consequences in interactive ways.

Other Approaches to Parenting Self-Efficacy

Other researchers who have been interested in parenting self-efficacy include Donovan and Leavitt (1989; Donovan, Leavitt, & Walsh, 1990), who have identified mothers described as having an "illusion of control." Although the illusion of control has been considered adaptive (e.g., Alloy & Abramson, 1979), Donovan et al. argue that individuals who greatly overestimate their own control mask feelings of inefficacy and exhibit behavior that has negative consequences for child outcomes. Thus illusory control becomes a defensive coping mechanism when parenting efficacy is challenged.

Donovan and her colleagues (1990) measured illusory control by asking mothers to engage in a simulated childcare task in which their actions (pressing a button) had no effect on an infant's crying, and then to estimate the extent of control they thought they had over the crying. On the basis of this estimation, the mothers were designated as high, moderate, or low in illusory control. Mothers high in illusory control seem similar in many of their characteristics to Bugental's low control mothers. They are relatively likely to attribute positive child-rearing outcomes to external and unstable factors, to report elevated levels of depression (measured by the Beck Depression Inventory), and to show heart rate changes indicative of aversion to impending baby cries. In contrast, mothers with more moderate levels of illusory control demonstrate heart rate changes indicative of attentive responding. Mothers with high illusory control also have more insecurely attached babies, presumably an indication of deficits in parenting skills. Finally, Donovan et al. report that mothers who are high in illusory control are more susceptible to learned helplessness; that is, they have great difficulty in finding a solution for what had initially been an insoluble child-rearing task. Presumably, individuals who have extremely high expectations of control are most disrupted when those expectations are disconfirmed.

Guided directly by Bandura's (1977) theory, Teti and Gelfand (1991) measured parenting self-efficacy by asking mothers to rate their feelings of efficacy in specific domains of infant care such as soothing a baby, understanding what it wants, amusing it, and disengaging from it. Like Bugental and Donovan and her colleagues, Teti and Gelfand report both behavioral and affective correlates of differential self-efficacy. Mothers who are low in self-efficacy are less competent at parenting, with competence determined by observers' ratings of their sensitivity, warmth, flatness of affect, disengagement, and anger during free play and feeding interactions with their infants. They are also high in depression on the Beck Depression Inventory. In contrast to Bugental, however, Teti and Gelfand argue that depression is a cause of low self-efficacy rather than an outcome, with evidence for direction of effect provided by their observation that both depression and self-efficacy were correlated with parenting competence, but that level of depression did not remain associated with competence after controlling for level of self-efficacy, whereas self-efficacy remained significantly associated after controlling for level of depression.

Kochanska, Radke-Yarrow, Kuczynski, and Friedman (1987) also suggest that depression is a cause of low self-efficacy. Self-efficacy was operationalized by asking mothers to rate the relative importance of maternal rearing practices, personality, paternal influences, other people, and luck on child outcomes in a variety of specific domains. These authors found that both bipolar and unipolar depressed mothers were more likely to attribute child outcomes to uncontrollable factors than were nondepressed mothers, a finding they attribute to feelings of helplessness and cognitive distortions that are a crucial component of affective illness.

Commentary

We conclude this section with three observations. The first has to do with the relation of depression to self-efficacy. Low self-efficacy may be the result of cognitive distortions that occur in depression, such as selective activation of memories of failure experiences (see Bandura, 1989, who uses Bower's 1983 affective-priming theory to explain this phenomenon). Or low self-efficacy may induce feelings of depression, possibly because it produces poor parenting, which leads to a lack of reinforcement in child interactions and resultant depression. Indeed, both mechanisms may be operating.

The second observation has to do with the varied ways in which self-efficacy has been measured. Although low parenting self-efficacy is clearly associated with specific patterns of physiological arousal and affective, behavioral, and cognitive deficits, the wide variety of ways in which it has been operationalized points to the necessity of care in making generalizations from various findings. Conceptually, for example, Bugental's definition involves considerations having to do with locus of control, whereas Teti and

Gelfand's does not. Empirically, the definitions appear to differ as well. Teti and Gelfand report a correlation of .74 between the Parenting Sense of Competence Scale from Abidin's (1986) Parenting Stress Index and their Maternal Self-Efficacy Scale, apparently indicating concurrent validity for their measure. In our own laboratory, we have administered the PAT and the Parenting Sense of Competence Scale to 105 mothers and fathers. The correlation between the Sense of Competence Scale and ACF is −.03, whereas the correlation with CCF is .12. Thus it appears that individuals who score low on perceived control over failure may be rather different from those who score low on the Maternal Self-Efficacy Scale. There is nothing wrong with this, of course, but it does suggest that a finer-grained analysis of what is being measured and how it relates to outcome variables is needed.

The final observation has to do with the inference that low attributions of control are likely to lead to uniformly negative outcomes. We raise the possibility that there are situations where believing oneself to have minimal control may serve a protective function. Where children are doing poorly, for example, claims of little control over outcomes, whether realistic or not, may serve to protect feelings of self-esteem. This "hedonic bias" is seen in mothers' lesser endorsement of their own control with respect to inferior academic achievement, as opposed to gifted or regular achievement, and with respect to the behavior of attention-deficit-disordered, hyperactive (ADDH) children, as opposed to non-ADDH children (Himelstein, Graham, & Weiner, 1991; Sobol, Ashbourne, Earn, & Cunningham, 1989). In fact, a variety of combinations of relative control may be attributed to parent and child under a variety of conditions that have an impact on parental affect and behavior. A discussion of the complex relation between control and stress and coping processes is beyond the focus of this chapter. For a detailed discussion, refer to Folkman (1984).

Inferences About Children's Behavior

We move now from a discussion of the inferences parents make about themselves in their relationships with their children to a discussion of inferences they make about their children. Studies of the latter have focused on parents' attributions for their children's behavior to dispositional versus situational factors. When children misbehave, for example, is it because they have done so intentionally or because they lack knowledge of more socially appropriate actions?

Attributions about the causes of children's misbehavior have been assumed to have an impact on parenting behavior and, ultimately, on the outcome of parents' socialization attempts. Historically, interest in parent attributions is evident in the suggestion that abusive parents characteristically interpret noncompliance as willful and indicative of a child's "bad" disposition (e.g., Steele & Pollack, 1968). Attempts to support this contention empirically have been both successful (Larrance & Twentyman, 1983) and unsuccessful (Rosenberg & Repucci, 1983), with the explanation for discrepant results not immediately obvious. More recently, Dix and his colleagues have drawn on attribution theory in particular to try to understand the broad range of both normal and abnormal parenting practices in terms of inferences made about the causes of a child's behavior.

Dix and Grusec (1985) describe four attributional models as relevant to parent-child interactions. One is Weiner's (1980), which is described earlier in this chapter. Heider's (1958) model of attributions of responsibility suggests that the degree of credit or blame parents assign to children for their behavior is a function of the extent to which the behavior causes an effect that was foreseen and intended. According to Kelly's (1967) covariation model, children's behavior is attributed to internal causes when the parent believes few other children would act that way (low consensus), that the child behaves that way across situations (low distinctiveness), and that the child acts in the same way in all similar situations (high consistency). The Jones and Davis (1965) model of correspondent inferences has been used to predict that parents will make dispositional attributions for their child's behavior if they believe that the effects of that behavior were knowingly and intentionally produced in the absence of serious constraints on the child's freedom.

Extrapolating from these attributional models, Dix and his colleagues (Dix & Grusec, 1985; Dix, Ruble, Grusec, & Nixon, 1986) propose that parents' behavioral responses to children follow a series of decisions about the children's behavior. Parents decide whether the effects of behavior were intentional; that is, whether the child knew what would happen, had the ability to make it happen, and was free from external control. If intentionality is assumed, then dispositional inferences are made. If the effects of behavior are assumed to be unintentional, then the behavior is assumed to reflect developmental or situational constraints.

Parents also decide whether children are responsible for or, in the case of negative acts, deserving of blame for their noncompliance. These causal attributions and attributions of responsibility are then hypothesized to lead to affect that is either positive or negative, with implications for parenting reactions. Attributions of intentionality and blameworthiness for negative out-comes make adults angry and incline them to punitive interventions, whereas attributions to situational pressures evoke sympathetic responses and a ten-dency to react in ways that impart knowledge. (In addition to the anger they arouse, attributions of intentionality and blame also promote punishment be-cause Western ethical systems dictate that punishment is appropriate when actions are intentional.) When parents make incorrect attributions about negative behavior, for example, inferring knowledge and intentionality where it does not exist, they will not make efforts to instruct or explain why behavior was unacceptable. This lack of instruction, as well as anger aroused in the child by harsh parental discipline, will not encourage the child to be-have in accord with parental wishes. In this way, faulty attributional thinking maintains itself. Moreover, when the anger aroused by attributions of blame and intentionality reaches inappropriately high levels, it runs the danger of promoting abusive parenting behavior. When attributions about negative be-havior are accurate, parents can appropriately tailor their reactions so that they instruct when behavior results from lack of knowledge or apply some power assertive pressure when the behavior is known by the child to be an-tisocial in nature. In this case parents are more likely to be successful in obtaining desired outcomes.

The model is supported by a series of studies in which parents rate the relative importance of various attributions—intent, disposition, responsibil-ity, knowledge, and control—for children's appropriate and inappropriate behavior (Dix et al., 1986, Dix & Lochman, 1990; Dix & Reinhold, 1991; Dix, Reinhold, & Zambarano, 1990; Dix, Ruble, & Zambarano, 1989). These studies have found that, with a child's increasing age, mothers are more likely to hold children responsible for their misdeeds and to think that their behav-ior is caused by dispositions, both of which are outcomes one would expect as knowledge and ability to control behavior increase. The more intentional behavior is seen to be and the more responsibility is assigned to the child, the more angry mothers report they feel, and the more likely mothers are to in-dicate that they would use power-assertive discipline. Behavior seen as less intentional and less blameworthy, on the other hand, is more likely to elicit proposals for egalitarian or inductive interventions.

As with parenting self-efficacy, studies by Dix and his colleagues indicate that affect is an outcome of negative attributions. In addition, parallel to the self-efficacy literature, affect also appears to be a determinant of negative attributions. Dix et al. (1990) asked mothers to monitor their moods at home and, when they were experiencing anger or were in a neutral mood, to watch videotapes of children being asked to respond to a request. Angry mothers, relative to those who were experiencing neutral feelings, blamed children more for noncompliance, chose more derogatory traits to describe the children, reported greater upset, and indicated stronger disapproval. As with self-efficacy and the effects of depression, the argument is that affect has an impact on cognitive functioning, in this case priming anger-related cognitions such as memories of difficult interactions with children or beliefs that children are difficult to control.

Not only negative affect has an impact on causal attributions, however. Dix and Reinhold (1991) found that the induction of feelings of happiness also led mothers to hold children more responsible for misdeeds, to become more upset, and to advocate stronger disapproval relative to mothers who were experiencing neutral feelings. Several explanations are offered by Dix and Reinhold for this seemingly anomalous finding, including the possibility that people in positive moods find negative events particularly aversive because they threaten their positive frame of mind.

Attributions of intentionality, disposition, and responsibility can serve a protective function for parents, just as do attributions of self-efficacy. Mothers studied by Dix et al. (1986), for example, thought children's altruism was more intentional, dispositional, and under their control than was misconduct. Although these mothers possibly felt that outcomes requiring self-sacrifice logically imply stronger intentions and dispositions, it is also plausible that a preponderance of such attributions for positive behavior emphasizes the success of parents at certain socialization tasks and helps maintain their self-esteem and feelings of self-efficacy, with consequent positive effects on parenting behavior. In like fashion, Gretarsson and Gelfand (1988) note that mothers see positive characteristics as stable and inborn and negative characteristics as transitory; the authors explain this view as a way for these mothers to enhance their own feelings of self-worth.

SOURCES OF PARENTING COGNITIONS

Having described two major classes of parenting cognitions, self-efficacy and attributions for children's behavior, we now turn to the developmental question: Where do these cognitions come from? We have already suggested that depression may alter parental thinking by priming memories of difficult interactions with children. In this section we discuss three other possible sources of parenting cognitions. The first proposal is that cognitions are acquired as a function of specific experiences parents have interacting with their own children and trying to change their behavior. The second proposal is that cognitions are acquired as a result of experiences parents had when they themselves were children, particularly in discipline situations, and that the specific ways in which parents were socialized, including child-rearing tactics and verbalized cognitions used by their own caregivers, are responsible for the beliefs that they bring to social interactions and discipline with their own children. The third proposal is that parenting cognitions have their basis in the way that parents think about relationships in general, including relationships with their children, and that ways of construing relationships are a reflection of parents' ways of thinking about early attachment experiences. We deal with this latter proposal in greatest detail.

Sources in Experiences With Children

The simplest source for parenting cognitions is the experiences that parents have with temperamentally difficult or easy children. Accordingly, children who are easily socialized may have parents who come to think of themselves as effective and children who are difficult to socialize may have parents who come to think of themselves as ineffective. This suggestion is supported by Teti and Gelfand's (1991) finding of a relationship between maternal self-efficacy and infant temperament. Similarly, difficult children may elicit more dispositional attributions for negative outcomes than easy children. However, although we know that children have marked impacts on parental functioning, and although we argue that the behavior of difficult or easy children maintains parenting cognitions, there is considerable evidence that attributional styles are already in place before parents gain direct experience with their own offspring. The fact that parents who have low self-efficacy can have either easy or difficult children (Bugental & Shennum, 1984) and that infant temperament scores do not differentiate mothers with varying degrees of illusory control (Donovan et al., 1990) indicates that child characteristics do not always carry primary responsibility for parental thinking. Several additional studies suggest that we need to look for the source of attributional styles in experiences individuals have before they take on the parenting role.

Negative attitudes and attributions about children that exist in parents before their children are born are predictive of problematic relationships postnatally (Moss & Jones, 1977). Further, negatively biased attributions occur among parents of aggressive boys even when they are making attributions about children who are not their own (Dix & Lochman, 1990), and negatively biased attributions occur in dysfunctional parents even when there is no difference between the behavior of their own children and that of control children (Mash & Johnston, 1982). These findings suggest that a profitable way of understanding parenting cognitions is to consider the developmental history of individuals before they become parents. Although we recognize that there may be biologically determined propensities to think poorly of the self or of others, we confine ourselves here to speculation about experiential determinants in part because few data are pertinent to genetically determined propensities.

Sources in Parents' Childhood Experiences With Control Strategies

A possible prototype for how parents respond to difficult interactions between themselves and their children is the experiences they themselves had as children in similar situations. In the discipline situation, for example, children learn about interactions in conflict situations, including information about their own roles and abilities, as well as expectations about the roles and abilities of others. They learn about their own abilities to handle conflicts as well as about the characteristics of those with whom they are in conflict, information that is important not only for peer relations but for parenting.

We propose here a set of mechanisms for understanding how parenting cognitions might be acquired that involves consideration of the way parents were disciplined when they were children. Relevant data are minimal and the ideas must be regarded as remaining to be tested, although Tiggemann, Winefield, Goldney, and Winefield (1992) report some weak relations between adults' attributional style and their memories of parental rearing style.

The first set of hypotheses has to do with the development of parenting self-efficacy. Baumrind (1991) reports that adolescent girls whose mothers use authoritarian control strategies to enforce restrictive and traditional values are less likely to be individuated, that is, to possess a well-formulated sense of identity and internal locus of control. In contrast, for both adolescent boys and girls, parental reasoning and openness to negotiation appear to foster individuation. These data support the contention that parental child-rearing styles have an impact on children's developing feelings of control.

We propose that feelings of control exhibited by children whose parents reason and are responsive to their thoughts and needs may come about in two ways. First, it has been demonstrated that children whose parents employ authoritative and egalitarian methods attribute their behavior to personal choice and self-direction (Dix & Grusec, 1983). Second, parents who listen to and are responsive to their children's point of view may well be teaching their children that they have the ability to modify outcomes in situations of disagreement. In these two distinct ways, children acquire feelings of power and efficacy they can carry into later conflict situations they have with their own children.

Children reared by authoritarian parents, on the other hand, rarely have the opportunity to acquire feelings of control. They are more likely to make attributions for their behavior to external pressure (Dix & Grusec, 1983) and are likely to learn that no one is ready to respond to their needs and wishes in conflict situations. Accordingly, they are more likely to carry feelings of powerlessness into later conflict situations they have with their own children, presumably resorting to harsh power-assertive techniques as a way of trying to attain some degree of control in a generally threatening situation. Baumrind's (1991) findings suggest that this style of interaction is especially likely to be learned by girls. (Skinner, 1985, presents a similar model, noting that sensitive and contingent child-rearing practices lead children to become more active in controlling their environments, which, in turn, results in the children's increased beliefs that they possess control.)

The second set of hypotheses has to do with the sources of causal attributions for children's behavior. Authoritarian child-rearing techniques may be responsible for an attributional style of assigning blame and responsibility to children for their misdeeds and making dispositional explanations for their misbehavior. The argument is in two parts. First, we know that authoritarian parents attribute higher levels of knowledge and responsibility to their misbehaving children than parents who are less authoritarian (Dix et al., 1989, Dix & Reinhold, 1991). In this way, their children may be exposed to dispositional forms of explanation for negative behaviors. Second, this attributional style is modeled when individuals find themselves in situations where they search for reasons for someone else's misbehavior, situations that include the behavior of their own children at a future point in time.

In summary, it has been suggested that authoritarian parenting promotes low parenting self-efficacy by teaching individuals to feel their behavior is under external control and that others are unresponsive to their wishes; and that authoritarian parenting promotes dispositional attributions for others' misdeeds because such attributions are characteristic of authoritarian parents and are modelled. These suggestions remain to be tested.

Early Sources in Attachment Relationships

The final proposal for how parenting cognitions are acquired uses attachment theory as its starting point. This theory currently enjoys a position of prominence in developmental psychology as an explanation for how early experiences with significant figures have enduring effects on subsequent social, emotional, and cognitive outcomes. The suggestion here is that how adults think about their attachment relationships with their own parents affects the way they think about parent-child interactions when they are parenting. We begin with a brief overview of attachment theory's basic tenets.

Attachment Theory

According to attachment theory (Ainsworth, Blehar, Waters, & Wall, 1978), parental responsiveness and sensitivity to children's emotional needs determine the way in which children organize emotional experience, as well as the strategies they employ to maintain a state of "felt security." Responsive and sensitive parents produce an environment in which the (secure) child can actively seek comfort and support from the attachment figure when lack of security is felt. If a parent is rejecting or inconsistently available and inept, then different strategies are developed to achieve a sense of security.

The insecure avoidant child of rejecting parents cuts off anger- or distress-related displays while experiencing anger and hostility inwardly; the insecure ambivalent child of an inconsistently available parent or a parent who is inept at comforting openly expresses heightened distress and directs fear and anger toward the attachment figure. These two patterns of adjustment are less adaptive, and a multitude of studies in the last decade suggest that maladaptive strategies developed in the first year of life continue to affect behavior throughout the course of childhood development (Bretherton, 1992).

Mediating these outcomes are working models of relationships (Bowlby, 1973) that are formed very early in childhood and that reflect early attachment experiences. These models tend to shape the individual's construction of subsequent social relationships, providing rules that direct both social behavior and appraisals of experience (Main, Kaplan, & Cassidy, 1985). These working models, which continue to direct behavior throughout the life span, function outside conscious experience, and so they are strongly resistant to change (Bretherton, 1985).

Measurement of Attachment Style

Currently there is considerable interest in manifestations of working models of relationships in adults. One technique for assessing these models that is of particular interest to researchers interested in the parenting process is the Adult Attachment Interview, or AAI (Main & Goldwyn, 1991). From answers to a variety of questions about childhood attachment experiences, one can assess the adult's current state of mind with respect to early attachment experiences. Attachment history, the presumed nature of previous attachments, or presumed previous states of mind do not form the basis of the assessment. What is relevant is the adult's state of mind with respect to these experiences. Three major patterns of organization have been identified.

Adults classified as secure/autonomous appear to value attachment but are able to be objective in evaluating their own particular experience. Actual experience may be inferred to have been either positive or negative, but the state of mind with respect to this experience is coherent, open, and objective. Adults classified as dismissing of attachment attempt to limit the influence of attachment relationships in their thinking, feeling, and behavior, while making an implicit claim to strength, normality, and independence. Finally, individuals classified as preoccupied with early attachments or past experiences seem confused, unobjective, and mentally entangled in their descriptions, being either passive and vague, fearful and overwhelmed, or angry, conflicted, and unconvincingly analytical. The AAI also identifies individuals who are unresolved with respect to the loss of an attachment figure or some other traumatic event. Individuals given primary assignment to this category are also categorized in terms of whether they are secure/autonomous, dismissive, or preoccupied.

Categories identified by the AAI mirror the patterns of attachment identified by Ainsworth et al. (1978), with the secure/autonomous adult pattern matched to the secure infant pattern, the dismissive adult pattern matched to the insecure avoidant infant pattern, and the preoccupied adult pattern matched to the insecure ambivalent infant pattern. The corresponding infant category for unresolved adults is disorganized: Disorganized infants, unlike those who are secure, avoidant, or ambivalent, do not demonstrate a consistent mode of dealing with feelings of anxiety aroused by threats to security. An impressive feature of the AAI is the high level of concordance that has been identified between mothers' attachment classifications based on the AAI and the attachment classification of their infants; secure/autonomous mothers tend to have secure babies, dismissing mothers tend to have avoidant babies, and preoccupied mothers tend to have ambivalent babies (Fonagy, Steele, & Steele, 1991; Main et al., 1985; Ward et al., 1990). This agreement suggests that the way a mother acts toward her child may be mediated by her mental constructions of attachment relationships.

Attachment Style and Parenting Behavior

Parental constructions of attachment relationships bear a relationship not only to the infant's attachment behavior, but also to the way in which parents act toward their preschool-aged children in laboratory situations. Crowell and Feldman (1988, 1991) report that secure/autonomous mothers are warm and supportive and give clear, helpful assistance that encourages learning and efficient problem solving in their toddlers. Dismissive mothers are less emotionally supportive and helpful, with a controlling, task-focused style characterized by coolness and remoteness. "Task completion, not learning, was the apparent goal of these mothers" (Crowell & Feldman, 1988, p. 1283). Preoccupied mothers also are not helpful and supportive, often presenting instructions in a confusing way. They are inconsistent in their behavior, at times being warm and gentle while at other times seeming coercive, puzzled, or angry. Preoccupied mothers also occasionally exhibit controlling behavior. When preparing to separate from their children, secure mothers prepare the toddlers well; dismissive and preoccupied mothers do not. Dismissive mothers leave easily, whereas preoccupied mothers have difficulty. At reunion, secure mothers move close to their children, whereas dismissive and preoccupied mothers do not. Cohn, Cowan, Cowan, and Pearson (1992) found that mothers and fathers who were secure/autonomous were more interactive, confident, and effective in their interactions with their children than those who were dismissive or preoccupied, and provided more information about a task to be solved.

Attachment Style, Parenting Cognitions, and Parenting Behavior

Parental mental representations of relationships, then, appear to predict parenting behavior. From evidence reviewed earlier in this chapter, we know that parenting cognitions are also predictive of parenting behavior. It appears, therefore, that researchers interested in parenting cognitions and those interested in attachment have been working independently toward an understanding of parenting strategies. Indeed, Bugental (e.g., 1991; Bugental et al., 1993) speculates about the relation between perceived control and

mental models of relationships, noting the consistency between her deline-
ation of a schema or cognitive construction of relationships and Bowlby's
(1973) notion of a working model of relationships.

As with Bowlby's (1973) notion of models that serve heuristic functions
by providing guidelines for behavior in a variety of interpersonal relationships, schemas about perceived control provide chronically accessible constructions that operate below the level of awareness and that can sensitize
individuals to specific events in the environment. However, only recently
(Grusec, Adam, & Mammone, 1993) has there been an attempt to map out
specific and explicit correspondences between mental representations, parenting cognitions, and parenting behavior. In the next part of this chapter, we
review possible relations between different mental models of relationships
and parenting cognitions that have guided the work of Grusec et al. Our suggestion is that working models of relationships include beliefs about the self
and about others, and that these beliefs are elicited in any interpersonal relationship, including one that involves parent and child. From this it follows
that parenting cognitions elicited during the process of parent-child interactions may have their basis in and be generated by working models parents
have about relationships in general. The parenting cognitions of particular
interest are those that form the basis of this chapter: parenting self-efficacy
and attributions about children's behavior.

Hypotheses and Evidence

We begin with a description of the characteristics of secure/autonomous,
dismissive, and preoccupied individuals, based on the research already described, and then move to hypotheses about the specific parenting cognitions
they might be expected to exhibit. Finally, we provide some data relevant to
these hypothesized relations between ways of construing relationships and
parenting cognitions.

Secure/autonomous adults are coherent, open, and objective in their deal-
ings with other individuals, presumably less inclined to biased and/or threatening interpretations of ambiguous events. In their specific interactions with
children, they are emotionally supportive, clear and consistent in their attempts at socialization, responsive, sensitive, and self-confident. They see
themselves and their parents as both bearing responsibility for child-rearing
outcomes. They should be reasonably high in self-efficacy and moderate in
their attributions of intentionality and knowledge and in their dispositional
attributions for children's behavior.

Dismissive adults, who frequently report the experience of childhood rejection, limit the importance of attachment relationships in their thinking, feeling, and behavior, while making an implicit claim to strength, normality, and independence. Their mental representations of parent-child relationships, then, should involve a parent who has little impact on the child and a child who is strong and independent. This mental representation ought to manifest itself in feelings of low parenting efficacy, supported by dispositional attributions about children's behavior as well as attributions of responsibility and blame.

In sharp contrast to dismissive ways of thinking and behaving are the thoughts and behavior of preoccupied adults. In their social interactions they are inconsistent, confused and confusing, and enmeshed in relationships in such a way that differentiation between themselves and others becomes difficult. A feature of their perceptions of attachment relationships having possible implications for their own parenting cognitions is their predisposition to assign blame for difficulties to the parent and their inability to understand their own role in these difficulties (Main & Goldwyn, 1991). Thus, in their working models of relationships, the parent is associated with responsibility for relationship failure and the child is identified as the innocent victim. Their mental representation of parent-child relationships, then, should be the opposite of dismissive individuals, with the parent as the powerful member of the dyad and the child as dependent and weak. Thus preoccupied individuals might be expected to assign high self-efficacy to themselves as parents and low control to their children. Similarly, preoccupied parents might be expected to make fewer dispositional attributions to their children.

Initial exploration of relations between attachment classification and parenting cognitions is reported by Grusec et al. (1993). We studied 20 fathers and 74 mothers who had a child between the ages of 4 and 7 years. The sample was a mixture of parents who were included in the research because of their involvement with child protection agencies and a control group matched for education and income. Parents who participated by virtue of their association with a protection agency had identified histories of either physical abuse or neglect.

To assess their mental representations of relationships, parents were administered Main and Goldwyn's Adult Attachment Interview. In addition, Bugental's Parent Attribution Test (Bugental & Shennum, 1984) was used to measure parenting self-efficacy. Attributions for children's behavior were obtained by asking parents to respond to a series of vignettes describing children's misdeeds. They were asked to imagine it was their child (the 4- to

7-year-old who had determined their eligibility for participation in the first place and, in the case of maltreating parents, their physically abused or neglected child between the ages of 4 and 7 years) and to answer a number of questions having to do with whether the child knew he or she had behaved badly, how much blame he or she deserved for the bad behavior, and whether the behavior was due to his or her personality or to the situation. Each question was accompanied by a 7-point scale ranging from low to high in terms of knowledge, blame, and personality, and parents were asked to circle the number that most closely approximated their evaluation of the child on each attributional dimension.

Given that no specific predictions had been made with respect to the unresolved category, Grusec et al. (1993) assigned parents to one of the three main classifications of secure/autonomous, dismissive, and preoccupied. Thus individuals whose primary classification was unresolved were placed into their secondary category. Intercoder agreement, based on number of agreements divided by number of agreements plus number of disagreements, was 87%. Two coders independently categorized each of the 94 AAI transcripts and, when there was disagreement, a third coder also categorized the transcript, with final agreement reached after discussion by all three coders. Each of the three coders had independently achieved satisfactory agreement on another set of AAI transcripts coded by Mary Main. Hence, there is a reasonable degree of certainty that AAI categorizations reported here were reliable not only within this one laboratory, but also with respect to those who developed the assessment system.

What of the correspondence between attachment classifications and parenting cognitions? PAT scores are displayed in Table 3.1 as a function of attachment classification. The picture that emerges conforms, by and large, to expectation. Overall, preoccupied parents reported themselves to have the most control over failure and dismissive parents the least control, with scores for total perceived control determined by subtracting perceptions of child control from those of adult control. The scores for secure parents fell in between and were significantly different from those for dismissive and preoccupied parents. Considering adult control over failure and child control over failure separately, preoccupied parents believed themselves to have more control over failure than secure or dismissive parents. Dismissive parents saw children as having more control over failure than secure parents, whereas preoccupied parents saw children as having least control. In essence, dismissive parents saw themselves as relatively low in power in child-rearing situations, whereas preoccupied parents saw themselves as high in power;

TABLE 3.1 Scores on the Parent Attribution Test and Attributions for Children's Behavior as a Function of Attachment Classification

	Attachment Classification		
Parenting Cognition	*Secure*	*Dismissive*	*Preoccupied*
Perceived control over failure	.24[b]	−.35[a]	1.40[c]
Adult control over failure	4.26[a]	4.15[a]	4.94[b]
Child control over failure	4.02[b]	4.50[c]	3.54[a]
Attributions to knowledge/blame	4.82[a]	4.35[a]	4.47[a]
Attributions to personality	2.64[a]	3.07[a]	3.87[b]

NOTE: High scores indicate high control over failure, high knowledge/blame, and high attribution to personality. Different superscripts across each line indicate statistically significant differences between groups.

these parents seem to have taken over, or incorporated, what they perceive as the role of their own parents. In the case of dismissive individuals, this means an adult who has little influence over an independent and self-sufficient child. In the case of preoccupied individuals, it means an adult who has great influence over a child who is relatively powerless in comparison.

Answers to questions about knowledge and blame were intercorrelated, so a summary score is presented, the average of the scores for each of the four relevant questions. This summary score does not distinguish between attachment categories. Attributions to personality do, however. Preoccupied parents were much more likely to attribute failure to the personality of their child than dismissive or secure parents. Thus parental attributions about children's knowledge of right or wrong and the extent to which they deserved blame for their misdeeds did not appear to be grounded in mental schemas that guide expectations about the behavior of others. Attributions about personality, however, were highly related to attachment classification. Preoccupied parents, enmeshed as they are in relationships, may find it difficult to differentiate between themselves and others, thus assuming responsibility for negative outcomes themselves, but also ascribing problem behavior to enduring features of their children because such behavior would be an indication of their own failure. Reasons for the failure to find differences between dismissive, secure, and preoccupied individuals in attributions of knowledge and blame are not entirely clear. Decisions about a child's knowledge or intentions may involve fewer inferences about the child in relation to the parent than those about relative control. If this is the case, then these decisions should be less influenced by mental representations of relationships. Ongoing research will attempt to clarify the issue.

CONCLUSION

There has been a major and rapid advance in our knowledge of parenting cognitions and their relation to affect and behavior in the last 10 years. In this chapter we have focused on two classes of cognitions that have received particular attention: those having to do with parenting self-efficacy and those having to do with the attributions parents make for the causes of their children's behavior. The fundamental question of how these cognitions develop has been raised, and we have provided evidence that these cognitions may be grounded in the parent's own child-rearing experiences. We have suggested that one such experience involves situations of parent-child disagreement and the techniques parents use to settle those disagreements. On a broader level, we have suggested these cognitions also may have their source in early attachment relationships and the models of relationship styles that emerge from those experiences. The empirical data we have offered support these suggestions and indicate that attempts to understand, predict, and control parenting cognitions must involve a focus on general representations of relationships and their associated affect, rather than on specific parenting cognitions alone.

REFERENCES

Abidin, R. R. (1986). *Parenting stress index—Manual.* Charlottesville, VA: Pediatric Psychology Press.

Abramson, L. Y., Seligman, M. E. P., & Teasdale, J. (1978). Learned helplessness in humans: Critique and reformulation. *Journal of Abnormal Psychology, 87,* 49-74.

Ainsworth, M. D. S., Blehar, M. C., Waters, E., & Wall, S. (1978). *Patterns of attachment: A psychological study of the strange situation.* Hillsdale, NJ: Erlbaum.

Alloy, L. B., & Abramson, L. Y. (1979). Judgments of contingency in depressed and nondepressed students: Sadder but wiser? *Journal of Experimental Psychology: General, 108,* 441-487.

Bandura, A. (1977). Self-efficacy: Toward a unifying theory of behavior change. *Psychological Review, 84,* 191-215.

Bandura, A. (1989). Regulation of cognitive processes through perceived self-efficacy. *Developmental Psychology, 25,* 729-735.

Baumrind, D. (1991). Effective parenting during the early adolescent transition. In P. A. Cowan & M. Hetherington (Eds.), *Family transitions: Advances in family research series.* (pp. 111-163). Hillsdale, NJ: Erlbaum.

Bower, G. H. (1983). Affect and cognition. *Philosophical Transactions of the Royal Society of London* (Series E), *302,* 387-402.

Bowlby, J. (1973). *Attachment and loss: Vol. 2, Separation.* New York: Basic Books.

Bretherton, I. (1985). Attachment theory: Retrospect and prospect. In I. Bretherton & E. Waters (Eds.), Growing points of attachment theory and research. *Monographs of the Society for Research in Child Development, 50* (1-2, Serial No. 209).

Bretherton, I. (1992). The origins of attachment theory: John Bowlby and Mary Ainsworth. *Developmental Psychology, 28,* 759-775.

Bugental, D. B. (1991). Affective and cognitive processes within threat-oriented family systems. In I. Sigel, A. V. McGillicuddy-DeLisi, & J. J. Goodnow (Eds.), *Parental belief systems: The psychological consequences for children* (2nd ed., pp. 219-248). Hillsdale, NJ: Erlbaum.

Bugental, D. B., Blue, J., Cortez, V., Fleck, K., Kopeikin, H., Lewis, J. C., & Lyon, J. (1993). Social cognitions as organizers of autonomic and affective responses to social challenge. *Journal of Personality and Social Psychology, 64,* 94-103.

Bugental, D. B., Blue, J., & Cruzcosa, M. (1989). Perceived control over caregiving outcomes: Implications for child abuse. *Developmental Psychology, 25,* 532-539.

Bugental, D. B., Blue, J., & Lewis, J. (1990). Caregiver beliefs and dysphoric affect directed to difficult children. *Developmental Psychology, 26,* 631-638.

Bugental, D. B., Mantyla, S. M., & Lewis, J. (1989). Parental attributions as moderators of affective communication to children at risk for physical abuse. In D. Cicchetti & V. Carlson (Eds.), *Current research and theoretical advances in child maltreatment* (pp. 254-279). New York: Cambridge University Press.

Bugental, D. B. & Shennum, W. A. (1984). "Difficult" children as elicitors and targets of adult communication patterns: An attributional-behavioral transactional analysis. *Monographs of the Society for Research in Child Development, 49* (1, Serial No. 205).

Cohn, D., Cowan, P., Cowan, C. P., & Pearson, J. (1992). Mothers' and fathers' working models of childhood attachment relationships, parenting styles, and child behavior. *Development and Psychopathology, 4,* 417-431.

Crowell, J. A., & Feldman, S. S. (1988). Mothers' internal models of relationships and children's behavioral and developmental status: A study of mother-child interaction. *Child Development, 59,* 1273-1285.

Crowell, J. A., & Feldman, S. S. (1991). Mothers' working models of attachment relationships and mother and child behavior during separation and reunion. *Developmental Psychology, 27,* 597-605.

Dix, T., & Grusec, J. E. (1983). Parental influence techniques: An attributional analysis. *Child Development, 54,* 645-652.

Dix, T. H., & Grusec, J. E. (1985). Parent attribution processes in child socialization. In I. Sigel (Ed.), *Parent belief systems: Their psychological consequences for children* (pp. 201-233). Hillsdale, NJ: Erlbaum.

Dix, T., & Lochman, J. E. (1990). Social cognition and negative reactions to children: A comparison of mothers of aggressive and nonaggressive boys. *Journal of Social and Clinical Psychology, 9,* 418-438.

Dix, T., & Reinhold, D. P. (1991). Chronic and temporary influences on mothers' attributions for children's disobedience. *Merrill-Palmer Quarterly, 37,* 251-271.

Dix, T., Reinhold, D. A., & Zambarano, R. J. (1990). Mothers' judgments in moments of anger. *Merrill-Palmer Quarterly, 36,* 465-486.

Dix, T., Ruble, D. N., Grusec, J. E., & Nixon, S. (1986). Social cognition in parents: Inferential and affective reactions to children of three age levels. *Child Development, 57,* 879-894.

Dix, T. H., Ruble, D. N., & Zambarano, R. J. (1989). Mothers' implicit theories of discipline: Child effects, parent effects, and the attribution process. *Child Development, 60,* 1373-1391.

Donovan, W. L., & Leavitt, L. A. (1989). Maternal self-efficacy and infant attachment: Integrating physiology, perceptions, and behavior. *Child Development, 60,* 460-472.

Donovan, W. L., Leavitt, L. A., & Walsh, R. O. (1990). Maternal self-efficacy: Illusory control and its effects on susceptibility to learned helplessness. *Child Development, 61,* 1638-1647.

Folkman, S. (1984). Personal control and stress and coping processes: A theoretical analysis. *Journal of Personality and Social Psychology, 46,* 839-852.

Fonagy, P., Steele, H., & Steele, M. (1991). Maternal representations of attachment during pregnancy predict the organization of infant-mother attachment at one year of age. *Child Development, 61,* 891-905.

Goodnow, J. J., & Collins, A. W. (1990). *Development according to parents: The nature, sources, and consequences of parents' ideas.* Hillsdale, NJ: Erlbaum.

Gretarsson, S. J., & Gelfand, D. M. (1988). Mothers' attributions regarding their children's social behavior and personality characteristics. *Developmental Psychology, 24,* 264-269.

Grusec, J. E., Adam, E., & Mammone, N. (1993). *Mental representations of relationships, parent belief systems, and parenting behavior.* Paper presented at the biennial meeting of the Society for Research in Child Development, New Orleans, LA.

Heider, F. (1958). *The psychology of interpersonal relations.* New York: John Wiley.

Himelstein, S., Graham, S., & Weiner, B. (1991). An attributional analysis of maternal beliefs about the importance of child-rearing practices. *Child Development, 62,* 301-310.

Holden, G., & Edwards, L. (1989). Parental attitudes toward child rearing: Instruments, issues, and implications. *Psychological Bulletin, 106,* 29-58.

Jones, E. E., & Davis, K. E. (1965). From acts to dispositions: The attribution process in person perception. In L. Berkowitz (Ed.), *Advances in experimental social psychology: Vol. 2* (pp. 219-266). New York: Academic Press.

Kelly, H. H. (1967). Attribution theory in social psychology. In D. Levine (Ed.), *Nebraska Symposium on Motivation* (pp. 192-238). Lincoln: University of Nebraska Press.

Kochanska, G., Radke-Yarrow, M., Kuczynski, L., & Friedman, S. L. (1987). Normal and affectively ill mothers' beliefs about their children. *American Journal of Orthopsychiatry, 57,* 345-350.

Larrance, D. T., & Twentyman, C. T. (1983). Maternal attributions and child abuse. *Journal of Abnormal Psychology, 92,* 449-457.

Main, M., & Goldwyn, R. (1991). *Adult attachment rating and classification systems.* Unpublished manuscript.

Main, M., Kaplan, N., & Cassidy, J. (1985). Security in infancy, childhood and adulthood: A move to the level of representation. In I. Bretherton & E. Waters (Eds.), Growing points of attachment theory and research. *Monographs of the Society for Research in Child Development, 50* (1-2, Serial No. 209).

Mash, E. J., & Johnston, C. (1982). A comparison of mother-child interactions of younger and older hyperactive and normal children. *Child Development, 53,* 1371-1381.

Moss, H. A., & Jones, S. J. (1977). Relations between maternal attitudes and maternal behavior as a function of social class. In P. H. Leiderman, S. R. Tulkin, & A. Rosenfeld (Eds.), *Culture and infancy* (pp. 439-465). New York: Academic Press.

Rosenberg, M. S., & Repucci, N. D. (1983). Abusive mothers: Perceptions of their own and their children's behavior. *Journal of Consulting and Clinical Psychology, 51,* 674-682.

Sigel, I. E., McGillicuddy-DeLisi, A. V., & Goodnow, J. J. (Eds.). (1991). *Parental belief systems: The psychological consequences for children* (2nd ed.). Hillsdale, NJ: Erlbaum.

Skinner, E. A. (1985). Action, control judgments, and the structure of control experience. *Psychological Review, 92,* 39-58.

Sobol, M. P., Ashbourne, D. T., Earn, B. M., & Cunningham, C. E. (1989). Parents' attributions for achieving compliance from attention-deficit-disordered children. *Journal of Abnormal Child Psychology, 17,* 359-369.

Steele, B. F., & Pollack, C. (1968). A psychiatric study of parents who abuse infants and small children. In R. Helfer & C. Kemp (Eds.), *The battered child* (pp. 103-147). Chicago: University of Chicago Press.

Teti, D. M., & Gelfand, D. M. (1991). Behavioral competence among mothers of infants in the first year: The mediational role of maternal self-efficacy. *Child Development, 62,* 918-929.

Tiggemann, M., Winefield, H. R., Goldney, R. D., & Winefield, A. H. (1992). Attributional style and parental rearing as predictors of psychological distress. *Personality and Individual Differences, 13,* 835-841.

Ward, M. J., Carlson, E. A., Altman, S., Levine, L., Greenberg, R. H., & Kessler, D. B. (1990). *Predicting infant-mother attachment from adolescent's parental working models of relationships.* Paper presented at the Seventh International Conference on Infant Studies, Montreal, Canada.

Weiner, B. (1980). A cognitive (attribution)-emotion-action model of motivated behavior: An analysis of judgments of help-giving. *Journal of Personality and Social Psychology, 39,* 186-200.

Naturally Occurring Interpersonal Expectancies

4

LEE JUSSIM
JACQUELYNNE ECCLES

Lee Jussim is Associate Professor of Psychology at Rutgers University. His research addresses relations among social perception, self-perception, and social reality. This work, which includes research on self-fulfilling prophecies, bias, accuracy, stereotypes, and reactions to evaluations, has won numerous awards, including a 1993 Rutgers' University Board of Trustees Fellowship for Scholarly Excellence, the 1991 Gordon Allport Award from the Society for the Psychological Study of Social Issues, and the 1988 Society for Experimental Social Psychology Dissertation Award. Much of his current research on relations between teacher expectations and student achievement is supported by a FIRST award from the National Institute of Child Health and Development.

Jacquelynne Eccles is Professor of Psychology, Chair of the Combined Program in Education and Psychology, and Research Scientist at the Institute for Social Research at the University of Michigan. She has authored or coauthored more than 50 articles and book chapters on topics ranging from gender-role socialization, teacher expectancies, and classroom influences on student motivation to adolescent development in family and school contexts.

Social psychology has long emphasized the power of social beliefs to create reality (see Eccles & Wigfield, 1985; Jussim, 1991, 1993; Merton, 1948, for reviews). According to many perspectives, people become what significant others, such as friends, parents, teachers, and employers, expect them to become. But are people so malleable that they readily fulfill others' erroneous expectations? How erroneous are interpersonal expectations? To address these questions, this chapter presents a critical review of evidence on relations between naturally occurring interpersonal expectations and others' behavior. First, we identify three sources of expectancy confirmation, strengths and weaknesses in experimental research on expectancies, and how expectancy effects may be identified under naturalistic conditions. Then we review studies investigating behaviors and achievements in educational and other settings. Finally, we discuss research addressing whether self-fulfilling

AUTHORS' NOTE: Preparation of this chapter was supported in part by NICHD grant 1 R29 HD28401-01A1 to Lee Jussim.

prophecies accumulate or dissipate over time, and briefly review factors that may moderate effects of interpersonal expectancies.

THREE SOURCES OF EXPECTANCY CONFIRMATION

Expectancy confirmation can occur via several processes (see Jussim, 1989, 1991, 1993, in press; Jussim & Eccles, 1992, for more detail). First, perceivers' expectations can be confirmed because they create self-fulfilling prophecies: For example, initially erroneous expectations may lead targets to behave in ways consistent with those expectations. Because self-fulfilling prophecies result from social interactions and social influence over time, because they involve changes in behavior and/or other personological characteristics, and because their magnitude likely depends on the maturity of both the target and the perceiver and on the specific situation, understanding the extent and nature of self-fulfilling prophecies is an important issue for social, personality, and developmental psychology. In addition, because self-fulfilling prophecies may be especially likely when people engage in major life transitions (Jussim, 1990), when individuals confront new situations, and when targets are uncertain of their own abilities and self-perceptions, self-fulfilling prophecies may contribute fundamentally to the development and change of social and personality attributes from the cradle to the grave.

Second, interpersonal expectations can be confirmed because they lead to perceptual biases—perceivers may interpret, remember, and/or explain targets' performance in ways consistent with their expectations. This type of expectancy-confirmation exists in the mind of the perceiver rather than in the behavior of the target. Consequently, perceptual bias is likely to be influenced by all the social and developmental processes linked to social perceptions including social stereotypes, attribution biases, and cognitive maturity.

Self-fulfilling prophecies and perceptual biases represent biasing effects of perceiver expectations on either the targets' actual behavior or the perceivers' evaluations of targets' characteristics. Expectations may also be confirmed because they are accurate. That is, expectations may accurately reflect or predict, without influencing, target behavior (Brophy, 1983; Jussim, 1991).

EXPERIMENTS AND NATURALISTIC STUDIES

The classic self-fulfilling prophecy paradigm involves providing teachers with false information (e.g., bogus high or low standardized test scores) about some randomly selected students (e.g., Rosenthal & Jacobson, 1968). Differences in subsequent performance between these and control students can be attributed only to the expectancy manipulation—that is, self-fulfilling prophecy. The procedure of creating erroneous expectations by providing perceivers with false information about targets has served as the prototype for hundreds of expectancy experiments in social, organizational, personality, and educational psychology (see Eden, 1986; Miller & Turnbull, 1986; Snyder, 1984, 1992, for reviews). Social psychologists often interpret the early studies as showing that (a) self-fulfilling prophecies are a powerful and pervasive phenomenon and (b) the influence of teachers' expectations on students' achievement equals or exceeds the influence of students' achievement on teacher expectations (see, for example, Fiske & Taylor, 1984; Jones, 1986; Miller & Turnbull, 1986).

However, because of several limitations, experimental studies do not definitively support these conclusions. First, conclusions regarding pervasiveness require documentation of naturally occurring, rather than experimentally induced, self-fulfilling prophecies. Second, experiments that require perceivers to develop erroneous expectations do not (and were never intended to) assess the extent to which expectations might be accurate. They provide no basis for comparing the extent of self-fulfilling prophecies to the extent of accuracy. Third, experiments that create false expectations only permit conclusions to be drawn about the relationship between erroneous beliefs and behavior. Under naturalistic conditions, however, expectations may be accurate. Accurate beliefs cannot create self-fulfilling prophecies, because, by definition, self-fulfilling prophecy refers to initially false beliefs becoming true.

NATURALISTIC STUDIES: OVERVIEW

These limitations of experimental studies have led some researchers to study relations between naturally occurring interpersonal expectancies and targets' behavior and motivation. We describe these studies and critically evaluate their ability to meet the conditions necessary for separating self-fulfilling prophecies, perceptual biases, and accuracy. We have not included the following types of studies.

1. Experiments inducing erroneous expectations, even if they were conducted in field settings
2. Studies reporting only simple correlations, which cannot distinguish between self-fulfilling prophecy, perceptual bias, or accuracy
3. Studies examining only relations between perceivers' expectations and their behavior toward targets
4. Studies examining only relations between perceivers' expectations and targets' beliefs about how they are treated by perceivers (see, for example, Brophy & Good, 1974; Darley & Fazio, 1980; Jussim, 1986; Rosenthal, 1974; Snyder, 1984, for reviews of such studies)

Before presenting our basic model for identifying the various components of expectancy confirmation, we need to define self-fulfilling prophecy, perceptual bias, and accuracy (see Jussim, 1989, 1991, 1993; Jussim & Eccles, 1992, for more details). Within our framework, three conditions must be met to identify naturally occurring self-fulfilling prophecies. First, perceivers' expectations must successfully predict targets' future behavior: Perceivers' expectations at time 1 must positively correlate with targets' behavior at time 2 (see Jussim, 1991, for a possible exception). Second, this predictive validity cannot result entirely from accuracy. If perceivers' expectations successfully predict but do not influence targets' behavior, no self-fulfilling prophecy has occurred. Third, perceivers must not be the main judges of targets' behavior.

Alternatively, perceivers' expectations may influence their judgments of targets' behavior through perceptual biases. When a perceptual bias occurs, perceivers' expectations influence their judgments of targets. Perceivers may evaluate targets' behavior as being more consistent with their expectations than is warranted on the basis of targets' actual behavior. Therefore, perceivers' expectations should more strongly predict their own judgments of targets' behavior than they predict independent assessments of targets' behavior.

Finally, perceivers' expectations can also be confirmed due to accuracy. There are two conceptually distinct aspects of accuracy. Impression accuracy concerns the basis of interpersonal expectations. Expectations based on more valid information can be considered more accurate than expectations based on less valid information. For example, teacher expectations based on previous grades may be considered more accurate than those based on physical attractiveness or falsified test scores. However, even expectations based on valid information often inaccurately predict future behavior (Kahneman & Tversky, 1973). Consequently, the second aspect of accuracy involves determining the extent to which interpersonal expectations predict targets' behavior without causing it. This is predictive accuracy—predictive validity without (self-fulfilling or biasing) influence.

The Basic Model

Figure 4.1 presents a general model of the role of perceiver expectations in self-fulfilling prophecies and represents the core basis of many of the naturalistic studies. The main ideas are that background information about targets may influence perceiver expectations (Path A); and that perceivers' expectations may influence targets' behavior, achievements, or attributes (Path B) and their own evaluations of targets (Path D). This basic model, in part or total, underlies most naturalistic studies of interpersonal expectancies. Although not specified in Figure 4.1, we assume that developmentally relevant characteristics such as age, cognitive maturity, prior experience, and certainty of one's social and self-perceptions can moderate the strength of all paths. We discuss these possible influences later in the chapter. Unfortunately, few researchers have directly assessed these moderating effects.

NATURALISTIC STUDIES IN THE CLASSROOM: TEACHER EXPECTANCY EFFECTS

We divide naturalistic studies of teacher expectations into three broad groups: Rist (1970), which is a highly cited and methodologically unique study; quasi-experimental studies; and longitudinal path analytic studies, which typically rely on regression and structural equation modelling techniques.

Rist (1970)

Rist's (1970) study is often cited as evidence of powerful naturally occurring self-fulfilling prophecies (e.g., Miller & Turnbull, 1986; Myers, 1987; Snyder, 1984). However, the study was based almost entirely on Rist's observations of a single inner-city kindergarten class over a school year (and

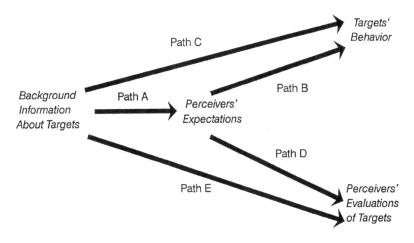

Figure 4.1. Basic Model for Assessing Relations Among Perceivers' Expectations and Targets' Behavior

first- and second-grade follow-ups). Consequently, the extent to which Rist's observations were influenced by his own hypotheses and expectations is not known. Even if Rist's observations were objective, the study provides no basis for concluding that self-fulfilling prophecies are powerful or pervasive. Because the study was based on interactions between a single teacher and a class of 30 students, it provides little basis for broad conclusions about relations between teacher expectations and student achievement. Furthermore, even Rist's own data and observations provide little evidence of self-fulfilling prophecy. Rist observes that, by the 8th day of class, the teacher had divided the class into three groups—a supposedly smart, average, and dumb group. Each group sat at its own table (Tables 1, 2, and 3, respectively). However, there were no mean differences in IQ scores among the three tables on a test administered at the end of the school year. Instead, the main difference was social class. In comparison with the other students, Table 1 students came from homes that had greater income and were more likely to have both parents present; they were also better dressed. There were comparable differences between the students at Tables 2 and 3. Table 1 was positioned closest to the teacher, and she directed nearly all of her time, attention, and personal warmth to those students. Such differences in treatment would be inappropriate and unjustified even if there were real differences in the intelligence of the children at the different tables. Nonetheless, there was no evidence of self-fulfilling prophecy. The only objective performance data provided were the IQ test scores, and they did not differ by group at the end of the school year.

In contrast, Rist provides good evidence of perceptual bias. He quotes the teacher as claiming several times throughout the year that the children at Table 1 were interested and involved in learning, whereas the other children seemed to "have no idea of what is going on in the classroom." Rist provides numerous examples of behavior suggesting that this was an inaccurate perception of differences in the children's motivation and interest. In addition, given the absence of differences in IQ score, these statements likely reflect perceptual bias stemming from the teacher's stereotypes regarding people from various socioeconomic groups.

Rist's study provides only indirect and incomplete evidence regarding accuracy. Any inferences regarding accuracy must be indirect because he did not assess the teacher's expectations. To the extent that the teacher used social class as a basis for her expectations, those expectations were probably inaccurate (because there were no social class differences in IQ). Whether the teacher's expectations were also based on other, more appropriate, factors cannot be determined.

The Quasi-Experimental Studies

Palardy (1969)

This study examined whether teachers' beliefs about sex differences in ability to learn how to read might be self-fulfilling. Palardy (1969) started with a pool of 42 first-grade teachers and identified two groups: One group believed that boys and girls learn to read equally well (Group A), and a second group believed that girls learn to read more quickly than boys (Group B). Five teachers from each group were then matched on demographics, teaching experience, and teaching methods. Reading readiness scores at the beginning of first grade and reading achievement scores at the end of first grade were obtained for 53 boys and 54 girls in Group A, and for 58 boys and 51 girls in Group B. The reading readiness scores were nearly identical for all four groups. The end of first grade reading achievement scores were then submitted to a two (student gender) by two (teacher expectancy group: A, B) analysis of covariance (with IQ scores as the covariate). The self-fulfilling prophecy prediction is that gender and teacher expectancy groups will interact so that there would be little difference between boys' and girls' reading achievement in Group A, whereas girls would outperform boys in Group B. This is exactly what Palardy found. The interaction was statistically significant and reflected an effect size of .14.[1] There were no main effects of student gender or group. The main strengths of this study are the careful matching of teachers with different expectations and the inclusion of initial reading readiness scores as a covariate. Although naturalistic studies can never eliminate alternative explanations to the same extent as experiments, Palardy's procedures kept such alternatives to a minimum.

Doyle, Hancock, and Kifer (1972)

This study of 11 teachers and 245 students focused on three predictions: First-grade teachers have higher expectations for girls than boys; these different expectations are erroneous; and erroneous expectations will be self-fulfilling. All three predictions were supported. Although there were no objective differences in boys' and girls' IQ scores, teachers estimated that boys had IQ scores averaging 99.9 and girls had scores averaging 104.5. The teachers underestimated the IQs of nearly 59% of the boys and overestimated the IQs of nearly 57% of the girls. Doyle, Hancock, and Kifer (1972) then divided the students into two groups: those whose IQ scores were overestimated and those whose scores were underestimated. The main outcome variable, reading achievement scores, was then submitted to a discrepancy (over- versus underestimated) by gender ANCOVA (using actual IQ scores as a covariate). Results were consistent with a self-fulfilling prophecy: Despite slightly lower IQ scores, girls had higher reading achievement scores. In addition, the effect for discrepancy was highly significant: Students with a mean IQ of 98 (those in the overestimated group) actually outperformed those with a mean IQ of 107 (those in the underestimated group). The expectancy effect size was .3.

Seaver (1973)

Seaver (1973) examined effects of expectations originating from teachers' experiences instructing older siblings. Seaver assumed that teachers would hold higher expectations for a child if they had taught a high achieving older sibling than if they had taught a low achieving older sibling. Although Seaver did not directly assess teacher expectations, research shows that teachers do base their expectations, in part, on experiences with siblings (Thurlow,

Christensen, & Ysseldyke, 1983). Seventy-nine sibling pairs and an unspeci-fied number of teachers were included in the study. The students were di-vided into two teacher expectancy groups based on whether the older sibling's performance was high or low in first grade. Twenty-seven of the younger siblings were assigned to the same first-grade teacher who had taught their older sibling. There were eight measures of achievement in first grade: six achievement test scores (five verbal and one math, all assessed in May) and winter and spring grade point averages. The performance of high and low expectation students was compared with the performance of "no expectation" students, whose teachers had had no prior contact with their older siblings. Consistent with the self-fulfilling prophecy hypothesis, chil-dren with high achieving older siblings performed better when their sibling had been taught by the same teacher (i.e., when their teacher held high ex-pectations for them) than when their sibling had been taught by another teacher. Similarly, children with low achieving older siblings performed worse when their teacher had had prior experience instructing their older sibling. However, of these differences, only two reading achievement scores and the math achievement score reached statistical significance. The effect sizes ranged from near 0 to .28. Because there were weaker effects for grades than for standardized test scores, Seaver found no evidence of perceptual biases.

The main strength of Seaver's study is its nonreactivity. The study was conducted entirely from school archival records. However, because teacher expectations were not measured, and because Seaver did not control for any student background variables, there may be alternative explanations for the main findings (see, for example, Mitman & Snow, 1985) and there is no way to estimate accuracy. The results do suggest, however, that teachers may rely too heavily on their experiences with siblings as a basis for their expecta-tions.

Sutherland and Goldschmid (1974)

Sutherland and Goldschmid (1974) focused on effects of inaccurate teacher expectations. Six first- and second-grade teachers provided their ex-pectations for all students in their classes 2 months into the school year. Ninety-three students were divided into five teacher expectation groups (ranging from "poor" to "superior"). The students were administered two intelligence tests (the WISC for children and the Lorge-Thorndike Group Intelligence Test) twice: 2 months and 7 months into the school year. Students with below average IQ scores were divided into two groups: those whom teachers believed had average intelligence (erroneously high expectation) and those whom teachers believed had below average intelligence (accurately low expectation). The self-fulfilling prophecy prediction is that students in the first group would show greater increases in IQ over the year. The pattern of increases confirmed the prediction for both IQ tests, but the difference was not statistically significant (effect sizes of .1 to .2).

Next, Sutherland and Goldschmid divided students with above average IQ test scores into two groups: those whom teachers believed had above average intelligence (accurately high expectation) and those whom teachers believed had average intelligence (inaccurately low expectations). The self-fulfilling prophecy prediction is that students in the second group would show lower increases or greater decreases in IQ test scores than students in the first group. This prediction was confirmed for both measures; in addition, these differences were statistically significant, and quite strong (*r*s of .45-.55).

The Path Analytic Studies

The path analytic studies differ from the other studies in several important respects. They generally include much larger samples of teachers and students, enhancing both their statistical power and their generalizability. They often include a wider array of student variables, which strengthens their ability to identify and control for sources of accuracy. They often include more than one teacher variable, which allows for examination of whether various types of teachers' perceptions and expectations are related differently to students' motivation and achievement. And the authors of path analytic studies generally present explicit models underlying their theoretical approach and empirical analyses.

Basic Assumptions

The model presented in Figure 4.1 captures the main ideas of most of the path analytic studies. Before describing how this model can be used to separate and identify self-fulfilling prophecies, perceptual biases, and accuracy, several clarifications are needed. First, the model requires that there be some time lag between variables as one moves from left to right—student background variables should be assessed prior to the assessment of teacher expectations, which, in turn, should be assessed prior to students' grades and standardized test scores. Second, in this chapter we focus exclusively on standardized path coefficients (which we will refer to as "betas," regardless of whether regression, LISREL, or some other technique was used to estimate them). Third, in any given study, each path in Figure 4.1 may correspond to several operational paths. Models may include many different aspects of students' background, multiple measures of teacher expectations, multiple standardized test scores, and final grades for more than one course. Fourth, the model makes no assumptions regarding the values any of the paths may take.

Paths C and E represent influences of students' background on their future achievement. Paths B and D represent the extent to which teacher expectations predict students' standardized test scores and final grades, respectively, after controlling for student background. Positive values for Path B represent self-fulfilling prophecy effects. If Path D is similar in magnitude to Path B (and if both are positive and significant), then Path D represents self-fulfilling prophecy. Results showing that Path D exceeds Path B represent perceptual bias. Such results mean that teachers evaluate students' performance in a manner more consistent with teachers' expectations than is justified on the basis of students' objective achievement (standardized test scores). Path A represents the influence of student background characteristics on teacher expectations, and is an index of impression accuracy. To the extent that teachers base their expectations on appropriate factors, such as students' achievement and motivation, those expectations may be considered accurate. If teachers base their expectations on inaccurate information, the expectations, too, will be inaccurate.

The model can also be used to identify predictive accuracy. It shows that teacher expectations will correlate with students' future standardized test scores and grades even if teacher expectations do not influence student achievement (i.e., if Paths B and D are both zero). The extent to which teacher expectations predict but do not influence standardized test scores equals Path A times Path C; the extent to which teacher expectations predict but do not influence final grades equals Path A times Path E. Predictive accuracy is statistically identical to a spurious correlation—to the extent that teacher expectations and student future achievement are both related to some third variable(s), teacher expectations will predict without causing student achievement. In practice, it is easier to estimate predictive accuracy by subtracting Path B from the zero-order correlation between teacher expectations and standardized test scores, and by subtracting Path D from the zero-order correlation between teacher expectations and grades. This is mathematically identical to Path A times Path C and Path A times Path E, respectively. Figure

4.1 shows $r(\text{TEs, STD}) = (\text{Path A} \times \text{Path C}) + \text{Path B}$; and $r(\text{TEs, Grades}) =$ (Path A $\times$ Path E) + Path D, where r = Pearson's correlation, TEs = teacher expectations, Grades = final grades, and STD = standardized test scores. Thus simple algebraic manipulation of these equations shows Path A $\times$ Path C = $r(\text{TEs, STD})$—Path B, and (Path A $\times$ Path E) = $r(\text{TEs, Grades})$—Path D.

The Omitted Variables Problem

All path analytic studies are subject to one major limitation: Paths assessed in the model are valid estimates of causal effects only if all influences on the dependent variable(s) are included. In the social sciences, one can never be certain that this assumption has been met. This is known as the *omitted variables problem*. For example, if a variable that influences both teacher expectations and student future achievement is excluded from a model, the paths representing self-fulfilling prophecy and perceptual bias will be inflated and accuracy will be underestimated. Nonetheless, an effort can be made to include as many potential influences as possible. Therefore, our review of the path analytic studies includes a particular emphasis on evaluating their success at including potential influences on teacher expectations and student achievement.

Williams (1976)

This study included more than 10,000 high school students in Ontario (no information on the number of teachers was provided). Williams's (1976) model is nearly identical to Figure 4.1, except that it included multiple operationalizations of nearly every variable. Student background variables included socioeconomic status (SES), IQ scores, their educational ambitions, previous grades, and their track (vocational or college). Two types of teacher expectations were assessed: cognitive (beliefs about students' performance) and behavioral (beliefs about students' cooperativeness, reliability, and industry). Measures of future achievement included two standardized achievement tests and final grades. Williams's results provide very little evidence of self-fulfilling prophecy. Of the eight possible coefficients (two types of expectations relating to two standardized tests, computed separately by student gender) only one reached statistical significance and even this effect was quite small (beta = .13) and only true for boys. In contrast, Williams found clear evidence of perceptual biases. Both types of expectations significantly predicted grades for boys and girls (betas = .14 to .27), after controlling for

IQ, previous grades, motivation, and SES. These results suggest that teachers' expectations influence their evaluations of students' performance (grades) more strongly than they influence students' actual learning (as indicated by the standardized tests). Williams's results also provide strong evidence of impression accuracy. Teachers' expectations were largely based on appropriate factors (IQ scores, grades, and motivation), and not on students' SES or gender. Results also show considerable evidence of predictive accuracy. Teachers' cognitive expectations correlated .40 to .63 with future standardized achievement test scores and .25 to .40 with their behavioral expectations. However, the path coefficients relating both types of teacher expectations to future standardized test scores (in the context of the model including all the student background variables as controls) were near zero. Consequently, there was no evidence that teacher expectations influenced these test scores. Instead, teacher expectations predicted, without causing, future standardized achievement test scores—that is, they were accurate. Furthermore, the main reason teacher expectations predicted grades was because they were accurate. Zero-order correlations of both types of expectations with grades were between .62 and .67; path coefficients ranged from .14 to .27. Thus path coefficients accounted for only 20% to 40% of the zero-order correlations. This means that about 60% to 80% of the zero-order correlations reflected predictive accuracy, and the remaining 20% to 40% reflected perceptual bias.

This early path analytic study remains one of the strongest naturalistic studies to date. By including so many student background variables, Williams's (1976) study reduced the omitted variables problem to a minimum. However, he does not report when teacher expectations were assessed. If they were assessed late in the school year (e.g., March or April), accuracy is a plausible alternative explanation for path coefficients relating teacher expectations to grades. By spring, teachers may simply know what grades they are going to assign.

West and Anderson (1976)

West and Anderson (1976) were among the first to present an explicit model of relations between naturally occurring teacher expectations and student achievement. Their model is captured by Paths A, B, and C in Figure 4.1 (they did not address perceptual biases). In particular, they address whether the association of teacher expectations with student achievement (self-fulfilling prophecy—Path B) was larger than the association of student achievement with teacher expectations (impression accuracy—Path A). Although West and Anderson indicated that their data were based on 3,000 high school students, they did not provide much additional detail (e.g., there is no information about the timing of the data collection, the number of teachers, correlations among variables, or even what constituted "student achievement"). Their results clearly showed that student achievement freshman year predicted sophomore year teacher expectations (beta = .37) more strongly than teacher expectations freshman year predicted student sophomore year achievement (beta = .12). However, the lack of detail makes it difficult to critically evaluate specific aspects of the study. Nonetheless, the study does represent an early attempt to compare accuracy to self-fulfilling prophecy, and its results are consistent with those of nearly all other path analytic studies.

Parsons, Kaczala, and Meece (1982)

This study of 275 fifth- to ninth-grade students in 17 math classrooms in southeastern Michigan investigated the role of teacher expectations in shaping gender differences in students' expectations for their own performance in math and students' ratings of their own math ability. It included the following measures: teachers' expectations for each student in their math class (teachers' ratings of how good they thought each student was at math and how well they expected each student to perform in an advanced math class), students' prior performance in math, students' expectations for their own performance in future math courses, and students' estimates of their own math ability. These measures can be used to evaluate Paths A, B, and C in Figure 4.1, with student expectations and ability self-concepts as the outcomes. First, there was strong evidence of accuracy (Path A, the zero-order correlation of teacher expectations with the indicator of prior math achievement, was .47). Second, students' expectations and ability self-concepts were significantly related to prior achievement levels (Path C); these correlations ranged from .28 to .49 depending on the sex of the child and the specific dependent measure. Finally, and most importantly for this chapter, teachers' expectations were significantly related to students' expectations and self-concepts even after the association of these measures with past performance was controlled (partial *r* of teacher expectancy to students' self-concept of math ability was .43 and to students' future expectations was .26). The study has two limitations: Prior student expectations and ability self-concepts were not included in the analyses, and all data were collected in the spring. The extent to which differences in student motivation and self-perceptions during the fall and winter influenced teachers' expectations in the spring cannot be determined. If this influence is large, it could account for the partial correlations reported above.

Brattesani, Weinstein, and Marshall (1984)

Brattesani, Weinstein, and Marshall (1984) addressed influences of teacher expectations on students' own performance expectations and their reading achievement test scores among 234 fourth-, fifth-, and sixth-grade students in 16 classrooms. The authors' model is a variation of that depicted in Figure 4.1. One student background variable was assessed: prior reading achievement scores. Teacher expectations for students' schoolwork and reading achievement were assessed in April. Brattesani et al. indicated that reading achievement scores were assessed at "the end of the school year." These authors reported proportion of variance accounted for by teacher expectations (after adding them to a model that already included prior reading achievement). Consistent with the self-fulfilling prophecy hypothesis, teacher expectations accounted for about 7% of the variance in reading achievement scores and 2% to 4% of the variance in student expectations. Brattesani et al. also provided evidence of impression accuracy. Because there was only a single student background variable, Path A is simply the correlation between prior reading achievement and teacher expectations. That correlation was .69 and .77 for high and low perceived differential treatment classes, respectively, indicating substantial accuracy in teachers' impressions of students.

The main goal in this study, however, was to discover whether student perceptions of differential treatment moderate expectancy effects. To address this question, Brattesani et al. divided classrooms into two groups: one in which students believed teachers treated high ability students more favorably than they treated low ability students; and one in which students believed teachers treated high and low ability students similarly. Supporting the moderation hypothesis, teacher expectations accounted for more variance in student expectations (R^2 increments of 6% to 12%) and achievement (R^2 increments of 14% to 16%) in high differential treatment classes than in low differential treatment classes (for student expectations, R^2 increments were near zero; for achievement, R^2 increments were 3%).

However, there are several important limitations to this study. First, teacher expectations were assessed late in the school year (April). After 8 months, teachers have had ample opportunity to discover how students' achievement differed in the current year from the previous year. Therefore, teachers' expectations might have predicted changes in future achievement, not because of self-fulfilling prophecies, but because teachers accurately perceived genuine changes in students' achievement. Second, there was only one control variable—initial reading achievement. Teachers may also base their expectations on students' grades and motivation levels (which were not controlled and which may enhance accuracy). Omitting these variables might inflate estimates of self-fulfilling prophecy effects. Third, students' initial expectations were not controlled. Therefore, the small R^2 increments in predicting student expectations may have resulted almost entirely from a spurious influence of students' initial expectations on both teachers' expectations and students' subsequent expectations. Fourth, by April, perhaps both teachers and students knew how students' current achievement differed from their previous achievement. This represents another source of correspondence between students' and teachers' expectations that is not explicitly incorporated into the model. Thus the R-squared increments in predicting student expectations probably were inflated. This study probably does show that self-fulfilling prophecies are stronger in classes where students perceive more differential treatment, although the absolute magnitude of self-fulfilling prophecies was probably lower than indicated by the researchers' analyses.

Jussim (1989) and Jussim and Eccles (1992)

These two studies were the first to assess and compare self-fulfilling prophecy, perceptual bias, and accuracy explicitly. Together, they included about 100 teachers and 1,700 students in sixth-grade math classes. Both studies assessed models that were more complex versions of the model presented in Figure 4.1. Several student background variables were included: previous standardized test scores, previous year grades, several motivational variables (self-concept of math ability, self-perceptions of effort and time spent on homework, and intrinsic and extrinsic value of math), and gender. Fall and spring assessments of the motivational variables were included in Jussim's (1989) study; only fall assessments were included in Jussim and Eccles's (1992) study. There were two outcome measures of achievement: final math grades and math scores on the Michigan Educational Assessment Program (MEAP, a standardized test administered to students in Michigan early in seventh grade). Three teacher expectation variables were assessed in early

October of sixth grade: teacher perceptions of students' performance, talent, and effort at math. Because results reported here are from two studies, they are presented in pairs. The first reference refers to Jussim (1989) and the second refers to Jussim and Eccles (1992). Although the main analyses were performed using the LISREL VI program, results are reported below as betas because they are standardized path coefficients.

Consistent with the self-fulfilling prophecy hypothesis, teacher perceptions of students' performance in October were significantly related to sixth-grade final grades (betas = .21 and .34) and MEAP scores (betas = .10 and .15). In Jussim's (1989) study, teacher perceptions of students' talent at math significantly related to both standardized test scores (beta = .17) and final grades (beta = .12); and teacher perceptions of performance significantly predicted changes in students' self-concept of math ability in the spring (beta = .11).

Results consistent with the perceptual bias hypothesis showed that teacher perceptions of students' effort significantly predicted grades (betas = .19 and .19) to a larger extent than they predicted standardized achievement test scores (betas = 0 and −.07). Teachers apparently assigned higher grades to students whom they perceived to be hard workers than to students whom they perceived to be lazy (see Jussim, 1989; Jussim & Eccles, 1992, for the basis for concluding that this represents bias rather than teachers simply rewarding hard-working students).

Teacher impressions were both accurate and inaccurate. Teacher impressions were largely accurate because they were most strongly based on appropriate factors: previous grades and standardized test scores, teacher perceptions of in-class performance, and student motivation (the multiple correlation of these factors with teacher expectation variables ranged from about .6 to .8). However, both studies showed that teacher expectations were biased by student gender. Teachers believed that boys were slightly more talented at math than girls (betas = .07 and .08) even though there was no gender difference in standardized test scores; girls received slightly higher grades than boys; and the analyses controlled for any differences in performance and motivation. Teachers also believed that girls tried harder than boys (betas = −.15 and −.11), even though there were no gender differences in self-perceptions of effort or time spent on homework and even though the analyses controlled for differences in performance and motivation. These results provided evidence of a small but consistent pattern of gender bias in teacher perceptions of students' effort and talent at math. Results from both studies also provided considerable evidence of predictive accuracy. The zero-order correlations of teacher perceptions with MEAP scores ranged from .34 to .57, and the path coefficients ranged from –.07 to .15. The path coefficients relating teacher perceptions to MEAP scores accounted for about 20% to 30% of the zero-order correlations; the remaining 70% to 80% represented predictive validity without influence, that is, accuracy. There was a similar pattern for final grades. Zero-order correlations of teacher perceptions with grades ranged from .50 to .71. Path coefficients ranged from .04 to .34. The path coefficients relating teacher perceptions to grades accounted for about 30% to 40% of the zero-order correlations; the remaining 60% to 70% represented accuracy.

Jussim (1989) and Jussim and Eccles (1992) address some of the major ambiguities and limitations in previous path analytic studies. Teacher expectations were assessed in early October, reducing the likelihood that teachers could accurately perceive clear achievement discrepancies in the current year as compared to the previous year. In addition, Jussim and Jussim and Eccles are among the few studies that include multiple measures of teacher expectations and grades and standardized test scores. These are the only studies to include multiple measures of motivation. When many potential sources of spurious relations are included in a model, path coefficients are more likely to reflect influences of teacher expectations on student achievement.

NATURALISTIC STUDIES OUTSIDE OF THE CLASSROOM

Berman (1979)

Berman assessed relations among clinicians' expectations for their clients and the outcome of therapy. Forty-four therapists were divided into 22 pairs. Each pair of therapists interviewed two patients. After the interview, Berman assessed each therapist's expectations regarding the outcome of therapy for the two patients they had interviewed. Each therapist then treated one of the two patients for 1 month. There were several outcome measures: therapist and patient reports of distress (global and specific), improvement, and self-concept; patient scores on a clinical questionnaire (the Hopkins Symptom Checklist); and therapist ratings of the patients on a scale assessing psychiatric symptoms (the Brief Psychiatric Rating Scale). If therapists' expectations were accurate, they should predict (correlate with) the outcome of the patients they did not treat. There was no evidence of accuracy. Therapist expectancy did not significantly correlate with any outcome measures for the patients they did not treat. If therapists' expectations created self-fulfilling prophecies, they should have correlated more strongly with the outcome of the patients they did treat than with the outcome of the patients they did not treat.

The results regarding self-fulfilling prophecy were mixed. Among the patients they did treat, therapists' expectations significantly correlated (around .3) with two of the five patient-reported outcome measures but with none of the five therapist-reported outcome measures. There also was no evidence of perceptual bias. If therapists' expectations biased their interpretations of patient outcomes, then they should have correlated more strongly with therapists' own ratings of the patients' improvement and distress than with patients' ratings. However, therapist expectations predicted patient-reported outcomes more strongly than therapist-reported outcomes.

The implications of this study are limited by the small sample, the brief time frame, and the lack of an independent assessment of patient outcome. However, it is an important study. The methodology of having perceivers provide expectations for targets and then interact only with a subset of those targets may be extremely useful for disentangling self-fulfilling prophecy, perceptual bias, and accuracy in other settings. In addition, the modest expectancy effects are consistent with results obtained from the classroom studies.

Eccles and Colleagues

Eccles and her colleagues have done a series of studies looking at the potential impact of parents' expectations for their children's performance on children's self-perceptions and expectations. Although these studies do not use course grades or achievement on standardized tests as the outcome variable, they are relevant to this chapter because they use the primary psychological predictors of achievement performance according to most theories of motivation and achievement.

(Eccles) Parsons, Adler, and Kaczala (1982)

(Eccles) Parsons, Adler, and Kaczala (1982) involved 270 fifth- to twelfth-grade students and their parents from southeastern Michigan. Although extensive information was gathered from the participants, we focus here on those aspects of the study most directly relevant to the model presented in Figure 4.1. Multiple measures assessed parents' perceptions of their children's math ability and difficulty in math. Comparable items assessed the adolescents' own expectations and ability self-concepts. The adolescents' prior math grades and math test scores were used as independent indicators of the adolescents' math aptitude. Parents' ratings of their children's math ability and of the difficulty of math for their child were reasonably accurate. The betas for the association of these perceptions with the child's past performance in math ranged from –.36 (for the difficulty items) to .53 (for the ability/expectancy items). In turn, parents' perceptions significantly related to adolescents' own ability self-concepts (betas ranged from .37 to .53). Finally, and most important for this chapter, despite the fact that past performance was significantly correlated with the adolescents' ability self-concepts and expectations (*r*s ranged from .25 to .34), the Path C coefficient (the link between prior grades and the adolescents' own ability self-concepts and expectations once parent expectations are entered into the path model) was nonsignificant for each of the adolescents' self-ratings.

Although this study provides preliminary evidence consistent with a self-fulfilling prophecy interpretation, it also provides evidence of accuracy in parents' expectations. It also does not control for the adolescents' prior self-perceptions, and the study was not longitudinal. Consequently, the possibility that the adolescents' own prior self-concepts and expectations are responsible for the association between their parents' expectations and their own subsequent self-concepts cannot be ruled out. This problem was dealt with in the studies summarized next.

Eccles et al. (1991), Eccles (1993), and
Eccles, Yoon, Wigfield, and Harold (1993)

This series of studies replicated the (Eccles) Parsons et al. (1982) study on a sample of 1,500 families of sixth- and seventh-graders, extended the domains to English and sports, and used the longitudinal results of the replication sample (the Michigan Study of Adolescent Life Transitions—MSALT) and two additional longitudinal studies to do cross-lagged analyses of possible reciprocal causal relations between parent and child expectations. Parents' expectations for their children's math and English ability and future performance were strongly related to the children's previous performance in these subjects and to the current teachers' rating of the children's ability (betas ranged from .48 to .64). Parents' expectations were also significantly related to the children's rating of their own abilities in each domain (betas, controlling for teachers' ratings, ranged from .20 to .38). Finally, despite significant zero-order correlations between teachers' ratings and children's ability self-concepts, these relations (the Path A coefficients) were nonsignificant once parents' expectations were entered into the model. However, like the (Eccles) Parsons et al. (1982) study, these replications suffered from the omission of an indicator of the children's prior ability self-concepts.

Eccles (1992) and Eccles, Yoon, Wigfield, and Harold (1993) used cross-lagged structural equation modeling to deal with this problem. First, using just the subjects from MSALT, these investigators estimated the path coefficients for the model illustrated in Figure 4.2. Figure 4.2 shows the path coefficients for sons in the domain of math. Similar results emerged for both sons and daughters in math, English, and sports. In all three domains, both mothers' and children's perceptions of the children's ability were strongly related to the teacher's assessment of the child's ability, suggesting that there is a strong element of accuracy in these expectations. In addition, by Grade 6 both mothers' and children's perceptions of the children's ability were quite stable over a 6-month period (the time between Wave 1 and Wave 2). Finally, and most important for assessing the self-fulfilling prophecy hypothesis, the relation of mothers' expectations at Wave 1 to children's self-perceptions at Wave 2 was significant in each domain, but the relation of children's expectations at Wave 1 to mothers' expectations at Wave 2 was not. This shows that parents' expectations produce changes in the children's self-perceptions over time, not vice versa.

Eccles et al. (1993) replicated these cross-lagged analyses across ages by using information from three similar longitudinal studies. The first study included approximately 300 children initially in Grades 1, 2, and 4. The second study was the MSALT study already described. The third study involved 260 children in Grades 5 to 6 and 9 to 12. Interesting developmental differences emerged. In Grades 2 through 6, results were similar to those reported in the paragraph above. The betas for the time 1 mother to time 2 child path ranged from .23 to .28. In contrast, these beta coefficients were not significant for children initially in Grade 1 or Grades 9 to 12. For these children, there was no evidence of a self-fulfilling prophecy effect for mothers' expectations.

Taken together, these results suggest that although parents' expectations for their children's ability may be largely accurate, parents' expectations also influence their children's ability self-concepts and expectations for future performance. However, these studies, too, may overestimate self-fulfilling effects of parents' expectations. Parents may use other cues, such as their perception of their children's motivation and interest, when they form their

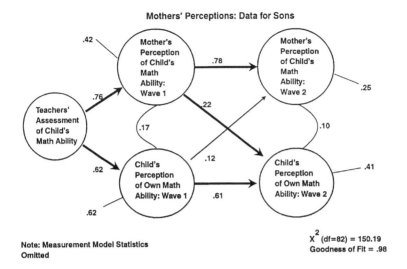

Figure 4.2. Cross-Lagged Structural Equation Modelling of Causal Directions and Mediating Influence

expectations for their children. If so, then these analyses also suffer from the omitted variable problem. Future research needs to examine this possibility.

Jacobs and Eccles (1992)

Many theoreticians argue that self gender-role stereotypes create self-ful-filling prophecies that lead to gender differences in adolescents' achievement expectations and self-perceptions of ability (see Eccles, Jacobs, & Harold, 1990). Jacobs and Eccles (1992) explicitly tested this prediction. Eccles et al. (1991) and Eccles (1992) present evidence that, by the time children are in Grade 6, parents have gender-stereotypic perceptions of their children's ability and future potential in math, English, and sports. Are these differences accurate or biased, and do they relate to children's own ability self-concepts once an independent rating of the children's actual ability is taken into account? Jacobs and Eccles's (1992) research was designed to answer these questions, using data from MSALT. In addition to the measures already reported, parents in MSALT indicated the extent to which they endorsed tradi-

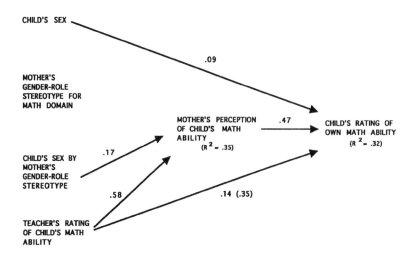

Figure 4.3. Moderating Effect of Mother's Gender-Role Stereotype for the Math Domain on the Impact of Child's Sex on Mother's Perceptions of Her Child's Abilities in Math
SOURCE: Data from Jacobs and Eccles (1992).

tional gender-role stereotypes regarding the ability of males and females in math and sports, and the relative importance of having high ability for males and females in each of these domains. The extent to which parents endorsed the traditional gender-role stereotypes was estimated, with scores ranging from no endorsement (egalitarian beliefs) to strong endorsement. Path analyses then estimated the various effects illustrated in Paths A, B, and C in Figure 4.1. Several background characteristics of both the target and the perceiver were taken into account. The specific model estimated for the math domain is shown in Figure 4.3.

The impression accuracy hypothesis predicts a significant relation between an independent indicator of the child's ability and the perceiver's expectation (in this case the mothers' ratings of their children's math ability). This prediction was confirmed. The expectancy bias hypothesis predicts a significant child-sex-by-parental-stereotyping interaction once the effect of the teacher rating and child sex has been controlled. Again this prediction was confirmed. By controlling for both child's sex and the teacher's ratings of each child's ability, this analysis controls for the possibility that the zero-order relation of children's sex to mothers' rating of their children's math ability reflects accuracy. The results suggest that there is a small element of bias (inaccuracy) in the mothers' expectations. The fact that the path from the mothers' expectations to the children's own ability self-perception is substantially larger (beta = .47) than the direct path from the teachers' rating to the children's ability self-concept (beta = .14) is consistent with a self-fulfilling prophecy hypothesis. Similar results emerged for sports.

Jacobs (1992)

Using data from the third study described under Eccles et al. (1993), Jacobs (1992) employed path analyses to examine the link between parents' expectations and children's math grades. Jacobs first assessed the relation of mothers' (and fathers') expectations for children's future performance in math to the children's previous math grade; these relations were strong (betas were .41 and .53, respectively). She then assessed the relation of both previous grade and mothers' (fathers') rating on the children's own future expectations. Like the other studies presented thus far, Jacobs found significant betas for all four relations, with the betas from each parents' expectation being larger (.37 for mothers and .43 for fathers) than the betas from previous grades (.24 for mothers and .19 for fathers). Finally, she regressed the children's year-end math grade on their mothers' (fathers') expectation, their own expectation, and their previous grade. Year-end grade was more strongly related to parents' expectations (.34 for mothers and .28 for fathers) than to either the children's own expectation (.22) or to previous grade (.25). These results show substantial impression accuracy, some predictive accuracy, and small self-fulfilling prophecy. However, like the other studies in this series, this study potentially suffers from the omitted variable problem by not including children's prior motivation and interest.

Frieze, Olson, and Russell (1991)

Although Frieze, Olson, and Russell (1991) focused on relations between physical attractiveness and income, this study is included here because the authors frame their predictions almost entirely in self-fulfilling prophecy terms. On the basis of experimental research showing that people often view attractive targets more favorably than unattractive targets and that these views can be self-fulfilling (see reviews by Hatfield & Sprecher, 1986;

Snyder, 1984), these authors predicted that attractive recipients of master's in business administration (MBAs) would receive higher starting salaries than unattractive MBAs, and that these differences would increase over time. Four raters evaluated the attractiveness of MBAs based on head-and-shoulders photographs in a picture book taken early in students' matriculation in their MBA program. Questionnaires were sent to more than 2,000 MBAs who graduated between 1973 and 1982. More than 70% responded and Frieze et al. had pictures of 737 of those. Analyses were based on this sample.

Frieze et al. estimated separate regression equations for men and women. Starting salaries were predicted from attractiveness, years of full-time work prior to receiving the MBA, and the year in which subjects took their first full-time job after receiving the MBA (to control for real time differences in salaries). A second set of analyses added height and whether or not the MBA was overweight as predictors of starting salary. Analyses partially supported the self-fulfilling prophecy hypothesis. Attractive men received significantly higher starting salaries than unattractive men, but attractiveness was not significantly related to the starting salaries of women. The second analysis showed that more attractive and less overweight men received significantly higher starting salaries, but again there were no effects of attractiveness or weight for women. A third set of analyses showed that physical attractiveness significantly predicted subsequent salaries for both men and women. Frieze et al. concluded that their research confirmed that "underlying beliefs about people based on their physical appearance affect their judgments and behaviors toward those individuals" (p. 1053).

Several important limitations, however, may undermine the viability of this conclusion. Perhaps most important, there was no assessment of employers' expectations for individual employees. The study clearly shows that MBAs' physical attractiveness predicts subsequent income. Whether this effect is mediated by employers' physical attractiveness stereotypes, however, is unknowable given the data available in this study. Further, the study likely suffers from at least one omitted variable problem. More attractive adults are in fact more socially skilled than less attractive adults, and self-fulfilling prophecies are unlikely to account for these social skill differences (Feingold, 1992). More socially skilled MBAs might deserve and receive higher salaries than less socially skilled MBAs. Finally, Frieze et al. also report only unstandardized regression coefficients and *t* values; no information is provided regarding means, standard deviations, correlations, or standardized coefficients. This renders it difficult to compare their results with those of other studies or to compare the extent of self-fulfilling prophecy versus accuracy. However, results seem to provide considerable evidence of accuracy. In nearly all models, the work-experience variables significantly and substantially predicted income. Further, the *t* values for these effects were generally much higher than those for attractiveness, height, and weight.

ACCUMULATION OF EXPECTANCY EFFECTS

Even small self-fulfilling prophecy effects, if they accumulate over time, might lead to large differences between targets of high versus low expectations. The idea that self-fulfilling prophecy effects accumulate over time lies at the heart of claims emphasizing the power of social beliefs to create social reality (e.g., Snyder, 1984). Consider a hypothetical example in which teachers' high expectations increase an average student's IQ by 3 points each year, and teachers' low expectations decrease an average student's IQ by 3 points each year. If this occurs each year from first grade through sixth, a student with an originally average IQ of 100, but who was the target of high teacher expectations, would have an IQ of 118. An originally identical student who was the target of low teacher expectations would have an IQ of 82 by the end of sixth grade. Such is the power of "small" effects that accumulate. But do expectancy effects actually accumulate? Perhaps they dissipate over time. Even if a teacher does create a 6-point IQ difference between two students, perhaps the next year that difference will lessen or disappear completely. We know of only four studies that have empirically assessed accumulation of expectancy effects.

Rosenthal and Jacobson (1968)

Rosenthal and Jacobson (1968) manipulated teachers' expectations in the first year by randomly selecting students and designating them as "late bloomers." However, in the second year, teachers developed expectations without direct intervention by the experimenters. The accumulation hypothesis predicts that there would be greater differences between late bloomers and controls in the second year than in the first year. In fact, the opposite was found: The differences between these students significantly declined after 2 years. On average, late bloomers had a 3.80 IQ point advantage over controls at the end of the first year, but only a 2.67 IQ point advantage at the end of the second year.

Rist (1970)

Rist (1970) followed a class of kindergarten students through second grade. Unfortunately, however, he provided no quantitative information regarding students' learning, IQ scores, or achievement in first or second grade. Thus it is impossible to determine clearly whether expectancy effects accumulated. Although Rist concludes that he observed a rigid castlike system based on social class, which suggests large and powerful accumulation effects, his observations actually suggest dissipation instead. As did the kindergarten teacher, the first-grade teacher assigned students to three tables (apparently according to her beliefs about the smart, average, and dumb students). All of the Table 1 ("smart") students in kindergarten were assigned to Table A in first grade. However, students at Tables 2 and 3 in kindergarten were all assigned to Table B. Thus, if table assignment is the criterion, kindergarten differences between Tables 2 and 3 disappeared by first grade, although differences between those children and Table 1 students were maintained. Rist reports further reduction of apparent differences in second grade. Again, the Table A students were all assigned to their own table (they were referred to as "Tigers"). Students from Tables B and C were assigned to a second table (referred to as "Cardinals"). None of the students from first grade were assigned to the "slow" table (called "Clowns"). In addition, Rist observes that in January, two of the Tigers were moved to the Cardinals' table, and two of the Cardinals were moved to the Tigers' table. Thus, although some of the differences among students in kindergarten were maintained through second grade, overall differences among the groups seem to have declined.

West and Anderson (1976)

West and Anderson (1976) included data on students in freshman, sophomore, and senior years of high school. The accumulation hypothesis predicts that the coefficients relating freshman year teacher expectations to senior year achievement will be larger than those relating to sophomore year achievement. However, the results supported the dissipation hypothesis: The coefficient relating freshman year teacher expectations to senior year achievement (.06) was smaller than the coefficient relating to sophomore year achievement (.12).

Frieze et al. (1991)

Frieze et al. (1991) addressed the accumulation issue by comparing the extent to which MBAs' attractiveness predicted starting salary versus salary in 1983. The unstandardized coefficients relating attractiveness to 1983 salary (2.60, 2.13 for men and women, respectively) were higher than those relating to starting salary (1.13, 0.28). Although these results are consistent with the accumulation hypothesis, they are also consistent with the social skills interpretation discussed earlier. Perhaps attractiveness differences in income increase over time (in part or in total) because attractiveness is a proxy for social skill. More socially skilled MBAs are likely to be more capable and deserving managers, administrators, and executives. Therefore, they would also be likely to receive higher salaries than their less socially skilled peers.

ARE EXPECTANCY EFFECTS UNIMPORTANT?

Although self-fulfilling prophecies and perceptual biases may not be as large as once claimed, nor are they trivial. A naturally occurring effect of "only" .2 means that, on average, of all targets of high expectations, 10% show substantial improvement and, of all targets of low expectations, 10% show substantial decreases in performance (see Rosenthal, 1984). Most researchers agree that such effects are important (e.g., Brophy, 1983; Jussim, 1990, 1991; Rosenthal & Jacobson, 1968). One way to get a sense of just how important this might be is to consider the effect as if it were the result of a large-scale social program (Rosenthal & Jacobson, 1968). A program that led 10% of the students who had been performing below average to perform above average probably would be viewed as a major accomplishment; a social policy that undermined students' performance so that 10% of those who had been above average achievers became below average probably would be considered an outrage. In addition, even though accuracy may prevent self-fulfilling prophecies from pervading and dominating dyadic social interactions, stereotype-based expectations may create differences between social groups (based on gender, ethnicity, social class) where none previously existed. This is the power of "small" expectancy effects.

FACTORS MODERATING EXPECTANCY EFFECTS

The small expectancy effect sizes in the naturalistic studies represent average effect sizes. It is likely that there are conditions under which expectancy effects are much larger or smaller. The experimental laboratory evidence is reviewed elsewhere (e.g., Snyder, 1992; see Cooper & Hazelrigg, 1988, for a meta-analysis; see also Jussim, 1990, 1993, for general reviews of moderating factors). Although few naturalistic studies have addressed factors moderating expectancy effects, three factors seem likely: characteristics of the perceiver; characteristics of the target; and situational factors.

Perceiver Characteristics: Prejudice, Cognitive Rigidity, and Belief Certainty

Prejudiced individuals seem especially unlikely to be motivated to be accurate. Instead, they seem likely to prefer to conclude that members of a stigmatized group have negative, enduring attributes. People high in cognitive rigidity or belief certainty also may not be motivated to consider viewpoints different than their own. People high in cognitive rigidity or belief are similar in that they may be unlikely to alter their beliefs when confronted with disconfirming evidence. Whether the source is prejudice, cognitive rigidity, or belief certainty (which may tend to co-occur within individuals—see Adorno, Frenkel-Brunswick, Levinson, & Sanford, 1950), people overly confident in their expectations may be most likely to maintain biased perceptions of individuals and to create self-fulfilling prophecies.

Target Characteristics

Self-Concept

When people have unclear self-perceptions, they are more susceptible to all sorts of social influence, including self-fulfilling prophecies. In contrast, when people have clear self-perceptions, they are not only less likely to fulfill others' expectations, but they often convince perceivers to view them much as they view themselves (see Jussim, 1986, 1990, 1993, for reviews).

Age

There are several reasons why age might be an important moderator. First, to the extent that targets need to understand the perceiver's expectations, cognitive maturity is an important moderator. Second, targets' confidence in their self-perceptions is likely to vary with age. Children between ages 4 and 7 are very positive and very confident in their ratings of their own abilities. Consequently, they may be less influenced by the subtle types of messages associated with some self-fulfilling prophecy mechanisms. However, by Grade 2 some of this confidence begins to wane and, because children at this age have had limited experience on which to base their estimates of their own academic abilities, children between Grades 2 and 6 may be especially susceptible to teacher expectancy effects. In contrast, given their cognitive maturity, their social comparison abilities, and the number of years of experience they have had to form their ability self-concepts, high school students may be less susceptible to erroneous teacher expectancies. Finally, children of different ages are more or less likely to undergo various life transitions. The impact of new situations and transition is discussed below.

Unfortunately, few researchers have looked at age as a moderator variable. Self-fulfilling prophecies were strongest among the youngest students in the original Rosenthal and Jacobson (1968) study, suggesting that younger children may be more malleable than older children and adults. However, a meta-analysis shows that the strongest teacher expectation effects occur in first, second, and seventh grade (Raudenbush, 1984). Further, the largest self-fulfilling prophecy effects yet reported were obtained in a study of adults (Eden & Shani, 1982). In Eccles et al.'s (1993) study of parents' expectations, larger expectancy effects were found in Grades 2 to 6 than in Grades 1 or 9 to 12. Although these findings do not deny a moderating role for age, they suggest that situational factors may also influence targets' susceptibility to self-fulfilling prophecies.

It also seems likely that targets' perceptions of the legitimacy of the perceivers' evaluations would affect the extent to which the target paid attention to messages from the perceivers about the target's abilities. Again this possible moderator is likely to vary with age and the specific role of the perceiver. It is also likely to vary with the status differential between the target and the perceiver. We know of no studies that have assessed these hypotheses.

Situational Factors

People may be more susceptible to confirming others' expectations when they enter new situations. Whenever people undergo major life transitions, such as entering a new school or starting a new job, they may be less clear and confident in their self-perceptions. As previously discussed, unclear self-perceptions render targets more susceptible to confirming perceivers' expectations. This analysis may help explain the seemingly inconsistent findings regarding age. Students in first, second, and seventh grade and new military inductees are all in relatively unfamiliar situations. Therefore, all may be more susceptible to self-fulfilling prophecies than other students or adults in more familiar surroundings. This may also account for Eccles et al.'s (1993) finding of minimal effects of parents' expectations in Grades 9 to 12 (by this time, students usually have clear ideas about their academic and athletic abilities).

Why were there larger effects in Eccles et al.'s (1993) study in Grades 2 to 6 than in first grade? Perhaps parents become more involved in students' schoolwork in Grades 2 to 6 than in first grade. There may be less academic work, such as homework and papers, in first grade than in later elementary school grades. Receiving larger amounts of parental time and attention focusing on schoolwork may be relatively new for most younger children, who might therefore be more susceptible to confirming their parents' expectations. Greater involvement also provides parents with greater opportunity to act on their expectancies and to influence their children. Alternatively, as we discussed earlier, perhaps younger children are simply insensitive to the types of subtle messages parents might be communicating about their view of their children's abilities.

CONCLUSION

This review yields several broad conclusions and suggests important directions for future naturalistic research on expectancy effects. First, perceivers' naturally developed expectations sometimes create self-fulfilling prophecies and perceptual biases. Expectancy effects clearly occur in educational settings and between parents and children. Although studies suggest that naturally occurring expectancy effects may also occur in clinical and business settings (Berman, 1979; Frieze et al., 1991), this research has sufficient limitations to render premature any conclusion about the size or even the existence of expectancy effects in these contexts. Additional research on naturally occurring expectancy effects outside of the classroom is greatly needed.

The evidence across the entire set of studies reviewed also clearly indicates that naturalistic self-fulfilling prophecies and perceptual biases tend to be relatively modest in size, ranging from about .1 to about .3 (although some studies fail to show any evidence of self-fulfilling prophecy—Rist, 1970, and Williams, 1976; and others show no evidence of perceptual bias—Berman, 1979, and Seaver, 1973). Further, with the exception of Berman (1979), all studies that provide evidence about accuracy (Brattesani et al., 1984; Eccles, 1992; Eccles et al., 1991; Eccles et al., 1993; Eccles Parsons, Adler, & Kaczala, 1982; Frieze et al., 1991; Jacobs, 1992; Jacobs & Eccles, 1992; Jussim, 1989; Jussim & Eccles, 1992; Parsons, Kaczala, & Meece, 1982; West & Anderson, 1976; Williams, 1976) show more evidence of accuracy than of self-fulfilling prophecies or perceptual biases. The difference in perceiver accuracy between Berman's (1979) study and the teacher expectation studies may have broader implications for understanding the nature of accuracy in person perception. Berman's (1979) therapists generated expectations after a single 30-minute session with their patients, but teachers often had weeks, and sometimes months, to observe students in the education studies. In general, it seems likely that initial impressions of targets based on limited information are far less likely to be accurate than impressions based on rich and extensive information obtained within the context of ongoing social relationships lasting weeks, months, or more.

Both the naturalistic studies and the meta-analyses (e.g., Rosenthal & Rubin, 1978; Smith, 1980), which focused primarily on experiments, converge on the conclusion that although expectancy effect sizes may occasionally be quite large, they are generally quite small. Social psychological perspectives on expectancy effects were once dominated by claims emphasizing their power and pervasiveness (see Jussim, 1991, 1993, for reviews). Neither the experimental nor naturalistic evidence, however, supports such claims. Despite the current lack of support, it remains possible that there are conditions under which naturally occurring expectancy effects are pervasive and powerful. Although small expectancy effects hypothetically may accumulate to create large differences among targets, existing research provides more evidence that expectancy effects dissipate over time than that they accumulate. Of course, even the typically "small" effects are practically and theoretically important. Unfortunately, however, few naturalistic studies have examined the conditions under which expectancy effects are large or small. Given the potential to contribute to social and intellectual development, inequality, and injustices, we believe an important challenge for future research is to identify naturally occurring conditions under which expectancy effects are powerful and pervasive.

NOTE

1. Throughout this chapter, whenever we use the term *effect size,* we refer to the correlation coefficient, *r,* except where otherwise noted.

REFERENCES

Adorno, T., Frenkel-Brunswick, E., Levinson, D., & Sanford, R. N. (1950). *The authoritarian personality.* New York: Harper.

Berman, J. S. (1979). Social bases of psychotherapy: Expectancy, attraction, and the outcome of treatment (doctoral dissertation, Harvard University). *Dissertation Abstracts International, 40,* 5800B.

Brattesani, K. A., Weinstein, R. S., & Marshall, H. H. (1984). Student perceptions of differential teacher treatment as moderators of teacher expectation effects. *Journal of Educational Psychology, 76,* 236-247.

Brophy, J. (1983). Research on the self-fulfilling prophecy and teacher expectations. *Journal of Educational Psychology, 75,* 631-661.

Brophy, J., & Good, T. (1974). *Teacher-student relationships: Causes and consequences.* New York: Holt, Rinehart & Winston.

Cooper, H., & Hazelrigg, P. (1988). Personality moderators of interpersonal expectancy effects: An integrative research review. *Journal of Personality and Social Psychology, 55,* 937-949.

Darley, J. M., & Fazio, R. H. (1980). Expectancy-confirmation processes arising in the social interaction sequence. *American Psychologist, 35,* 867-881.

Doyle, W. J., Hancock, G., & Kifer, E. (1972). Teachers' perceptions: Do they make a difference? *Journal of the Association for the Study of Perception, 7,* 21-30.

Eccles, J. S. (1993). School and family effects on the ontogeny of children's interests, self-perceptions, and activity choice. In J. E. Jacobs (Ed.), *Nebraska symposium on motivation, 1992* (pp. 145-218). Lincoln: University of Nebraska Press.

Eccles, J. S., Jacobs, J. E., & Harold, R. D. (1990). Gender role stereotypes, expectancy effects, and parent's socialization of gender differences. *Journal of Social Issues, 46,* 183-201.

Eccles, J. S., Jacobs, J. E., Harold, R., Yoon, K. S., Arbreton, A., & Freedman-Doan, C. (1991, August). *Expectancy effects are alive and well on the home front.* Invited address, Annual Meeting of the American Psychological Association, San Francisco.

Eccles, J. S., & Wakefield, A. (1985). Teacher expectations and student motivation. In J. B. Dusek (Ed.), *Teacher expectancies* (pp. 185-228). Hillsdale, NJ: Erlbaum.

Eccles, J. S., Yoon, K. S., Wigfield, A., & Harold, R. E. (1993). *Causal relations between mothers' and children's beliefs about the children's abilities.* Manuscript submitted for publication.

Eccles Parsons, J., Adler, T. F., & Kaczala, C. M. (1982). Socialization of achievement attitudes and beliefs: Parental influences. *Child Development, 53,* 310-321.

Eden, D. (1986). OD and self-fulfilling prophecy: Boosting productivity by raising expectations. *Journal of Applied Behavioral Science, 22,* 1-13.

Eden, D., & Shani, A. B. (1982). Pygmalion goes to boot camp: Expectancy, leadership, and trainee performance. *Journal of Applied Psychology, 67,* 194-199.

Feingold, A. (1992). Good-looking people are not what we think. *Psychological Bulletin, 111,* 304-341.

Fiske, S. T., & Taylor, S. E. (1984). *Social cognition.* Reading, MA: Addison-Wesley.

Frieze, I. H., Olson, J. E., & Russell, J. (1991). Attractiveness and income for men and women in management. *Journal of Applied Social Psychology, 21,* 1039-1057.

Hatfield, E., & Sprecher, S. (1986). *Mirror, mirror . . .: The importance of looks in everyday life.* Albany: State University of New York Press.

Jacobs, J. E. (1992). The influence of gender stereotypes on parent and child math attitudes. *Journal of Educational Psychology, 83,* 518-527.

Jacobs, J. E., & Eccles, J. S. (1992). The impact of mothers' gender-role stereotypic beliefs on mothers' and children's ability perceptions. *Journal of Personality and Social Psychology, 63,* 932-944.

Jones, E. E. (1986). Interpreting interpersonal behavior: The effects of expectancies. *Science, 234,* 41-46.

Jussim, L. (1986). Self-fulfilling prophecies: A theoretical and integrative review. *Psychological Review, 93,* 429-445.

Jussim, L. (1989). Teacher expectations: Self-fulfilling prophecies, perceptual biases, and accuracy. *Journal of Personality and Social Psychology, 57,* 469-480.

Jussim, L. (1990). Social reality and social problems: The role of expectancies. *Journal of Social Issues, 46*(2), 9-34.

Jussim, L. (1991). Social perception and social reality: A reflection-construction model. *Psychological Review, 98,* 54-73.

Jussim, L. (1993). Accuracy in interpersonal expectations: A reflection-construction analysis of current and classic research. *Journal of Personality, 61,* 637-668.

Jussim, L. (in press). Self-fulfilling prophecies. In A. S. R. Manstead & M. Hewstone (Eds.), *Blackwell dictionary of social psychology.* Oxford, UK: Blackwell.

Jussim, L., & Eccles, J. (1992). Teacher expectations II: Construction and reflection of student achievement. *Journal of Personality and Social Psychology, 63,* 947-961.

Kahneman, D., & Tversky, A. (1973). On the psychology of prediction. *Psychological Review, 80,* 237-251.

Merton, R. K. (1948). The self-fulfilling prophecy. *Antioch Review, 8,* 193-210.

Miller, D. T., & Turnbull, W. (1986). Expectancies and interpersonal processes. *Annual Review of Psychology, 37,* 233-256.

Mitman, A. L., & Snow, R. E. (1985). Logical and methodological problems in teacher expectancy research. In J. B. Dusek (Ed.), *Teacher expectancies* (pp. 93-131). Hillsdale, NJ: Erlbaum.

Myers, D. G. (1987). *Social psychology* (2nd ed.). New York: McGraw-Hill.

Palardy, J. M. (1969). What teachers believe—What children achieve. *Elementary School Journal, 69,* 370-374.

Parsons, J. E., Kaczala, C. M., & Meece, J. L. (1982). Socialization of achievement attitudes and beliefs: Classroom influences. *Child Development, 53,* 322-339.

Raudenbush, S. W. (1984). Magnitude of teacher expectancy effects on pupil IQ as a function of the credibility of expectancy inductions: A synthesis of findings from 18 experiments. *Journal of Educational Psychology, 76,* 85-97.

Rist, R. (1970). Student social class and teacher expectations: The self-fulfilling prophecy in ghetto education. *Harvard Educational Review, 40,* 411-451.

Rosenthal, R. (1974). *On the social psychology of the self-fulfilling prophecy: Further evidence for Pygmalion effects and their mediating mechanisms.* New York: MSS Modular Publications.

Rosenthal, R. (1984). *Meta-analytic procedures for the social research.* Beverly Hills, CA: Sage.

Rosenthal, R., & Jacobson, L. (1968). *Pygmalion in the classroom: Teacher expectations and student intellectual development.* New York: Holt, Rinehart & Winston.

Rosenthal R., & Rubin, D. B. (1978). Interpersonal expectancy effects: The first 345 studies. *The Behavioral and Brain Sciences, 3,* 377-386.

Seaver, W. B. (1973). Effects of naturally-induced teacher expectancies. *Journal of Personality and Social Psychology, 28,* 333-342.

Smith, M. L. (1980). Teacher expectations. *Evaluation in Education, 4,* 53-55.

Snyder, M. (1984). When belief creates reality. *Advances in Experimental Social Psychology, 18,* 247-305.

Snyder, M. (1992). Motivational foundations of behavioral confirmation. *Advances in Experimental Social Psychology, 25,* 67-114.

Sutherland, A., & Goldschmid, M. (1974). Negative teacher expectation and IQ change in children with superior intellectual potential. *Child Development, 45,* 852-856.

Thurlow, M. L., Christensen, S., & Ysseldyke, J. E. (1983). *Referral research: An integrative summary of findings.* Minneapolis: University of Minnesota.

West, C., & Anderson, T. (1976). The question of preponderant causation in teacher expectancy research. *Review of Educational Research, 46,* 613-630.

Williams, T. (1976). Teacher prophecies and the inheritance of inequality. *Sociology of Education, 49,* 223-236.

5

Self-Conceptions, Person
Conceptions, and Their Development

DIANE N. RUBLE
CAROL S. DWECK

Diane N. Ruble is a Professor of Psychology and Coordinator of the Developmental Concentration at New York University. She received a Ph.D. from the University of California at Los Angeles, and taught at Princeton and the University of Toronto, before assuming her present position. Her research interests include gender development and self-evaluative processes, as well as the development of person perception.

Carol S. Dweck is a Professor of Psychology at Columbia University. She received a Ph.D. from Yale University. Her research focuses on motivational processes and their development.

Self-conceptions and conceptions of persons have received considerable attention in both social psychology and developmental psychology, but often from different perspectives. These conceptions are not only interesting in their own right, but have also been shown to play important roles in motivational processes. In this chapter, we review recent research on the development of trait conceptions and their role in motivational processes, integrating what is known and formulating questions for future research. In addition, we discuss the ways in which developmental work does or could make contact with current work in social psychology.

OVERVIEW OF CHAPTER

Until recently, it was widely assumed that children below the age of about 8 did not have psychological self-conceptions or person conceptions. Several lines of work converged to lend credence to this view. First, young children's self-descriptions were found to be "physicalistic," focusing on their posses-

AUTHORS' NOTE: Preparation of this chapter was supported, in part, by a National Institute of Mental Health Research Scientist Development Award (00484) and research grant (37215) to Diane Ruble. The authors are grateful to Donal Carlston, Shuping Lu, and Leonard Newman for reading and commenting on an earlier version of this chapter.

sions or physical appearance rather than on psychological characteristics. Second, young children did not appear to understand traits or stable dispositions in the way that older children did. Third, young children did not appear to show the maladaptive motivational patterns in the face of failure that accompany negative trait (ability) inferences in older individuals; this was taken as further evidence for the absence of trait conceptions. In short, it was believed that not until middle to late grade school, when the requisite cognitive abilities developed, could children understand psychological characteristics and respond to events in terms of them.

Recent research, however, suggests that young children (as young as 3 or 4) do in fact have some aspects of psychological self-conceptions and, moreover, show the accompanying motivational patterns found in older children. Specifically, their self-conceptions appear to revolve around notions of goodness and badness, with a sizable proportion of young children believing they are "bad" when they fail a task. These children show virtually all of the characteristics of a helpless reaction. These findings indicate that many important questions remain about young children's self-conceptions and person conceptions, and about how these conceptions and their motivational impact may change with development.

There is increasing evidence that, during the grade school years, children's conceptions of self and others become more differentiated. That is, they may move away from more global good-bad conceptions and begin to refer to more distinct domains of personhood. In this chapter, we examine past findings of increased understanding or use of stable dispositional concepts over the early school years and focus on the question of whether young children's use of global evaluative terms (good, bad, mean) for themselves and others represents a true understanding of psychological dispositions. We also discuss theories and findings in the adult social-personality literature (particularly the literature on dispositional inference) showing how these approaches may inform our analysis, as well as how our developmental analysis may inform these approaches.

BACKGROUND

Developmental Changes in Children's Impressions of People

What does personhood mean to children of different ages? When children think about what people are like, what features are salient? There has been considerable interest in such questions over the past 30 years. Many studies suggest that the features of people that are most salient change with age and that the perception that people possess stable, dispositional characteristics is a particularly important aspect of these changes. Moreover, considerable research suggests that such changes have important implications for personal and interpersonal choices and behaviors. In this section, we briefly summarize the data that support these conclusions (see Rholes, Newman, & Ruble, 1990, and Shantz, 1983, for reviews).

A common approach to the study of person perception is to ask children for open-ended descriptions of themselves (e.g., Livesley & Bromley, 1973; Mohr, 1978) or others (e.g., Barenboim, 1981; Livesley & Bromley, 1973; Peevers & Secord, 1973). Livesley and Bromley's (1973) research illustrates the typical findings using this method. Their main analysis groups children's descriptions into two categories: peripheral (concrete, perceptually salient facts or behaviors, such as physical appearance, and routine habits or behaviors); and central (inner, psychological aspects, such as personality traits, motives, and needs). Livesley and Bromley found that, prior to 8 years of age, children rely heavily on peripheral descriptors, whereas older children are much more likely to refer to various central personal features. One of the most interesting aspects of their data was the finding that many differences between 7- and 8-year-old children are greater than those between 8- and 15-year-old children. This observation led them to suggest that "the eighth year is a critical period in the developmental psychology of person perception" (p. 147).

One obvious problem interpreting age differences in impression formation from open-ended data is that differences in references to traits may reflect language facility or understanding of what the question calls for, rather than true differences in perceptions of what people are like. Partly in response to this problem, a number of studies have turned to forced-choice methods or rating scales to assess children's perceptions of others. A common procedure is to show or tell subjects about a target child's behavior that is intended to suggest a dispositional characteristic (e.g., generous, athletic). Subjects are then asked to predict what the actor will do in a new situation that involves that characteristic. The reasoning is that if children understand a disposition to be a stable characteristic of the individual, they should predict a cross-situationally consistent pattern of behavior.

Studies using this methodology have, in general, found an age-related increase in consistent behavior predictions between 5 and 9 years of age. For example, even though younger children can label a behavior in terms of appropriate trait terms (that an actor who failed to share her sandwich is self-ish), they are less likely to predict that the actor will be selfish in a different situation than are older children (e.g., Ferguson, van Roozendaal, & Rule, 1986; Rholes & Ruble, 1984). Similar findings occur for self-ratings; several studies suggest that evaluative feedback has relatively little overall impact on young (under 7 years) children's predictions for future performance (Parsons & Ruble, 1977; Stipek & Hoffman, 1980). Younger children's be-havior predictions often do not differ from chance responding. These studies suggest that an important development in person perception is the belief that people possess stable traits that influence their behavior across different, trait-relevant situations.

This conclusion is further supported by findings that changing perceptions about the nature of persons appear to have important behavioral conse-quences. For example, Grusec and Redler (1980) found that attributing a child's own generous behavior to his or her generous nature led to more subsequent generosity in new settings than did social reinforcement. This advantage of trait attribution did not hold for younger (5 to 6 years) children, however, possibly because, as the authors suggest, they "have difficulty in thinking of themselves in terms of enduring dispositional traits that produce consistency in behavior" (p. 532). Similarly, Eisenberg, Cialdini, McGreath, and Shell (1987) found that the likelihood that children's compliance with a small request to behave altruistically would generalize to a larger request (the "foot-in-the-door" effect) depended on children's understanding of invariant traits. These studies and others (see Rholes et al., 1990, for a review) suggest children's growing understanding of people in dispositional terms may have important implications for personal and interpersonal behaviors.

Self-Conceptions and Helpless Reactions to Failure

Another line of evidence relevant to the development of children's under-standing of stable dispositions consists of findings suggesting that young children do not show the "helpless" reactions to failure found in many older children (Miller, 1985; Rholes, Blackwell, Jordan, & Walters, 1980). Spe-cifically, children above the age of about 10 respond to failure with self-denigration (negative inferences about their intelligence), markedly reduced expectations, negative affect, and performance impairment or low persist-ence. In these older children, the helpless response is predicted by the belief that intelligence is a fixed trait (rather than a more malleable quality). These findings fit nicely with findings suggesting that young children cannot yet understand ability or intelligence in a traitlike way. Because the helpless pattern in older children is associated with a belief in fixed ability, the absence of a helpless pattern in younger children provides another source of evidence (albeit indirect) that young children lack an understanding of stable traits, that they do not see failure as reflecting on a fixed and important aspect of the self and do not fall into a helpless pattern of responding.

This pattern of findings also seems reasonable because of its adaptive implications. It is in the early years that children master many of the most difficult and important tasks of a lifetime, such as locomotion, language, and reading. Many of these tasks are extremely challenging ones, requiring extended periods of time for mastery, and are fraught with obstacles and failure along the way. Viewed in this way, it makes sense that young children are spared the self-consciousness and vulnerability that appear to go with stable self-conceptions. They are thus able to approach highly difficult tasks and to confront failure without concerns about how negative outcomes reflect on their attributes. This pattern is a happy tableau of youthful innocence and invulnerability. Unfortunately, it is not an accurate one.

EVIDENCE FOR HELPLESSNESS AND SELF-CONCEPTIONS IN YOUNG CHILDREN

Dweck and her colleagues (Cain, 1990; Hebert & Dweck, 1985, reported in Dweck, 1991; Heyman, Dweck, & Cain, 1992; Smiley & Dweck, in press) provide clear evidence of a helpless pattern in young children—one that is linked to beliefs about the self. Four studies with preschoolers (Hebert & Dweck, 1985; Smiley & Dweck, in press), kindergartners (Heyman et al., 1992) and first graders (Cain, 1990) indicate that a sizable proportion of young children (37% to 51% across studies) exhibit critical aspects of the helpless pattern in the face of failure or criticism: low persistence, lowered expectancies, negative affect, and self-denigration or self-blame. These studies differ from many previous studies in that the tasks (like jigsaw puzzles of well-known cartoon characters) had clear, visible successes and failures. In addition, great care was taken to make the assessments of children's reactions comprehensible and compelling to children of that age. Moreover, because it was suspected that young children's inferences might revolve around issues of goodness and badness (rather than issues of intelligence), procedures were developed to probe specifically for such ideation.

It should be noted that the finding of helplessness in young children does not necessarily contradict findings of developmental change in reactions to failure. Developmental studies typically examine each age group as a whole and compare the responses of one age group to another. By doing so, such studies obscure individual differences within age groups. In a study that looked at age changes as well as at individual differences in reactions to failure, Cain (1990) found evidence for clear age changes in failure responses. Older children overall showed much greater reactions in their success expectancies than did younger children. However, Cain also found a sizable proportion of young children (first graders) who exhibited helpless responses (low persistence, lowered expectations, negative affect). Older children as a group may become more sensitive to failure, but a subgroup of young children may already be exhibiting a marked sensitivity. Thus it appears that when the tasks and the assessments are age appropriate, when the failures are salient and meaningful, and when individual differences are looked for, some young children do indeed reveal their vulnerability.

However, although many of the manifestations of helplessness are similar in younger and older children, the self-inferences of young children are quite different. When they confront failure, older helpless children conclude that they are not smart; young helpless children conclude that they are bad (Hebert & Dweck, 1985; Heyman et al., 1992). Moreover, young children endorse the belief that badness is a stable characteristic. This means that helplessness in young children is linked to a belief in a stable characteristic, but that characteristic is a more global goodness/badness, not intelligence.

It is reasonable that young children's concerns should revolve around issues of goodness rather than issues of intelligence. They are in the thick of being socialized and being taught what is good and bad, right and wrong. Moreover, lacking extensive experience with tasks and feedback in the intellectual domain, many young children may not make a clear distinction between good-bad/right-wrong feedback received for their conduct (Dweck & Elliott, 1983; Heyman et al., 1992; Stipek & Daniels, 1990). At any rate, it is plausible that young children's focal concern is a more global goodness of the self. What is the evidence for these global self-conceptions?

The suggestion that young children perceive task failure to fall within the general domain of goodness comes from a study by Hebert and Dweck (1985; reported in Dweck, 1991). In this study, preschool children role-played socialization agents' (teachers' and parents') reactions to children's puzzle outcomes (three failed puzzles and one completed one). The children who showed helpless reactions role-played far more punishment and criticism from these agents than did children who showed more persistent, mastery-oriented reactions. The more mastery-oriented children also seemed concerned with goodness-badness and reward-punishment, but they tended to role-play teachers and parents praising and rewarding the effort they had expended or the progress they had made.

Heyman et al. (1992) looked more directly at young children's self-inferences from negative outcomes and their beliefs about goodness-badness. In this study, kindergartners were led through vivid role plays of three scenarios. In each scenario, the child pretended to perform a task (write numbers, build a house from blocks, draw a family) as a nice surprise for the teacher, but in each case, before giving the product to the teacher the child noticed a mistake. In two of the three scenarios the teacher criticized the child for the mistake. When children received the no-criticism story first, virtually all of them thought their product was excellent despite the mistake. More than 94% gave their work a rating of 5 or 6 on a 6-point scale. Following criticism, 60.7% of the children continued to award themselves one of the top ratings, but 39.3% gave their products lower ratings. These "low product raters" showed other aspects of the helpless pattern, including self-blame.

Specifically, low-product raters were more likely to report negative affect, were less likely to agree to persist in the task, and were less likely to come up with constructive solutions for dealing with the situation. In addition, as in the Hebert and Dweck (1985) study, low product raters were more likely than high product raters to role-play negative reactions from parents, and were less likely to role-play positive reactions. Most interesting, however, is a new measure that tapped the degree to which children believed that the situation reflected on them as a person, that is, the degree to which they called major aspects of themselves into question.

Following each episode with criticism, children were asked to think about everything that had happened in that episode and to decide how what happened made them feel: like they were good or not good at the activity; smart or not smart; a good or not good girl/boy, or a nice or not nice girl/boy. Low product raters rated themselves significantly more negatively than did high product raters in each of the four categories of self-ratings. These differences were quite large, with almost none of the high product raters feeling that they were not a good person, but more than half of the low product raters feeling this way. Moreover, the low product raters were not discriminatory in their self-denigration. They were as likely to say they were not a nice person as to indict their specific skills on the task. Thus young children are not immune to negative self-evaluation or indictment of their traits following a negative event.

Were these evaluations simply affect-driven responses that might be specific to the failure context? In other words, were these children just feeling bad about themselves and then agreeing that they were bad? Children were asked in a separate (prior) session whether a child who gets things wrong on his or her schoolwork is bad. Almost half (47.6%) of the low product raters believed that this was the case, whereas only 18.5% of the high product raters made this inference. Thus the tendency of low product raters to ascribe a global evaluative trait on the basis of mistakes is a tendency that generalizes beyond themselves and their immediate experience.

Heyman et al. (1992) also identify another general belief that distinguishes the low product raters from the high product raters—a belief in the stability of bad behavior. Children were told to imagine that a new boy (girl) was in their class and that this child performed a series of naughty acts ("steals your crayons, scribbles on your paper"). They were then asked whether they thought the child would always act this way. Twice as many of the low product raters as the high product raters (50% versus 24.6%) expressed a belief in bad behavior as a stable characteristic. Thus this study shows that, just as with older children, where a belief in fixed intelligence predicts inferences about intelligence and helpless responses in the face of failure, a belief in stable badness appear to be associated with inferences about badness and helpless responses in the face of failure or criticism for younger children.

These findings suggest that young children may well have a conception of self—at the very least a conception of self as an object that can be evaluated (and whose negative evaluation has clear motivational consequences). Do these conceptions qualify as trait conceptions? How might they differ from the trait conceptions held by older children? In the next section, we suggest that although these self-conceptions may be the beginning of or prerequisites for later dispositional conceptions, they differ from them in several ways.

TRAIT CONCEPTIONS IN YOUNG CHILDREN

What does the literature suggest about the possibility that children under 7 years of age are capable of conceiving of people in terms of stable personality characteristics? Several studies question the portrait of young children as lacking the skills to see the stable characteristics of themselves and others.

Studies Using
Open-Ended Response Measures

Although most open-ended studies show an increase with age in the proportion of traitlike statements when children are asked to describe themselves or someone else, a few studies show that, under some conditions, young children can be induced to use such descriptors more frequently. Feldman and Ruble (1988) report that 5- to 6-year-olds who expected to interact later with a target child they viewed on videotape were more likely to describe that child in central, traitlike terms than were children who did not expect future interaction. It should be noted, however, that although the proportion of central statements for young children was quite high in the expectation condition (50% to 60%), it was significantly higher for the older children (9-10 years) in this condition. Nevertheless, the findings suggest that previous low levels of spontaneously generated central characteristics by young children may have been due to the lack of motivation to understand the child. Similarly, Ferguson, Olthof, Luiten, and Rule (1984) found that under some conditions, 50% to 60% of their kindergarten subjects spontaneously generated traitlike terms.

The findings of these two studies are impressive and suggest a need to look closer at the impression formation skills of young children. There are reasons to be cautious, however, about jumping to the conclusion that previous failures to show high levels of spontaneous trait statements by young children necessarily imply that young children have a much more advanced understanding about people's stable characteristics than they show. Specifically, it seems likely that the nature of young children's traitlike impressions may be quite different than those of older children and adults. The concept of trait implies an internal, causal structure that underlies and motivates an actor's behavior (Alston, 1975; Barenboim, 1985; Rholes et al., 1990). It is not clear that the trait terms used by young children imply such psychological mechanisms. In their review of the literature on impression formation in children, Rholes et al. (1990) suggest as a working hypothesis that children's initial category system is valence based and egocentric in the sense that behavioral groupings are based on whether they have a positive or negative impact on the child. In fact, considerable evidence suggests that when young children use traitlike terms, these terms are global and evaluative in nature. Thus children's increased use of traitlike terms in some conditions may indicate that the children have a clearer indication of how they feel about the person, rather than that they have an understanding of personality dispositions.

In a very early (though nonsystematic) study of the development of impression formation, Watts (1944) concludes that on the rare occasions that children younger than 7 went beyond concrete, observable characteristics in describing a person, they divided people into two categories—those who pleased them (kind, good, nice) and those who did not (unkind, bad, horrid). Similarly, in a large, careful study by Livesley and Bromley (1973), the incidence of global evaluations by the youngest children in their sample (7-year-olds) was found to be relatively high. Although the young children rarely referred to traitlike terms, when they did, the only terms used by more than 3 out of 40 children were globally evaluative in nature: nice, good, kind, bad, bossy, silly, naughty. The use of such global evaluative terms did not vary much by age, even though the incidence of other, more specific, traitlike terms increased dramatically with age, more than doubling by age 8.

In a more recent study, Smetana (1985) found that about 50% of young children's descriptors of others were either global (bad, not nice, naughty) or conduct-relevant evaluations (rude, messy), but that such descriptors declined substantially with age. She considered these to be dispositional statements because they were considered so by others (e.g., Livesley and Bromley, 1973), and because such global evaluations may represent a primitive form of dispositional qualities (dishonest, selfish) that are used by older children who have a more sophisticated vocabulary. This is a tenable position, but the argument directing the present analysis is that such statements may be more clearly evaluative, rather than dispositional; compelling evidence that they reflect true traitlike inference remains to be offered. Within this context, it is important to note that such global evaluative terms were included among those counted as stable traits by both Feldman and Ruble (1988) and Ferguson et al. (1984). It is thus possible that the relatively high levels of traitlike terms in some conditions of these studies reflect primarily an increase in such evaluative statements. If so, the findings might be better interpreted as reflecting a context effect on the salience of liking, rather than on stable traits.

In summary, open-ended studies purporting to show traitlike thinking by 5- to 6-year-old children may be interpreted as global, evaluative thinking. The distinction suggested here is a subtle but important one. Young children's statements about a person's qualities as good or bad (nice or mean) may be more relational or emotional in nature (I like him or her, or myself) and say more about feelings and evaluations than about the actual characteristics of the person. Such a distinction is similar to the division of attitudes into their cognitive (what is) and affective (how I feel about it) components

(Eagly & Chaiken, 1992), and, like the area of attitudes, this distinction may have important implications for personal and interpersonal choices and behaviors.

Studies Using Judgment/Prediction Measures

Several other studies conclude that children younger than 7 years of age understand stable characteristics of others; in some cases children make predictions about a target's future behaviors consistent with trait inferences that could have been drawn from prior behavioral information provided about the target. Can these findings also be interpreted as reflecting children's global evaluations of the targets rather than an understanding of their dispositional qualities? In this section, we consider how well this and other hypotheses may apply to these studies.

The Global Evaluation ("Liking") Hypothesis

Does a liking or evaluative orientation explain the predictions of young children? If so, a higher likelihood of behavior generalization by young children would be seen when liking of the target is made salient and when the behaviors portrayed involve a clear evaluative dimension (nice/mean). Consistent with these hypotheses, most observations of predicted behavioral consistency by young children have, in fact, been limited to behaviors that are highly associated with liking. Several studies have found that kindergarten subjects predict behavioral consistency for selfish/mean and generous/nice targets (Cain & Heyman, 1993; Dozier, 1991; Heller & Berndt, 1981).[1] In Cain and Heyman (1993) and Dozier (1991), the likability dimension may have been highlighted by the procedure that involved an explicit comparison between a nice and a not-nice target. For example, in Cain and Heyman (1993), the comparison was between Cinderella and her stepsister, and in Dozier (1991), the comparison was between a target who did one or more prosocial behaviors and one who did one or more antisocial behaviors. Although these data indicate that young children can discriminate between targets who do nice and not nice things, it is not clear that children's predictions are based on inferred dispositional prosocial motivation. It seems probable that, in all cases, subjects liked one target more than the other and were disposed to assign good things to him or her. Indeed, in Dozier's procedure, subjects were told they would hear stories about children their age and make judgments about how much they liked the peers and how many pennies the peer would give them. Thus children were primed to think about how they felt about the targets rather than what the target's attributes were.

Liking may also explain the traitlike judgments of kindergarten children reported by Ferguson et al. (1984). Children described an actor on videotape and were then asked to explain why the actor engaged in a negative act in a future situation. The findings for all age groups showed that the children's ratings of the positivity and negativity of the actor's initial behaviors were significantly correlated with their subsequent expectations. Although the size of these correlations increased with age, these ratings may have reflected impressions of the actor's stable dispositions even for the youngest children. Because the ratings were of a highly evaluative nature (e.g., mean), however, the relation observed may have reflected consistency in evaluation (not likable), rather than dispositional inference. Somewhat more impressive was the additional finding that these adjective-rating-expectation correlations were higher for younger children, whose spontaneous descriptions contained a higher number of central statements (e.g., nice, mean). As suggested by Ferguson et al., these data suggest that a subset of children younger than 7 years may view people in terms of dispositional stabilities. Alternatively, however, only a subset of these young children may apply their evaluative reactions (not likable) consistently.

Results from two other studies provide more direct evidence for the liking hypothesis. In Feldman and Ruble (1988), children were told they could win prizes at some games and asked to select partners for the different games among targets displaying different characteristics they had seen on videotape. Older children selected partners based on instrumental goals, maximizing the number of prizes they could win, whereas younger children selected partners based on their liking as friends, even though the best choice for winning at the games was not always the most likable target. Across the two studies, 70% to 80% of the "errors" made by young children (i.e., choosing a partner who would not maximize prizes) could be considered a liking bias).

In a recent follow-up study (Thompson, Boggiano, Costanzo, Matter, & Ruble, 1994), this idea that such choices have different meanings to older and younger children was examined in terms of an experimental manipulation that provided an opportunity to see if older children could be induced to think more like younger children (i.e., evaluatively, in terms of affect or liking) and vice versa. Children were asked to form impressions of two targets shown on videotape and were given either an affective focus (think about how you feel about the target, whether you like him or her or not) or a descriptive focus (think about what the target is like, how you would describe him or her to someone else). Consistent with the present hypothesis, previously observed differences between older and younger children appeared only in the descriptive set. Specifically, the affective focus eliminated age differences in strategic partner choices, behavior-consistent predictions, and partner/friend overlap. Thus the data support the idea that inducing older children to think about people evaluatively makes their choices and predictions appear more like younger children. The reverse did not seem to work, however. There was no evidence that a descriptive set made younger children think about people more like older children. This basic difference in younger and older children's choices is further supported by the finding that younger children's general evaluative impressions (nice, mean, I like him or her) were related to their choices, whereas older children's more central, abstract impressions (she's good at sports, he shares things) were related to choices.

The "Good-Bad" Category Hypothesis

An alternative explanation of the above data is that children may group behaviors (or people) into two categories, good and bad, much like they sort characteristics and activities according to gender (Huston, 1983; Ruble, 1994). Watts (1944) argues that young children view people in terms of this dichotomous classification and view their social world according to rigid distinctions. Similarly, Paley's (1988) observations of preschoolers suggests that young children are almost obsessed with distinguishing good from bad. They are preoccupied with stories about being bad at home, such as being hurt by flaunting safety rules and playing with knives. Moreover, in Paley's classrooms, no character is more rule governed than the bad guy; he cannot even have a birthday. Such observations are supported by research showing that young children have great difficulty cross-cutting categories: A person who is good (e.g., a father) cannot do bad things (e.g., be a thief) (Saltz & Medow, 1971).

Thus, as an alternative to the liking explanation of young children's trait-consistent behavior predictions, children may place targets into good or bad categories based on the initial description of the behavior. Their subsequent predictions, then, may be cognitively mediated by perceptions of what is good and bad, rather than affectively mediated by liking. It is not possible from data currently available to distinguish clearly between these explanations. One study, however, seems more compatible with the category hypothesis.

Stipek and Daniels (1990) found that kindergarten children predicted that a classmate rated high in reading would perform better than a classmate rated low in reading in every situation whether or not the situation was relevant to reading ability (e.g., sharing, jumping hurdles). Because reading skill is much less clearly linked to liking than the prosocial behaviors used in the studies described previously, the liking hypothesis does not appear to provide a satisfactory account of these data. Instead, as concluded by Stipek and Daniels, these data suggest that young children do not make disposition relevant distinctions and instead predict behavior on the basis of a global "good-bad" dimension.

The "First Trait" Hypothesis

A third hypothesis is that the first stable disposition that young children become aware of involves a particular set of evaluative characteristics, namely nice/not nice or good/bad, attributes that may be particularly relevant to young children because they deal with conduct and liking. In this case, one might find that young children predict stabilities in behaviors on the basis of these characteristics but not on others. One would further expect, if goodness and niceness are indeed perceived as traits, that children's predictions would be specific to these attributes and would not generalize to other attributes that can also be labeled positive or negative (e.g., smart/stupid). A few studies are consistent with this hypothesis.

Cain and Heyman (1993) asked children to rate nice and not-nice targets on an intellectual task (knowing colors) and on an athletic task (ring-toss) as well as on sharing. Consistent with the global evaluation or good/bad category hypotheses, the children rated the nice actor higher on all three judgments. Consistent with the first-trait hypothesis, however, the difference between the nice and not-nice target was greater for sharing than for the other two judgments (significantly so for the athletic task). Similarly, consistent with the first-trait hypothesis, Heller and Berndt (1981) found that kindergarten children predicted that a generous target would share and help significantly more than a selfish target, but the differences for the other domains examined (e.g., doing well on a test) were not significant (though in the same direction).

Thus both studies appear to suggest that even 5-year-olds may distinguish different types of stable dispositions when evaluating a target exhibiting traits with clear nice/not nice evaluative implications. Whether or not these reflect true trait inferences in the sense of recognizing an underlying prosocial motivation or simply a linking together of common behaviors is not possible to determine from these data (Barenboim, 1985; Rholes et al., 1990). Nevertheless, these studies do appear to indicate that something more than a simple good-bad distinction is being made. It also seems possible that evaluation (liking) is determining the kindergartners' predictions, but that knowing colors or doing well on a test are perceived as less relevant to liking than other attributes. Future research controlling for the likability of children engaging in different behaviors is needed to interpret these findings more fully.[2]

Evidence of Differentiated Traits in Young Children

Three studies report evidence that children under 7 years of age make generalized behavioral predictions for multiple, differentiated characteristics, including those that are not conduct or liking related (Droege & Stipek, 1993; Gnepp & Chilamkurti, 1988; Ruble, Newman, Rholes, & Altshuler, 1988). These studies appear to provide the clearest evidence of true trait understanding by young children. In each case, however, procedural aspects of the data raise alternative explanations.

Gnepp and Chilamkurti (1988) presented children with six different story themes, two of which did not involve prosocial or conduct characteristics (shy and clown). Although generalized predictions increased with age, even kindergartners showed significant trait-consistent predictions. Unfortunately, these data are somewhat difficult to interpret unambiguously because they are not presented separately for type of trait. This effect may be driven primarily by the four more global, evaluative traits. An additional reason to question whether the kindergartners' responses really involved a trait inference about the protagonist is that they rarely used a trait-related explanation for their responses. The proportion of trait-related explanations for fourth graders was .80; it was only .36 for kindergartners. Again, it would be interesting to know whether the traits provided by the kindergartners were primarily of the global, evaluative type (nice, mean).

In the Droege and Stipek (1993) study of kindergartners, third graders, and sixth graders, kindergartners' ratings of two of their classmates' characteristics (likability and academic) were found to be related to their choices of whom they would like to have as playmates or as members of their team for an academic contest, providing apparent evidence of differentiated traits. Other aspects of the data, however, add some confusion to the interpretation of these results. The association between ratings and choices increased with age for partner choices in the academic but not the social dimension. More importantly, the rated academic competence of classmates did not correspond to teacher ratings of competence for kindergartners. It is not clear what their academic rating meant, and one possibility (not tested) is that it reflects a global, evaluative judgment (nice, likable). Finally, children were asked about the perceptions of stability of their classmates' competencies (e.g., How would a child rated as not too smart be rated next year or if he or she moved to a different school?). The results showed that children in third and sixth grades assumed considerable stability in both domains, but that kindergartners did not assume stability for academic competence. Thus, although there is evidence that kindergartners make choices (predictions) based on rated characteristics of their peers, it is not clear that these are differentiated judgments regarding stable traits, representing more than a global good-bad or likability dimension.

Finally, one other (admittedly speculative) interpretation for some of these results is that certain contexts may prime different behaviors and thereby change the standards that children use to decide what behavior is reasonable to expect. For example, in the Gnepp and Chilamkurti (1988) study, the children were first given an extensive set of trait-relevant behaviors (e.g., Tommy helps old people walk down the stairs; he shows new kids around the school, he sets the table for his mom whenever he can). This listing may have the unintended effect of changing the norms, so that future helpful behavior was predicted because it was seen as a common behavior, rather than because the target was a helpful person.[3] An interesting control condition for future research would be to ask children to make predictions for a different target after they have heard the trait list for the first target.

Summary

In short, there are alternative explanations for previous findings suggesting that children under 7 to 8 years of age draw inferences about others' dispositions from behavior and then use those dispositional inferences to make predictions about their subsequent behavior in new situations. We have highlighted three primary alternatives. First, much of the data may be viewed as reflecting a global, evaluative bias, that young children's apparent understanding of traits revealed in behavioral predictions reflects instead consistency in evaluations or "liking." Second, the good-bad category hypothesis suggests that children's trait-consistent predictions may in some cases reflect more of a cognitive categorization, rather than affective, evaluative process.

Third, some data are consistent with the first-trait hypothesis that young children's initial understanding of dispositions is limited to a particular type of characteristic, that concerned with prosocial behavior or conduct.

The issue is far from resolved. A number of researchers argue that young children may engage in differentiated, dispositional thinking and that consistent behavioral predictions shown under certain circumstances may reflect this capacity. As we suggest in this analysis, however, the few results seeming to support this conclusion are ambiguous and can be interpreted in other ways. It is also possible that a global evaluation or good-bad category reflects dispositional thinking not unlike that of adults. As discussed in the next section, there is considerable ambiguity about what constitutes dispositional inference in adults, as well. Future research is needed to examine directly the alternative hypotheses being suggested here.

MOTIVATIONAL IMPLICATIONS
OF DEVELOPMENTAL CHANGES

What motivational/behavioral differences might arise from having the more domain-specific, differentiated dispositional conceptions of older children versus the more global, undifferentiated evaluative concepts of younger children?

First, because one of the main distinguishing features of dispositional inference is the notion of internal, psychological causality, one prediction is that emerging conceptions of persons as possessing such characteristics should lead to an active interest in soliciting information relevant to assessing underlying motives and goals. A new realization of the impact of underlying personal stabilities implies that one must learn a previously unrecognized set of material in order to master one's social environment. Thus, at this point in development, a child may show a heightened interest in dispositional characteristics or information relevant to him or her (Ruble, 1994). There is little direct evidence relevant to this hypothesis. One exception is a recent study that found that 7- to 8-year-old children who were high versus low on a measure of understanding stable, dispositional concepts were more likely to select dispositional-relevant questions (e.g., "Do you like to play tricks") rather than disposition-peripheral questions (e.g., "How do you get to school?") to ask a child whom they were about to meet (Camhy & Ruble, 1994). Another prediction is that individual differences in viewing people as possessing stable traits (Dweck & Leggett, 1988) should have similar effects.

Indeed, Gervey, Chiu, Hong, and Dweck (1993) found that when trying to arrive at a guilty-innocent verdict, college subjects who believed in fixed traits requested significantly more dispositional information than did subjects who did not view people in this way.

Second, although viewing oneself or others in dispositional terms or in evaluative terms should influence subsequent behaviors and judgments regarding the target (as we suggest above), in many circumstances the nature of the reaction should differ. In particular, only the dispositional inference should lead to behaviors directly relevant to the dispositional inference, whereas evaluative inference may be expected to lead to affective or liking-relevant behaviors, such as choice of partner. Thus age-related differences in the behavioral impact of information about a target may depend on the nature of the dependent measure. For example, Feldman and Ruble (1988) found that young children responded differentially to "nice" versus "not-nice" targets when asked to allocate toys to them, a behavior that seems consistent with a liking, rather than an attributional, interpretation. In contrast, studies in which the behaviors are presumably attributionally mediated have found behavioral consequences of disposition-relevant information for children older than 7 to 8 years of age (Eisenberg et al., 1987; Grusec & Redler, 1980). This distinction between evaluation- versus disposition-relevant consequences may also prove useful in sorting out the different meanings of trait labels in studies with adults.

A similar implication, directly relevant to our emphasis on achievement-related self-conceptions, is that self-assessment processes may be quite different if performance standards are based on inferences of competence versus global good-bad evaluations. Standards based on inferences of competence involve various diagnostic criteria, such as comparing one's performance over time or with others (temporal or social comparison) or assessing level of performance relative to the difficulty of the task (Trope, 1986). In contrast, global evaluation as good or bad implies meeting an implicit or explicit standard for the performance, such as completing it, or actual or anticipated feedback from others about the product.

Thus one would expect to see quite different forms of self-assessment among children younger or older than 7 to 8 years of age; indeed, this is the case. Social comparison directed toward competence assessment rather than mastery goals develops during these years (Butler, 1989; Ruble & Frey, 1991). More directly relevant is a recent study showing age-related differences in evaluative biases (Ruble, Eisenberg, & Higgins, 1994). This study was based on findings that when people feel threatened, they are more likely to engage in self-enhancement strategies (e.g., Pyszcynski, Greenberg, & Laprelle, 1985), and one way to do this is to minimize or ignore the consequences of failure feedback for self-evaluation. Ruble et al. (1994) conclude that both younger and older children engage in these self-enhancement strategies, as shown by differences in the impact of failure information when evaluating themselves versus another child, but that they do so for different types of judgments. Older children were less likely to incorporate failure information when evaluating their own general ability, consistent with the idea that they are oriented toward drawing inferences about specific competence from performance feedback. In contrast, young children were less likely to incorporate failure information when evaluating whether their own specific performance was good or bad, consistent with the idea that immediate performance feedback by an adult indicating failure has direct implications for being a bad child.

Another implication of having a general evaluative response versus dispositional conceptions is that young children's motivational vulnerability may be of a more "reactive" nature, with helpless young children revealing their vulnerabilities only when salient evaluation leads them to question themselves. Because of older children's understanding of dispositions and concern with their own status on a dispositional continuum, they may enter situations with dispositional concerns and may try to structure situations in terms of their dispositional concerns. Consistent with this proposal is the finding by Benenson and Dweck (1986) that only when trait explanations emerged in a domain did children begin to show defensive behavior in that domain.

The finding of global evaluations in young children and their link to helplessness raises a number of interesting questions about the relation between early vulnerability and later vulnerability. What happens to a child's early vulnerability when more differentiated dispositional concepts are developed? On the one hand, early belief in global, stable goodness/badness may predispose children to beliefs in stable traits and vulnerability later on. On the other hand, new, specific dispositions may be conceptualized *de novo,* meaning that some children who were previously vulnerable may adopt more mastery-promoting beliefs, whereas some children who were previously mastery-oriented may adopt beliefs that render them vulnerable.

It is also possible that in addition to developing new, more differentiated dispositional concepts, children who are prone to global self-evaluations continue to be so. Evidence for this possibility comes from a recent study of college students by Zhao and Dweck (1993), in which subjects who believed in fixed intelligence were more likely to exhibit global self-derogation in the face of intellectual failure (in addition to ability derogation) than subjects who did not believe in fixed intelligence. These findings suggest that at least a subset of these older individuals continue to engage in global self-evaluations on the basis of specific outcomes.

Finally, the study of dispositional beliefs in older individuals leads to the conclusion that although most individuals develop an understanding of dispositions, this can take several forms (Dweck, Hong, & Chiu, 1993). Some individuals conceive of dispositions as relatively fixed traits that can be readily diagnosed. The beliefs lead to rapid, confident trait inferences and the prediction of a high degree of individual consistency. Other individuals do not believe in fixed traits, and instead appear to view behavior as being mediated by more dynamic psychological processes, such as a person's beliefs, goals, intentions, and affective states. These individuals often do not predict a high degree of consistency in behavior across situations, because for them, consistency depends on the same beliefs, goals, intentions, or affective states being elicited across situations. Ironically, these individuals' behavioral predictions may sometimes look quite similar to young children who do not have an understanding of dispositions, but the predictions of these individuals are based on a sophisticated understanding of the dynamics of psychological causality.

RELATION TO SOCIAL PSYCHOLOGICAL
THEORIES ON TRAIT INFERENCE

The analysis of possible developmental changes in the meaning or representation of trait-related terms overlaps in some important ways with recent concerns about trait inference processes among adults. Theoretical analyses of the trait inference process in general note that trait terms may have multiple meanings, only one of which reflects true dispositional inference in the sense of "enduring internal states that are believed to predispose an individual to behave in a certain manner" (Trope & Higgins, 1993, p. 493). For example, one series of studies (Uleman, 1987) presented subjects with sentences about an actor that could be interpreted as reflecting traits. When subjects were later asked to recall the sentences, the findings showed that traits corresponding to the behaviors were particularly effective retrieval cues. These findings were interpreted as indicating that individuals are inclined to make "spontaneous dispositional inferences" without explicit impression formation goals. In subsequent research, however, it was discovered that these trait terms were not necessarily linked to the actor (as would be true in a dispositional inference), but rather often reflected a summary of the behavior (Uleman & Moskowitz, 1994). To illustrate, the term "generous" apparently cued only the fact that some generous behavior was performed, rather than that the actor was a generous person. Such a distinction between trait-as-action-descriptors and trait-as-person-attributes is widely discussed in the person perception literature (Bassili, 1989; Fletcher, 1984).

Newman and Uleman (1993) refer to five different ways trait-related terms can be used; that is, to describe a particular behavior, a person at a particular time, a person's frequent behaviors, a person over time, and a dispositional cause, with only the final meaning representing dispositional inference as implied by models of impression formation. Even for adults, reference to a term, such as *generous,* may not imply a dispositional inference. Moreover, the different representations of terms may well have different judgmental and behavioral implications (Newman & Uleman, 1993; see also Dweck et al., 1993).

These recent theoretical analyses in the social psychological literature provide many reasons to suspect that true dispositional inference is likely to be a relatively late developmental phenomenon. Current models of impression formation suggest that there are multiple stages involved in the process, and all of them argue that dispositional inference is a later stage (Newman & Uleman, 1993; Trope & Higgins, 1993). For example, Trope (1986) proposes that dispositional attributions occur in two stages, behavior identification and inference; Gilbert and his associates (e.g., Gilbert, Pelham, & Krull, 1988) propose a 3-stage model in which 2 stages of dispositional inference (characterization and correction) are preceded by behavior categorization (identification).

These models propose that dispositional inference requires considerably more cognitive effort than behavior identification or classification. The final inference stage is disrupted when it is difficult or when the cognitive system is overloaded (Gilbert et al., 1988), suggesting that under many conditions (such as being an immature processor), dispositional inference is unlikely to occur by simply presenting behavioral information about a person. Models of person memory lead to a similar conclusion. For example, Hastie and Kumar (1979) present a hierarchical model in which specific behaviors occur at the lowest level, their organization into traits occur at a middle level, and a connection of these traits to a person (i.e., dispositional inference) occurs at the highest level and may require additional inferential work (Bassili,

1989; Newman & Uleman, 1993). Similarly, Wyer and Srull's (1989) model of social information processing consists of three levels of processing units. At the lowest level, the "comprehender" interprets information in terms of action and attribute concepts, not including trait concepts. This interpretation is then available to the second level unit, called the "encoder/organizer," which organizes the behaviors into trait-behavior clusters and evaluative person representations. Finally, an inference that a person possesses a disposition is performed by a separate processing unit called the "inference maker," and considerable computation may be required. Thus, once again, organizing behaviors into trait clusters is viewed as relatively primitive, whereas representing those traits in terms of dispositions of a person requires much more effort and sophisticated processing.

Getting to the stage of dispositional inference may require specific impression formation goals (Newman & Uleman, 1993). Indeed, in some accounts even organization of behavior into traits may require such goals (Bassili, 1989; Wyer & Srull, 1989), though other models are silent on this issue. The lack of goal-related aspects of many models may be due to common assumptions that person inference is an ever-present goal of person perception, because it allows people to predict future behavior from the past and thereby gain a sense of control (Fiske, 1993; Jones & Davis, 1965; Trope & Higgins, 1993), though developmental research suggests that such goals may not characterize the person perception behavior of children younger than 7 to 8 years of age (Feldman & Ruble, 1988; Thompson et al., 1994).

Taken together, these analyses clearly indicate that the use of trait terms often reflects a relatively automatic and low level of processing trait-relevant information. Such a contention seems even more likely for younger children given that they are likely to be less skilled and deliberate at processing such information. Thus theoretical models of impression formation and person memory processes seem supportive of previous developmental conclusions that when children are exposed to a trait-relevant behavior (whether their own or that of another), they will not likely draw a dispositional inference about the target, nor will subsequent behavior-consistent predictions reflect such an inference stored in memory (Rholes et al., 1990).

Does this literature have anything to say about our further contention that when such behavioral generalizations occur, they often reflect evaluative rather than trait consistency? Somewhat surprisingly, relatively few of the impression formation or person memory models include an affective or evaluative component. There are a few exceptions, however.

Wyer and Srull (1989) place behavioral clustering into traits and person evaluation at the middle level of processing, such that prior to dispositional inference, a general evaluative concept is formed to determine whether or not the target is likable. The implication of this model is that in the experimental situations presented to children, relative to dispositional inferences, likability evaluations of the target are more likely to be made and are more likely to be accessible when making further judgments about the target.

Some impression formation models include affect or evaluation as one of several ways persons might be represented (Carlston, 1992; Fiske & Taylor, 1984). Carlston's (1992) associated systems theory, for example, proposes that people's impressions of others can be represented in terms of four major mental systems governing stimulus input: visual perception, language, physiological or affective responding, and action. One's impression of a person is a composite of four distinct features corresponding to these mental systems, involving appearance, traits (verbal labels), feelings, and behavioral responses toward the target. The question generated from the present developmental analysis is whether the affective system has some priority over the verbal system in representing persons. Carlston presents no hypotheses regarding a possible advantage of any of these systems, and indeed argues that there is no reason to suspect that affective information would have primacy in the sense of degrading more slowly, as others have suggested (Zajonc, 1980). Carlston does propose, however, the possibility that such information may be preserved as evaluations, a more cognitive form of affect.

In short, the person perception literature does include a role for evaluation as part of the process of representing others; this role is viewed by some as coming earlier in the process than dispositional inference. From the perspective of the present analysis, however, there are a number of unanswered questions. It is not clear from this literature whether such evaluations are as basic or as fundamental as we are implying here. Certainly the importance of evaluation is supported by a long tradition of research on the semantic differential, in which factor analyses of people's ratings of various concepts on bipolar adjectives (e.g., active-passive, valuable-worthless) typically find that the evaluative dimension accounts for a larger proportion of total variance than other dimensions (e.g., potency; Osgood, Suci, & Tannenbaum, 1957). Although the literature on categorization and stereotyping involves evaluation as a central concept influencing perceptions and judgment (Fiske & Taylor, 1984; Markus & Zajonc, 1985; Stangor & Lange, 1994), this is not an issue that has had much influence on person perception research.

Recent research suggests that evaluative processes may be more basic than usually assumed. Fazio, Sanbonmatsu, Powell, and Kardes (1986) show that highly accessible attitudes act as evaluative primes, so that the speed with which subjects can classify an adjective as positive or negative is influenced by the evaluation associated with the attitude (e.g., priming with the attitude object gun would lead to faster classification of repulsive as bad than appealing as good). More interestingly, a recent study has shown that this evaluative priming effect works for virtually any attitude object, whether strong or weak (Bargh, Chaiken, Govender, & Pratto, 1992). These data suggest that exposure to any information that can be classified as good or bad will be so classified and will affect subsequent judgments. Applied to the present analysis, these findings seem to lend support to our proposal that initial behavior of a target is represented evaluatively, and that these evaluations affect the subsequent judgment about the target's future behavior, whether or not more advanced processes (i.e., dispositional inference) are involved.

So far we have argued that recent social psychological research has been concerned with distinctions similar to ours in the meaning of ascribing traits to behaviors, and that the findings are consistent with several features of our developmental analysis. Does our analysis raise any further questions or generate hypotheses that may broaden these social psychological theories? One obvious question emerging from the preceding discussion is where evaluations fit into models of impression formation and memory. In the Carlston (1992) model, for example, evaluative associations may be connected, perhaps automatically, to any input about a target person, be it visual, behavioral, or verbal, as well as affective. More generally, is it misleading to have models of social perception that do not include an evaluative component at all?

A second, related question concerns how the associative structure of person representations may relate to developmental changes. Models of person memory involving trait information focus on three components: specific behaviors, behavior clusters or traits, and a person node (Hastie & Kumar, 1979; Wyer & Carlston, 1979). To illustrate, representation of Nancy as a generous person would consist of paths between the person node—Nancy— and trait node—generous—and links between generous and specific behaviors, such as donates money to charity and always gives presents on birthdays. Whether or not there is a direct connection between the specific behaviors and the person node varies by model (Newman & Uleman, 1993). As Newman and Uleman (1993) point out, such models can incorporate the distinction between dispositional inference and representations of traits as

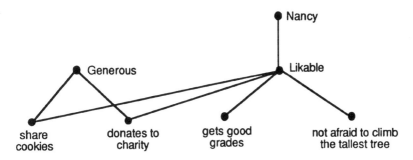

Figure 5.1. Model of Person Representation in Which Global Evaluation or Liking Links

behavior identifications by eliminating the connection between the person and trait nodes. Observation of the two behaviors would still lead to the label "generous," but the further inference that Nancy has an internal quality that leads her to generous behaviors would be missing. Such a model reflects the person perception process of young children.

To accommodate the data presented in the foregoing developmental review, however, some concept must link to the person node. We suggest that this would be an evaluation node. Observation of generous behaviors would lead both to a behavior categorization—generous—and to a positively valenced evaluation. Consistent with Wyer and Srull's (1989) model, this evaluation would be linked with the person, whereas the trait, which requires additional processing and motivation, would not. Thus Nancy would be liked and this positive evaluation would be elicited when questioned about Nancy's subsequent behavior. Moreover, to the extent that this positive evaluation is abstracted from specific behaviors, these predictions might involve any positive behavior, such as bravery or competence, in addition to generosity. A graphic depiction of such a model is presented in Figure 5.1.

Finally, as implied above, theories of dispositional inference and person representation may also need to consider dispositional inferences that are not trait inferences and do not involve the attachment of trait terms to the target. Some individuals (those who do not believe in fixed traits) appear to favor person analyses that focus on the mediating psychological processes that guide people's behavior (e.g., beliefs, goals, intentions, affective states) (Dweck et al., 1993), and Chiu, Sacks, and Dweck (1994) show that these individuals' person representations tend to be built around perceived motivational characteristics rather than around trait judgments. Shoda and Mischel

(1993) also set forth an approach to dispositional inference in which perceivers may attend to process-oriented variables (such as the individual's stable expectations, goals, and values) in forming impressions of a target's personality. One task for developmental research and for theories of dispositional inference is to consider different ways in which people may conceptualize dispositions and draw inferences about them.

SUMMARY AND CONCLUSIONS

Most adults understand people to have internal psychological dispositions that cause observable patterns of behavior. They may disagree about the nature of these dispositions, with some believing in inherent traits that have causal status and others leaning toward more dynamic views of dispositions, with underlying beliefs and values guiding patterns of behavior. Nevertheless, much of social psychological theorizing on person perception assumes that people have some psychological theory of behavior and of individual differences in behavior.

In contrast, developmental research presents a much more mixed account of children's understanding of dispositional qualities. Early research suggests that children under 7 do not have such an understanding, whereas more recent research appears to question this conclusion. We have reviewed evidence that young children are able to make global good-bad inferences about or evaluations of themselves and others, but we have questioned what these global good-bad inferences mean.

Our analysis of the literature on the development of person perception has led us to suggest that young children's application of good-bad labels to themselves and others probably reflects something other than an understanding of internal causes of behavior. For example, good and bad may simply reflect liking or positive and negative evaluations (like attractive or unattractive) that can be applied to people, but have no implications for internal psychological mechanisms. Alternatively, they may be ways that young children have of classifying people, sorting them into categories the way that they avidly sort boys and girls into gender categories at that age. In this case, children could have detailed theories about the characteristics that accrue to people in each category, but little idea of psychological causality.

We have suggested that future research into the nature of these trait representations has important implications for our understanding in other areas. Domain-specific dispositional conceptions versus global, undifferentiated evaluative concepts are likely to have quite different motivational and behavioral consequences. For example, early forms of helplessness may have a more reactive quality, coming to the fore only after salient evaluations are presented, whereas later forms may reflect an active trait-relevant construction or self-presentation (e.g., looking smart) that guides behavior even before evaluation takes place. Moreover, if the basis of helplessness does indeed shift with developmental changes in person conceptions, interesting questions are raised about the developmental continuity of helpless responding.

A developmental analysis of the different meanings of trait concepts raises questions about current social psychological models of person perception and memory. For example, how central are evaluation and liking to the social perception process, and how should such notions be incorporated into the associative structure of person representation? A number of fascinating questions remain concerning the nature of developmental changes in children's understanding of dispositions and about their implications for general theories of social perception.

NOTES

1. Smetana (1985) also reports results consistent with this conclusion. She asked children in first, fourth, and seventh grades to make predictions for two actors who exhibited negative moral acts (e.g., stealing) and negative conventional acts (e.g., using bad table manners). She does not present evidence that the youngest children made better-than-chance predictions, however, but only that there was no significant interaction with grade.

2. There is another possible interpretation. There may be a positivity bias for the skill domains. The nice target is rated as high on these skills as on nice behaviors, but the not-nice target is rated higher on skills than on not-nice behaviors. Such behaviors as knowing colors or doing well on a test may be perceived by kindergartners as showing less variation across different individuals than niceness (e.g., they believe everyone can do these things) or that kindergartners are more reluctant to attribute negative outcomes in these domains. Comparison conditions in which smart or athletic behaviors are initially presented as the stimulus traits being inferred are needed in order to interpret these results.

3. A similar phenomenon may partly explain why Ruble et al. (1988) found that young children made trait-consistent predictions for athletic ability but not for generosity when pictures of the actors engaging in the target behaviors were left in view to serve as a memory aid, but the reverse was found when the pictures were removed. Evidently, the pictures highlighted contextual or normative information that sometimes worked in favor of and sometimes worked against perceiving cross-situational consistency.

REFERENCES

Alston, W. P. (1975). Traits, consistency, and conceptual alternatives for personality theory. *Journal for the Theory of Social Behavior, 5,* 17-47.

Barenboim, C. (1981). The development of person perception in childhood and adolescence: From behavioral comparisons to psychological constructs to psychological comparisons. *Child Development, 52,* 129-144.

Barenboim, C. (1985). A response to Berndt and Heller. In S. R. Yussen (Ed.), *The growth of reflection in children* (pp. 61-67). Orlando, FL: Academic Press.

Bargh, J. A., Chaiken, S., Govender, R., & Pratto, F. (1992). The generality of the automatic attitude activation effect. *Journal of Personality and Social Psychology, 62,* 893-912.

Bassili, J. N. (1989). Traits as action categories versus traits as person attributes in social cognition. In J. N. Bassili (Ed.), *On-line cognition in person perception* (pp. 61-89). Hillsdale, NJ: Erlbaum.

Benenson, J., & Dweck, C. S. (1986). The development of trait explanations and self-evaluations in academic and social domains. *Child Development, 57,* 1179-1187.

Butler, R. (1989). Mastery versus ability appraisal: A developmental study of children's observations of peer's work. *Child Development, 60,* 1350-1361.

Cain, K. M. (1990). *The development of children's motivational patterns and conceptions of intelligence.* Unpublished doctoral dissertation.

Cain, K. M., & Heyman, G. D. (1993, March). *Can Cinderella solve puzzles? Preschoolers' ability to make dispositional predictions within and across domains.* Poster presented at the Biennial Meeting of the Society for Research in Child Development, New Orleans, LA.

Camhy, M., & Ruble, D. N. (1994). Becoming acquainted with a peer: Social-cognitive and motivational influences. *Social Development, 3,* 89-107.

Carlston, D. E. (1992). Impression formation and the modular mind: The associated systems theory. In L. L. Martin & A. Tesser (Eds.), *The construction of social judgments* (pp. 87-96). Hillsdale, NJ: Erlbaum.

Chiu, C., Sacks, R., & Dweck, C. S. (1994). *Bases of categorization and person cognition.* Unpublished manuscript.

Dozier, M. (1991). Functional measurement assessment of young children's ability to predict future behavior. *Child Development, 62,* 1091-1099.

Droege, K. L., & Stipek, D. J. (1993). Children's use of dispositions to predict classmates' behavior. *Developmental Psychology, 29*(4), 646-654.

Dweck, C. S. (1991). Self-theories and goals: Their role in motivation, personality and development. In R. Dienstbier (Ed.), *Nebraska symposium on motivation, 1990* (pp. 199-235). Lincoln: University of Nebraska Press.

Dweck, C. S., & Elliott, E. S. (1983). Achievement motivation. In S. R. Yussen (Ed.), *Handbook of child psychology: Vol. IV. Social and personality development* (pp. 643-691). New York: John Wiley.

Dweck, C. S., Hong, Y., & Chiu, C. (1993). Implicit theories: Individual differences in the likelihood and meaning of dispositional inference. *Personality and Social Psychology Bulletin, 19,* 644-656.

Dweck, C. S., & Leggett, E. L. (1988). A social-cognitive approach to personality and motivation. *Psychological Review, 95,* 256-273.

Eagly, A. H., & Chaiken, S. (1993). *The psychology of attitudes.* New York: Harcourt Brace and Company.

Eisenberg, N., Cialdini, R., McCreath, H., & Shell, R. (1987). Consistency-based compliance: When and why do children become vulnerable? *Journal of Personality and Social Psychology, 52,* 1174-1181.

Fazio, R. H., Sanbonmatsu, D. M., Powell, M. C., & Kardes, F. R. (1986). On the automatic activation of attitudes. *Journal of Personality and Social Psychology, 50,* 229-238.

Feldman, A. S., & Ruble, D. N. (1988). The effect of personal relevance on dispositional inference: A developmental analysis. *Child Development, 59,* 1339-1352.

Ferguson, T. J., Olthof, T., Luiten, A., & Rule, B. G. (1984). Children's use of observed behavioral frequency versus behavioral covariation in ascribing dispositions to others. *Child Development, 55,* 2094-2105.

Ferguson, T. J., van Roozendaal, J., & Rule, B. G. (1986). Informational basis for children's impressions of others. *Developmental Psychology, 22,* 335-341.

Fiske, S. T. (1993). Social cognition and social perception. *Annual Review of Psychology, 44,* 155-194.

Fiske, S. T., & Taylor, S. E. (1984). *Social cognition.* Reading, MA: Addison-Wesley.

Fletcher, G. J. O. (1984). Psychology and common sense. *American Psychologist, 39,* 203-213.

Gervey, B., Chiu, C., Hong, Y., & Dweck, C. S. (1993, June). *Processing and utilizing information in social judgment: The role of implicit theories.* Paper presented at the Fifth Annual Convention of the American Psychological Society, Chicago.

Gilbert, D. T., Pelham, B. W., & Krull, D. S. (1988). On cognitive busyness: When person perceivers meet persons perceived. *Journal of Personality and Social Psychology, 54,* 733-740.

Gnepp, J., & Chilamkurti, C. (1988). Children's use of personality attributions to predict other people's emotional and behavioral reactions. *Child Development, 59,* 743-754.

Grusec, J. E., & Redler, E. (1980). Attribution, reinforcement, and altruism: A developmental analysis. *Developmental Psychology, 16,* 525-534.

Hastie, R., & Kumar, P. A. (1979). Person memory: Personality traits as organizing principles in memory for behaviors. *Journal of Personality and Social Psychology, 37,* 25-38.

Hebert, C., & Dweck, C. S. (1985). *The mediators of persistence in preschoolers.* Unpublished manuscript.

Heller, K. A., & Berndt, T. J. (1981). Developmental changes in the formation and organization of personality attributions. *Child Development, 52,* 683-691.

Heyman, C. D., Dweck, C. S., & Cain, K. M. (1992). Young children's vulnerability to self-blame and helplessness: Relationship to beliefs about goodness. *Child Development, 63,* 401-415.

Huston, A. C. (1983). Sex-typing. In E. M. Hetherington (Ed.), *Social development: Vol. 4* in P. H. Mussen (Gen. Ed.), *Carmichael's manual of child psychology* (4th ed., pp. 387-467). New York: John Wiley.

Jones, E. E., & Davis, K. E. (1965). From acts to dispositions: The attribution process in person perception. In L. Berkowitz (Ed.), *Advances in experimental social psychology: Vol. 2* (pp. 219-266). New York: Academic Press.

Livesley, W. J., & Bromley, D. B. (1973). *Person perception in childhood and adolescence.* Chichester, UK: Wiley.

Markus, H., & Zajonc, R. B. (1985). The cognitive perspective in social psychology. In G. Lindzey & E. Aronson (Eds.), *Handbook of social psychology* (3rd ed., pp. 137-230). Reading, MA: Addison-Wesley.

Miller, A. T. (1985). A developmental study of the cognitive bases of performance impairment after failure. *Journal of Personality and Social Psychology, 49,* 529-538.

Mohr, D. M. (1978). Development of attributes of personal identity. *Developmental Psychology, 14,* 427-428.

Newman, L. S., & Uleman, J. S. (1993). When are you what you did? Behavior identification and dispositional inference in person memory, attribution, and social judgment. *Personality and Social Psychology Bulletin, 19,* 513-525.

Osgood, C. E., Suci, G. J., & Tannenbaum, P. H. (1957). *The measurement of meaning.* Urbana: University of Illinois Press.

Paley, V. G. (1988). *Bad guys don't have birthdays.* Chicago: University of Chicago Press.

Parsons, J. E., & Ruble, D. N. (1977). The development of achievement-related expectancies. *Child Development, 48,* 1075-1079.

Peevers, B. H., & Secord, P. F. (1973). Developmental changes in attribution of descriptive concepts to persons. *Journal of Personality and Social Psychology, 27,* 120-128.

Pyszcynski, T., Greenberg, J., & Laprelle, J. (1985). Social comparison after success and failure: Biased search for information consistent with a self-serving conclusion. *Journal of Experimental Social Psychology, 21,* 195-211.

Rholes, W. S., Blackwell, J., Jordan, C., & Walters, C. (1980). A developmental study of learned helplessness. *Developmental Psychology, 16,* 616-624.

Rholes, W. S., Newman, L. S., & Ruble, D. N. (1990). Understanding self and other: Developmental and motivational aspects of perceiving people in terms of invariant dispositions. In E. T. Higgins & R. Sorrentino (Eds.), *Handbook of motivation and cognition: Foundations of social behavior: Vol. II* (pp. 369-407). New York: Guilford.

Rholes, W. S., & Ruble, D. N. (1984). Children's understanding of dispositional characteristics of others. *Child Development, 55,* 550-560.

Ruble, D. N. (1994). A phase model of transitions: Cognitive and motivational consequences. *Advances in Experimental Social Psychology, 26,* 163-214.

Ruble, D. N., Eisenberg, R., & Higgins, E. T. (1994). Developmental changes in achievement evaluation: Motivational implications of self-other differences. *Child Development, 65,* 1095-1110.

Ruble, D. N., & Frey, K. S. (1991). Changing patterns of comparative behavior as skills are acquired: A functional model of self-evaluation. In J. Suls & T. A. Wills (Eds.), *Social comparison: Contemporary theory and research* (pp. 79-113). Hillsdale, NJ: Erlbaum.

Ruble, D. N., Newman, L. S., Rholes, W. S., & Altshuler, J. (1988). Children's naive psychology: The use of behavioral and situational information for the prediction of behavior. *Cognitive Development, 3,* 89-112.

Saltz, E., & Medow, M.L. (1971). Concept conservation in children: The dependence of belief systems on semantic representation. *Child Development, 42,* 1533-1542.

Shantz, C. U. (1983). Social cognition. In J. H. Flavell & E. M. Markman (Vol. Eds.), *Handbook of child psychology: Vol. 3* (4th ed., pp. 495-555). New York: John Wiley.

Shoda, Y., & Mischel, W. (1993). Cognitive social approach to dispositional inferences: What if the perceiver is a cognitive-social theorist? *Personality and Social Psychology Bulletin, 19,* 574-585.

Smetana, J. G. (1985). Children's impressions of moral and conventional transgressors. *Developmental Psychology, 21,* 715-724.

Smiley, P. A., & Dweck, C. S. (in press). Individual differences in achievement goals among young children. *Child Development.*

Stangor, C., & Lange, J. E. (1994). Mental representations of social groups: Advances in understanding stereotypes and stereotyping. *Advances in Experimental Social Psychology, 26,* 357-416.

Stipek, D., & Daniels, D. (1990). Children's use of dispositional attributions in predicting the performance and behavior of classmates. *Journal of Applied Developmental Psychology, 11,* 13-28.

Stipek, D., & Hoffman, J. (1980). Development of children's performance-related judgments. *Child Development, 51,* 912-914.

Thompson, E. P., Boggiano, A. K., Costanzo, P. E., Matter, J. A., & Ruble, D. N. (1994). *Developmental changes in children's affective vs. instrumental orientations toward peers.* Manuscript submitted for publication.

Trope, Y. (1986). Identification and inference processes in dispositional attribution. *Psychological Review, 93,* 239-257.

Trope, Y., & Higgins, E. T. (1993). The what, when, and how of dispositional inference: New answers and new questions. *Personality and Social Psychology Bulletin, 19,* 493-500.

Uleman, J. S. (1987). Consciousness and control: The case of spontaneous trait inference. *Personality and Social Psychology Bulletin, 13,* 337-354.

Uleman, J. S., & Moskowitz, G. B. (1994). Unintended effects of goals on unintended inferences. *Journal of Personality and Social Psychology, 66,* 490-501.

Watts, A. F. (1944). *The language and mental development of children.* London: Harrap & Co.

Wyer, R. S., & Carlston, D. E. (1979). *Social cognition, inference and attribution.* Hillsdale, NJ: Erlbaum.

Wyer, R. S., Jr., & Srull, T. K. (1989). *Memory and cognition in its social context.* Hillsdale, NJ: Erlbaum.

Zajonc, R. B. (1980). Feeling and thinking: Preferences need no inferences. *American Psychologist, 35,* 151-175.

Zhao, W., & Dweck, C. S. (1993). *Implicit theories and vulnerability to depression-like responses.* Unpublished manuscript, Columbia University.

6

The Role of Normative Beliefs in Children's Social Behavior

NANCY G. GUERRA
L. ROWELL HUESMANN
LAURA HANISH

Nancy G. Guerra is an Associate Professor of Psychology at the University of Illinois at Chicago and the University of Michigan. She received her doctorate degree in Human Development from Harvard University. Her major research interests are prevention of antisocial behavior and the role of cognitive factors in the development of aggression and delinquency. She is the author of *Viewpoints Violence Prevention Curriculum* and has published numerous articles about aggression and delinquency.

L. Rowell Huesmann is Professor of Communication and Psychology and Research Scientist at the Institute for Social Research at the University of Michigan. He earned a doctorate from Carnegie-Mellon University in Psychology. His research and scientific contributions have ranged from mathematical and computer models of human information processing and media effects on behavior to experimental studies of social behavior. He is the author of numerous journal articles and two books about aggressive behavior.

Laura Hanish is a graduate student in clinical and developmental psychology at the University of Illinois at Chicago. Her research interests include aggression and victimization among children, gender differences in children's social behavior, and social cognition.

A major task of social development is children's acquisition of the ability to monitor and control their own behavior. Such self-regulation occurs, in part, as a function of the child's developing cognitive system. The central role of cognition in the regulation of social behavior is evident in a number of recent conceptual models (Bandura, 1991; Dodge, 1986; Huesmann, 1988; Rubin & Krasnor, 1986). Several cognitive mechanisms have been enumerated, and their relation to specific types of social behavior has been demonstrated in a number of empirical studies. Moreover, efforts have been directed at identifying stable individual differences in social cognition that contribute to the relative stability of behavior across time and situations (Huesmann & Eron, 1984).

Much of this work has focused on examining the link between specific social information-processing skills and social behavior during childhood and adolescence. In particular, a number of investigators have applied an information-processing model to the study of children's aggressive behavior. For example, Dodge (1986, 1993) identifies five interrelated, sequential information-processing skills (encoding of cues, interpretation of cues, response search, response decision, enactment). In several studies, aggressive children have been found to display biases and deficits in each of these processing skills (Dodge, 1980; Dodge & Frame, 1982; Dodge, Petit, McClaskey, & Brown, 1986). Furthermore, this relation is strongest when comprehensive assessments of multiple skills are utilized (Slaby & Guerra, 1988).

Sequential models provide a framework for understanding how social information in a specific situation is processed and translated into a behavioral response. However, equally important are children's preexisting social schemata, or their organized prior knowledge in the social domain. Such schemata represent abstracted general knowledge and guide and shape how information is processed. One of the main purposes of schemata is to simplify reality, enabling individuals to function in a world that otherwise would be of paralyzing complexity (Abelson, 1981; Rumelhart & Ortony, 1977). The schemata concept has been applied to knowledge about the self, others, social roles, and events (Fiske & Taylor, 1984).

Most theoretical models of the cognition-behavior link have paid little attention to the role of cognitive schemata. This is particularly true for social-cognitive models of children's aggression. Although researchers often mention concepts such as rule structures (Dodge, 1986) or goals (Rubin & Krasnor, 1986), the identification of relevant social schemata and the assessment of their relation to information processing and behavior have been largely overlooked.

In our own recent work on the cognitive regulation of behavior, we have identified a particular type of social schemata that we refer to as *normative beliefs*. We define normative beliefs as an individual's cognitions about the acceptability or unacceptability of behaviors that regulate his or her corresponding behaviors. Such beliefs are both situation specific and general. A broad range of interpersonal actions falls under this type of normative regulation, from acceptable forms of addressing authority figures to acceptable behaviors within the context of close personal relationships. An example of a situation-specific normative belief would be "It's okay to hit others if they hit you first." An example of a general belief would be "It's okay to hit others."

In this chapter, we examine the link between normative beliefs and children's aggressive behavior. First we draw on research in social and developmental psychology in an effort to distinguish normative beliefs from other related constructs. Following this, we discuss the process by which normative beliefs are acquired and examine their role in the cognitive regulation of behavior. Then we present a recently developed measure of children's normative beliefs about aggression, and discuss the relations between children's normative beliefs and their aggressive behavior in two studies. Finally, we discuss the limitations of our approach and suggest directions for future research, including the importance of normative beliefs in behavior change programs.

THE NATURE OF NORMATIVE BELIEFS

We use the term *normative beliefs* to refer to an individual's cognitions about the acceptability or unacceptability of social behaviors that regulate his or her behavior. Such beliefs delineate the range of allowable and prohibited behaviors for that individual. A number of related constructs can be found in the social and developmental literature. We examine some of these constructs below, paying particular attention to how normative beliefs differ.

Social psychologists have tended to focus on *consensual social norms* and on how individual behavior conforms to these group norms. The notion that behavior is governed, in part, by consensual social norms draws on several major traditions in social psychology, including work on role theory (Cooley, 1902; Mead, 1934), conformity (Sherif, 1936), and norm formation (Deutsch & Gerard, 1955). Across these traditions, social norms most frequently have been defined as shared proscriptions for behavior that are accepted by a majority of group members and enforced by informal or formal sanctions. Such norms may exist at a number of levels, including dyads (Thibaut & Kelley, 1959), groups (Sherif, 1936), and cultures (Mead, 1969).

Some writers have also distinguished between social norms as descriptors of behavior ("what is") and social norms as directives for behavior ("what ought to be"). For example, Cialdini, Kallgren, and Reno (1991) refer to norms that describe what most people will do as *descriptive norms,* and norms that characterize what people are expected to do as *injunctive norms.*

Similar contrasts have been made by other social scientists; Deutsch and Gerard (1955) distinguish between informational and normative social influence, and Gibbs (1965) differentiates between collective expectations and collective evaluations.

Although such distinctions are valuable for a clearer understanding of norms, we prefer to define social norms only as injunctive rules, while allowing that commonly used rules may become injunctive simply because they are common. Even restricting oneself to injunctive norms, the definition of social norms as shared proscriptions creates problems in identifying social norms and relating them to individual behavior. For example, what if a few individuals in a social group are not favorably disposed toward a rule? Is it then not a social norm? Or what if an individual misperceives whether others are favorably disposed toward a rule? Is it then not a social norm? Perhaps most important, by what process does a group characteristic, a social norm, affect an individual's behavior?

A number of recent social psychological theorists have addressed the issue of how social norms should relate to individual behavior by incorporating terminologies reflecting an individual's belief system in regard to social norms. For instance, according to the theory of reasoned action (Fishbein & Ajzen, 1975), volitional or planned behavior is determined by the behavioral intention to perform a behavior. A person's behavioral intention results from his or her "attitude" toward the behavior (defined by these authors as an evaluation based on perceived consequences) and his or her "subjective norms" (defined by these authors as derived from perceptions of what important specific others think should be done and the person's motivation to comply with those norms). Fishbein and Ajzen use the term *normative beliefs,* although this refers to an individual's perceptions that specific persons or groups think he or she should perform a behavior, which is quite distinct from our definition of normative beliefs.

By defining normative beliefs as individualistic standards or cognitions about the acceptability of a behavior for oneself, and not as shared proscriptions whose genesis lies within the social group, we avoid many of these problems. We can easily distinguish normative beliefs from social norms, which we define as the actual social consensus on what individuals are expected to do. *Perceived social norms,* in turn, are defined as the individual's perception of the social consensus. However, an individual's normative beliefs may or may not be consistent with social norms or with the individual's perceived social norms. Clearly, there should be considerable overlap between a person's normative beliefs and the prevailing social norms. However, it is important to remember that individuals (particularly children) receive normative information across a broad range of settings.

We propose that normative beliefs serve primarily to regulate behavior. Believing that a behavior is acceptable does not mean it will be performed. An acceptable behavior is okay to do and okay not to do. However, believing that a behavior is unacceptable means that it should not be performed. Although our conception of normative beliefs contains a "should not" component, it does not specify a "should" (injunctive) component.

Personal beliefs about behaviors that should be performed (that is, personal standards for required behaviors) have been addressed more regularly in the developmental literature as they relate to motivation to perform prosocial or altruistic acts. A number of theories of altruism rely on concepts such as personal norms, personal values, or internalized norms (Eisenberg, 1986; Schwartz, 1977; Staub, 1978). Although there is often considerable variation in the use of these terms, they generally are described as internalized standards for behavior that are constructed by the individual and that motivate behavior through self-evaluation. Because such standards are internalized, they are experienced as feelings of personal obligation. Performance of behavior consistent with these standards results in positive self-reactions such as pride and enhanced self-esteem, whereas nonperformance produces negative self-reactions such as guilt and loss of self-esteem.

In our conceptualization of normative beliefs, they are neither directives for behavior nor internalized standards that motivate behavior through self-evaluation. Rather, consistent with the information-processing perspective, normative beliefs represent abstracted general knowledge about acceptable and unacceptable behaviors and enable individuals to simplify reality by providing guides for behavior. In some cases, normative beliefs may be backed by internalized self-evaluative processes, and in other cases they may be linked to external sanctions.

It is important to bear in mind that self-regulation of behavior occurs regardless of whether a behavior is considered unacceptable because it results in external sanctions or internal self-evaluation. In fact, in understanding mechanisms of self-regulation, the distinction between external and internal controls is often blurred. Very early in development, actual external sanctions are quickly replaced by cognitive representations of sanctions, and behavior is regulated by the child's own inhibitory processes. As Maccoby and Martin (1983) point out, "Inhibition that is based on external commands or fear of punishment (frequently called external control), as well as inhibition that is based on a child's self-accepted prosocial values (frequently called internal controls), call on a common nexus of self-regulatory processes" (p. 36). Related studies have shown that children as young as 2 years of age exercise some degree of self-regulation based on an awareness of what is allowed and what is not (e.g., Lytton, 1980).

This conception of cognitive self-regulation as a system of beliefs about allowable/prohibited behaviors is somewhat at odds with traditional cognitive-developmental theory. Rather than emphasizing beliefs about appropriate behaviors, per se, cognitive-developmental approaches have focused on developmental changes in how children reason about or judge the appropriateness of different courses of action. Such work has focused largely on moral development and the mechanisms by which children create moral meaning (Kohlberg, 1969; Piaget, 1965). The construction of moral meaning is believed to be dependent on the child's progression through an invariant sequence of stages. Each stage is believed to represent a qualitative transformation in reasoning that reflects movement from external controls toward internal controls based on universal principles.

The utility of this approach for understanding children's social behavior is compromised by the weak relation between stages of moral reasoning and moral action (for a review, see Blasi, 1980). In our conceptualization of normative beliefs, we propose that they regulate behavior regardless of whether they are backed by internal or external sanctions. However, normative beliefs that are supported by internalized sanctions would be expected to be more stable and resistant to situational and contextual influences.

THE ACQUISITION OF NORMATIVE
BELIEFS AND THEIR RELATION TO BEHAVIOR

We propose that normative beliefs are acquired through a socialization process involving perception of social norms, identification with specific reference groups, and personal evaluation. For very young children who identify almost exclusively with the parent or primary caregiver, normative beliefs are likely to be anchored in parental rules—young children are frequently overheard verbalizing parental prohibitions (such as "don't touch") when contemplating a behavior. Such verbalizations should contribute to the active construction of the child's own normative beliefs, although these beliefs should also undergo changes with development as individuals integrate information from diverse social groups into their own evaluative framework. When individuals are exposed to normative information from different sources (for instance, family and peers) their normative beliefs should be influenced by the social norms of the reference group they identify with most closely.

The acquisition of normative beliefs also involves an evaluative process. Judging a behavior to be acceptable for oneself involves more than just a reiteration of a social norm. If this were the case, socialization would, in fact, be an extremely simple task of providing information about socially approved or prohibited behaviors. Rather, individuals construct normative beliefs in accordance with their own evaluative schema. This evaluative schema is likely to include one's assessment of self-efficacy for the behavior, response-outcome expectancies, and self-concept.

In developing an unambiguous terminology for dealing with the role of normative influence in guiding social behavior, the social/developmental scholar is faced with numerous obstacles. As discussed in the preceding section, social psychology has a rich history of research on social norms, attitudes, and beliefs, out of which several terminologies relevant to the norm construct and its relation to behavior have emerged. Similarly, developmental psychologists have a long-standing interest in both socialization and cognitive development, although the cognition-behavior relation has come to the forefront only recently.

From a social psychological standpoint, consensual social norms facilitate social interaction by providing individuals with a uniform language of shared symbols and concepts. Such consensual norms also engender group cohesiveness over time by specifying appropriate behaviors of group members, and they foster obligatory relations necessary for social systems to endure. Beyond their role in promoting group cohesion, social norms also provide individuals with information regarding adaptive responses. This is particularly relevant in ambiguous or novel situations when the appropriate response is unclear. In such situations, it is reasonable to believe that if most people have chosen a certain course or action, such action is probably appropriate.

However, consensual norms provide weak explanations of individual behavior independent of the social group. One problem is that social norms are often defined in vague, global terms (such as the *norm of reciprocity* and the *norm of social responsibility*), providing vastly oversimplified conceptions of social behavior. Writers such as Darley and Latane (1970) have noted that incompatible social norms often exist simultaneously in a given social situation, making any behavior explainable by attributing it to the corresponding social norm.

Even theorists who have examined the role of normative influence on specific types of individual behavior have limited their focus to perceptions of and compliance with prevailing social norms and have failed to integrate other relevant cognitive mechanisms. For instance, although Fishbein and Ajzen's (1975) theory of reasoned action represents a sincere attempt to clarify the role of norms, it has probably introduced as many ambiguities as it has resolved. Although the role of "beliefs about consequences," that is, Fishbein and Ajzen's "attitude about the behavior," might seem to be separated from the role of subjective norms, this is an illusion, unless one believes that consequences are unrelated to social norms. Empirical evidence suggests that the attitudinal and normative structures defined in this way may not be independent, with attitudes being more influential than subjective norms in predicting planned behavior (Vallerand, Deshaies, Cuerrier, Pelletier, & Mongeau, 1992).

In contrast, cognitive-developmental researchers have derived a terminology appropriate for discussing the child's evolving reasoning structure, how this structure unfolds with development, and how environmental feedback and developmental processes interact. However, they have attended little to how beliefs should be represented cognitively or how such beliefs actually influence behavior within a given social context. Other investigators of children's social behavior have examined the mechanisms of learning and the relative influence of diverse socialization practices. Their studies include investigations of the relations between children's behavior and reinforcement contingencies and the role of observation of models (Bandura, Ross, & Ross, 1963). Only recently have socialization researchers "gone cognitive" and begun to study how children's cognitions influence their behavior.

A basic premise of social cognitive theory is that, with development, children's behavior is regulated increasingly by a number of cognitive mechanisms (Bandura, 1986). Impulsive responding gives way to cognitive processing, although there is substantial variation across both individuals and situations in the extent to which cognitive mechanisms are engaged. Furthermore, although unfamiliar situations require deliberate, conscious cognitive strategies that demand some effort, often referred to as "controlled processing," such processes become "automatic" over time with repeated exposure to similar situations (Schneider & Shiffrin, 1977).

In postulating specific mechanisms by which normative beliefs influence behavior, one must consider their role in both controlled and automatic processing. However, because our own recent work has focused primarily on automatic social behavior, and because the everyday social interactions of school-aged children typically involve automatic behaviors performed with little contemplation, we attempt to account for the normative belief-behavior relation within a process model that primarily accounts for automatic behavior. Many of the proposed mechanisms of influence should apply equally to more controlled processing steps articulated in other models (e.g., Dodge, 1986).

According to our model (Huesmann, 1988), automatic social behavior is determined to a great extent by programs for behavior. These programs can be described as *cognitive scripts* (Abelson, 1981) that are stored in a person's memory and are used as guides for behavior. Scripts enable people to manage the complexities of the social world by specifying the prototypical sequence of events and appropriate responses. A typical scripted response is the sequence of events associated with ordering food in a restaurant. With increasing age, children are more likely to encounter similar situations repeatedly and develop "scripted" responses.

The primary process through which scripts are formed is a learning process involving both observational and enactive components. However, the outcome of this process is heavily influenced by the child's environment and a range of predisposing factors such as temperament. Furthermore, through a process of cognitive abstraction, subsets of learned scripts are converted into more general scripts that provide overall guiding principles for social behavior. Thus the scripts that guide the child into typical aggressive behavior sequences found among children also form the basis for more general scripts guiding the adult into antisocial behavior.

A fundamental premise of this model is that a child will encode into a script any problem-solving strategy he or she observes if it seems to work and is consistent with his or her normative beliefs. Whether or not a script can be utilized later depends on how well it is encoded and maintained. The rehearsal of aggressive acts through fantasizing about aggression, for example, should strengthen encoding. From an information-processing perspective, therefore, normative beliefs play an important role by providing standards and values against which the child can compare potential scripts and decide if they should be encoded and rehearsed. The encoding of nonaggressive rather than aggressive scripts should be facilitated by normative beliefs that prohibit aggression.

Scripts are cast as the central cognitive component of a complex psychological process that generates social behavior. A person's affective response to a situation and that person's concomitant cognitive interpretations play roles in the process. Normative beliefs have also been presumed to play a critical role in the utilization of scripts. Huesmann (1988) argues that not all scripts that occur to a child (that is, are retrieved from memory) are employed by the child. Before acting out the script, according to Huesmann, the child reevaluates the appropriateness of the behaviors suggested by the script in light of his or her current normative beliefs. This view of normative beliefs depicts them as filters for behavior that eliminate behaviors that seriously violate current normative beliefs. However, although a particular set of normative beliefs may have been influential during the encoding of a given script, with development, such normative beliefs regularly change in response to both structural cognitive changes and changing social influences.

We have now come to the conclusion, however, that this is too narrow a view of the role normative beliefs play in the activation and utilization of scripts. In Figure 6.1, we diagram our revised conception. In our revised view, normative beliefs exert an influence on behavior in three different ways.

First, normative beliefs directly affect the relative salience of situational cues and the ways in which cues are evaluated (particularly under conditions of ambiguity). People are more likely to attend to cues that are relevant to their normative beliefs. Once an individual attends to a cue, his or her normative belief may influence how the cue is interpreted. For instance, a child who believes it is unacceptable to let another child tease him or her may be overly sensitized to such behavior and misread situational cues accordingly.

Second, normative beliefs can serve as cues for retrieving scripts consistent with beliefs. In other words, people do not simply generate possible scripts for behavior and reject those that violate normative beliefs. The active beliefs serve as cues in the retrieval process. For example, a male whose normative belief supports female subservience, when engaged in an argument with his wife, may retrieve scripts suggesting violence because his normative belief cues that script.

Third, normative beliefs act as filters for behavior to reduce the likelihood of behaviors that violate normative beliefs. One can view the filtering process as assigning an evaluative valence to the behavior suggested by the script. The total valence will depend on other factors as well, and might be called one's "attitude toward the behavior." The value contributed by the normative belief may be greater or lesser depending on the proscribed acceptability of the behavior, and may depend on cues in the environment.

It is important to realize that the processes through which normative beliefs exert their influence on behavior do not require conscious reflection by the individual. Normative beliefs affect cue interpretation, trigger the recall

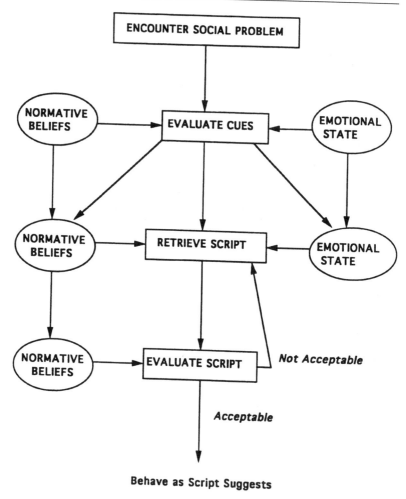

Figure 6.1. Three Ways That Normative Beliefs Influence Behavior

of specific scripts, and filter out unacceptable behaviors suggested by scripts. At the same time, the effects of more complex normative beliefs likely increase as time for reflection before behaving increases. Under conditions of high arousal and reactive responding, cue interpretation will be affected by only the simplest, most automatically engaged beliefs, and well-learned scripts will be retrieved and executed with little filtering by complicated beliefs. The adolescent inner-city boy who fears for his life may shoot before his normative beliefs about the acceptability of that response are engaged. Along these lines, Zelli, Huesmann, and Cervone (1993) demonstrate that aggressive people make more hostile attributions about nonhostile scenarios when they are forced to respond rapidly than when they are given time for reflection.

NORMATIVE BELIEFS AND CHILDHOOD AGGRESSION

We have drawn from both the developmental and the social literature to derive a definition of normative beliefs that assigns such beliefs a critical role in children's social behavior, particularly automatic or "scripted" behaviors. We have presented a model for the role of such beliefs that suggests that they influence the learning and performance of aggressive behavior in several ways. We now describe a measure we have developed to assess normative beliefs about aggression in children, and discuss a few studies we have completed that demonstrate that normative beliefs about aggression are related to children's aggressive behavior.

Study 1

When we began our initial investigation of normative beliefs and social norms, many of the ideas expressed in this chapter had not coalesced. However, we recognized a number of the difficult measurement problems inherent in any attempt to assess children's beliefs about the acceptability of aggressive behaviors. Children's reports could be expected to be very sensitive to the demand characteristics of the questioning and to the perceived social desirability of the possible responses. Children's beliefs could be expected to change radically with age, and very young children might not have any stable beliefs of their own and might simply respond to situational cues.

In the initial study (Huesmann, Guerra, Miller, & Zelli, 1992; Huesmann, Guerra, Zelli, & Miller, 1992), we derived a 35-item scale for assessing beliefs about the approval of aggression. Beginning with the conception that beliefs about aggression are cognitions about the acceptability of specific aggressive behaviors in specific contexts, we first developed a set of 88 questions that might be appropriate for elementary school children. Taking Fishbein and Ajzen's (1975) categorization of social behaviors on the basis of "action, target, context, and time" as a point of departure, we described aggressive acts that varied in characteristics of actor, target, and provocation. Specifically, the items varied on four dimensions: severity of provocation; severity of response; gender of provoker; and gender of responder.

The questions followed a format that Guerra and Slaby (Guerra & Slaby, 1990; Slaby & Guerra, 1988) developed, and asked children, "How often do you think _____ is okay? Never, Sometimes, Often, Always." To minimize demand characteristics and to make the phrasing easier for young children to understand, questions were asked in the third person. For example, one question was "It's okay for a boy, Tom, to hit a girl, Julie, if Julie says something bad to Tom first." The strong/weak provocation manipulation was accomplished by substituting "if Julie hits" for "if Julie says something bad to." Similarly, the severity of response manipulation was accomplished by changing "It's okay for _____ to hit _____" to "It's okay for _____ to scream at _____."

In the pilot study with 25 second graders, questions were included to assess not only whether children thought a behavior was acceptable, but whether they thought other children and other adults would think it was acceptable (similar to our notion of perceived social norms). The pilot study revealed that it did not matter whether one asked a child about whether he or she thought the behavior was okay or asked the child about whether most children thought the behavior was okay. If a child believed most children thought a behavior was okay, the child thought it was okay himself or herself. In other words, the children's normative beliefs were highly correlated with their perceived social norms for other children. However, on average the children thought that adults were less likely to approve of children's aggression. Because of this, we deleted the items related to perceived children's social norms but retained the items about adult's beliefs. To reduce the number of items, other items were deleted that the children could not understand or that had very low item total correlations in the pilot study.

Subjects

The resulting 35-item scale was then administered to 293 second-, third-, and fourth-grade children to determine the psychometric properties of the scale and to examine the relations between children's normative beliefs and their aggressive behavior. The subjects attended four inner-city schools in neighborhoods in Chicago in which crime was a serious problem. All the children for whom permission could be obtained participated (155 boys, 138 girls; 104 second graders, 92 third graders, 98 fourth graders). The sample was more than 85% African American and Latino. One hundred of these subjects were reassessed after 3 months to determine stability.

Results

Our findings (Huesmann, Guerra, Miller, & Zelli, 1992) reveal that one can reliably assess individual differences in normative beliefs on a variety of subscales with these questions. These include overall approval of aggression at children (alpha = .90), aggression at boys (alpha = .83), aggression at girls (alpha = .84), aggression under weak provocation (alpha = .80), and aggression under strong provocation (alpha = .84). The 3-month stability of scores on the overall aggression at children scale was .48, with the stabilities on the subscales ranging from .36 to .47.

The children's scores on many of these preliminary scales also correlated significantly with boys' and girls' self-reports of aggressive behavior and significantly with boys' peer nominations of aggressive behavior. The overall score for approval of aggression at children correlated .15 ($p < .10$) with boys' peer nominations of aggression and .41 ($p < .001$) with boys' self-reports. The correlation with girls' self-reports was .23 ($p < .05$). However, the correlation with girls' peer nomination scores was not significant.

On all the scales listed above, except aggression at boys and aggression under weak provocation, the mean approval of aggression score for boys was significantly higher than for girls. In this sample there was also a tendency for approval of aggression to increase with age, though the increase was only significant for boys on aggression under strong provocation.

Study 2

Although the results of the initial study demonstrate that children's approval of aggression can be measured reliably, they also suggest that the scale would benefit from further refinement. The correlations with actual aggressive behavior were not significant except when the aggressive behavior was also measured by self-reports. The differences one might expect as a function of age and gender were not large, even though the questionnaire was quite long. Finally, the questionnaire seemed to be measuring more than one belief structure, as questions assessing what we have now defined as individual normative beliefs were mixed with questions assessing perceived social norms of adults with regard to children's behavior.

On the basis of these considerations, a revised 20-item scale was developed to assess children's normative beliefs as concisely as possible. The 20-item scale included 12 of the 35 items from the original scale. We eliminated the questions that did not fit theoretically with our conception of normative beliefs (e.g., questions about adults' beliefs), questions that did not increase the internal consistency of the scale they were on because they had very little variance (e.g., "It's okay to hit someone back after being hit"), and questions that correlated highly with other questions and did not explain any unique variance of relevance (e.g., questions with "out of control" as the provocation). In addition, to tap more general normative beliefs about aggression, we added 8 questions that did not include any provocation, but simply asked the child if it was generally okay to use aggression; for instance, "It is usually okay to push and shove other people around."

Sample

This revised measure was tested on a sample of 2,035 urban elementary school children. These children were from 16 urban schools located in economically disadvantaged communities. The sample was about evenly split between boys and girls and was approximately 40% African American, 40% Latino, and 20% Caucasian. A subsample of 1,104 first and fourth graders was retested 1 year later when they were in the second and fifth grades.

Results

Although the resulting scales had fewer items than the original scales, their internal consistency remained high. The internal consistency for the total normative beliefs about aggression scale was .87, and the subscale reliabilities ranged from .68 to .82. Furthermore, the children's scores on their normative beliefs about aggression correlated more significantly ($r = .23$, $p < .001$) with their peer-nominated aggression score than in Study 1. The correlations remained significant when the data were analyzed separately by gender.

Of greatest interest for this chapter, however, are the changes over time that we discovered with the longitudinal sample. According to our conception that normative beliefs evolve through observational and enactive learning as the child develops, one would expect some stability for normative beliefs over time, coupled with longitudinal causal relations between beliefs and behavior. One would expect that more approving beliefs about aggression would lead to more aggressive behavior and that engaging in more aggressive behavior would lead to the development of more approving normative beliefs. This is exactly what the data suggest. When aggressive behavior is predicted from aggressive behavior and normative beliefs 1 year previously, the normative beliefs add significantly to the prediction of later aggressive behavior beyond what early aggressive behavior predicts. Similarly, when normative beliefs about aggression are predicted from normative beliefs and aggression 1 year previously, aggressive behavior adds significantly to the prediction of later normative beliefs beyond what early normative beliefs predict. Thus it appears that normative beliefs influence a child's behavior and a child's behavior also influences his or her future normative beliefs.

Finally, Study 2 revealed a clearer pattern of gender and age trends than did Study 1. Although boys and girls did not differ significantly on normative beliefs in the first grade, boys' approval of aggression increased much more rapidly with age than did girls. As a result, boys approved of aggression significantly more than girls during the latter elementary grades (grade 3 and beyond).

DISCUSSION

In this chapter, we argue that normative beliefs serve as cognitive schemata that are central to the regulation of social behavior. We propose that normative beliefs play an important role in children's information processing. Specifically, we discuss a model that emphasizes how normative beliefs influence the development of scripts for behavior, as well as how they exert their influence on behavior in relation to the interpretation of social cues, retrieval of potential scripts, and evaluation of such scripts (see Figure 6.1).

We differentiate normative beliefs from social norms and perceived social norms; social norms refer to consensual group standards and perceived social norms refer to an individual's perception of those standards. However, because normative beliefs deal with whether a behavior is considered acceptable or unacceptable, they are likely to be highly correlated with the prevailing social norms of the reference group an individual identifies most closely with. To explain how social norms relate to individual behavior, however, it is important to determine the standards an individual applies to himself or herself, regardless of whether such standards are consistent with prevailing social norms.

We also differentiate normative beliefs from constructs referring to internalized standards that motivate behavior through self-evaluation, such as Schwartz's (1977) notion of personal norms, although we believe that normative beliefs can be consistent with and reflect such internalized standards. However, the distinction between external and internal controls is often misleading, because self-regulation of behavior occurs regardless of whether external or internal sanctions are anticipated. However, to the extent that normative beliefs are influenced by variations in social context, we expect normative beliefs based on internalized standards to be more stable, particularly under conditions where external contingencies change markedly.

Although we provide empirical evidence of a relation between normative beliefs and children's aggressive behavior, several concerns remain. Perhaps the most important issue involves a better understanding of the extent to which we can accurately measure children's normative beliefs, particularly for behaviors such as aggression, where demand characteristics are high. The fact that children's own beliefs differ from their beliefs about what most adults would say is encouraging, although children's own beliefs do not differ from their perceptions of other children's beliefs.

Another issue concerns the lack of inclusion of "required" behaviors in both our conceptualization and our measurement of normative beliefs. If a behavior is unacceptable, regulation should occur by inhibiting performance of the behavior. However, if a behavior is acceptable, it is allowable but not required. Regulatory cognitions may be better understood as filters to eliminate negative behaviors, whereas constructs such as personal norms may be more useful in explaining prosocial or altruistic behavior. Another possibility is that items that also tap children's perceptions of whether they believe a behavior is required should be included, for instance, "You should hit another child if he hits you first."

Our interest in normative beliefs extends to behavior change programs. We propose that the effectiveness of programs that teach children skills or problem-solving strategies should be limited if efforts are not made simultaneously to modify children's corresponding normative beliefs. In our own intervention work with aggressive adolescents, we have found that change in normative beliefs about aggression is the best overall predictor of postintervention change in aggressive behavior (Guerra & Slaby, 1990). In an intervention study currently underway (Guerra, in press) we emphasize changing individuals' normative beliefs about aggression and, simultaneously, changing peer group social norms about aggression. We believe that behavior change is most effectively accomplished by fostering the development of normative beliefs that are consistent with the skills and behaviors targeted by the intervention.

REFERENCES

Abelson, R. P. (1981). The psychological status of the script concept. *American Psychologist, 36,* 715-729.

Bandura, A. (1986). *Social foundations of thought and action: A social-cognitive theory.* Englewood Cliffs, NJ: Prentice-Hall.

Bandura, A. (1991). Social cognitive theory of moral thought and action. In W. M. Kurtines & J. L. Gewirtz (Eds.), *Moral behavior and development: Advances in theory, research, and applications: Vol. 1* (pp. 45-103). Hillsdale, NJ: Erlbaum.

Bandura, A., Ross, D., & Ross, S. A. (1963). A comparative test of the status envy, social power, and secondary reinforcement theories of identification learning. *Journal of Abnormal and Social Psychology, 67,* 527-534.

Blasi, A. (1980). Bridging moral cognition and moral action: A critical review of the literature. *Psychological Bulletin, 88,* 1-45.

Cialdini, R. B., Kallgren, C. A., & Reno, R. R. (1991). A focus theory of normative conduct. *Advances in Experimental Social Psychology, 24,* 201-234.

Cooley, C. H. (1902). *Human nature and the social order.* New York: Scribner.

Darley, J. M., & Latane, B. (1970). Norms and normative behavior: Field studies of social interdependence. In J. Macaulay & L. Berkowitz (Eds.), *Altruism and helping behavior* (pp. 83-102). New York: Academic Press.

Deutsch, M., & Gerard, H. B. (1955). A study of normative and informational social influence upon individual judgment. *Journal of Abnormal and Social Psychology, 51,* 629-636.

Dodge, K. A. (1980). Social cognition and children's aggressive behavior. *Child Development, 51,* 162-170.

Dodge, K. A. (1986). A social information processing model of social competence in children. In M. Perlmutter (Ed.), *Minnesota symposium on child psychology* (pp. 77-125). Hillsdale, NJ: Erlbaum.

Dodge, K. A. (1993). Social-cognitive mechanisms in the development of conduct disorder and depression. *Annual Review of Psychology, 44,* 559-584.

Dodge, K. A., & Frame, C. L. (1982). Social cognitive biases and deficits in aggressive boys. *Child Development, 53,* 629-635.

Dodge, K. A., Petit, G. S., McClaskey, C. L., & Brown, C. (1986). Social competence in children. *Monographs of the Society for Research in Child Development, 51*(2).

Eisenberg, N. (1986). *Altruistic emotion, cognition, and behavior.* Hillsdale NJ: Erlbaum.

Fishbein, M., & Ajzen, I. (1975). *Belief, attitude, intention, and behavior.* Reading, MA: Addison-Wesley.

Fiske, S. T., & Taylor, S. E. (1984). *Social cognition.* Reading, MA: Addison-Wesley.

Gibbs, J. P. (1965). Norms: The problem of definition and classification. *American Journal of Sociology, 70,* 586-594.

Guerra, N. G. (in press). Violence prevention. *Preventive Medicine.*

Guerra, N. G., & Slaby, R. G. (1990). Cognitive mediators of aggression in adolescent offenders: II. Intervention. *Developmental Psychology, 26,* 269-277.

Huesmann, L. R. (1988). An information-processing model for the development of aggression. *Aggressive Behavior, 14,* 13-24.

Huesmann, L. R., & Eron, L. D. (1984). Cognitive processes and the persistence of aggressive behavior. *Aggressive Behavior, 10,* 243-251.

Huesmann, L. R., Guerra, N. G., Miller, L., & Zelli, A. (1992). The role of social norms in the development of aggression. In H. Zumkley & A. Fraczek (Eds.), *Socialization and aggression* (pp. 139-152). New York: Springer-Verlag.

Huesmann, L. R., Guerra, N. G., Zelli, A., & Miller, L. (1992). Differing normative beliefs about aggression for boys and girls. In K. Bjorkqvist & P. Niemela (Eds.), *Of mice and women: Aspects of female aggression* (pp. 77-87). Orlando, FL: Academic Press.

Kohlberg, L. (1969). Stage and sequence: The cognitive-developmental approach to socialization. In D. A. Goslin (Ed.), *Handbook of socialization theory and research* (pp. 347-480). Chicago: Rand McNally.

Lytton, H. (1980). *Parent-child interaction: The socialization process observed in twin and singleton families.* New York: Plenum.

Maccoby, E. E., & Martin, J. A. (1983). Socialization in the context of the family: Parent-child interaction. In P. H. Mussen (Ed.), *Handbook of child psychology: Vol. IV* (pp. 1-101). New York: John Wiley.

Mead, G. H. (1934). *Mind, self, and society.* Chicago: University of Chicago Press.

Mead, M. (1969). *Sex and temperament in three primitive societies* (2nd ed.). New York: Dell.

Piaget, J. (1965). *The moral judgement of the child.* New York: Free Press.

Rubin, K. H., & Krasnor, L. R. (1986). Social-cognitive and social behavioral perspectives on problem solving. In M. Perlmutter (Ed.), *Minnesota symposium on child psychology: Vol. 18* (pp. 1-68). Hillsdale, NJ: Erlbaum.

Rumelhart, D. E., & Ortony, A. (1977). The representation of knowledge in memory. In R. C. Anderson, R. J. Spiro, & W. E. Montague (Eds.), *Schooling and the acquisition of knowledge* (pp. 99-136). Hillsdale, NJ: Erlbaum.

Schneider, W., & Shiffrin, R. M. (1977). Controlled and automatic human information processing: I. Detection, search, and attention. *Psychological Review, 84,* 1-66.

Schwartz, S. H. (1977). Normative influences on altruism. *Advances in Experimental Social Psychology, 10,* 222-279.

Sherif, M. (1936). *The psychology of social norms.* New York: Harper.

Slaby, R. G., & Guerra, N. G. (1988). Cognitive mediators of aggression in adolescent offenders: I. Assessment. *Developmental Psychology, 24,* 580-588.

Staub, E. (1978). *Positive social behavior and morality: Social and personal influences: Vol. 1.* New York: Academic Press.

Thibaut, J. W., & Kelley, H. H. (1959). *The social psychology of groups.* New York: John Wiley.

Vallerand, R. J., Deshaies, P. J., Cuerrier, J. P., Pelletier, L. G., & Mongeau, C. (1992). Ajzen and Fishbein's theory of reasoned action as applied to moral behavior: A confirmatory analysis. *Journal of Personality and Social Psychology, 62,* 98-109.

Zelli, A. Z., Huesmann, L. R., & Cervone. (1993). *Beliefs and hostile attributions.* Manuscript under review.

7

Influences of Affect on Cognitive Processes at Different Ages: Why the Change?

DAPHNE BLUNT BUGENTAL
ETA K. LIN
JOSHUA E. SUSSKIND

Daphne Blunt Bugental is Professor of Developmental Psychology and Social Psychology and Director of the Interdisciplinary Program in Human Development at the University of California at Santa Barbara. She serves on editorial boards within both social psychology and developmental psychology and is currently an Associate Editor of *Personality and Social Psychology Bulletin.*

Eta K. Lin is a graduate student in the Department of Psychology at the University of California at Santa Barbara. She is in the Social/Personality Program and is completing an emphasis in Human Development. Her research interests focus on adult responses to the eliciting properties of children's nonverbal behaviors.

Joshua E. Susskind is a graduate student in the University of California at Santa Barbara's Department of Psychology. He is in the Social/Personality Program and is completing an emphasis in Human Development. His research interests focus on developmental changes in stereotyping processes.

Interest in the impact of affect on cognition has emerged across many areas within psychology. Attention has been directed to the effects of affect on the encoding and retrieval of information, and on the performance of tasks that require cognitive effort. Concern with such effects has appeared in the areas of social cognition, social development, cognition, and personality—fields that often fail to cross-reference each other. Empirical interest has been directed to such diverse outcomes as language acquisition (e.g., Bloom, 1993), eye witness memory (e.g., Christianson, 1992), memory for story content (e.g., Forgas, Burnham, & Trimboli, 1988), acceptance of persuasive messages (Mackie & Worth, 1989), and problem solving, judgment, and decision making (Isen, 1990).

AUTHORS' NOTE: The authors would like to express their appreciation to Bert Moore for his valuable comments on an earlier draft of this paper. Order of authorship among the two junior authors was determined randomly.

In this chapter, we are concerned with changes in the effect of affect on cognition across developmental levels. In accounting for observed differences, we consider the processes that may mediate such relations and the extent to which such mediators vary with age. We propose that changes with age are influenced not only by changes in capacity or experience but also by the emergence of regulation processes that are engaged in response to affective states. Our focus is on the effects of affect on memory; but we also consider the effects of affect on other cognitively demanding activities.

Traditional views of the relation between affect and cognition have focused on the role of associative networks and/or autonomic arousal as mediators. We argue that the changing relation between affect and cognition can be better understood by additional consideration of the mediating role of affect regulation. Both the developmental literature (e.g., Campos, Campos, & Barrett, 1989; Kopp, 1989) and the social psychological literature (e.g., Mayer, Salovey, Gomberg-Kaufman, & Blainey, 1991) have directed increasing attention to affect regulation processes. Affect exists for the sake of its capacity to inform and motivate adaptive responses to the environment (Frijda, 1986; Schwarz, 1990). But just as affect itself regulates responses, affective states must in turn be regulated for an individual to maintain effective transactions with the environment. For example, one may reduce attentional engagement with aversive stimuli, problem solve with respect to them, get help from someone else. Variations in regulatory mechanisms, in turn, have direct consequences for the effectiveness of state management as well as for the attentional resources that are available for other processing activities.

Definitions

Affect has been defined and operationalized in many different ways in the literature. In this chapter, we use the term *affect* to include both mood and emotions. *Mood* is used to refer to generalized feeling states that are relatively long in duration; "emotion" is used to designate relatively brief reactions or signals displayed in response to specific events. In talking about affect, we typically refer to positive versus negative affect. Although little effort has been made to induce discrete mood states in children (see Nasby & Yando, 1982, for an exception), efforts to do so have been made with adults. Often such efforts have been unsuccessful in that depression, anger, and anxiety are likely to co-occur as a function of mood induction procedures.

Just as affect and emotion have been subject to varying definitions, the concept of affect or emotion regulation has been variously conceived. As noted by Dodge and Garber (1991), affect regulation represents an ambiguous concept. It may refer to the effects of affect as a regulator of other processes. It may refer to one specific type of regulatory process. Or it may imply that affect itself is regulated by other processes. Our focus in this chapter is on the ways in which affective states are modulated by regulatory activities that are generated within individuals themselves or by others within their environment.

Organization of Chapter

In exploring the ways in which and reasons why developmental change may occur in the impact of affect on cognitive processes, we first summarize the general mechanisms that have been suggested to account for the relation between affect and cognition. We then consider the developmental processes and age changes that may serve to influence this relation. In a review of the support that is available for suggested processes, we summarize the current state of empirical evidence. Finally, we present results of a research program that has focused on changes across middle childhood in memory of witnessed affect-eliciting events.

MECHANISMS THAT MAY ACCOUNT FOR THE RELATION BETWEEN AFFECT AND COGNITION

Within the adult literature, the impact of affect on cognition is conceptualized from a variety of theoretical frameworks. It is represented within a social cognition framework that focuses on the nature of associative processes. It also is conceptualized in terms of the influences of autonomic arousal on cognitive processes. Finally, affect is understood from the standpoint of its motivational sequelae.

Associative Networks

Bower (1981) suggests that affective states (mood) may influence information processing as a function of the associations between affect and other material. That is, affect is linked to the conceptual content of memory through a network of associations.

Affect may influence processing in different ways. Mood states may increase the accessibility of associated material in working memory. When the individual accesses a large body of associated material in active memory, there is a reduction in the overall capacity that is available for other cognitive activities. So individuals in a happy, sad, or any other mood state may show a decrease in their ability to engage in tasks that require a lot of thought. This process is based on the premise of a fixed pool of attentional resources (Kahneman, 1973). The notion of capacity constraints has been invoked to explain processing interference shown in response to positive (e.g., Mackie & Worth, 1989) or negative (e.g., Ellis & Ashbrook, 1988) affect.

At the same time, mood states may also have processing advantages through the priming of associated cognitions. That is, an individual's mood state makes it easy for associated ideas to come to mind. Material that is associated with a particular mood state may be easily learned or remembered. For example, individuals who are in a happy mood may easily recall past happy events, or they may easily learn new material that is positive in nature. From this view, affect is interpreted as a node within an associative network and acts as a retrieval cue for related concepts.

Arousal

Attention has been directed to the role of arousal as a mediator in the relation between affect and cognition. The assumed relation is of two basic types. The classic Yerkes-Dodson law predicts optimal processing at moderate levels of arousal. The curvilinear model has long been invoked as an explanation of the effects of stress on performance and processing. This view argues that optimal processing and performance occur at moderate levels as opposed to very high or very low levels of arousal. Low levels of arousal lead to insufficient attentional deployment. Very high levels of arousal may lead to an overload on attentional mechanisms, with the net effect that deficits are shown in the ability to acquire information from the environment or from associated memory stores. Although proponents of this position still exist, recent reviews (e.g., Christianson, 1992) have led to skepticism concerning the generality of such effects.

Increasing support has been found for the effects suggested by Easterbrook (1959). According to this position, the presence of intense affect or arousal leads to a focus on central features of the environment and reduced attentional deployment to the periphery. Thus an individual witnessing an accident may have a detailed memory for accident-related events but may be unable to provide a description of the surrounding environment. With heightened levels of arousal, there is an increasing restriction or narrowing of cue utilization. This restriction may have different consequences for processing based on the nature of the task; that is, restriction of cue utilization may lead to greater attentional deployment to central information but reduced attention to peripheral information.

Christianson (1992), in his review of this area of research, argues for an adaptation of the Easterbrook position. He proposes that affective events may trigger attention automatically, that is, before the individual is fully aware of eliciting stimuli and without the requirement that the observer first engage in a conscious appraisal of events. Once the nature of the event has been recognized, however, deliberate attention and analytic effort is directed to understanding and coping with the event. As this higher level of controlled processing requires effort and attentional resources, it imposes constraints on the attentional resources that are available for other cognitively demanding activities. Thus an individual attempting to cope with the aftermath of an accident may experience exceptional difficulty in looking up an emergency number in a phone book.

Motivational Models

A third position accounts for the relation between affect and cognition in terms of motivational processes. The individual is conceptualized as engaged in a motivated attempt to optimize his or her mood state; that is, the presence of affect leads to responses that are directed to maintaining and extending positive states and eliminating or reducing negative states (Isen, 1990). For example, an individual in a happy mood may spend little time in careful analysis of the event that produced this state; to do so might in itself break the positive mood.

CHANGES WITH AGE THAT MAY CONTRIBUTE TO THE RELATION BETWEEN AFFECT AND COGNITION

The focus of our concern here is on the age changes in the relation between affect and cognition. At younger ages, regulatory activities are more under the control of biologically preprogrammed regulatory mechanisms, as well as the interventions of others. With middle childhood, regulatory activities increasingly move under the child's cognitive control, and the relation between affect and cognition more closely resembles that seen in adulthood.

Changing Processing Capacities

One of the first considerations in discussing age-related changes in information-processing patterns is the presence of developmental changes in processing capacity. It has been suggested that the attentional requirements of mental operations are greater at younger ages—which in turn may lead to production deficiencies (Craik & Byrd, 1982). Alternately, information may be processed more efficiently with age; as a result, less "space" is needed for processing operations and more space is free for storage operations (Case, 1985). Hashers and Zaks (1979) argue that age differences are greater on memory tasks that require high use of attentional resources (e.g, tasks that require recording information) than they are for tasks that involve automatic, noneffortful encoding operations (e.g., memory for relative frequencies). Additionally, younger children are less effective than older children in their use of deliberate memory strategies (e.g., complex mnemonics)—operations that place a heavy demand on attentional capacity.

With respect to the processing of affect-eliciting stimuli, arousing events may require more of young children's limited capacity resources (Leichtman, Ceci, & Ornstein, 1992). As a result, young children may show a reduced capacity to encode, store, and retrieve information.

Biologically Determined Affect Regulation Programs

In early infancy, affect regulation may be thought of as organized by biologically set "programs" (Kopp, 1989) and as occurring without intention. Early regulatory activity is consistent with Christianson's (1992) perceptual/automatic level of response. These early regulatory systems may be thought of as biologically designed to optimize the infant's transactions with the environment. For example, visual engagement facilitates social interaction and information acquisition; but at the same time, excess levels of visual engagement carry the risk of stimulus overload and excess levels of arousal. Visual engagement and disengagement in infancy thus serve as important regulators of ongoing transactions. As with many regulatory abilities, however, there are variations in children's adaptive management of visual behavior and thus the adaptive management of their negotiations with the environment. For example, infants who disengage visual attention in response to unpleasant stimuli are less susceptible to negative affects such as fear, and are also more soothable when distressed (Derryberry & Rothbart, 1988). Age changes in the adaptive alternation of visual engagement and disengagement reflect the child's increasing ability to regulate negotiations with the environment (Rothbart, Ziaie, & O'Boyle, 1992). For example, Fabes, Eisenberg, and Eisenbud (1993) found that older children experiencing autonomic arousal in response to a vicarious emotional event (witnessing the distress of another child) were likely to visually disengage from the source of distress.

Preprogrammed regulatory activities also occur within the autonomic nervous system. For example, heart rate changes are regulated by respiratory processes (vagal tone). It has been suggested that this process modulates the infant's reactivity to the environment (Porges, 1991). Infants who show a relatively high vagal tone tend to be less reactive to stressful events. As the integration of the sympathetic and parasympathetic nervous system increases during infancy, vagal tone increases—along with general increases in self-regulation ability. And throughout this developmental progression, children with higher vagal tone tend to show higher self-regulation ability.

In short, some regulatory systems are present at birth to serve homeostatic needs in the regulation of adaptive negotiations with the infant's internal and external environment. At the same time, these systems also show developmental change and individual variation. Additionally, they may ultimately influence the socializing environment itself.

Social Regulation

A child's affective state may also be regulated by the actions of others (Kopp, 1989). Such regulatory involvement is more direct at younger ages but continues to influence affect regulation in more indirect ways at older ages. The relatively higher involvement of others in the child's affect regulation at younger ages has implications for the importance of the caregiver's social regulation activities for the child's effective information processing and negotiations with the environment. If, for example, a caregiver responds to an infant cry with soothing activities, processing deficits following from excess arousal may be attenuated. At all ages, the socialization provided by caregivers is influenced by children's affective reactivity as well as their self-regulatory ability (e.g., Snow, Jacklin, & Maccoby, 1983).

Across infancy, children show increases in their strategic use of communication signals and in their ability to use the expressive behavior of others to manage their own actions and affect. The emergence of social referencing allows children to make use of the expressive behavior of others in their cognitive analysis of the environment (Walden, 1991). Young children—when experiencing an affective state—actively seek information about the responses and coping strategies employed by others under such circumstances (Dunn & Brown, 1991). Additionally, children acquire proficiency in their use of communication to elicit information and support from others (e.g., Jones & Raag, 1989). Social overtures become increasingly efficient as children make expanding use of language in their efforts to engage others in meeting their own needs (Dunn & Brown, 1991). As Kopp (1989) notes, "with language, children can state their feelings to others, obtain verbal feedback about the appropriateness of their emotions, and hear and think about ways to manage them" (p. 349).

The social scaffolding provided by others may directly influence children's information-processing ability—including their memory for distressing events. Supportive others may provide affect modulation or structuring that assists children in their encoding and retrieval of to-be-remembered (TBR) events. Goodman, Bottoms, Schwartz-Kenney, and Rudy (1991) found that memory differences between children age 3 to 7 were attenuated if the interviewer had a supportive manner. Other people may also structure TBR events. Moston and Engleberg (1992) found that differences in recall between 7- and 10-year-olds were sharply attenuated when children had the opportunity to discuss TBR events with a friend and were accompanied by that friend to the interview.

With increasing levels of development, the possibilities for affect regulation are expanded on the basis of the direct instruction provided by socializing agents. Caregivers typically show a large investment of effort in helping children learn to regulate their affective states and their expressions of emotion. It has been suggested that the mother-child dyad serves as an affect regulation unit (Thompson, 1990). Even with very young children, mothers show a continuous involvement in managing children's affective states and assisting children in acquiring strategies for regulation of their own affects (e.g., Capitides & Bloom, 1993; Kopp, 1989). By middle childhood, agents of socialization (adults and peers) show a high investment in transmission of explicit cultural norms concerning displays of affect (e.g., Saarni, 1984). By the later years of middle childhood, children have become proficient in the understanding and use of display rules. Socialization influences not only the regulation of affective displays, but also what children report regarding past events. As a result, children's "memory" for past events may be confounded with the "rules" they have acquired for reporting those experiences (Steward, 1993).

Cognitive Regulation

Ultimately, developmental changes in the management of affect reflect the emergence of expanded cognitive regulation options. At very early ages (early infancy), children may show what Kopp (1989) describes as "elemental cognitive" mechanisms in response to distress acquired on the basis of learned associations. During middle childhood, however, striking increases are shown in children's capacity for complex information integration and planning. As noted by Labouvie-Vief, Hakim-Larson, DeVoe, and Schoeberlein (1989),

> The transfer from one set of processes to the other forms the major theme of theories of cognitive and interpersonal development. As the individual's cognitive capacities mature, regulations occur less often in terms of the urgent dictates of individual homeostasis and more often in terms of shared cultural rule and symbol systems. (p. 279)

During middle childhood, children show a number of changes that facilitate cognitive regulation of affect: increased integration of information from multiple sources, increased use of dispositional inferences, increased understanding of the links between personal dispositions and behavior, and increasing social competencies and social control options. Changes in cognitive development combine with expanded knowledge and skills to foster a more mature appraisal of affect-eliciting events and coping options.

One of the most extensively noted changes during these years is the child's expanded ability to integrate information from multiple sources and along different dimensions as a guide to appraisal processes (Case, 1985). The integration of the full range of information that is relevant to affect-eliciting events and affective responses may be understood in terms of these broader developmental processes. For example, older children have a better understanding of the psychological implications of events. Additionally, older children are less likely than younger children to rely on the direct implications of the expressive behavior of others in interpreting emotional cues; instead, they integrate expressive cues with inferences about the possible inner states and motives of others (e.g., Gnepp & Gould, 1985). At older ages, children's evaluations and representations of social events are increasingly based on relational notions; for example, older children engage in greater social comparison activity, and their affective responses are increasingly influenced by comparison processes (Frey & Ruble, 1985). As a result of increases in cognitive integration activities, children should be less bound by the stimulus features of immediate affect-eliciting situations and better able to appraise events in terms of multiple causation.

Beginning with the seminal work of Livesley and Bromley (1973), attention has been directed to children's increased use of dispositional inference in making judgments about themselves and others (see Rholes, Newman, & Ruble, 1991). In early childhood, the free descriptions given of self and others focus on peripheral, external characteristics (identity, appearance, possessions) rather than central, personal dispositions (motives, values). Rholes and Ruble (1984) present evidence to show that young children are able to use trait terms, but their use of such terminology indexes behaviors rather than generalized personal characteristics or traits.

In middle childhood, there is an increased understanding that behavior has predictive implications for future events (Rholes et al., 1991). Younger children's ability to label behavior in terms of dispositions is not reflected in their understanding of the cross-situational consistency of relevant behavior. If, for example, young children (5 to 6 years) learn that a child consistently behaves in a helpful way, they draw the correct dispositional inference; but this inference has little impact on their expectations of the future behavior of this child. In contrast, older children (9 to 10 years) use dispositional information to predict future behaviors that are congruent with earlier behaviors (Rholes & Ruble, 1984). A number of studies support this conclusion, including Gnepp and Chilamkurti's (1988) findings of age differences in children's ability to use dispositional information to predict emotional responses. It should be noted that older children are more likely than younger children to understand the temporal stability of their own characteristics as well as those of others (Rotenberg, 1982). Thus their regulatory options in response to affect-eliciting events may be enhanced by their understanding that current behaviors have implications for future events.

With the increased experience and expanded social contacts of middle childhood, children also acquire social knowledge and social skills that are relevant for affect-regulation strategies. Although older children may differ little from younger children in the extent to which they engage in affect-regulation activities, they are more likely to engage in cognitive strategies (Masters, 1991). Children report increasing utilization of cognitive strategies such as denial or distraction (as opposed to reliance on situational management) in regulating distress (e.g., Altshuler & Ruble, 1989). Older children are more likely to recognize that mental processes can redirect emotion.

Finally, relevant schematic structures become increasingly differentiated (Leichtman et al., 1992) across middle childhood. Embedded within the regularities in social cognitive development are variations that reflect individual differences in ways of cognitively representing social experience. That is, the knowledge structures that children bring to bear on affect-eliciting events vary as a function of their unique histories. As with adults, older children differ in the ways in which they cope with feelings of distress; they may focus on direct attempts to resolve a problem (problem-focused coping) or they may focus on the management of their feelings of distress (emotion-focused coping; Lazarus & Folkman, 1984).

Variations in children's understanding of interpersonal relationships may influence their coping styles. From the standpoint of the developmental literature, the "working models" of relationships that emerge from early attachment experiences may influence the interpretations and expectations that children bring to their transactions with their social environments (Bowlby, 1980). Integrating social psychological theory and social cognitive developmental theory, one may predict that social attributions emerging in middle childhood produce differential vulnerability to affect-eliciting events and subsequent regulatory responses (Bugental & Cortez, 1993; Dodge & Coie, 1987; Dweck & Leggett, 1988).

EVIDENCE CONCERNING THE RELATION BETWEEN AFFECT AND INFORMATION PROCESSING IN THE ADULT LITERATURE

Before reviewing the developmental changes that have been found in the relation between affect and cognition, we briefly summarize our state of knowledge within adult populations. Research has tended to focus on three topics: the effect of the congruence between mood state and valence of informational content, the effect of positive mood on information processing, and the effect of negative mood on information processing.

Mood Congruence Effects

The adult literature supports superior encoding and retrieval of material that is congruent with the individual's current affective state (Blaney, 1986).

Some controversy exists, however, concerning the extent to which mood congruence is stronger for positive or negative moods. In general, stronger mood congruence effects have been obtained for positive mood states than for negative mood states (e.g., Singer & Salovey, 1988). The observed asymmetry has been explained as resulting from greater mood repair efforts in response to negative affect, or alternately, as due to the less extensive network of associated material for negative material. It has also been suggested that greater mood congruence effects are present for some negative affects (e.g., anger) than others (e.g., sadness; Isen, 1990).

Positive Affect and Information Processing

The adult literature is sometimes summarized as indicating that the presence of positive affect provides processing advantages. This conclusion is most defensible from the standpoint of evidence drawn from mood congruence studies, for example, access to positive material in positive mood states. However, the main beneficial effects of positive mood appear to be limited to certain aspects of processing. The overall advantage of positive moods appears to focus on the "looser" access they provide to associative networks (Fiedler, 1988)—thus facilitating more creative processes. Positive mood has been found to influence categorizational processes, such that individuals in a positive mood perceive items as more related than individuals in other moods (Isen, 1990). If an activity requires skills involving divergent thought, benefits follow from the presence of positive affect.

At the same time, positive mood may have disadvantages for the quality of processing. It has generally been observed that positive affect leads to low use of systematic or analytic processing and high reliance on simpler, heuristic processing (Isen, 1990). Adults in a positive mood are likely to engage in strategic shortcuts and nonanalytic thought. In response to persuasive arguments, adults are equally influenced by weak and strong arguments—suggesting the nonsystematic nature of their processing style (Worth & Mackie, 1987). To the extent that tasks require focused, analytic thought, positive affect may lead to processing deficits.

Negative Affect and Information Processing

Asymmetrical effects have been observed for positive and negative moods. Individuals in negative moods, like those in positive moods, appear to have a smaller working memory capacity to devote to other cognitive tasks (Darke, 1988). At the same time, negative mood states inform the individual of the possibility of threat or negative outcomes—which, in turn, may lead the individual to become more analytical in subsequent activities (Schwarz, 1990). Increases in systematic processing are directed to those events that caused the negative affect or that are relevant to eliciting events. Fiedler (1988) suggests that, under these circumstances, thoughts are characterized by "tightening."

As might be expected, the effects of negative affect on information processing are dependent on task demands. Advantages may be observed for tasks that benefit from an analytic focus. For example, individuals who have been given a problem-solving failure experience (Pittman & D'Agostino, 1985) show subsequent enhancement in the quality of their social inferences—an activity may be thought of as consistent with an analytic focus. Disadvantages are more often found for tasks that suffer from the presence of concurrent analytic activity. For example, attempts to remember a word list may be impaired following a failure experience (Ellis & Ashbrook, 1988).

Additionally, there is evidence that the effect of negative affect on memory depends on the nature of the TBR events. As suggested by Revelle and Loftus (1992), researchers who observe enhanced accuracy in memory of distressing events typically are concerned with the gist of events; researchers who find evidence for the impairment position more typically are concerned with memory for details that precede or follow an affective event. This distinction supports the notion of affect as leading to narrowed attention to central features of the event and away from peripheral components.

It appears that during negative moods, processing benefits accrue for central information or for activities that involve inference or analysis. But at the same time, processing deficits accrue for peripheral information or for activities that are resource demanding but noninferential in nature. Whereas positive affect leads to regulatory activity directed to broad approach and maintenance activities, negative affect leads to narrowly focused state-altering activities. Regulatory processes activated in response to negative affect are diverse and depend on the nature of the specific affect. Individuals in a sad mood might seek solace in the company of supportive others, whereas those in an angry mood might involve themselves in a highly active physical activity. Ultimately, the means by which states may be altered depend on characteristics of the individual and the situation.

EVIDENCE FOR THE RELATION BETWEEN AFFECT AND INFORMATION PROCESSING IN THE CHILD LITERATURE

Researchers concerned with the influence of affect on information processing in children have explored some of the same relationships as those concerned with adult processes. In summarizing the child literature, one must give close consideration to the developmental level of those studied as well as to the observational context employed. Unfortunately, there has been a tendency in this literature to make comparisons of adults versus children, without consideration of developmental level. Age comparisons are also complicated by differences in task, setting, and procedure, as well as developmental processes. At all ages, the social nature of the setting may influence the effect of affect on cognition. The presence of others may increase the demands on attentional resources. Alternately, the presence (and action) of others may facilitate affect regulation.

Mood-Congruence Effects

It has been suggested that mood-congruence effects are not as robust for children as for adults (Forgas et al., 1988). Forgas et al. (1988) conducted an impression-formation task with children between the ages of 8 and 10 who were exposed to happy or sad mood inductions. The children were then exposed to information that was consistent or inconsistent with that mood state (e.g., a picture and description of a child who was happy or sad following the viewing of mood-inducing videos). A day later, children were placed in moods that were congruent or incongruent with their initial mood state and assessed for their memory of previous events. Incongruence between initial mood and TBR events facilitated memory. Additionally, Potts, Morse, Felleman, and Masters (1986) observed that a mismatch between story valence and original subject mood facilitated memory among 7- and 8-year-olds. Forgas et al. (1988) suggest three explanations for the apparent absence of mood congruence effects among children. First, children may lack the controlled processing skills needed to maintain a focus on mood-consistent stimuli. Second, they may be more sensitive to information that is discrepant from their current mood, and thus may process inconsistent information to a greater depth. Finally, they may lack the inferential skills needed for person perception judgments.

Nasby and Yando (1982) studied 10- to 12-year-old children—an age grouping for which social cognitive competencies are well advanced. These authors observed that positive mood during encoding and retrieval facilitated recall of positive material. On the other hand, the effects of negative moods differed on the basis of the specific affects induced. Sad mood during encoding interrupted recall of positive material and had no advantage for recall of negative material. Conversely, anger during encoding interrupted recall of positive material but facilitated recall of negative material. The authors suggest that children are not as successful as adults in their ability to regulate affect, and thus show greater memory interference effects as a function of negative mood state. Alternately, one could argue that both adults and children show a consistent pattern of enhancement for recall of positive material when in a positive mood, but fail to show a uniform pattern of enhanced recall of negative material when in a negative mood. Adults appear to be more likely to show greater mood congruence effects for anger than for sadness (Isen, 1990).

No conclusions with respect to age changes in mood congruence effects can be drawn without a comparison of children of different ages exposed to the same or equivalent procedures. Nonetheless, there are some indications of greater mood congruence effects at older ages. At younger ages, children appear to be more influenced by incongruence effects and direct greater attention to stimuli that are divergent from their mood.

Positive Affect and Information Processing

Research assessing the effects of positive mood on children's cognitions yields different findings based on the nature of tasks employed. For example, Isen (1990) induced positive mood states (with a gift) among first graders, and then gave them instructions to sort stimuli. She found that children placed in a positive mood state were more likely to sort items into atypical dimensions. Additionally, Williams and Isen (reported in Isen, 1990) found that 4-year-olds showed an enhanced ability to see relations among diverse stimuli under conditions of positive affect.

Positive mood has also been observed to produce benefits for learning. Masters, Barden, and Ford (1979) asked 4-year-old children to generate thoughts about positive, neutral, and negative events; subsequently, observations were made of the children's performances on a shape discrimination learning task. The positive induction was found to increase children's performance, and the negative induction was found to lead to performance deficits. These findings are consistent with a motivational explanation of the effects of positive affect. Bartlett and Santrock (1979), studying 5-year-olds, found advantages for positive mood over negative mood in memory for words presented in affect-inducing stories. Performance advantages for positive mood state were found for recall rather tnan for recognition. This selective advantage for recall over recognition can be explained from both motivational and cognitive perspectives. Positive affect may serve as a retrieval cue for positive material (Isen, 1990)—a process that is more likely to influence recall than recognition (Bower, 1981). On the other hand, children placed in a positive mood state may be highly motivated, and thus demonstrate greater effort or more efficient use of retrieval routines.

Less evidence is available concerning potential cognitive deficits resulting from children's positive affect. As a possible exception, Bloom and Capatides have explored the age-linked association between affect and one particular type of cognitive activity—language generation (Bloom, 1993; Capatides & Bloom, 1993). These investigators observed an inverse relation between the onset and rate of language acquisition and the tendency to manifest nonverbal expressions of affect (in particular, positive affect). The authors suggest that there is a competition for limited attentional resources for children who are first acquiring language. That is, the processes involved in experiencing and expressing emotions compete for resources with the processes involved in early speech production. Bloom and Capatides do not argue that positive affect yields language production deficits; but that it may be difficult during this transitional period for the child to manage the simultaneous demands of both activities.

In summary, positive affect (at all ages) affords motivational benefits and provides a loosening of associations. But positive affect may under some circumstances compete for attentional resources with the demands of particular tasks.

Negative Affect and Information Processing

Differences in the options available for regulating negative affect at different ages can be expected to yield different consequences for cognitive processing at different stages of development. Additionally, differences may be found as a function of the observation settings employed for children of different ages (and the significance of those settings at different ages).

The most striking differences in findings within this area have emerged in the eyewitness literature. Goodman and her colleagues (Goodman, Hirschman, Hepps, & Rudy, 1991) and Peters (1991) have debated the extent to which young children show deficits in their processing of events under conditions of high anxiety. Goodman et al. (1991) report that higher levels of anxiety are associated with superior memory or are unassociated with memory. Peters (1991), on the other hand, reports that higher levels of anxiety tend to be associated with memory deficits.

In one study, Goodman and her colleagues (1991) assessed young children's memory for event-related information following a painful medical procedure (venipuncture) versus a comparable but painless procedure in the same setting (a design being rubbed onto the child's arm by a nurse). Typically, children (aged 3 to 7 years) were held on their mother's lap. Children who manifested a high level of distress were found to show greater memory of witnessed events than children who showed less distress. Although Goodman and her colleagues did not find differential recall of central versus peripheral events as a function of children's distress, they argue that the memory questions employed were primarily focused on affect-relevant information, and thus may have been subject to the enhancement effects associated with attentional narrowing. The same essential findings were replicated in a series of studies, and have been supported in other programs (e.g., Steward, 1993).

Peters (1991) assessed children's memory following their exposure to several types of stress-eliciting events. In one study, 3- to 8-year-old children experienced a (nonpainful) visit to the dentist. In a second study, 6-year-olds in a nursery school setting were exposed to a strange man who came into the room and vigorously rubbed their head while he took their pulse. In these and other situations, higher levels of distress were associated either with no difference in recall or with lower levels of recall. Some support for attentional narrowing was found; children who experienced higher levels of distress showed memory deficits that were limited to peripheral information, that is, details of the room in which the stress-inducing procedures took place.

In attempting to resolve conflicting findings between these two research programs, one must consider the social affordances typically present with the two research programs (as well as the other methodological and measurement differences that have been noted by others). In Goodman et al.'s (1991) research, children typically were in direct physical contact with their mothers during procedures. No such contact appears to have been present in Peters's (1991) observations. Close physical contact between mother and child during these procedures may have facilitated the child's ability to direct and maintain attention to stress-inducing events (rather than engaging in avoidance activities). Additionally, children in Goodman et al.'s research may have showed a pattern of affect (and autonomic) recovery as a function of the presence of the mother, whereas less opportunity for socially assisted recovery appears to have been available in Peters's research. Additionally, the context provided by caregivers for memory (at encoding, subsequent discussion, or later retrieval) may have differentially influenced children's recall of witnessed events.

AN INVESTIGATION OF AGE CHANGES IN MEMORY AS INFLUENCED BY CHANGING REGULATORY STRATEGIES

There are striking changes in the regulatory options that are available to children at different ages—in particular, with respect to negative events. We have suggested that there may be increased variability between children in the regulatory strategies they engage in middle childhood as a function of the increased role of cognitive structures (and variability in cognitive structures) at this age. Differences in regulatory processes, in turn, may be expected to have differential consequences for information processing. Consistent with this view, we explored the role of social attributions as moderators of the affect-memory tie, as well as the role of both arousal and attention as mediating mechanisms (Bugental, 1993; Bugental, Blue, Cortez, Fleck, & Rodriguez, 1992; Bugental, Cortez, & Blue, 1992). As Leichtman et al. (1992) note, "No work to date has explored the developmental implications of an attentional explanation of the affect-memory relationship" (p. 188).

Children between the ages of 5 and 10 were initially measured on a picture attribution test. Their responses were scored in terms of the control attributed to children within interpersonal interactions; on this basis, children were categorized as having high or low perceived control. Children subsequently watched a short videotape of a child having a routine medical exam. The tape was ambiguous in that no painful or distressing procedures were shown, but the room contained equipment that might be seen in an examining room. Tapes varied only in the expressive cues briefly shown for the doctor and child: smiling expressions for both (positive), a fearful expression for the child and an annoyed expression for the doctor (negative), and neutral expressions for both. These brief displays were found to induce congruent affective responses in children. Tapes were filled with various types of TBR information. After an intervening activity, children were interviewed to assess their memory for witnessed events.

As a whole, younger children were found to make significantly more errors in their recall of the miscellaneous TBR events seen in the negative condition. Older children, on the other hand, were somewhat more likely to show processing enhancement in response to negative cues (a trend that approached significance; Bugental et al., 1992). It is interesting to note that Oates and Shrimpton (1991) obtained a similar reversal between 4- to 6-year-olds and 10- to 12-year-olds in accuracy of memory for information acquired during stress-inducing (venipuncture) versus nonstressful events. Although evidence in that study was based on small samples (and no statistical information was reported regarding the interaction between age and condition), older children tended to show enhanced recall (free recall, cued recall, and response to objective questions) during stress-inducing conditions, whereas younger children showed reduced recall under the same circumstances.

In our research, significant variations were also found as a function of social attributions; but the significant effects of attributions were limited to older children. Older children with low perceived control showed processing deficits after witnessing negative social cues. In contrast, older children with high perceived control showed processing enhancement after witnessing negative social cues.

So what mediates the differential processing patterns shown at different ages and among children with high or low perceived control? An initial possibility was that of differential autonomic responses. Younger (but not older) children were found to be more likely to show elevations in autonomic arousal in response to negative social cues. Among the youngest group (5- and 6-year-olds), the greater that elevations in autonomic arousal were manifested, the higher the subsequent level of processing errors was shown (partialling out the effect of other variables in a regression analysis). This supports the expectation (Leichtman et al., 1992) that arousal has a greater effect on memory at younger ages. One may speculate that the observed pattern reflects the memory deficits that have typically been found for short-term recall as a function of high arousal. At younger ages, children appeared to be directly reactive to the experimental inductions—showing arousal and processing errors in negative inductions.

At older ages, processing patterns were sensitive to variations in children's cognitions. Children with high perceived social control responded to negative social cues with attentional engagement—a pattern that is consistent with attempts to understand a controllable stimulus. As suggested by Rholes et al. (1991), older children may show a more active, information-seeking approach to the social environment as a function of their increased under-

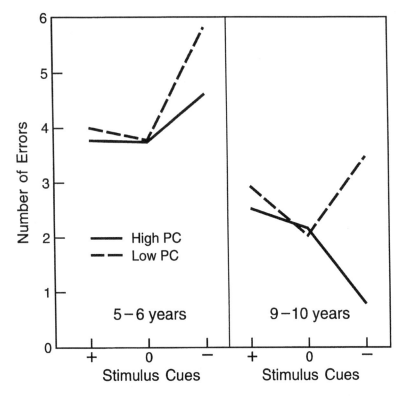

Figure 7.1. Memory Errors Shown as a Function of Induction and Perceived Control (PC)

standing of the invariance of person constructs. To this conclusion, we add that such an approach is more probable if the child's representation of a relationship with adults includes an agentic role for self.

Older children who believed they lacked control were more likely to engage regulatory processes consistent with "defense," that is, attentional avoidance. Their increasing pattern of attentional disengagement may be thought of as producing benefits for affect management but losses for the acquisition of relevant information. Memory errors for the two groups are shown in Figure 7.1.

This research is an early foray into the exploration of the complex ways in which children of different ages acquire and retain information in affect-inducing settings. We need to know more about the role of affect regulation as a mediator of this process. Additionally, more information is needed concerning variations in children's memory for salient versus peripheral events, as well as the differences that might be found in different social contexts. As a caveat, it is important to note that the children in our study faced no immediate threat but instead were exposed vicariously to the distress of another child in a personally relevant situation, that is, in a situation that they themselves had experienced. Observations were made of children who were exposed to mildly distressing stimuli while alone—a factor that may have led to unrelieved distress and greater memory impairment among younger children or among children who had a low sense of their own control.

Findings obtained for older children are consistent with the general model proposed by Bugental and her colleagues (Bugental, 1993; Bugental & Cortez, 1993; Bugental, Blue, Cortez, Fleck, & Rodriguez, 1992; Bugental, Cortez, & Blue, 1992) for caregiving adults. It is suggested within this model that caregiver attributions moderate affective responses and information-processing patterns demonstrated in interactions with challenging children. Adult caregivers with low perceived control, like older children with low perceived control, show deficits in their ability to process information when they think about or engage in challenging interactions with others (Bugental, 1993). Within the adult literature, similar processes have been studied for learned helplessness. Individuals with a pessimistic attributional style have been found to show deficits in their problem-solving ability after exposure to a helplessness induction (Abramson, Seligman, & Teasdale, 1978).

SUMMARY AND CONCLUSIONS

We have suggested that an enhanced understanding of developmental and individual variation in the relation between affect and cognition may be afforded by consideration of the role of affect regulation. Across developmental levels, individuals do not simply experience affective states—they also regulate those states in increasingly sophisticated and diverse ways. The selection of regulatory strategies in turn determines the ways in which and the effectiveness with which information processing and performance are managed.

At all ages, positive affect appears to have similar regulatory consequences and similar implications for information processing. Events that trigger positive affect foster enhanced engagement with those events. These motivational consequences produce benefits on tasks that profit from divergent thought; for example, creative activities. They also appear to produce benefits for activities that are influenced by effort. Additionally, positive mood facilitates access to or acquisition of congruent material at all ages. At the same time, positive affect may lead to deficits in cognitively demanding activities in children as well as adults. The nature of the tasks that pose cognitive demands may, of course, differ across developmental levels. Our understanding of such processes would be increased by a systematic consideration of developmental change (or invariance) in the effects of positive affect on processing patterns.

Processing changes in response to negative affect appear to be more subject to developmental variations. Our own research reveals more striking autonomic reactions to negative events at younger ages; autonomic reactions in turn, have negative consequences for memory of witnessed events. Thus the simpler biologically based regulatory processes more typically engaged at younger ages may have direct consequences for memory deficits.

In infancy and early childhood, the regulation of the child's affective state is strongly influenced by others; for example, the close presence of a supportive caregiver. For this reason, the social context (and social regulation possibilities) associated with affect-eliciting events has particular significance for the young child's ability to process and recall distressing events. Variations in the observed association between negative affect and memory may be influenced by the availability and salience of others as sources of affect regulation.

Across middle childhood, regulatory options available for the management of distress increasingly move under the control of the child's cognitive processes. Older children have a greater ability than younger children to appraise cognitively the nature of negative eliciting events and the ways in which they might cope with such events—as well as the actual skills and knowledge to cope with these events. At the same time, differences between children in their ways of thinking about relationships increasingly foster different regulatory strategies and differential success in information acquisition. Children with high perceived control are likely to show attentional engagement with negative stimuli and manifest memory enhancement effects. In contrast, children with low perceived control regulate their distress through attentional disengagement, but at a "cost" of deficits in their memory for witnessed events.

Both the social psychological literature and the developmental literature would benefit from further consideration of the role of stable representations of self and others as sources of influence on affect regulation strategies—and corresponding changes in information processing. Up to this point, concern with individual differences has focused on the effects of variations in affective reactivity, temperament, or affective disorders. Little attention has been directed to variations in affect regulation as a source of influence on information processing. Our findings with older children suggest that stressful events may trigger different regulatory strategies for children who differ in their ways of thinking about relationships. Regulatory strategies, in turn, influence children's acquisition of information. In future research, it will be useful to explore further the implications of adult as well as child regulatory processes for the effective processing of affect-eliciting events.

REFERENCES

Abramson, L. Y., Seligman, M. E. P., & Teasdale, J. (1978). Learned helplessness in humans: Critique and reformulation. *Journal of Abnormal Psychology, 87,* 49-74.

Altshuler, J. L., & Ruble, D. N. (1989). Developmental changes in children's awareness of strategies for coping with uncontrollable stress. *Child Development, 60,* 1337-1349.

Bartlett, J. C., & Santrock, J. W. (1979). Affect-dependent episodic memory in young children. *Child Development, 50,* 513-518.

Blaney, P. H. (1986). Affect and memory: A review. *Psychological Bulletin, 99,* 229-246.

Bloom, L. (1993). *The transition from infancy to language: Acquiring the power of expression.* New York: Cambridge University Press.

Bower, F. H. (1981). Mood and memory. *American Psychologist, 36,* 129-148.

Bowlby, J. (1980). *Attachment and loss: Loss, sadness, and depression.* New York: Basic Books.

Bugental, D. B. (1993, March). *Maladaptive attentional responses of children with low perceived control.* Paper presented at the Meetings of the Society for Research in Child Development, New Orleans, LA.

Bugental, D. B., Blue, J., Cortez, V., Fleck, K., & Rodriguez, A. (1992). Influences of witnessed affect on information-processing in children. *Child Development, 63,* 774-786.

Bugental, D. B., & Cortez, V. (1993, April). *Parental views of the caregiving relationship as a risk factor for child maltreatment.* Paper presented at the Meetings of the Western Psychological Association, Phoenix, AZ.

Bugental, D. B., Cortez, V., & Blue, J. (1992). Children's affective responses to the expressive cues of others. In N. Eisenberg & R. Fabes (Eds.), *New directions in child development* (pp. 75-90). San Francisco: Jossey-Bass.

Campos, J. J., Campos, R. B., & Barrett, K. C. (1989). Emergent themes in the study of emotion development and emotion regulation. *Developmental Psychology, 25,* 394-401.

Capatides, J. B., & Bloom, L. (1993). Underlying process in the socialization of emotion. In C. Rovee-Collier & L. Lipsett (Eds.), *Advances in infancy research: Vol. 8* (pp. 99-135). Norwood, NJ: Ablex.

Case, R. (1985). *Intellectual development: Birth to adulthood.* New York: Academic Press.

Christianson, S. (1992). Emotional stress and eyewitness memory: A critical review. *Psychological Bulletin, 112,* 284-309.

Craik, F. I. M., & Byrd, M. (1982). Aging and cognitive deficits: The role of attentional resources. In F. I. M. Craik & S. E. Trehub (Eds.), *Aging and cognitive processes* (pp. 191-212). New York: Plenum.

Darke, S. (1988). Effects of anxiety of inferential reasoning on performance. *Journal of Personality and Social Psychology, 55,* 499-505.

Derryberry, D., & Rothbart, M. K. (1988). Arousal, affect, and attention as components of temperament. *Journal of Personality and Social Psychology, 55,* 958-966.

Dodge, K. A., & Coie, J. D. (1987). Social information-processing factors in reactive and proactive aggression in children's peer groups. *Journal of Personality and Social Psychology, 53,* 1146-1158.

Dodge, K. A., & Garber, J. (1991). Domains of emotion regulation. In J. Garber & K. A. Dodge (Eds.), *The development of emotional regulation and dysregulation* (pp. 3-14). New York: Cambridge University Press.

Dunn, J., & Brown, J. (1991). Relationships, talk about feelings, and the development of affect regulation in early childhood. In J. Garber & K. A. Dodge (Eds.), *The development of emotional regulation and dysregulation* (pp. 89-110). New York: Cambridge University Press.

Dweck, C. S., & Leggett, E. L. (1988). A social-cognitive approach to motivation and personality. *Psychological Review, 95,* 256-273.

Easterbrook, J. A. (1959). The effect of emotion on cue utilization and the organization of behavior. *Psychological Review, 66,* 183-201.

Ellis, H. C., & Ashbrook, P. W. (1988). Resource allocation model of the effects of depressed mood on memory. In K. Fiedler & J. Forgas (Eds.), *Affect, cognition, and social behavior* (pp. 25-43). Toronto: Hogrefe.

Fabes, R. A., Eisenberg, N., & Eisenbud, L. (1993). Behavioral and physiological correlates of children's reactions to others in distress. *Developmental Psychology, 29,* 655-663.

Fiedler, K. (1988). Emotional mood, cognitive style, and behavior regulation. In K. Fiedler & J. Forgas (Eds.), *Affect, cognition, and social behavior* (pp. 100-119). Toronto: Hogrefe.

Forgas, J. P., Burnham, D. K., & Trimboli, C. (1988). Mood, memory, and social judgments in children. *Journal of Personality and Social Psychology, 54,* 697-703.

Frey, K. S., & Ruble, D. N. (1985). What children say when the teacher is not around: Conflicting goals in social comparison and performance assessment in the classroom. *Journal of Personality and Social Psychology, 48,* 550-562.

Frijda, N. H. (1986). *The emotions.* Cambridge, UK: Cambridge University Press.

Gnepp, J., & Chilamkurti, C. (1988). Children's use of personality attributions to predict other people's emotional and behavioral reactions. *Child Development, 59,* 743-754.

Gnepp, J., & Gould, M. E. (1985). The development of personalized inferences: Understanding of other people's emotional reactions in light of their prior experience. *Child Development, 56,* 1455-1464.

Goodman, G. S., Bottoms, B. L., Schwartz-Kenney, B. M., & Rudy, L. (1991). Children's memory for a stressful event: Improving children's reports. *Journal of Narrative and Life History, 1,* 69-99.

Goodman, G. S., Hirschman, J. E., Hepps, D., & Rudy, L. (1991). Children's memory for stressful events. *Merrill Palmer Quarterly, 37,* 109-158.

Hasher, L., & Zacks, R. T. (1979). Automatic and effortful processes in memory. *Journal of Experimental Psychology: General, 108,* 356-388.

Isen, A. M. (1990). The influence of positive and negative affect on cognitive organization: Some implications for development. In N. Stein, B. Leventhal, & T. Trabasso (Eds.), *Psychological and biological approaches to emotion* (pp. 75-94). Hillsdale, NJ: Erlbaum.

Jones, S. S., & Raag, T. (1989). Smile production in older infants: The importance of a social recipient for the facial signal. *Child Development, 60,* 811-818.

Kahneman, A. (1973). *Attention and effort.* Englewood Cliffs, NJ: Prentice-Hall.

Kopp, C. B. (1989). Regulation of distress and negative emotions: A developmental view. *Developmental Psychology, 25,* 341-354.

Labouvie-Vief, G., Hakim-Larson, J., DeVoe, M., & Schoeberlein, S. (1989). Emotions and self-regulation: A life-span view. *Human Development, 32,* 279-299.

Lazarus, R. S., & Folkman, S. (1984). *Stress, appraisal, and coping.* New York: Springer-Verlag.

Leichtman, M. D., Ceci, S. J., & Ornstein, P. A. (1992). The influence of affect on memory. In S. Christianson (Ed.), *Handbook of emotion and memory* (pp. 181-200). Hillsdale, NJ: Erlbaum.

Livesley, W. J., & Bromley, D. G. (1973). *Person perception in childhood and adolescence.* Chichester, UK: Wiley.

Mackie, D. M., & Worth, L. T. (1989). Cognitive deficits and the mediation of positive affect in persuasion. *Journal of Personality and Social Psychology, 57,* 27-40.

Masters, J. C. (1991). Strategies and mechanisms for the personal and social control of emotion. In J. Garber & K. A. Dodge (Eds.), *The development of emotional regulation and dysregulation* (pp. 182-207). New York: Cambridge University Press.

Masters, J., Barden, R. C., & Ford, M. (1979). Affective states, expressive behavior, and learning in children. *Journal of Personality and Social Psychology, 37,* 380-389.

Mayer, J. D., Salovey, P., Gomberg-Kaufman, S., & Blainey, K. (1991). A broader conception of mood experience. *Journal of Personality and Social Psychology, 60,* 106-111.

Moston, S., & Engelberg, T. (1992). The effect of social support on children's eyewitness testimony. *Applied Cognitive Psychology, 6,* 61-76.

Nasby, W., & Yando, R. (1982). Selective encoding and retrieval of affectively valent information: The cognitive consequences of children's mood states. *Journal of Personality and Social Psychology, 43,* 1244-1253.

Oates, K., & Shrimpton, S. (1991). Children's memories for stressful and non-stressful events. *Medicine, Science, and the Law, 31,* 4-10.

Peters, D. (1991). The influence of stress and arousal on the child witness. In J. Doris (Ed.), *The suggestibility of children's recollections* (pp. 60-76). Washington, DC: American Psychological Association.

Pittman, T. S., & D'Agostino, P. R. (1985). Motivation and cognition: Control deprivation and the nature of subsequent information-processing. *Journal of Experimental Social Psychology, 25,* 465-480.

Porges, S. W. (1991). Vagal tone: An autonomic mediator of affect. In J. Garber & K. A. Dodge (Eds.), *The development of emotional regulation and dysregulation* (pp. 111-128). New York: Cambridge University Press.

Potts, R., Morse, M., Felleman, E., & Masters, J. C. (1986). Children's emotions and memory for affective narrative content. *Motivation and Emotion, 10,* 39-57.

Revelle, W., & Loftus, D. A. (1992). The implications of arousal effects for the study of affect and memory. In S. Christianson (Ed.), *Handbook of emotion and memory* (pp. 113-150). Hillsdale, NJ: Erlbaum.

Rholes, W. S., Newman, L. S., & Ruble, D. N. (1991). Understanding self and others. In E. T. Higgins & R. M. Sorrentino (Eds.), *Handbook of motivation and cognition* (pp. 369-407). New York: Guilford.

Rholes, W. S., & Ruble, D. N. (1984). Children's understanding of dispositional characteristics of others. *Child Development, 55,* 550-560.

Rotenberg, K. J. (1982). Development of character constancy of self and other. *Child Development, 53,* 505-515.

Rothbart, M. K., Ziaie, H., & O'Boyle, C. (1992). Self-regulation and emotion in infancy. In N. Eisenberg & R. A. Fabes (Eds.), *New directions in child development: The development of self-regulation and emotion* (pp. 7-24). San Francisco: Jossey-Bass.

Saarni, C. (1984). An observational study of children's attempts to monitor their expressive behavior. *Child Development, 15,* 424-429.

Schwarz, N. (1990). Feelings as information: Informational and motivational functions of affective states. In R. Sorrentino & E. T. Higgins (Eds.), *Handbook of motivation and cognition: Foundations of social behavior: Vol. 2* (pp. 527-561). New York: Guilford.

Singer, J. A., & Salovey, P. (1988). Mood and memory: Evaluating the network theory of affect. *Clinical Psychology Review, 8,* 211-251.

Snow, M. E., Jacklin, C. N., & Maccoby, E. E. (1983). Sex-of-child differences in father-child interaction at one year of age. *Child Development, 54,* 227-232.

Steward, M. S. (1993). Understanding children's memories of medical procedures: "He didn't touch me and it didn't hurt!" *Minnesota Symposia on Child Psychology, 26,* 171-226.

Thompson, R. A. (1990). Emotion and self-regulation, socioemotional development. *Nebraska Symposium on Motivation, 1988: Vol. 36* (pp. 367-467). Lincoln: University of Nebraska Press.

Walden, T. A. (1991). Infant social referencing. In J. Garber & K. A. Dodge (Eds.), *The development of emotional regulation and dysregulation* (pp. 69-88). New York: Cambridge University Press.

Worth, C. T., & Mackie, D. M. (1987). Cognitive mediators of positive affect in persuasion. *Social Cognition, 5,* 76-94.

8

The Development of Emotional Self-Regulation in Infancy and Early Childhood

LISA J. BRIDGES
WENDY S. GROLNICK

Lisa J. Bridges is an Assistant Professor of Developmental Psychology at the University of California at Riverside. She received a Ph.D. in Psychology from the University of Rochester. Her current research interests include the development of emotional self-regulation; component process approaches to attachment, social interaction, and temperament; the role of the father in early development; and the impact of family organization and structure on children's emotional development. She has authored and coauthored numerous articles on these topics.

Wendy S. Grolnick is Assistant Professor of Psychology in the Clinical Psychology Program in the Frances L. Hiatt School of Psychology at Clark University, where she is a William T. Grant Foundation Faculty Scholar in the area of Children's Mental Health. She received a Ph.D. in Psychology from the University of Rochester. She has published numerous papers in the areas of motivational and emotional development and is particularly interested in the development of motivation and self-regulation within both family and school contexts.

Numerous perspectives on emotion and the relations among emotion, cognition, and behavior have been presented in the psychological literature. Emotions have been described as part of a motivational system leading an individual to act (Tomkins, 1970). Emotions also serve as communicative gestures (Ekman, 1984; Emde, Kligman, Reich, & Wade, 1978); the ability to express emotion adequately and to interpret the expressions of others is considered an aspect of social competence (Dodge, 1991; MacDonald & Parke, 1984; Saarni, 1979).

For emotions to fulfill these functions, however, the individual must have the capacity to regulate both the experiential and the expressive aspects of emotion (Thompson, 1990). Over the past several years, the importance of emotion regulation has gained recognition in literature on early socioemotional development. This increased recognition is reflected in face-to-face interaction research (e.g., Field, 1987; Tronick, 1989), discussions of infant-parent attachment relationships (Cassidy, in press), infant temperament research (Rothbart, 1991), and descriptions of developmental trends and

185

individual differences in the expressions of discrete emotions (Malatesta, Culver, Tesman, & Shepard, 1989).

Research in which the development of emotion regulation is the central focus is quite new, however, and much of the existing literature relevant to discussions of emotion regulation, particularly within the first few years of life, has not been well integrated. This chapter presents a theoretical perspective on emotional self-regulation and its development. We focus on normative changes and individual differences in emotional self-regulation during the infant-toddler period (from birth through approximately 3 years of age), with an emphasis on the regulation of negative emotions. However, our perspective is a life-span, developmental one that has been informed by research and theory relevant to older ages as well, and part of our goal in this chapter is to present a perspective that is relevant far beyond early childhood.

EMOTIONAL SELF-REGULATION:
STRATEGIES AND EMOTIONAL RESPONSIVENESS

We define emotional self-regulation (ESR) as the set of processes involved in initiating, maintaining, and modulating emotional responsiveness, both positive and negative. This is similar to Kopp's (1989) definition of emotion regulation as processes involved in coping with heightened levels of both positive and negative emotions, with an additional emphasis placed on initiating emotion as an integral component of emotion regulation. The term *emotional self-regulation* is used to emphasize our interest in how, over the course of development in infancy and childhood, the regulation of emotions increasingly comes under the control of the individual.

Like Kopp (1989), Tronick (1989), and others, we take as a basic premise that regulating emotion is an intrinsic goal of the individual. Functional and discrete emotion approaches (e.g., Barrett & Campos, 1987; Izard & Malatesta, 1987) emphasize the role that emotions play in motivating and directing behavior. Negative emotions signal to the individual, as well as to his or her social partners, that some action is required to alleviate negative conditions, such as hunger, boredom, or the presence of excessively unfamiliar or overwhelming stimuli. Positive emotions signal the individual to continue ongoing behavior or to increase approach behavior. Emotions can fulfill these roles because negative emotion states are inherently uncomfortable, and positive emotion states are inherently pleasurable. Hence, the individual is motivated to engage in activities that will bring high levels of negative arousal to tolerable levels, and to initiate or continue behaviors that promote positive emotion.

The ability and the tendency to self-regulate emotion depend on interdependent component processes. We distinguish between two such components: emotional responsiveness and strategy use. This distinction is similar to that made by Eisenberg and her colleagues (e.g., Eisenberg & Fabes, 1992; Eisenberg et al., 1993) between emotional intensity and regulatory processes, or emotion regulation. In our view, however, it is conceptually useful to include both responsiveness and strategy use as interacting components in an emotional self-regulatory system.

Emotional responsiveness includes the ability of individuals to regulate both the expression and the experience of various emotions, and the extent to which they do so. Individual differences in emotional responsiveness are reflected in variations in the intensity of expressions of particular emotions and in temporal characteristics of emotion such as rise time and duration of emotion states. Further, individuals differ in physiological responsiveness to stimuli in ways that are likely to influence both the experience and expression of emotional arousal (Rothbart & Posner, 1985).

ESR strategies include behaviors used by the individual to regulate emotional experience. Similar constructs have been proposed by Kopp (1989) and Gianino and Tronick (1988). ESR strategies may involve a number of different behavioral tendencies described by Rothbart (1991; Rothbart & Derryberry, 1981), such as approach or withdrawal from a stimulus, orientation of attention toward or away from a stimulus, and physical self-comforting and self-stimulation, as well as cognitive and symbolic manipulations of a situation, such as when a young child repeats "She's coming back" while waiting for the return of an absent parent.

Some ESR strategies, particularly those involving physical self-soothing, have been described as part of the expression of emotion (Fogel & Reimers, 1989) or as anxiety symptoms (Main & Solomon, 1986). Although we do not view these approaches as wrong, our focus on emotional self-regulation as an organizational construct leads us to describe these behaviors in terms of their adaptive, emotion-regulating functions, rather than as symptoms of distress.

Emotional responsiveness and ESR strategy use are interdependent components of an integrated emotional self-regulatory system. The extent to which cognitive and behavioral strategies are used within and across particular contexts by an individual depends in part on his or her general levels of responsiveness for specific emotions or types of emotion (see Barrett &

Campos, 1987). In turn, emotional responsiveness may be modified across development through the acquisition of more or less effective cognitive and behavioral ESR strategies.

THE DOMAIN OF EMOTIONAL SELF-REGULATION

Our conceptualization of emotional self-regulation is informed by work on early emotional expressiveness (Izard & Malatesta, 1987), temperament (Rothbart & Derryberry, 1981), early infant-parent interaction (Gianino & Tronick, 1988; Tronick, 1989), attachment (Ainsworth, Blehar, Waters, & Wall, 1978), behavioral self-control and delay of gratification (e.g., Block & Block, 1980; Mischel, 1974), and emotion socialization (Parke et al., 1989; Saarni, 1979). Although each of these areas of research has used terms such as *emotion regulation, emotion regulation strategies,* and *self-regulation,* the terms are used in a variety of ways. Research and theory from these areas are discussed below, when we turn to issues of developmental change and individual differences. Before doing so, however, it may be useful to describe the associations between emotional self-regulation and several of these constructs.

Attachment and Emotional Self-Regulation

Attachment and emotional self-regulation are highly related constructs (Cassidy, 1993; Kobak & Sceery, 1988). Attachment is described as an affective bond between an infant and his or her caregiver(s) (Ainsworth et al., 1978; Bretherton, 1987) that develops over the first year of life. This bond is seen in the tendency of the mobile infant to seek proximity and contact with the caregiver when facing stress or uncertainty, and to use him or her as a "secure base" for exploring the environment under more relaxed conditions.

Qualitative differences in infant-parent attachment are usually assessed in the "strange situation," a laboratory procedure developed by Ainsworth and Wittig (1969). This procedure includes two brief separations from the mother (first with an unfamiliar female in the room with the infant, later with the infant alone and then reunited with the same female "stranger"), each followed by a reunion episode with the mother. Based primarily on behaviors during reunion episodes, infant-parent relationships are classified into one of three major categories—secure, avoidant, and ambivalent—in most studies.

Secure infants use their parents as bases for exploration prior to separation. They may or may not be distressed by separation, but they clearly prefer the parent to the stranger and they engage the parent upon her return, either distally or proximally. If they are distressed by separation, they can be comforted by the parent upon her return. Avoidant and ambivalent relationships are considered insecure. Infants in avoidant relationships may not appear distressed by separation, but they demonstrate a tendency to ignore, turn away from, or move away from the parent, particularly during reunions. Infants in ambivalent relationships tend to be highly distressed by separations. During reunions, they may engage in proximity and contact-seeking behavior, but this behavior is mixed with a tendency to resist contact as well, thus giving the impression that the infants do not derive comfort from the return of the parent. Often these infants appear markedly angry, although some may also be characterized by extreme passivity. Insecure infants demonstrate little exploratory behavior, even prior to separation.

Recently, the concept of attachment has been used to describe relationships among older children, adolescents, and adults and their parents (e.g., Cassidy & Kobak, 1988; Kobak & Sceery, 1988; Main, Kaplan, & Cassidy, 1985), and between older individuals and their peers and romantic partners (Collins & Reed, 1990; Hazan & Shaver, 1987). Although the procedures for classification differ, most of these approaches derive a set of classifications that are parallel to the secure, avoidant, and ambivalent classifications in the infant-parent attachment work.

The focus of attachment research is on relationship quality, with an emphasis on the infant-mother relationship. Emotion regulation is of interest because it impacts, and is impacted by, these attachments. Variations in emotion regulation styles assist individuals in maintaining relationships that they are biologically prewired to maintain. In other words, because these relationships are seen as crucial for survival, infants develop strategies for expressing emotion that maintain the relationships to the best of their ability. For example, the avoidant behaviors and dampened emotional expressiveness of some infants may be due in part to the parent's rejection of dependent behaviors and expressions of negative emotion in the past. Because the infant relies on the parent for safety and caregiving, emotional and social behaviors that threaten to push the caregiver away from the infant are suppressed. In this sense, patterns of emotional responsiveness may become strategies for regulating the attachment relationship (Cassidy, 1993).

Different attachment styles have also been described as strategies for regulating emotion in interpersonal relationships (Cassidy, 1993; Kobak &

Sceery, 1988). The secure infant, for example, whose parent is consistently and appropriately responsive to the infant's distress signals, learns that it is acceptable to exhibit distress and to seek out actively the assistance of the parent to provide comfort in stressful situations. In contrast, the avoidant infant, due to the parent's nonresponsiveness to his or her distress signals, may be learning to inhibit emotional expressiveness as well as other-directed self-regulatory strategies such as contact-seeking and maintaining behaviors, and instead to rely on more nonsocial forms of emotion regulation.

These approaches are not entirely inconsistent with our approach to ESR development. Our view, however, is that emotion regulation is a distinct goal of the individual, partially overlapping with, and yet separable from, the goals of attachment and social interaction. Our focus is on the developing ability to self-regulate emotion across a variety of contexts—social and non-social. As Malatesta et al. (1989) note, "The affective system . . . is another organ of individual adaptation that has a broader and more differentiated mission" than the attachment system (p. 80).

Self-Control and Delay of Gratification

Two other bodies of research that have influenced our conceptualization of emotional self-regulation are the literature examining children's ability to delay gratification in favor of larger promised rewards in the future (Mischel, 1974) and that examining children's ability to refrain from touching or playing with prohibited objects (Block & Block, 1980; Funder, Block, & Block, 1983; Vaughn, Kopp, & Krakow, 1984). Despite considerable differences in these two approaches to the control of behavior, both speak to the important associations between behavior and emotion.

Mischel (1974) views delay of gratification as a cognitive competency that allows individuals to control behavior in the service of longer-range goals. Although research on delay of gratification has focused on observed behavior, using measures such as the number of seconds a child delays in obtaining an object, Mischel discusses associations between emotion regulation and behavioral self-control. In his studies, the children who were most able to delay obtaining a reward when told that they would receive a more desired reward in return for such delay were those who used techniques such as talking, singing, making up games, and resting their heads on the table, thus "converting the aversive waiting situation into a more pleasant nonwaiting one" (p. 267). Clearly these behaviors fall within the scope of the ESR strategies that are our central concern.

The perspective developed by Block and Block (e.g., 1980; Funder et al., 1983) differs from that of Mischel (1974) in that self-control is not seen as a discrete competency. Delay of gratification is a behavioral manifestation of two personality characteristics, ego control and ego resiliency. *Ego control* is the tendency to express or inhibit impulses, feelings, and desires across many domains of functioning. High levels of ego control are associated with the suppression of action and expression across contexts, regardless of the appropriateness or inappropriateness of such actions and expressions. *Ego resiliency,* on the other hand, is the extent to which ego control is modifiable based on contextual input.

The link between ESR and behavioral self-control is even stronger in the Blocks' work. Both behaviors are seen as dual manifestations of ego control and ego resiliency. The tendency to suppress impulses extends to the tendency to suppress emotions as well. Ego resiliency is exhibited both in the extent to which behavioral self-control can be modified to meet contextual demands, and in the extent to which the individual's general tendencies to express or inhibit the expression of emotions are similarly modifiable.

Our conceptual and empirical work has been strongly influenced by this literature. Given our focus on development in the infant-toddler period, as well as our view that emotional self-regulation is a central organizing construct in early development, however, we have moved the focus away from behavioral self-control. We are interested in the manner in which young children regulate the negative emotions that go along with frustration, separation, and other emotion-arousing situations. Developmentally, emotional self-regulation is evident from early infancy, with relatively rapid changes both in the extent to which emotions are expressed and in the types of strategies available for self-regulation. In contrast, Vaughn and his colleagues (1984) suggest that behavioral self-control develops more slowly, with stable individual differences beginning to emerge in the third year of life. Early individual differences in emotional self-regulation may be associated with later individual differences in behavioral self-control (Kopp, 1989), and behavioral self-control may also be greatly influenced by the concurrent ability to regulate the experience of negative emotion within particular contexts and across contexts.

Emotion Socialization and Emotion Control

Emotion socialization and *emotion control* tend to be used to describe how individuals learn to express emotion appropriately and to control inappropriate responses in particular social contexts. Researchers concerned with emotion socialization are also concerned with the developing ability to interpret the nonverbal emotional signals of others. This ability is an important aspect of emotional self-regulation, facilitating competent social interactions (Dodge, 1991; Parke et al., 1989; Saarni, 1979). Emotional self-regulation is, however, a broader construct, the core of which involves regulation of the experience of emotion, rather than the social control of emotional expression. Our interest lies not only in the when and how much questions that are asked in the emotion socialization literature, but in how individuals regulate their emotions—what strategies they have developed to control emotional expression and experience.

Coping

Coping and emotional self-regulation are highly related concepts. Most or all behaviors identified as coping strategies are also considered ESR strategies. One difference is that theoretical and empirical approaches to coping among older children and adults place an appropriately greater emphasis on cognitive strategies and active behaviors designed to alleviate sources of stress. Lazarus and Folkman (1984) describe problem-focused and emotion-focused coping as distinct forms of coping observable in children and adults. *Problem-focused coping* involves active efforts to modify conditions that are aversive to the individual. *Emotion-focused coping,* on the other hand, involves efforts to modify or manage emotional responses to an aversive condition. Both problem-focused and emotion-focused coping behaviors are included in our conceptualization of ESR strategies.

Because of the limited, although rapidly developing, ability of young children to modify their environments through their own activities, there may be even less distinction between coping and emotional self-regulation in the infant-toddler period. Gianino and Tronick (1988) suggest that the principal difference between coping and emotional self-regulation in early childhood may be the types of conditions with which the individual is dealing. Self-regulation of emotion is an ongoing process, most obvious under conditions of stress. The term *coping* tends to refer to a response to a negative, stressful situation or condition that is objectively outside of the bounds of "normal" everyday stressors. Experiences of effective emotional self-regulation in the face of everyday stressors may promote effective coping under more extreme circumstances (Gianino & Tronick, 1988; Grolnick & Bridges, 1993; Kopp, 1989).

Summary

Much literature has served as the foundation for the study of emotional self-regulation. In this section, we attempted to provide some conceptual links between our views of emotional self-regulation and some of the work that may be more widely known to social and personality psychologists, as well as to developmental researchers. In the remaining sections, we focus on developmental trends and individual differences in emotional self-regulation in infancy and early childhood.

THE DEVELOPMENT OF EMOTIONAL SELF-REGULATION

Normative developmental changes in emotional responsiveness and in the use of ESR strategies are evident. Changes in the intensity and temporal patterning of emotional responses, as well as in the types of discrete or blended emotions elicited by particular stimuli, depend in part on physiological and cognitive development. Similarly, some ESR strategies await the development of cognitive abilities that are not present in the young infant. Other strategies that may be present in rudimentary form from earliest infancy require physical and cognitive maturation in order to be considered fully self-regulatory.

Over the infancy period, emotional responsiveness becomes less unstable, with emotion states tending to persist longer (given more or less constant contextual factors) and to transition more gradually (Izard & Malatesta, 1987). At the same time, given a contextual shift such as a parent's departure, negative emotional reactions may occur more rapidly and with higher intensity during later infancy than they did earlier (Thompson, 1990). Izard and his colleagues have conducted both cross-sectional (Izard, Hembree, Dougherty, & Spizzirri, 1983) and longitudinal (Izard, Hembree, & Huebner, 1987) examinations of age-related changes in the expression of discrete emotions, such as anger and sadness, and affects such as pain in response to DPT injections in children 2 to 19 months of age. Among their results, these researchers found that the length of time to recover from distress decreases with age, with a particularly strong decline between 2 and 4 months of age. These results, demonstrating age-related changes in aspects of emotional and, more generally, affective responsiveness, indicate that changes occur in the extent to which infants regulate their emotions.

Researchers examining the facial expression of discrete emotions have also found that there is an increasing tendency to express blended emotions, rather than single emotion expressions, with age. Lip compression, an expression that is not part of a discrete emotion and that is not seen in early infancy, is apparent in a substantial number of children by 2 years of age (Malatesta et al., 1989). The use of both blended emotion expressions and compressed lips has been suggested as an indicator that emotion expressions are being regulated. For example, lip compression may represent an effort to suppress a full-blown anger or fear response. Later in childhood, lip compression may also be used to suppress full-blown pleasure in conditions where such expressions may be deemed inappropriate. Differential emotions theory (e.g., Izard & Malatesta, 1987; Malatesta et al., 1989) suggests that the correspondence between expression and experience is very strong in the early years of life, with decreasing concordance across childhood and beyond. It may be suggested, then, that the experience of emotion is similarly more strongly regulated with development across the infant/toddler period.

Developmental changes in the use of particular ESR strategies have been less well documented empirically. However, there are developmental trends in the availability of a variety of ESR strategies. In early infancy, infant gaze may be captured by particular stimulus characteristics, leading to obligatory attention (see Rothbart, 1989). However, by 2 to 3 months, greater control of gaze is evident in infants (Olson & Sherman, 1983), and regulation of visual attention appears to be used by infants as a strategy for emotional self-regulation. This can be seen, for example, in the tendency of infants to avert their gaze periodically as arousal increases during face-to-face interactions (Tronick, 1989).

Physical self-soothing behaviors such as thumb sucking and hair twisting are also among the earliest actions that appear to have a self-regulatory function. Even prior to the age when infants can voluntarily move hand to mouth, nonnutritive sucking on a thumb or pacifier can produce temporary soothing (Kessen & Leutzendorff, 1963). By 4 months of age, these movements become purposeful and directed. At this point, such behaviors may be seen as ESR strategies (Demos, 1986). Physical self-soothing behaviors continue to be evident from early infancy onward in situations of stress. In one of the few studies to examine emotional self-regulatory behaviors in infancy specifically, Stifter (1993) reports that physical self-soothing behaviors are significantly more frequent than other self-regulatory behaviors during mildly frustrating situations at both 5 and 10 months of age. Further, these behaviors are more effective in reducing distress on the part of the infant than other behaviors assessed in this study, such as turning away from the frustrating object.

The capacity for emotional self-regulation during the first few months of life is limited, however, and tends to be possible only under conditions of low to moderate arousal (Kopp, 1989). In the face of stronger arousal, the young infant requires the participation of a responsive caregiver to assist in the regulation of his or her emotional state. For example, infants require caregivers to provide physical care and social interaction (including engagement and appropriate disengagement) in response to their emotion signals and levels of arousal.

Social partners continue to be important sources of emotion regulation throughout infancy and beyond. During the latter half of the first year, however, a change occurs in this initially external source of emotion regulation. Locomotor infants seek out proximity or contact with caregivers actively under conditions of uncertainty or stress, and they use the caregiver as a "secure base" for their exploratory efforts (Bowlby, 1969). Thus the use of the caregiver may be viewed as a self-initiated emotion regulation strategy.

Other ESR strategies become available as symbolic and linguistic capabilities increase toward the end of the second year and beyond. When the child develops the ability to understand the goals of an attachment partner who is an autonomous individual (i.e., when a *goal-corrected partnership* has been established; Bowlby, 1969), the child may be able to regulate distress during a separation by reminding himself or herself why the parent left and when he or she will return. Other phrases or suggestions, many provided by caregivers, may be adopted by the young child attempting to deal with a stressful situation (e.g., "I'm a big girl"; "I don't like that thing"). Children may also employ their newly acquired cognitive skills to create pretend scenarios or reenactments of situations that have caused them anxiety or distress. Piaget (1962) notes that this form of pretend play appears to serve an assimilative function for children, helping them integrate novel experiences, thus reducing their levels of uncertainty and distress.

In an ongoing cross-sectional study of infants and toddlers at 12-13, 18-19, 24-25, and 32-33 months of age, we are examining the use of ESR strategies in a laboratory playroom setting. Two separate visits, spaced 4 weeks apart, were conducted with each subject and his or her mother. One assessment included two mildly frustrating delay situations during which an attractive object (a snack or a brightly wrapped present) was placed out of reach but within sight of the infant. In one delay the mother was asked to read a magazine and to be minimally responsive to her child. In the other delay no such restriction was placed on the mother's interactions with her child. The other visit included a brief period when the child was left alone and then joined by a slightly familiar female experimenter. A parallel study with 3½- to 4½-year-olds, including frustrating delay situations only, was also conducted.

Our coding strategy for this work has been to note the presence of particular ESR strategies, such as those described earlier, in brief intervals across the duration of each episode of delay and separation. A preliminary examination of the mean percentages of intervals during which infants and toddlers engaged in each of the coded ESR strategies at each age for each situation suggests age trends for some strategies. Other strategies do not appear to vary across the ages examined. One strategy that appears to become more frequent involves *active engagement,* when the child reorients attention away from the potentially stressful aspect of the environment toward other objects and nonsocial activities. Active engagement includes actively playing with toys and other objects in the room (other than the delay object), and exploring the room in systematic and focused ways. Age-related increases were particularly evident in the delay situation during which the mother was asked to remain passive, where the presence of nonsocial active engagement increased from 13.06% of intervals at 12 months and 12.34% at 18 months to 18.86% at 24 months, 25.14% at 32 months, and 60.72% at 3½-4½ years.

Another type of active engagement possible in situations in which another individual is present involves attempts to engage that person in play or playful conversation. Directed smiling, showing toys, positive or neutral vocalizations, and verbal requests for play are included in this strategy. In the mother-passive delay situation, these social forms of active engagement increased in prevalence from less than 1% of all intervals at 12 months to 4.44% at 18 months, 8.50% at 24 months, 17.04% at 32 months, and 25.28% at 3½-4½ years. In the delay situation where the mother was available to be an active play partner, the mean percentage of intervals including adult-oriented active engagement increased even more dramatically, from a low of 16.66% of intervals at 12 months to 88.56% of intervals at 3½-4½ years, whereas nonsocial active engagement did not increase substantially.

At the same time that active engagement appears to increase across the ages studied, less focused orientation of attention and activity away from the potential source of stress within each of the playroom situations tends to decrease. There is also a sharp drop between 32 months and 3½-4½ years in another emotional self-regulatory strategy we examined, other-directed comfort-seeking attempts in the parent-passive frustrating delays (27.89% and 1.14% of intervals, respectively). The impression is, then, that older toddlers and preschool-aged children are more able to distract themselves from a potentially distressing or frustrating situation by playing on their own in situations where the parent is otherwise engaged and more able to make more playful initiatory attempts in their interactions with adults. At the same time, they demonstrate a decreased tendency to seek attention from a preoccupied parent by seeking proximity and comfort relative to the younger infants and toddlers.

Other ESR strategies examined in this study did not vary consistently across age. These include physical self-soothing behaviors in all situations and actively searching for the parent. Symbolic ESR strategies such as those described earlier were rare or nonexistent at all ages, as would be expected given the young ages of the subjects. Stronger age-related trends in more cognitive and symbolic ESR strategies may be more evident in examinations of older children using self-report as well as observational measures.

Summary

Developmental trends in emotional responsiveness in the infant-toddler period have been clearly described both by researchers who use discrete measures of specific facial expressions of emotion (e.g., Izard & Malatesta, 1987; Malatesta et al., 1989) and by those who use more global measures of distress (see Thompson, 1990). Fewer studies have been conducted to examine developmental trends in the acquisition and utilization of behavioral strategies for emotional self-regulation specifically. ESR strategies may be normatively developmentally acquired due in part to maturational changes in physical and cognitive capabilities (Rothbart, 1991) and to normative experiences, particularly in important social relationships (Malatesta et al., 1989; Thompson, 1990).

Strategies are not lost, however; nor are they completely replaced. Even as adults, we engage in physical self-soothing behaviors such as sucking our fingers or twisting strands of hair, and we seek out the company of loved ones when distressed. Over the course of development, the individual may acquire a repertoire of ESR strategies, any of which could be used in the appropriate circumstances. These strategies may become hierarchically organized, as part of an integrated emotional self-regulatory system, according to the extent to which they are appropriate for, and effective within, particular developmental periods (Cole & Kaslow, 1988).

INDIVIDUAL DIFFERENCES IN
EMOTIONAL SELF-REGULATION

Although normative developmental trends are expected in both emotional responsiveness and ESR strategy use, individual differences in emotional responsiveness in infancy and early childhood are well documented. Izard et al. (1987), for example, found stable individual differences in the expression of the discrete emotions of anger and sadness in response to DPT injections from assessments made in early infancy (at 2, $4\frac{1}{2}$, and 7 months) to an assessment at 19 months. Hyson and Izard (1985) found moderate to extremely strong relations between 13 and 18 months in the facial expression of negative emotion during the infant-alone separation episode of the strange situation.

Numerous other researchers have found consistent individual differences in irritability or distress-proneness during infancy and toddlerhood (e.g., Matheny, Riese, & Wilson, 1985; Riese, 1987; Rothbart, 1986). Connell and Thompson (1986) found significant consistency for measures of negative emotionality assessed during the strange situation at 13 and 19 months of age. In our work, we have found that infant emotional responsiveness in strange situation separation and reunion episodes is consistent across assessments with the mother and the father, conducted approximately 1 month apart at 12 and 13 months (Bridges & Connell, 1991; Bridges, Connell, & Belsky, 1988).

As in the area of developmental trends, few researchers have conducted studies examining individual differences in the use of ESR strategies. In one study designed to examine consistencies and inconsistencies in infant attachment-related behaviors with mothers and fathers, we found that the tendencies of infants to engage in proximity- and contact-seeking behaviors with parents during reunion episodes of the strange situation, and to seek proximity, contact, and distance interaction with unfamiliar adults during separation episodes, were significantly correlated across assessments with the mother and the father (Bridges & Connell, 1991). This suggests that behavioral strategies such as comfort seeking and active reorientation to a social partner are not exclusive to specific attachment relationships and may be indicative of developing ESR strategies.

CONTRIBUTORS TO INDIVIDUAL
DIFFERENCES IN EMOTIONAL SELF-REGULATION

What are the sources of individual differences in the functioning of the emotional self-regulatory system? In this section, we focus on two contributors to individual differences: temperamental characteristics and experiences within relationships (most notably parent-child relationships). A third potential contributor, context-specific experiences, has received considerably less empirical and theoretical attention, and is not discussed here. Although these contributors are mutually interrelated, we find it to be conceptually useful to discuss their influences on the development of individual differences in ESR strategies and emotionality separately.

Temperamental/Constitutional Influences

Several different perspectives on temperament are prominent in the literature on early emotional development (Goldsmith et al., 1987). These perspectives differ with respect to the boundaries they propose for the concept of temperament, including the particular dimensions of temperament, the extent to which temperamental characteristics are necessarily genetic or constitutional in origin, and the extent to which consistency or change in temperament may be expected across development.

Despite their differences, however, there are areas of convergence. Most temperament theorists agree that temperament involves individual differences in a set of personality characteristics that are evident from early in life, that demonstrate some stability across time, and that have some constitutional basis. Further, every major theory of temperament includes emotionality in some form in the definition of the construct (Goldsmith et al., 1987). For example, Goldsmith and Campos (1982) define temperament as individual differences in the expression of basic emotions such as anger, sadness, fear, pleasure, and interest. In an approach that is highly relevant to our work, Rothbart and her colleagues (e.g., Rothbart & Derryberry, 1981; Rothbart & Posner, 1985) define temperament as constitutionally based individual differences in reactivity and self-regulation. The primary way in which nontemperamental factors influence emotional self-regulation, according to Rothbart (1989), is when cognitive and linguistic skills develop sufficiently to allow an individual to override temperamental characteristics.

Support for temperamental influences on ESR comes from research, such as that cited above, indicating consistency in emotionality or patterns of discrete emotion expression across time. Other support comes from reports suggesting consistency in emotion-relevant observational and parent-report temperament assessments (see Bates, 1987, and Rothbart, 1991), research demonstrating associations between biological indicators of arousal and emotional expression and experience (Rothbart & Posner, 1985), and studies of monozygotic and dizygotic twins supporting the presence of a significant heritable component to individual differences in negative emotionality (Emde et al., 1992).

Relational Influences

Associations between emotional responsiveness and qualitative aspects of infant-parent interaction have been examined in a variety of ways. The types of research involved are diverse, including face-to-face interaction research and examinations of individual differences in infant-parent attachment security. Most of this work has been conducted with mothers. Some researchers have also begun to examine early father-child relationships and the contributions of these relationships to emotional development.

Early Infant-Parent Interaction

Much of the research on early infant-parent interaction has focused on the mutual expression and regulation of affect in dyadic, usually face-to-face, interactions. Similarities in maternal and infant emotional expressions have been found to appear quite early in infancy. Malatesta and her colleagues (Malatesta et al., 1989) found concordance in expressions of positive emotion and surprise at $2\frac{1}{2}$, 5, $7\frac{1}{2}$, and 22 months, and compressed lip expressions at $7\frac{1}{2}$ and 22 months. Other researchers have found that the ability of the mother to be appropriately responsive to the infant's interactive behaviors (e.g., smiling and vocalizing when the infant orients to her, quieting and sitting back when the infant turns away) is associated with increasing positive emotionality and longer and more smoothly transitioning bouts of attending to social partners on the part of the infant (e.g., Gianino & Tronick, 1988; Tronick, 1989).

On the other hand, it has been suggested that persistent maternal nonresponsiveness or misreading of infant cues may have long-term implications for the development of affective and interactive difficulties (Field, 1987; Tronick, 1989). Langhorst and Fogel (1982), for example, report that the frequency and intensity of avoidance in the strange situation at infant-age 12 months was inversely correlated with the maternal tendency to decrease activity when the infant averted his or her gaze during face-to-face interactions at 3 months. This suggests that maternal insensitivity to infant signals that stimulation is becoming overwhelming and that self-regulation is required may lead infants to become increasingly persistent in their efforts to self-regulate emotion through the use of avoidant behaviors.

Attachment and Emotion Regulation

The establishment of clear-cut attachment relationships toward the end of the first year of life is a well-researched milestone in socioemotional development. It has been suggested that attachment classifications may be conceptualized as styles of regulating emotions within relationships (Cassidy, 1993; Kobak & Sceery, 1988). Secure, avoidant, ambivalent infants do not neatly differentiate along the lines of emotional responsiveness, however. Secure infants are diverse with respect to emotional expressiveness and types of attachment behaviors exhibited. Whereas some secure infants are not highly distressed by separations and tend to engage in relatively high levels of affectively neutral-to-positive social interactions without particularly seeking contact or proximity with the parent during reunion episodes, others are more distressed during separations and are more likely to engage in high levels of proximity and contact-seeking behavior. Avoidant infants are often described as being lower in expressed negative emotionality than secure infants (however, see Braungart & Stifter, 1991), whereas ambivalent infants are described as being higher in distress.

Other studies examining discrete emotion expressions have found some differences between secure and insecure infants. Malatesta et al. (1989) found that insecure infants showed enhanced interest expressions in reunions, relative to secure infants. Insecure boys showed more compressed lip expressions during both preseparation play and in reunions. In Malatesta et al.'s study, almost all of the insecure infants were classified as avoidant. Ambivalent infants have been found to demonstrate fewer interest expressions and more sadness expressions than secure infants (Shiller, Izard, & Hembree, 1986).

Few studies have assessed relations between the infant-parent attachment and ESR strategy use, although most of the social interactive behaviors that differentiate attachment groups may be considered strategies for regulating emotion. Braungart and Stifter (1991) found that avoidant infants were more likely to use self-comforting behaviors such as thumb sucking than secure infants. In reunions, avoidant infants were also less likely to orient to the mother and more likely to play with toys.

Taken together, these studies support a strong association between developing styles of emotional self-regulation and infant-mother attachment. The presence of enhanced interest and compressed lip expressions among avoidant infants within situations that most infants find at least mildly stressful supports the suggestion that avoidant infants are developing a style of emotional self-regulation in the infant-mother relationship in which the expressive aspects of negative emotional responsiveness are suppressed. At the same time, the presence of avoidant behaviors that are the principal defining characteristics of avoidant infants suggests that the tendency to engage in other-directed self-regulatory strategies is being suppressed, and more nonsocial strategies (such as playing with or fingering toys and thumb sucking) are being utilized.

The Infant-Father Relationship

A small but growing number of reports suggest that the infant-father relationship may contribute uniquely to early emotional development, particularly to expressive aspects of emotional responsiveness. Parke (e.g., MacDonald & Parke, 1988) suggests that children learn a great deal about emotional expression in high-energy play, often described as characteristic of infant-father interactions. Fathers, at least those who are not primary caregivers, may feel somewhat freer than primary caregiving mothers to promote high levels of arousal in their children, rather than trying to keep their children in a mildly positive state of emotional arousal (see Malatesta, 1982). Therefore, father-child play may contain a wider range of emotion on the part of both parent and child than mother-child play. This extended range of emotional expressions on the part of both partners in father-child play may provide opportunities for the child to learn about appropriate and competent ways to express emotions in social interactions, as well as to interpret accurately the emotional expressions of others, thus providing unique emotion socialization opportunities for children.

Little empirical work has directly addressed the relative influence of the father-child relationship on emotional development. In examinations of preschool parent-child interactions, Parke and his colleagues (Parke et al., 1989) found stronger relations between children's peer competence and qualitative assessments of father-child play than mother-child play interactions, particularly for boys. Bridges et al. (1988) found that individual differences in negative emotion exhibited in the first reunion of the strange situation were more strongly and uniquely associated with emotionality with the stranger in a subsequent separation in the infant-father assessment than in the infant-mother assessment. Although highly speculative at this point, this work suggests that the father-child relationship in infancy and early childhood may have a particularly strong and unique influence on social, expressive aspects of emotional responsiveness.

Summary

Consistent individual differences in emotional responsiveness in the infant-toddler period have been demonstrated in numerous studies. Researchers examining facial expressions of discrete emotions have described changes in these facial expressions that may reflect increased self-regulation of emotions. Although little research has been conducted to examine individual differences in ESR strategy use directly, research on infant-parent relationships indicates that consistent individual differences in attachment-related behaviors may be considered emotional self-regulatory strategies. Contributors to these developing individual differences in the infant-toddler period include temperamental characteristics and characteristics of relationships with both mothers and fathers.

OPTIMAL DEVELOPMENT OF
EMOTIONAL SELF-REGULATION

In this section, we turn to the issue of how optimal development of emotional self-regulation should be characterized. Optimal development cannot be described in terms of specific ESR strategies, or in terms of levels of emotional responsiveness for different emotions. Rather, optimal development involves the flexibility of adaptiveness of the individual, reflected in the ability to use a range of possible strategies, depending on their appropriateness in given contexts. For example, seeking out the parent for comfort or security may be a highly effective strategy when the parent is available. It is not an effective strategy in the short run when the parent is absent, however. This approach is conceptually similar to the constructs of ego control and ego resiliency described by Block and Block (1980).

One example of the necessity for flexibility in ESR strategy use is provided by Compas (1993), who reports that children whose parents are suffering with severe medical conditions tend to display healthier psychological adjustment when their coping efforts are directed at their own thoughts and feelings about the situation, rather than at attempting to alleviate the parent's condition. Children and adults who are prone to use problem-focused coping efforts may tend to be more successful copers than those who rely on emotion-focused efforts. However, problem-focused coping may not be appropriate for every instance in which coping is required, such as when there is little that an individual can do to alter an objectively stressful situation. The individual must demonstrate sufficient flexibility to alter his or her modal forms of self-regulation in order to adequately function across contexts.

In the absence of adequate flexibility, behaviors that are optimal in a given context or relationship, or at a given age, may carry over into other contexts and relationships, where they become maladaptive (Cole & Zahn-Waxler, 1992; Malatesta & Wilson, 1988). An avoidant interactive style on the part of an infant whose parent is prone to reject contact and interactive bids may be highly adaptive in the short term. However, this avoidant style may lead the individual to develop persistent maladaptive patterns of interaction, leading to further emotional and social difficulties (Sroufe & Fleeson, 1985).

In one relevant study, Kobak and Sceery (1988) used procedures developed by Main and her colleagues (Main et al., 1985) to classify attachment organization in late adolescence. The focus of these procedures is on evaluating subjects' relationships with their parents during childhood. Three classifications are derived: secure, dismissive, and preoccupied. These classifications parallel the secure, avoidant, and ambivalent classifications used with infants and toddlers, and they are believed to be developmentally related as well. In other words, a secure attachment with the caregiver during early childhood is likely to predict secure attachment in adulthood; avoidant early relationships are reflected in a later dismissive attachment style; and early ambivalence is associated with continued anxious preoccupation with attachment issues in adulthood. In Kobak and Sceery's (1988) study, college students who were classified as dismissing of relationships (i.e., who consistently downplayed the importance of attachments and had difficulty recalling specific attachment experiences from childhood) were rated by their peers as higher in hostility than were secure or preoccupied students.

Kobak and Sceery (1988) suggest that this hostility toward peers may be displaced hostility engendered in the parent-child relationship. Other attachment researchers have suggested that this hostility is an additional manifestation of the internal working model of attachment relationships developed through a relationship history with a parent who is rejecting and hostile toward expressions of dependency and attachment needs (see Cassidy, 1993; Main et al., 1985; Sroufe & Fleeson, 1985).

A focus on emotional self-regulation suggests a somewhat different approach to explaining the hostility of these adolescents. Attachment figures who are nonresponsive to a child's distress, and who may also be somewhat punishing of signs of dependency on the part of the infant, are teaching their children to minimize negative emotion in stressful circumstances and to rely on their own, essentially nonsocial, ESR strategies to aid this minimization. One such strategy is redirecting attention away from the parent. Over time, this redirecting of attention away from social partners may become a general, inflexible strategy for regulating emotion. Interactive attempts by others may then become dysregulating experiences for the individual, potentially leading to expressions of more or less overt anger and hostility.

Flexibility may also be the hallmark of optimal development of expressive aspects of emotional responsiveness, such that the individual is able to express high intensity emotions when it is safe or appropriate to do so (e.g., crying and expressing intense sadness in the company of sympathetic others, expressing intense joy in the presence of a responsive partner), although at the same time being able to minimize emotional expressiveness when necessary. Optimal development in the experiential aspects of emotional responsiveness certainly does not lie in the persistent minimization of emotion. Rather, optimal functioning involves the ability of the individual to experience genuine emotions across a range of intensities without perceiving himself or herself to be "out of control" and overwhelmed by intense emotion (Cole & Kaslow, 1988).

Some additional work on children's coping supports the view that optimal functioning involves flexibility in choosing among ESR strategies. Siegel (1983) found that children who reported greater numbers of potential coping strategies demonstrated more successful coping with hospitalization for elective surgery than those who described fewer strategies. Consistent with the view that ESR strategies are not lost with the development of additional strategies, Weisz and Dennig (1993) suggest that children may develop hierarchies of coping strategies, "each focused on successively less desirable objectives" (p. 7). Such a hierarchy allows an individual (at any age) to continue to meet some goals, even though others may be temporarily or permanently unobtainable. As an example, these authors describe a possible sequence of coping behaviors for a child whose parents are engaged in violent conflict. The child might first attempt to intervene directly between the parents. If this is unsuccessful, the child might seek instrumental assistance from others, followed by attempting to withdraw from the situation, and eventually seeking out another individual for emotional support. With respect to the multiplicity of goals that a child has within a family (e.g., affiliation, safety, avoiding experiences of negative emotion), Weisz and Dennig are likely correct in describing each of these coping strategies as oriented to progressively more modest sets of goals. The ESR goal of these behaviors is consistent, however. The child is attempting, in the face of a highly nonresponsive environment and with whatever resources he or she has available, to reduce his or her experienced distress.

Optimal emotional self-regulation is flexible emotional self-regulation. Throughout childhood and into adulthood, flexibility may lead to a perception of autonomous functioning in the emotion domain. The well-regulated individual does not feel controlled by his or her emotions, and does not feel compelled to use one or a very few strategies to regulate them. Rather, the individual feels in control of his or her emotions. Although it cannot be said that an infant or toddler "feels autonomous" with respect to his or her emotions, we believe that the roots of flexibility and experience of autonomy begin in this early developmental period.

SUMMARY

In this chapter, we presented a new conceptualization of emotional self-regulation and its development. We suggested that emotional self-regulation is a central goal of the individual from early infancy that is not derived from other goals such as the maintenance of attachment relationships with caregivers. This goal is met through social interactive processes, as well as through processes that are not inherently social, such as physical self-soothing behaviors and orientation of attention. Viewing emotional self-regulation as an organizational construct leads us to an understanding that a variety of different ESR strategies may be utilized to achieve the same goal—the regulation of emotion. Some strategies may be more effective in the long run and across situations. Optimal functioning is facilitated, however, by the development of a repertoire of ESR strategies that may be chosen from according to their usefulness for particular contexts and situations.

Research is beginning to accumulate demonstrating that developmental trends and individual differences in emotional self-regulation occur within the infant-toddler period and beyond. Such individual differences are likely to be associated with variations in infant temperament and early experience, particularly experience in important caregiving relationships. A specific focus on emotional self-regulation is a recent trend in the literature on early socioemotional development; however, much work remains to be done. Several researchers (e.g., Gianino & Tronick, 1988; Stifter, 1993) are now using approaches to the assessment of emotional self-regulation that are similar to our own, examining infant utilization of a set of emotional self-regulatory strategies across a variety of contexts and the associations between strategy use and emotional responsiveness. Although much work remains to be done to assess the usefulness of this approach for evaluating individual differences in socioemotional functioning and the associations between such individual differences and later functioning, we feel that this is an exciting new approach that will add considerably to our understanding of social and personality development.

REFERENCES

Ainsworth, M. D. S., & Wittig, M. (1969). Attachment and exploratory behavior of one-year-olds in a strange situation. In B. M. Foss (Ed.), *Determinants of infant behavior: Vol. 4* (pp. 111-136). London: Methuen.

Ainsworth, M. D. S., Blehar, M. C., Waters, E., & Wall, S. (1978). *Patterns of attachment: A psychological study of the strange situation.* Hillsdale, NJ: Erlbaum.

Barrett, K. C., & Campos, J. J. (1987). Perspectives on emotional development II: A functionalist approach to emotions. In J. D. Osofsky (Ed.), *Handbook of infant development* (2nd ed., pp. 555-578). New York: John Wiley.

Bates, J. E. (1987). Temperament in infancy. In J. D. Osofsky (Ed.), *Handbook of infant development* (2nd ed., pp. 1101-1169). New York: John Wiley.

Block, J. H., & Block, J. (1980). The role of ego-control and ego-resiliency in the organization of behavior. In W. A. Collins (Ed.), *Minnesota Symposia on Child Psychology: Vol. 13* (pp. 39-101). Hillsdale, NJ: Erlbaum.

Bowlby, J. (1969). *Attachment and loss: Vol. I.* New York: Basic Books.

Braungart, J. M., & Stifter, C. A. (1991). Regulation of negative reactivity during the strange situation: Temperament and attachment in 12-month-old infants. *Infant Behavior and Development, 14,* 349-364.

Bretherton, I. (1987). New perspectives on attachment relations: Security, communication, and internal working models. In J. Osofsky (Ed.), *Handbook of infant development* (pp. 1061-1100). New York: John Wiley.

Bridges, L. J., & Connell, J. P. (1991). Consistency and inconsistency in infant emotional and social interactive behavior across contexts and caregivers. *Infant Behavior and Development, 14,* 471-487.

Bridges, L. J., Connell, J. P., & Belsky, J. (1988). Infant-mother and infant-father interaction in the strange situation: A component process analysis. *Developmental Psychology, 24,* 92-100.

Cassidy, J. (in press). Emotion regulation: Influences of attachment relationships. In N. Fox (Ed.), Biological and behavioral foundations of emotion regulation. *Monographs of the Society for Research in Child Development.*

Cassidy, J., & Kobak, R.R. (1988). Avoidance and its relation to other defensive processes. In J. Belsky & T. Nezworski (Eds.), *Clinical implications of attachment* (pp. 300-323). Hillsdale, NJ: Erlbaum.

Cole, P. M., & Kaslow, N. J. (1988). Interactional and cognitive strategies for affect regulation: Developmental perspective on childhood depression. In L. Alloy (Ed.), *Cognitive processes in depression* (pp. 310-343). New York: Guilford.

Cole, P. M., & Zahn-Waxler, C. (1992). Emotional dysregulation in disruptive behavior disorders. In D. Cicchetti & S. L. Toth (Eds.), *Rochester symposium on developmental psychology: Vol. 4: Developmental perspectives on depression* (pp. 173-210). Rochester, NY: University of Rochester Press.

Collins, N. L., & Reed, S. L. (1990). Adult attachment, working models, and relationship quality in dating couples. *Journal of Personality and Social Psychology, 58,* 644-663.

Compas, B. E. (1993, March). *An analysis of "good" stress and coping in adolescence.* Paper presented at the Biennial Meeting of the Society for Research in Child Development, New Orleans, LA.

Connell, J. P., & Thompson, R. A. (1986). Emotion and social interaction in the strange situation: Consistencies and asymmetric influences in the second year. *Child Development, 57,* 733-745.

Demos, V. (1986). Crying in early infancy: An illustration of the motivational function of affect. In T. B. Brazelton & M. Yogman (Eds.), *Affect in early infancy* (pp. 39-73). New York: Ablex.

Dodge, K. A. (1991). Emotion and social information processing. In J. Garber & K. A. Dodge (Eds.), *The development of emotion regulation and dysregulation* (pp. 159-181). Cambridge, UK: Cambridge University Press.

Eisenberg, N., & Fabes, R. A. (1992). Emotion, regulation, and the development of social competence. In M. S. Clark (Ed.), *Emotion and social behavior: Vol. 14. Review of personality and social psychology* (pp. 119-150). Newbury Park, CA: Sage.

Eisenberg, N., Fabes, R. A., Bernzweign, J., Karbon, M., Poulin, R., & Hanish, L. (1993). The relations of emotionality and regulation to preschoolers' social skills and sociometric status. *Child Development, 64,* 1418-1438.

Ekman, P. (1984). Expression and the nature of emotion. In K. Scherer & P. Ekman (Eds.), *Approaches to emotion* (pp. 329-343). Hillsdale, NJ: Erlbaum.

Emde, R. N., Kligman, D. H., Reich, J. H., & Wade, T. (1978). Emotional expression in infancy: 1. Initial studies of social signaling and an emergent model. In M. Lewis & L. Rosenblum (Eds.), *The development of affect* (pp. 125-148). New York: Plenum.

Emde, R. N., Plomin, R., Robinson, J., Corley, R., DeFries, J., Fulker, D., Reznick, J. S., Campos, J., Kagan, J., & Zahn-Waxler, C. (1992). Temperament, emotion, and cognition at fourteen months: The MacArthur Longitudinal Twin Study. *Child Development, 63,* 1437-1455.

Field, T. (1987). Affective and interactive disturbances in infancy. In J. Osofsky (Ed.), *Handbook of infant development* (pp. 972-1005). New York: John Wiley.

Fogel, A., & Reimers, M. (1989). Commentary: On the psychobiology of emotions and their development. *Monographs of the Society for Research in Child Development, 54*(1-2).

Funder, D. C., Block, J. H., & Block, J. (1983). Delay of gratification: Some longitudinal personality correlates. *Journal of Personality and Social Psychology, 44,* 1198-1213.

Gianino, A., & Tronick, E. Z. (1988). The mutual regulation model: The infant's self and interactive regulation coping and defense. In T. Field, P. McCabe, & N. Schneiderman (Eds.), *Stress and coping* (pp. 47-68). Hillsdale, NJ: Erlbaum.

Goldsmith, H. H., Buss, A. H., Plomin, R., Rothbart, M. K., Thomas, A., Chess, S., Hinde, R. A., & McCall, R. B. (1987). Roundtable: What is temperament? Four approaches. *Child Development, 58,* 505-529.

Goldsmith, H. H., & Campos, J. J. (1982). Toward a theory of infant temperament. In R. N. Emde & R. J. Harmon (Eds.), *The development of attachment and affiliative systems* (pp. 161-193). New York: Plenum.

Grolnick, W. S., & Bridges, L. J. (1993, March). *An analysis of "good stress" in infancy.* Paper presented at the Biennial Meeting of the Society for Research in Child Development, New Orleans, LA.

Hazan, C., & Shaver, P. R. (1987). Romantic love conceptualized as an attachment process. *Journal of Personality and Social Psychology, 52,* 511-524.

Hyson, M. C., & Izard, C. E. (1985). Continuities and changes in emotion expressions during brief separation at 13 and 18 months. *Developmental Psychology, 21,* 1165-1170.

Izard, C. E., Hembree, E. A., Dougherty, L. M., & Spizzirri, C. L. (1983). Changes in facial expressions of 2 to 19 month old infants following acute pain. *Developmental Psychology, 19,* 418-426.

Izard, C. E., Hembree, E. A., Huebner, R. R. (1987). Infants' emotion expressions to acute pain: Developmental change and stability of individual differences. *Developmental Psychology, 23,* 105-113.

Izard, C. E., & Malatesta, C. Z. (1987). Perspectives on emotional development: I. Differential emotions theory of early emotional development. In J. D. Osofsky (Ed.), *Handbook of infant development* (2nd ed., pp. 494-554). New York: John Wiley.

Kessen, W., & Leutzendorff, A. W. (1963). The effect of non-nutritive sucking on movement in the human newborn. *Journal of Comparative and Psychological Review, 56,* 69-72.

Kobak, R. R., & Sceery, A. (1988). Attachment in late adolescence: Working models, affect regulation, and perception of self and others. *Child Development, 59,* 135-146.

Kopp, C. B. (1989). Regulation of distress and negative emotions: A developmental view. *Developmental Psychology, 25,* 343-354.

Langhorst, B., & Fogel, A. (1982, March). *A cross-validation of microanalytic approaches to face-to-face play.* Paper presented at the Biennial Meeting of the International Conference on Infant Studies, Austin, TX.

Lazarus, R. S., & Folkman, S. (1984). *Stress, appraisal, and coping.* New York: Springer-Verlag.

MacDonald, K., & Parke, R. E. (1984). Bridging the gap: Parent-child play interaction and peer interactive competence. *Child Development, 55,* 1265-1277.

Main, M., Kaplan, N., & Cassidy, J. (1985). Security in infancy, childhood, and adulthood: A move to the level of representation. *Monographs of the Society for Research in Child Development, 50*(1-2).

Main, M., & Solomon, J. (1986). Discovery of a new, insecure-disorganized/disoriented attachment pattern. In T. B. Brazelton & M. Yogman (Eds.), *Affective development in infancy* (pp. 95-124). Norwood, NJ: Ablex.

Malatesta, C. Z. (1982). The expression and regulation of emotion: A lifespan perspective. In T. Field & A. Fogel (Eds.), *Emotion and early interaction* (pp. 1-24). Hillsdale, NJ: Erlbaum.

Malatesta, C. Z., Culver, C., Tesman, J. R., & Shepard, B. (1989). The development of emotion expression during the first two years of life. *Monographs of the Society for Research in Child Development, 54*(1-2).

Malatesta, C. Z., & Wilson, A. (1988). Emotion-cognition interaction in personality development: A discrete emotions, functionalist analysis. *British Journal of Social Psychology, 27,* 91-112.

Matheny, A. P., Riese, M. L., & Wilson, R. S. (1985). Rudiments of infant temperament: Newborn to nine months. *Developmental Psychology, 21,* 486-494.

Mischel, W. (1974). Processes in delay of gratification. In L. Berkowitz (Ed.), *Progress in experimental personality research: Vol. 3* (pp. 249-292). New York: Academic Press.

Olson, G. M., & Sherman, T. (1983). Attention, learning, & memory in infants. In P. H. Mussen (Ed.), M. M. Haith & J. J. Campos (Vol. Eds.), *Handbook of child psychology: Vol. II. Infancy and developmental psychobiology* (pp. 1001-1080). New York: John Wiley.

Parke, R. D., MacDonald, K. B., Burks, V. M., Carson, J., Bhavnagri, N., Barth, J. M., & Beitel, A. (1989). Family and peer systems: In search of the linkages. In K. Kreppner & R. M. Lerner (Eds.), *Family systems of life span development* (pp. 65-92). Hillsdale, NJ: Erlbaum.

Piaget, J. (1962). *Play, dreams, and imitation in childhood.* New York: Norton.

Riese, M. L. (1987). Temperamental stability between the neonatal period and 24 months. *Developmental Psychology, 23,* 216-222.

Rothbart, M. K. (1986). Longitudinal observation of infant temperament. *Developmental Psychology, 22,* 356-365.

Rothbart, M. K. (1989). Temperament and development. In G. A. Kohnstamm, J. E. Bates, & M. K. Rothbart (Eds.), *Temperament in childhood* (pp. 187-248). Chichester, UK: Wiley.

Rothbart, M. K. (1991). Temperament: A developmental framework. In J. Strelau & A. Angleitner (Eds.), *Explorations in temperament: International perspectives on theory and measurement* (pp. 61-74). New York: Plenum.

Rothbart, M. K., & Derryberry, D. (1981). Development of individual differences in temperament. In M. E. Lamb & A. L. Brown (Eds.), *Advances in developmental psychology: Vol. 1* (pp. 37-86). Hillsdale, NJ: Erlbaum.

Rothbart, M. K., & Posner, M. I. (1985). Temperament and the development of self-regulation. In L. C. Hartlage & C. F. Telzrow (Eds.), *The neuropsychology of individual differences* (pp. 93-123). New York: Plenum Press.

Saarni, C. (1979). Children's understanding of display rules for expressive behavior. *Developmental Psychology, 15,* 424-429.

Shiller, V. M., Izard, C. E., & Hembree, E. A. (1986). Patterns of emotion expression during separation in the strange situation procedure. *Developmental Psychology, 22,* 378-382.

Siegel, L. J. (1983). Hospitalization and medical care of children. In E. Walker & M. Roberts (Eds.), *Handbook of clinical child psychology* (pp. 1089-1108). New York: John Wiley.

Sroufe, L. A., & Fleeson, J. (1985). Attachment behavior and the construction of relationships. In W. Hartup & Z. Rubin (Eds.), *The nature and development of relationships* (pp. 176-199). Hillsdale, NJ: Erlbaum.

Stifter, C. A. (1993, March). *Infant emotion regulation: The effectiveness of certain behaviors to modulate negative arousal.* Paper presented at the Biennial Meeting of the Society for Research in Child Development, New Orleans, LA.

Thompson, R. A. (1990). Emotion and self-regulation. In R. A. Thompson (Ed.), *Socio-emotional development: Vol. 36. Nebraska Symposium on Motivation* (pp. 367-467). Lincoln: University of Nebraska Press.

Tomkins, S. S. (1970). Affect as the primary motivational system. In M. Arnold (Ed.), *Feelings and emotions* (pp. 101-110). New York: Academic Press.

Tronick, E. Z. (1989). Emotions and emotional communication in infants. *American Psychologist, 44,* 112-119.

Vaughn, B., Kopp, C., & Krakow. (1984). The emergence and consolidation of self-control from eighteen to thirty months of age: Normative trends and individual differences. *Child Development, 55,* 990-1004.

Weisz, J. R., & Dennig, M. D. (1993, March). *The search for an understanding of "good" stress and coping in childhood.* Paper presented at the Biennial Meeting of the Society for Research in Child Development, New Orleans, LA.

The Role of Emotion Beliefs and Values in Gender Development

9

STEPHANIE A. SHIELDS

Stephanie A. Shields is Professor of Psychology at the University of California at Davis. She received a Ph.D. from the Pennsylvania State University. Her two areas of research interest are human emotion, especially the relation between emotion as a quality of consciousness and emotion as a cultural construct, and gender. She also writes on the social context of psychological research, focusing on 19th-century scientific study of women and gender.

In the study of gender development, emotion is ordinarily construed as but one dimension of gender role behavior. There is reason to believe, however, that emotion beliefs, the representation of emotion in culturally shared emotion norms (Gordon, 1989; Stearns & Stearns, 1986), stereotypes, and folk theories of emotion play central roles in the acquisition and practice of a gendered identity. (*Gender* is the psychological and cultural representation of sex; because I am primarily concerned with the social meaning of emotion as it is deployed in the construction of psychological differences, I use the term *gender* throughout this chapter.)

The significance of emotion beliefs in gender development has been overlooked because, as Brody (1985) notes, the treatment of gender and gender-relevant variables in research on emotion has been largely atheoretical. Emotion researchers have tended to examine gender almost exclusively in terms of gender similarities and differences, which, as Jacklin (1981) and many others point out, constrains the formulation of explanatory theory. The identification of gender differences (or similarities) per se is not particularly informative: Finding a gender difference explains neither how the difference got there nor what maintains it. A more productive strategy is to theorize the context in which gender effects operate and to examine variables that drive when and how differences are likely to occur.

AUTHOR'S NOTE: Support for this research was provided in part by a Rockefeller Foundation grant and by University of California at Davis Faculty Research grants. Portions of this chapter were presented at meetings of the American Psychological Association (1991) and the American Psychological Society (1993). I would like to thank Nancy Eisenberg and several anonymous reviewers for their very helpful comments.

Recent advances in the study of emotion beliefs and the social context of emotional display and reported experience offer the foundation for a more theoretically informed investigation. The study of emotion and gender has benefitted from innovative methods (e.g., Egerton, 1988), systematic study of beliefs about emotion and gender (e.g., Fabes & Martin, 1991; Shields & Koster, 1989), and studies of the contextual variables that determine the presence and magnitude of gender effects (e.g., La France, 1993; Stoppard, 1993). These advances provide a point of departure for the next generation of research. Furthermore, if we move beyond the static model of gender implied by a gender difference/similarity approach and consider gender as multidimensional (Spence, 1993) and as an active construction of self-identity, emotion beliefs move to the foreground in their role as mediators of the individual's self-understanding and understanding of social expectations for girls and boys and women and men.

In this chapter, I first examine current literature on gender and emotion from a social-developmental perspective. The review replaces the conventional search for gender differences with an examination of what gender means and how it operates. By doing so, one moves from the descriptive (are there differences?) to the explanatory (what drives the extent to which differences are manifested?). This strategy shows clearly that measurement context (particularly its interpersonal dimensions) and beliefs about emotion and its social value are significant determinants of when and how gender and emotion are linked.

I then use themes evident in the literature review to develop an account of the role that beliefs about emotion play in the acquisition and practice of gender-coded behavior. By "gender coded" I mean behavior or experience that is expected to be more typical, natural, or appropriate for one sex than for the other. I accord a central role to emotion beliefs in proposing that they define cultural representations of masculinity/femininity, and, in that role, are the framework for the individual's acquisition and maintenance of a gendered identity. Throughout, my analysis is informed by Deaux and Major's (1987) model of gender in context as a framework for examining how emotion beliefs are implicated in generating gender effects.

Deaux and Major (1987) propose that gender-related behaviors are influenced by three aspects of the context: expectations of perceivers, self-systems of the actor, and situational cues. There is ample evidence that gender role socialization within the family and peer group is significant in initiating and sustaining the practice of gender-coded emotional behavior (Brody & Hall, 1993). What Deaux and Major add to a role socialization account is the capacity to predict variation within and across individuals and situations. Thus interpersonal context (perceivers' expectations and the nature of the situation) is construed as integral to gender performance, not simply the medium within which gendered behavior occurs. More important, Deaux and Major conceptualize gender-related behavior as a socially embedded negotiation of identity that aims at self-confirmation and self-presentation. It is precisely this question of identity on which this chapter ultimately focuses.

GENDER IN EMOTIONAL DEVELOPMENT

Three areas of gender-related emotions research are particularly germane to a social-developmental analysis: (a) understanding and use of emotion concepts (i.e., beliefs about emotion or specific emotions), including attributions regarding the causes and consequences of emotion; (b) producing and reading emotionally expressive behavior; (c) self-reports of experienced and expressed emotion. Because much of this work has recently been reviewed elsewhere (Brody & Hall, 1993; La France & Banaji, 1992; Manstead, 1992; Shields, 1991a), I discuss only a few representative studies in each area. Although I aim to provide a developmental account, few studies go beyond simple age-based comparisons. Furthermore, adults and children are rarely included in the same study, and so apparent age-related differences are difficult to uncouple from methodological differences among studies.

Understanding and Applying Emotion Concepts

Studies of emotion concepts generally involve people's descriptions of the antecedents, constituents, and consequences of emotions and their knowledge of emotion-relevant stereotypes. The majority of studies show no consistent gender differences in adults' emotion knowledge (e.g., Johnson & Schulman, 1988; Shields, 1984) or that of children (e.g., Lubin, Rinck, & Collins, 1986; Thompson, 1989). Nor are gender differences usually found in studies of affective influences on cognitive processes either for children (Bugental, Lin, & Susskind, Chapter 7, this volume) or adults (e.g., Clark & Teasdale, 1985).

Considering that girls' social development is typically more advanced relative to that of boys of the same age, it is noteworthy that gender differences in children's emotion understanding are generally absent, even in preschoolers (Adams, Summers, & Christopherson, 1993). This is the case even when social knowledge such as affective perspective taking is tapped (Eisenberg & Lennon, 1983). For example, Gnepp and Gould (1985) found a gradual increase in affective perspective-taking abilities across age (kindergarten, second grade, fifth grade, and college students), but no gender differences at any age.

The one area in which gender differences are likely to emerge suggests that interpersonal causes and consequences of emotion may be more salient to girls (e.g., Belle, Burr, & Cooney, 1987; Trepanier-Street & Romatowski, 1986) and women (e.g., Brabeck & Weisgerber, 1988; O'Leary & Smith, 1988) than to boys and men. In what appears to be a discrepancy between knowledge and performance, boys and men are less likely than girls and women to insert reference to the connection between emotion and social roles or relationships in their accounts of emotion. This is the case whether the experimental context emphasizes the interpersonal or whether subjects themselves have an opportunity to introduce the social or interpersonal aspects of emotion's context into their responses. For example, Egerton (1988) examined adults' accounts of anger and weeping episodes while they imagined themselves in an emotion-evoking scenario. Most notable of the gender differences obtained for the two types of emotion scenario was women's greater reported conflict about the anger episode (describing anger as effective, but upsetting and costly to relationships) and men's more frequent use of "passion schemas" that disembed emotion from its social framework (representing anger as externally caused and uncontrollable). The greater likelihood for girls to refer to the social causes and consequences of emotion is apparent even before middle childhood. Strayer (1986), for example, interviewed 4- to 5- and 7- to 8-year-old children regarding their beliefs about the antecedents of particular emotions. Girls volunteered more interpersonal themes as instigators of emotion than did boys.

Women also tend to report valuing the discussion of emotion; this adult pattern is evident in descriptions of emotional disclosure by early adolescence. For example, Papini, Farmer, Clark, Micka, and Barnett (1990) found that junior high school girls reported more emotional self-disclosure to parents and peers than boys. Slavin and Rainer (1990) surveyed high school students and found that girls and boys reported the same magnitude of support from family members, but girls also believed they got more support (e.g., talk about personal concerns, satisfaction with help and support) from nonfamily adults and peers.

The differences in females' and males' responses do not appear to reflect a gender difference in knowledge of the social components of emotion. For example, girls and boys are equally knowledgeable about affective display rules and the conditions for dissembling (Saarni, 1989). Women and men are equally responsive to the display rule differences between communal and exchange relationships (Clark & Taraban, 1991), even though they anticipate different rewards and costs of expressing emotion within social situations (Stoppard, 1993). When adults are specifically asked about the interpersonal aspects of emotion, women's and men's accounts may differ in detail, but men can describe significant interpersonal dimensions as readily as women (e.g., Buss, 1991).

Deaux and Major's (1987) model is useful in explaining the apparent emotion knowledge/performance discrepancy. In the area of expression management, for example, girls and boys appear to be equally knowledgeable about affective display rules and the social conditions that call for hiding or exaggerating one's true feelings about a situation; they differ, however, in performance of expressive control, and the difference is greater among older children (reviewed in Saarni, 1989). In one study, interviews about emotional dissembling revealed very few gender differences in children's reports (Saarni, 1988). Those few differences were primarily due to reports of the oldest girls (age 13 to 14), who were quite knowledgeable about the strategic functions of emotional communication in relationships. They endorsed the positive value of honest expression of emotion to peers, yet they also reported that expressive dissembling is very effective. Rather than view these as contradictory or disingenuous positions, we may regard these statements as expressions of values that constitute a gendered identity. Simply stated, girls learn how society values their being girls, and one way to be a genuine girl is to value emotion and to know how to use it.

Producing and Reading
Emotionally Expressive Behavior

Emotion is expressed in many modalities, but the bulk of research has focused on specific facial signals, the accuracy with which people encode discernible expressions, and the accuracy with which people can decode, that is, identify, another's discernible expression.

Researchers studying children's abilities to recognize and label facial expressions of emotion have obtained results similar to those when studying children's other emotion knowledge: Gender differences are essentially absent and older children outperform younger children (reviewed in Brody,

1985). Nor do there appear to be gender differences in children's knowledge about expressions or their expressive competence (e.g., Ekman, Roper, & Hager, 1980). Studies of children's production of spontaneous (i.e., unposed) and posed expressions similarly reveal no gender differences. Manstead (1992) and Brody (1985), whose reviews draw on somewhat different sets of studies, both conclude that there is no evidence of gender differences in readability of spontaneous expressiveness in infants or children, although individual studies may report a gender difference in the frequency with which specific emotional expressions occur. For the most part, these differences are consistent with emotion stereotypes. As these studies typically involve gross behavioral assessments in which the rater knows the child's sex, it is not possible to unconfound observer expectancies from the behavior that is observed.

I return later to the socialization of gender-stereotypic expressive styles. Here it is enough to note that some investigators (e.g., Malatesta, Grigoryev, Lamb, Albin, & Culver, 1986) have suggested that infants' earliest expressive interactions with caregivers are gender coded, that is, caregivers differentially respond to the specific emotional expressions of female and male infants.

In adults, a small but consistent gender difference is found in producing and recognizing specific emotions. Gender differences occur by early adolescence; in girls, but not boys, they may be related to social competence (Custrini & Feldman, 1989). Women tend to be better at identifying the emotion expressed in others' posed or, to a lesser extent, spontaneous expressions (e.g., Kirouac & Dore, 1985) and at having their own spontaneous expressions recognized accurately by others (e.g., Wagner, MacDonald, & Manstead, 1986). In the rare studies that find men more accurate at decoding or encoding expression, it is very likely for the expression to be anger (e.g., Rotter & Rotter, 1988; Wagner et al., 1986).

Adult gender differences may be accounted for in part by the measurement context. Hall (1987) points out that expressive behavior is often measured in settings in which there are demand characteristics for gender-appropriate behavior, such as "get acquainted" sessions whose social features may elicit sociable expressive behavior more successfully from females than from males.

Adult gender differences in expressive style and the frequency of expressive change may also contribute to gender differences in the production of readable expressions and how observers interpret expressive behavior. Buck and his colleagues (Buck, Baron, Goodman, & Shapiro, 1980) report that the readability of women's, but not men's, spontaneous facial expressions in response to emotionally loaded slides is positively related to the number of discrete expressions produced. In adults, some dimensions of behavioral tempo show consistent gender-typical differences. Women tend to be more expressive in the sense of modulating and changing facial expression, gesturing, and rate and inflection of speech (Gallaher, 1992). Furthermore, expressive style is dispositional in that it is relatively stable across situations (Gallaher, 1992), although it can be moderated depending on situational demands and constraints. However, females' greater spontaneous facial expressiveness is not apparent until adolescence (Manstead, 1992).

Social evaluation of expressive style is gender coded (Henley, 1977). Riggio and Friedman (1986), for example, suggest that women and men may be held to different standards of "appropriate" expressivity. They found that social impressions of male and female targets are moderated by gender-coded expressive patterns: Men who display other-oriented movements and gestures are more favorably evaluated than less nonverbally skilled men, whereas for women, spontaneous facial expressiveness most contributes to making a positive initial impression.

These baseline gender differences in expressivity suggest that expressive style is a component of "emotionality," a construct stereotypically identified with femininity. Expressiveness is not felt emotion, yet the conflation of the two may be at the core of culturally shared assumptions about emotionality. Such a conclusion remains to be tested, but it suggests a means by which gender beliefs contribute to observers' differential sensitivity to the content of others' expressive behavior (Shields, 1987). In other words, gender-coded beliefs about expressivity may prime observers to interpret some actors' behavior as more emotional (or less emotional) than others', not simply because observers see what they expect to see, but because expressive style is equated with emotion. Here again, Deaux and Major's (1987) gender-in-context model can be used to predict when gender-coded emotion beliefs will be likely to induce gender effects in behavior.

Self-Report of Emotional Experience

Different research strategies tend to be used to tap children's and adults' beliefs about their own emotional experiences. Children are usually presented with a hypothetical situation, asked to think about how they might feel in that situation, and then choose or rate the intensity of the emotion that would be likely to occur. Occasionally the child's self-ratings are obtained after mild emotion is induced. When these methods are used, gender similarities rather than differences generally are found for children from preschool through preadolescence (e.g., Harris, 1989; Wintre, Polivy, & Murray, 1990), though some investigators report a difference in the specific emotions that girls and boys attribute to themselves for emotion-eliciting scenarios (e.g., Strayer, 1989). With adults and adolescents, investigators are much more likely to rely on standardized scales and the subject's ability to recall a specific experience or set of experiences. When this method is used, gender differences are much more likely to be found for children as well as for adolescents and adults.

Like other kinds of events for which the individual may have a great deal of knowledge but little tangible or specific data, the occurrence of gender differences depends on how the question is asked (e.g., Eisenberg, Fabes, Schaller, & Miller, 1989; LaFrance & Banaji, 1992; Shields, 1991a). Gender differences, which tend to conform to gender stereotypes, are more likely when research participants make global, retrospective self-assessments about their experience and expression of emotion, and are much less likely when participants report on specific instances of emotion. When measures are concurrent, such as when people are asked to keep diaries in which they record occurrences of emotion shortly after they occur (e.g., Averill, 1983), gender differences are attenuated or disappear. In any event, self-reports are an index of what people believe to be true about themselves, and beliefs are representations of experience, not equivalent to the experience itself (Steinke & Shields, 1993). Self-report can therefore give some sense of what respondents notice and value in themselves.

There is one very interesting exception to the pattern of women reporting more intense or frequent emotion than men. For anger, a prototypically "masculine" emotion, the gender difference in reports usually disappears; occasionally anger is reported more frequently by men (e.g., Janisse, Edguer, & Dyck, 1986). A number of different investigators using a variety of techniques have observed this pattern (e.g., Allen & Haccoun, 1976; Averill, 1983; Burrowes & Halberstadt, 1987; Stoner & Spencer, 1987).

What drives the apparent age and context dependence of self-report? Two explanations stand out. First, the questions used to obtain self-report may be prone to measurement bias. Manstead (1992) notes, for example, that women report more hedonically negative emotion, but this may be due to differences in occupational roles: As women are more likely to be responsible for the care of home and children, "the average number of aversive events encountered by a woman who is a homemaker and/or mother may simply be greater" (p. 365). Second, the experiential dimension of emotion may not provide sufficient "hard" data on which to base a quantitative self-assessment. Moskowitz (1986) asserts that self-reports are most effective in assessing characteristics that have stability, coherence, and generality across situations. Gender-coded emotion beliefs have all of these features, whereas recall of felt emotion does not. When research participants do not have much immediate information about experience, the research context may trigger a heuristic in which participants compare themselves to a gender-coded emotional standard to produce a response (e.g., "I'm a man, so I'm probably less expressive than women"). Research participants are clearly aware of gender-coded emotion standards. Banaji and LaFrance (cited in LaFrance, 1993) found that self-reports of emotionality obtained in a public setting are more likely to conform to gender stereotypes than self-reports that are made anonymously and privately.

EMOTION BELIEFS AND VALUES IN GENDER DEVELOPMENT

How does the child's sense of gender and his or her gender-based self-assessment come to be shaped by emotion beliefs? What is it about social context that makes it such a powerful determinant of gender effects in emotion? Certainly innate differences between the sexes may set the stage for "biasing" emotional development in ways that result in male and female patterns of emotionality in adulthood. However, hypothesized innate biasing mechanisms alone cannot explain the loose connection between gender differences and age, lack of generality across modalities, or the knowledge/performance discrepancy that is so readily manipulated by measurement context. In this section I draw on socialization conceptions of emotion as a feature of gender roles, and, within the gender-in-context framework, formulate an account of how gender and emotion become linked in development. Evidence for this account is presented in the course of elaborating three core propositions:

1. Beliefs about emotion are gender coded.
2. Beliefs about emotion code gender.
3. Gender is learned by practicing emotion.

Beliefs About Emotion Are Gender Coded

Children and adults can recognize and name a number of gender-coded emotion beliefs, ranging from what could be considered the emotion "master stereotype," which equates emotionality with femaleness (e.g., Shields, 1987), to some of the social rules regarding appropriate display and experience of specific emotions. Emotion-specific gender stereotypes are held by preschoolers who report that males experience more anger but less sadness than females (Karbon, Fabes, Carlo, & Martin, 1992), and by adults who expect women to display less negatively sanctioned emotion (e.g., Johnson & Schulman, 1988). Emotion stereotypes also are linked to age and emotion type (Fabes & Martin, 1991).

Other emotion beliefs, however, are not so easily articulated. Tacitly held beliefs ground our understanding of emotion, and in ordinary discourse may seem no more than a manifestation of emotion's "natural" character. Tacit beliefs about emotion are as gendered as emotion stereotypes. One way to make implicit beliefs explicit is to examine how emotion is represented in popular culture. Advice literature, for example, is heavily concerned with guiding emotional behavior. As such, it is not a record of what people actually do, but instead it reveals what people believe they are and what they ought to do about it (Shields & Koster, 1989).

One example will illustrate this point. In studies of parent advice manuals, I have found strikingly different representations of mothers' and fathers' emotions (Shields & Koster, 1989; Shields, Steinke, & Koster, 1993). Whether directed to intact birth families, stepparents, adoptive parents, or single parents, maternal emotion (including that of stepmothers) is represented as a barely controllable disposition to "overreact" emotionally. All maternal emotions are represented as potentially dangerous to a child's healthy development, and even though female caregivers are cautioned to exercise sufficient vigilance and self-restraint, women are portrayed as ultimately likely to fail. Of course some mothers habitually overreact, but descriptions of maternal emotion out of control are made as if this behavior is normative. Furthermore, not simply expressiveness, but the female caregiver's emotion itself, is represented as destructive. Fathers, too, are cautioned about excessive emotion, but problematic emotion is portrayed as having external sources: his wife, his job, or the children themselves. Moreover, fathers are urged to be emotionally expressive and not to worry unduly about problem emotion. Representation of emotion in advice literature shows that gender coding of emotion beliefs includes some very basic notions about the nature of females and males—notions that are part of the core of who we come to believe we are as persons.

Implicit beliefs, such as these embedded in representation of parents' emotion, in combination with explicit gender-coded emotion stereotypes, reveal the density and complexity of gender-coded emotion beliefs. It is within this network of emotion beliefs that the child learns what it means to be a woman or to be a man.

Beliefs About Emotion Code Gender

If we examine the features that define the difference between concepts of masculine and feminine, we find that beliefs about emotion are at the core. The history of the constructs of psychological masculinity and femininity (M and F respectively) vividly illustrates this point (Shields, 1991b). Spence (1984, 1993) argues persuasively that gender is a multidimensional phenomenon that is only partially represented by the expressivity-instrumentality components of conventional M/F scales. The expressivity-instrumentality core is, in fact, recognizable on the basis of emotion-relevant items alone. In general, emotion-relevant F items indicate a kind of "delicacy of feeling," expressiveness (emotional or otherwise), or attentiveness to emotion's interpersonal dimension. Emotion-relevant M items indicate expressive control or self-assertion with some emotional component.

Terman and Miles's (1936) Attitude Interest Analysis Survey (AIAS) was the first of many paper-and-pencil M/F tests. The AIAS, used with children and adults, includes the subtest "Emotional and Ethical Attitudes" (weighted double in calculating M/F scores), and is essentially a test of emotion stereotype knowledge. M/F tests developed subsequently continue to emphasize emotion as a basis for differentiating masculine and feminine (e.g., MMPI Scale 5; California Psychological Inventory).

By the early 1970s, the assumption that masculinity and femininity represent opposite anchors on a unidimensional, bipolar continuum was replaced by the alternative view that M and F should be construed as orthogonal dimensions, each of which can be expressed as its own bipolar continuum. Emotion-related traits continued to figure prominently in measuring and defining psychological gender. About half of the 20 items on the Bem Sex-Role Inventory (BSRI; Bem, 1974) indicative of femininity (e.g., affectionate, eager to soothe hurt feelings, warm) reflect emotion or concern with emotion; the M scale contains only two obvious emotion-related items (assertive, aggressive), but the M dimension is recognizable as such. One quarter of the items on the Personal Attributes Questionnaire (PAQ; Spence & Helmreich, 1978) pertain directly to emotion: self-ratings of emotionality, excitability in a major crisis, easily hurt feelings, awareness of feelings of others, warmth in relations with others, and propensity to weep.

The constructs of masculinity and femininity are organized around emotion stereotypes. Spence (1993) showed that BSRI self-ratings on the single items "masculine" and "feminine" (which are negatively correlated with each other) are significantly correlated with BSRI and PAQ expressive items for women (positive correlation with "feminine," negative correlation with "masculine") and instrumental items for men (negative correlation with "feminine," positive correlation with "masculine"). Spence concludes that scores on the BSRI and PAQ should not be related to gender-linked characteristics and behaviors "except as they happen to be influenced by instrumentality and expressiveness per se" (p. 624). Spence's observation accounted for the general pattern of findings that subjects who rate themselves as possessing a high degree of masculine characteristics on M/F scales also endorse emotion beliefs/values that are stereotypically masculine, whereas subjects high on femininity scales conform to feminine emotion stereotypes (e.g., Brody, Hay, & Vandewater, 1990; Conway, Giannopoulos, & Stiefenhofer, 1990; Ganong & Coleman, 1985; LaFrance, 1993). The relation between M/F scores and emotion-related attributes may be explained by the fact that both measure the same attribute: the extent to which the individual believes he or she conforms to gender-coded emotion stereotypes.

Learning Gender by Doing Emotion

The "what" of gender is learned from physical appearance and from the artifacts of social organization, such as gender-typical or gender stereotyped toys, clothing, and occupations. Emotion beliefs distinctively add the "how" of being a gendered person—the feelings, values, and expression of feelings that signal the genuineness or authenticity of oneself as female or male. Apparent gender differences in the salience of emotional experience (evident in self-reports) and in the emphasis placed on interpersonal aspects of emotion in part reflect a gendered presentation of self grounded in learning and practicing a gendered identity. For example, the emotional sharing that especially characterizes girls' friendships (Maccoby, 1990) sets the stage for later regulation of one's emotional life. Thus both women and men are more willing to discuss their emotions with women friends, and women report more willingness than men to discuss emotions generally (e.g., Aukett, Ritchie, & Mill, 1988). Emotion beliefs also color the individual's expectations regarding the consequences of expressing or withholding felt emotion (e.g., Fuchs & Thelen, 1988); at least for adults, both prescriptive and proscriptive beliefs are gender coded (Stoppard & Gunn-Gruchy, 1993). Emotion beliefs do not simply reflect what we do, but how we do it and how we feel about ourselves doing it (Shields, 1993).

Children have ample opportunity to learn and practice emotion in a gender-coded way. Recent reviews provide a thorough overview of emotion socialization (Brody & Hall, 1993; Gordon, 1989; Saarni & Harris, 1989), so a few representative studies suffice to illustrate how finely tuned the gender repertoire can be.

Mothers and fathers of preschoolers talk about emotional aspects of events in similar ways, but employ a wider emotional vocabulary with daughters than with sons (Kuebli & Fivush, 1992). Adults also respond differently to girls' and boys' expressive styles, particularly rewarding girls' expressive behavior when they are friendly and talkative, that is when they behave "like girls" (Cantor & Gelfand, 1977). Within the peer group, children rehearse gender-coded emotional styles (e.g., von Salisch, 1988). For example, Sheldon (1992) found that preschool girls (white middle class) employ a conflict-management style within same-sex groups that is simultaneously self-assertive and conciliatory, whereas boys tend to engage in a larger proportion of coercive talk.

Emotion beliefs appear to be organized, and so should function like other gender-coded information or schemas. In the single study I have located that tests this hypothesis, Fabes and Martin and their collaborators found that emotion beliefs can define expectations concerning gender (Martin, Fabes, Eisenbud, Karbon, & Rose, 1990). Preschool children viewed pictures of people expressing emotions that were stereotypic (e.g., boy angry) and counterstereotypic (e.g., boy crying). Children were three times more likely to recall incorrectly the sex of the person expressing an emotion when the emotion was counterstereotypic. In other words, the children reported having seen a girl rather than a boy cry. Interestingly, boys were more likely to distort than were girls, and there was more distortion for boy targets than for girl targets. Furthermore, children were more likely to recall sex-consistent emotions as being more intense than sex-inconsistent emotions, even though pictures did not objectively differ in intensity of expression.

If emotion beliefs operate as gender schemas, they should also, like gender schemas, provide a basis for making inferences about ambiguous or partial information (Eisenberg, Martin, & Fabes, in press). There is suggestive data that this occurs. Biernat (1991) has found that the relation between judgments about masculinity and femininity becomes increasingly negative with age (kindergarten to college students), a trend that she interprets as a shift from viewing gender in dualistic terms to viewing it as a unidimensional construct. In other words, even though adults are more cognitively capable of making judgments about people based on their individuating characteristics than on their sex, adults also are more likely to view gender in oppositional terms: to be more masculine in a trait necessitates being less feminine in that trait. Gender-coded emotion beliefs, like a unidimensional conceptualization of gender, tend to dichotomize male/female, masculine/feminine as distinct, nonoverlapping categories: Feminine is emotional; masculine is not. If operating as a gender schema, emotion beliefs could thus reassert gender difference in the face of gender-ambiguous or contradictory information. For example, told that "the man cried," the hearer would be likely to infer gender-consistent causes (e.g., a grave loss) and consequences (e.g., a "manly" style of weeping). Emotion beliefs as gender schemas also may help to explain why gender differences in children's self-reported emotional experience begin to appear at about the same age at which children acquire the cognitive flexibility that allows them to understand and apply multiple classification dimensions to gender: A gender-based emotion dichotomy imposes order on a multidimensional concept.

The use of gender categories to codify ambiguous behavior also may be the impetus behind caregivers' gender-coded contingent responses to infants. Fagot and her colleagues (Fagot & Hagan, 1991; Fagot & Leinbach, 1993) hypothesize that caregivers are particularly susceptible to using gender stereotypes to guide their reactions to infants and toddlers because gender-ambiguous behavior lends itself to being "read" in gender stereotypic ways. The variety and intensity of infants' and toddlers' expressive behavior especially lends itself to contingent responding. Fagot, Hagan, Leinbach, and Kronsberg (1985) found that, even though boys and girls did not differ in their communicative behavior, adult caregivers responded to toddlers' self-assertive acts and their attempts to communicate with adults in gender-stereotypic ways. Adults attended more to boys' assertive acts and intense communications and more to girls' mild communications.

Because emotionally expressive behavior is highly gender coded, an important component of a child's learning how to "do" gender (i.e., enact a gendered identity) involves learning how to "do" emotion. Doing gender encompasses not only emotional display but also emotion values (e.g., emotional self-disclosure is good) and beliefs about emotional experience (e.g., anger is appropriate when one's rights are violated). Doing gender also reflects the operation of the individual's self-conceptualization. Deaux (1993) proposes that the individual's formulation and reformulation of identity is fashioned as a response to the events and circumstances of one's life. As a dimension of gender, emotion beliefs and values may provide the glue of continuity in the formation and change of the individual's social identities.

CONCLUSION

When research on gender and emotion is viewed from a new perspective, namely a focus on the variables that exaggerate or attenuate the occurrence of difference, the conventional way of thinking about gender differences in emotion is challenged. Whether children or adults are studied, what each sex knows about emotion differs far less than what each sex is likely to do with that knowledge. When gender differences occur, they conform by and large to emotion stereotypes, but differences are context dependent (e.g., self-reported emotion experience), of less magnitude than stereotypes would predict (e.g., adult encoding and decoding of facial expression), or altogether absent (e.g., most understanding and application of emotion knowledge).

With the change in focus comes the recognition that ideas about emotion are significant in defining and maintaining beliefs about gender differences. The nature of gender itself becomes the focus. This chapter accords a central role to emotion beliefs in proposing that, whether explicitly represented in emotion stereotypes or more subtly transmitted as in advice literature, emotional standards define the core of "masculine" and "feminine." In their role of defining cultural representations of masculinity/femininity, emotion beliefs are the medium for the individual's acquisition and maintenance of a gendered identity via the practice of gender-coded emotional values and behavior.

Despite the clear points of intersection, studies of gender development and emotional development have largely occupied separate spheres—different researchers, different theoretical models, and different empirical foci. Broadly speaking, "gender" and "emotion" each have a different conceptual status within their respective fields. Although research in both fields incorporates a cognitive approach, gender development researchers are likely to include consideration of gender knowledge in terms of its effects on person-oriented information processing across children's developmental levels (e.g., self-concept, inferences about others), whereas emotion researchers often view development simply in terms of the way in which children's knowledge and application of emotion concepts approach that of adults (e.g., understanding the antecedents and consequences of specific emotions). Furthermore, in gender development, gender roles and stereotypes tend to be viewed as culturally value laden and changing over historical time, but investigators studying emotional development are much less likely to problematize emotion (that is, make the concept of "emotion" itself the object of study). In emotion research, social context is viewed as functioning only to accelerate or retard "the inevitable emergence of universal cognitive abilities" (Gordon, 1989, p. 321). For example, children's understanding of emotion antecedents is tested, but not what it means to identify situations and experiences as "emotion." As progress is made in formulating theories that link gender and emotion (e.g., Brody & Hall, 1993) and emotion and social context (e.g., Saarni, 1989), the gap between these two fields will be bridged.

The separate trajectories of gender development and emotion development research have obscured the significant ways in which the two literatures should inform one another. As a consequence, few empirical studies directly test the association between emotion beliefs and gender development. The key questions that need to be tested concern how gender-coded emotion beliefs are organized and function as gender schemas. The ways in which emotion beliefs influence the processing of partial or ambiguous gender-relevant information deserve particular attention.

The ideas discussed in this chapter have both theoretical and practical implications. At the theoretical level, further study of beliefs about emotion can play a major role in revealing what gender means, how gender operates, and how gender is negotiated in our relationships with others. At the practical level, the significance of gender-coded emotion beliefs reminds us that identifying emotion in oneself or another is not a value-neutral activity.

REFERENCES

Adams, G. A., Summers, M., & Christopherson, V. A. (1993). Age and gender differences in preschool children's identification of the emotions of others: A brief report. *Canadian Journal of Behavioural Science, 25*, 97-107.

Allen, J. G., & Haccoun, D. (1976). Sex differences in emotionality: A multidimensional approach. *Human Relations, 29*, 711-722.

Aukett, R., Ritchie, J., & Mill, K. (1988). Gender differences in friendship patterns. *Sex Roles, 19,* 57-66.

Averill, J. R. (1983). Studies on anger and aggression: Implications for theories of emotion. *American Psychologist, 38,* 1145-1160.

Belle, D., Burr, R., & Cooney, J. (1987). Boys and girls as social support theorists. *Sex Roles, 11/12,* 657-665.

Bem, S. L. (1974). The measurement of psychological androgyny. *Journal of Consulting and Clinical Psychology, 42,* 155-162.

Biernat, M. (1991). Gender stereotypes and the relationship between masculinity and femininity: A developmental analysis. *Journal of Personality and Social Psychology, 61,* 351-365.

Brabek, M. M., & Weisgerber, K. (1988). Responses to the Challenger tragedy: Subtle and significant gender differences. *Sex Roles, 19,* 639-650.

Brody, L. (1985). Gender differences in emotional development: A review of theories and research. *Journal of Personality, 53,* 102-149.

Brody, L. R., & Hall, J. A. (1993). Gender and emotion. In M. Lewis & J. Haviland (Eds.), *Handbook of emotions* (pp. 447-461). New York: Guilford.

Brody, L. R., Hay, D. H., & Vandewater, E. (1990). Gender, gender role identity, and children's reported feelings toward the same and opposite sex. *Sex Roles, 7/8,* 363-387.

Buck, R., Baron, R., Goodman, N., & Shapiro, B. (1980). Unitization of spontaneous nonverbal behavior in the study of emotion communication. *Journal of Personality and Social Psychology, 30,* 587-592.

Burrows, B. D., & Halberstadt, A. G. (1987). Self- and family-expressiveness styles in the experience and expression of anger. *Journal of Nonverbal Behavior, 11,* 254-268.

Buss, D. M. (1991). Conflict in married couples: Personality predictors of anger and upset. *Journal of Personality, 59,* 735-747.

Cantor, N. L., & Gelfand, D. M. (1977). Effects of responsiveness and sex of children on children and adults' behavior. *Child Development, 48,* 232-238.

Clark, D. M., & Teasdale, J. D. (1985). Constraints on the effects of mood on memory. *Journal of Personality and Social Psychology, 48,* 1595-1608.

Clark, M. S., & Taraban, C. (1991). Reactions to and willingness to express emotion in communal and exchange relationships. *Journal of Experimental Social Psychology, 27,* 324-336.

Conway, M., Giannopoulos, C., & Stiefenhofer, K. (1990). Response styles to sadness are related to sex and sex-role orientation. *Sex Roles, 9/10,* 579-587.

Custrini, R. J., & Feldman, R. S. (1989). Children's social competence and nonverbal encoding and decoding of emotions. *Journal of Clinical Child Psychology, 18,* 336-342.

Deaux, K. (1993). Reconstructing social identity. *Personality and Social Psychology Bulletin, 19,* 4-12.

Deaux, K., & Major, B. (1987). Putting gender into context: An interactive model of gender-related behavior. *Psychological Review, 94,* 369-389.

Egerton, M. (1988). Passionate women and passionate men: Sex differences in accounting for angry and weeping episodes. *British Journal of Social Psychology, 27,* 51-66.

Eisenberg, N., Fabes, R. A., Schaller, M., & Miller, P. A. (1989). Sympathy and personal distress: Development, gender differences, and interrelations of indexes. In N. Eisenberg

(Ed.), *New directions for child development: No. 44. Empathy and related emotional responses* (pp. 107-126). San Francisco: Jossey-Bass.

Eisenberg, N., & Lennon, R. (1983). Sex differences in empathy and related capacities. *Psychological Bulletin, 94,* 100-131.

Eisenberg, N., Martin, C. L., & Fabes, R. A. (in press). Gender development and gender effects. In D. C. Berliner & R. C. Calfee (Eds.), *The handbook of educational psychology.* New York: MacMillan.

Ekman, P., Roper, G., & Hager, J. C. (1980). Deliberate facial movement. *Child Development, 51,* 886-891.

Fabes, R. A., & Martin, C. L. (1991). Gender and age stereotypes of emotionality. *Personality and Social Psychology Bulletin, 17,* 532-540.

Fagot, B. I., & Hagan, R. (1991). Observations of parent reactions to sex-stereotyped behaviors: Age and sex effects. *Child Development, 62,* 617-628.

Fagot, B. I., Hagan, R., Leinbach, M. D., & Kronsberg, S. (1985). Differential reactions to assertive and communicative acts of toddler boys and girls. *Child Development, 56,* 1499-1505.

Fagot, B. I., & Leinbach, M. D. (1993). Gender-role development in young children: From discrimination to labeling. *Developmental Review, 13,* 205-224.

Fuchs, D., & Thelen, M. H. (1988). Children's expected interpersonal consequences of communicating their affective state and reported likelihood of expression. *Child Development, 59,* 1314-1322.

Gallaher, P. E. (1992). Individual differences in nonverbal behavior: Dimensions of style. *Journal of Personality and Social Psychology, 63,* 133-145.

Ganong, L. H., & Coleman, M. (1985). Sex, sex roles, and emotional expressiveness. *The Journal of Genetic Psychology, 146,* 405-411.

Gnepp, J., & Gould, M. E. (1985). The development of personalized inferences: Understanding of other people's emotion reactions in light of their prior experiences. *Child Development, 56,* 1455-1464.

Gordon, S. (1989). The socialization of children's emotions: Emotional culture, competence, and exposure. In C. Saarni & P. L. Harris (Eds.), *Children's understanding of emotion* (pp. 319-349). Cambridge, UK: Cambridge University Press.

Hall, J. A. (1987). On explaining gender differences: The case of nonverbal communication. In P. Shaver & C. Hendrick (Eds.), *Review of personality and social psychology: Vol. 7* (pp. 177-200). Beverly Hills, CA: Sage.

Harris, P. L. (1989). *Children and emotion.* New York: Basil Blackwell.

Henley, N. M. (1977). *Body politics: Power, sex, and nonverbal communication.* Englewood Cliffs, NJ: Prentice-Hall.

Jacklin, C. N. (1981). Methodological issues in the study of sex-related differences. *Developmental Review, 1,* 266-273.

Janisse, M. P., Edguer, N., & Dyck, D. G. (1986). Type A behavior, anger expression, and reactions to anger imagery. *Motivation and Emotion, 10,* 371-386.

Johnson, J. T., & Shulman, G. A. (1988). More alike than meets the eye: Perceived gender differences in subjective experience and its display. *Sex Roles, 19,* 67-79.

Karbon, M., Fabes, R. A., Carlo, G., & Martin, C. L. (1992). Preschoolers' beliefs about sex and age differences in emotionality. *Sex Roles, 27,* 377-390.

Kirouac, G., & Dore, F. Y. (1985). Accuracy of the judgment of facial expression of emotions as a function of sex and level of education. *Journal of Nonverbal Behavior, 9,* 3-7.

Kuebli, J., & Fivush, R. (1992). Gender differences in parent-child conversations about past emotions. *Sex Roles, 27,* 683-698.

LaFrance, M. (1993, June). *Towards a reconsideration of the gender-emotion relationship.* Paper presented at the meeting of the American Psychological Society, Chicago.

LaFrance, M., & Banaji, M. (1992). Towards a reconsideration of the gender-emotion relationship. In M. Clark (Ed.), *Review of personality and social psychology: Vol. 14* (pp. 178-201). Newbury Park, CA: Sage.

Lubin, B., Rinck, C. M., & Collins, J. F. (1986). Intensity ratings of mood adjectives as a function of gender and age group. *Journal of Social and Clinical Psychology, 4,* 244-247.

Maccoby, E. E. (1990). Gender and relationships: A developmental account. *American Psychologist, 45,* 513-520.

Malatesta, C. Z., Grigoryev, P., Lamb, C., Albin M., & Culver, C. (1986). Emotion socialization and expressive development in preterm and full-term infants. *Child Development, 57,* 316-330.

Manstead, A. S. R. (1992). Gender differences in emotion. In M. A. Gale & M. W. Eysenck (Eds.), *Handbook of individual differences: Biological perspectives* (pp. 355-387). Chichester, UK: Wiley.

Martin, C. L., Fabes, R. A., Eisenbud, L., Karbon, M. M., & Rose, H. A. (1990, March). *Boys don't cry: Children's distortions of others' emotions.* Paper presented at the Southwestern Society for Research in Human Development, Tempe, AZ.

Moskowitz, D. S. (1986). Comparison of self-reports, reports by knowledgeable informants, and behavioral observation data. *Journal of Personality, 54*(1), 294-317.

O'Leary, V. E., & Smith, D. (1988, August). *Sex makes a difference: Attributions for emotional cause.* Paper presented at the American Psychological Association Convention, Atlanta, GA.

Papini, D. R., Farmer, F. F., Clark, S. M., Micka, J. C., & Barnett, J. K. (1990). Early adolescent age and gender differences in patterns of emotional self-disclosure to parents and friends. *Adolescence, 25,* 959-976.

Riggio, R. E., & Friedman, H. (1986). Impression formation: The role of expressive behavior. *Journal of Personality and Social Psychology, 50,* 421-427.

Rotter, N. G., & Rotter, G. S. (1988). Sex differences in the encoding and decoding of negative facial emotions. *Journal of Nonverbal Behavior, 12,* 139-148.

Saarni, C. (1988). Children's understanding of the interpersonal consequences of dissemblance of nonverbal emotional-expressive behavior. *Journal of Nonverbal Behavior, 12,* 275-294.

Saarni, C. (1989). Children's understanding of strategic control of emotional expression in social transactions. In C. Saarni & P. L. Harris (Eds.), *Children's understanding of emotion* (pp. 181-208). Cambridge, UK: Cambridge University Press.

Saarni, C., & Harris, P. L. (Eds.). (1989). *Children's understanding of emotion.* Cambridge, UK: Cambridge University Press.

Sheldon, A. (1992). Conflict talk: Sociolinguistic challenges to self-assertion and how young girls meet them. *Merrill-Palmer Quarterly, 38,* 95-117.

Shields, S. A. (1984). Distinguishing between emotion and nonemotion: Judgments about experience. *Motivation and Emotion, 8,* 355-369.

Shields, S. A. (1987). Women, men, and the dilemma of emotion. In P. Shaver & C. Hendrick (Eds.), *Review of personality and social psychology: Vol. 7* (pp. 229-250). Beverly Hills, CA: Sage.

Shields, S. A. (1991a). Gender in the psychology of emotion: A selective research review. In K. T. Strongman (Ed.), *International review of studies on emotion: Vol. 1* (pp. 227-245). New York: John Wiley.

Shields, S. A. (1991b, August). *Doing emotion/doing gender.* Paper presented at the American Psychological Association, San Francisco.

Shields, S. A. (1993, June). *The persistence of beliefs about gender and emotion: What difference do they make?* Paper presented at the meeting of the American Psychological Society, Chicago.

Shields, S. A., & Koster, B. A. (1989). Emotional stereotyping of parents in child rearing manuals, 1915-1980. *Social Psychology Quarterly, 52,* 44-55.

Shields, S. A., Steinke, P., & Koster, B. A. (1993). *The double bind of caregiving: Representation of emotion in American advice literature.* Manuscript submitted for publication.

Slavin, L. A., & Rainer, K. L. (1990). Gender differences in emotional support and depressive symptoms among adolescents: A prospective analysis. *American Journal of Community Psychology, 18,* 407-421.

Spence, J. T. (1984). Masculinity, femininity, and gender-related traits: A conceptual analysis and critique of current research. In B. A. Maher & W. B. Maher (Eds.), *Progress in experimental research in personality* (pp. 1-97). New York: Academic Press.

Spence, J. T. (1993). Gender-related traits and gender ideology: Evidence for a multifactorial theory. *Journal of Personality and Social Psychology, 64,* 624-635.

Spence, J. T., & Helmreich, R. (1978). *Masculinity and femininity: Their psychological dimensions, correlates, and antecedents.* Austin: University of Texas Press.

Stearns, C. Z., & Stearns, P. N. (1986). *Anger: The struggle for emotional control in America's history.* Chicago: University of Chicago Press.

Steinke, P., & Shields, S. A. (1993). *Self-report as a research method: Innovation from "limitations."* Manuscript submitted for publication.

Stoner, S. B., & Spencer, W. B. (1987). Age and gender differences with the anger expression scale. *Educational and Psychological Measurement, 47,* 487-492.

Stoppard, J. M. (1993, June). *Beyond gender stereotypes: Putting the gender-emotion relationship into context.* Paper presented at the meeting of the American Psychological Society, Chicago.

Stoppard, J. M., & Gunn-Gruchy, C. D. (1993). Gender, context, and expression of positive emotion. *Personality and Social Psychology Bulletin, 19,* 143-150.

Strayer, J. (1986). Children's attributions regarding the situational determinants of emotion in self and others. *Developmental Psychology, 22,* 649-654.

Strayer, J. (1989). What children know and feel in response to witnessing affective events. In C. Saarni & P. L. Harris (Eds.), *Children's understanding of emotion* (pp. 259-289). Cambridge, UK: Cambridge University Press.

Terman, L. M., & Miles, C. C. (1936). Sex and personality. New York: Russell & Russell.

Thompson, R. A. (1989). Causal attributions and children's emotional understanding. In C. Saarni & P. L. Harris (Eds.), *Children's understanding of emotion* (pp. 117-150). Cambridge, UK: Cambridge University Press.

Trepanier-Street, M. L., & Romatowski, J. A. (1986). Sex and age differences in children's creative writing. *Journal of Humanistic Education and Development, 25,* 18-27.

von Salisch, M. (1988). *Girls' and boys' ways of arguing with a friend.* Paper presented at the Third European Conference on Developmental Psychology, Budapest.

Wagner, H. L., MacDonald, C. J., & Manstead, A. S. R. (1986). Communication of individual emotions by spontaneous facial expressions. *Journal of Personality and Social Psychology, 50,* 737-743.

Wintre, M. G., Polivy, J., & Murray, M. A. (1990). Self-predictions of emotional response patterns: Age, sex, and of situational determinants. *Child Development, 61,* 1124-1133.

10

Social Development and Self-Monitoring

WILLIAM G. GRAZIANO
STEFANIE B. WASCHULL

William G. Graziano is a Professor in the Department of Psychology at Texas A&M University. He received a Ph.D. from the University of Minnesota in 1976. His research interests fall at the boundary of developmental, social, and personality psychology.

Stefanie B. Waschull is a Psychology Instructor at Athens Technical Institute in Athens, Georgia. She received a Ph.D. in Psychology from the University of Georgia in 1991. Her primary interests are in social and personality development, particularly children's self-esteem, and the development of motive systems.

In what would prove to be a series of exceptionally influential papers, Snyder (1974, 1979) introduced the construct of self-monitoring. According to Snyder (1979), adults differ in the extent to which they monitor, through self-observation and self-control, their expressive behavior and self-presentation. Subsequent research has shown that self-monitoring is related to processes of social cognition (e.g., Snyder & Cantor, 1980), cooperation and competition (e.g., Danheiser & Graziano, 1982), self-disclosure (e.g., Shaffer, Smith, & Tomarelli, 1982), social comparison (Elliott, 1979), friendship selection (e.g., Snyder, 1987) and self-evaluation (e.g., Ickes, Layden, & Barnes, 1978; Paulhus, 1982). This construct appears to be related to many basic processes underlying personality and social behavior.

There is debate about the factorial structure of self-monitoring, and there have been calls for greater theoretical elaboration of the construct itself (e.g., Briggs & Cheek, 1986; Gabrenya & Arkin, 1980; Hoyle & Lennox, 1991; West & Finch, in press). Nonetheless, even critics acknowledge that Snyder's

AUTHORS' NOTE: This work was supported by National Science Foundation grant BNS 8705780 to William G. Graziano. The authors are grateful to Gary Lautenschlager, Lynn Musser, Christopher Leone, David Ward, Rick Crelia, David Pittenger, Robert Frank Weiss, Shaun Campbell, Lauri Jensen-Campbell, and Cynthia Frame for their contributions to various aspects of the project. We also thank Philip Costanzo, David Funder, Charles Halverson, William Ickes, Louis Penner, Radmila Prislin, James Shepperd, Mark Snyder, Tedra Walden, and Thomas Ward for comments on an earlier version of this chapter.

self-monitoring construct has captured the attention of personality and social psychology researchers (Briggs & Cheek, 1986; West & Finch, in press). We agree with the critics that further theoretical elaboration is needed, but we suggest a new focus for the elaboration. Some questions potentially more important than factorial structure should be addressed. At a general level, we do not know how or from what interpersonal or dispositional substrate self-monitoring emerges, when self-monitoring emerges, or in what form self-monitoring differences are expressed in persons of different ages.

This chapter examines the construct of self-monitoring from a developmental perspective. First, we probe the idea that previous critiques of self-monitoring miss the point that self-monitoring links to the notion of self-as-process and self-as active-constructor-of-situations (but see Briggs & Cheek, 1986; Hoyle & Sowards, in press). Second, we discuss three different ways of conceptualizing the development of self-monitoring. In all three, we assume that self-monitoring differences are linked to the development of emotion and motivational systems. Finally, we consider self-monitoring in relation to the idea that social-cognitive representations may be modularized (Chomsky, 1980; Tooby & Cosmides, 1990, 1992) with "dedicated" sub-schemas (Costanzo, 1991) within a larger cognitive representation. Modules may not "shake hands" in certain contexts (Laboratory of Comparative Human Cognition, 1983).

SELF-MONITORING SITUATED IN THEORY AND HISTORY

Lewin's Legacy: Three Themes

Despite claims to the contrary, Lewin's ideas (1935, 1951) have left an enduring imprint on the field of social psychology, at least as it is practiced and taught in North America (Patnoe, 1988). Lewin's students have been productive researchers, and they have become the opinion leaders in the field. As such, their interests have influenced the definition of the "mainstream" issues in the field (Jones, 1985).

Three Lewinian themes are widespread, and all three are relevant to the analysis of self-monitoring. These three themes involve skepticism about personality characteristics as causal agents of social behavior, the importance of a perceiver's phenomenology of the immediate situation, and the role of motives in generating structure for cognition and behavior. The first theme, skepticism about personality characteristics, is embedded within a distinction originally applied to physics that Lewin draws between Aristotelian and Galilean modes of thought. In Aristotelian thought, the focus is on the classification of objects or persons in terms of their inherent characteristics, with attention to attributes essential for inclusion in a class. This leads to the segregation of elements. Earth, fire, and water are mutually exclusive, clearly separate categories of basic elements.

Lewin believes that in psychology, Aristotelian thinking is rampant. It is manifest in efforts to classify people (e.g., "child" versus "adolescent") or phenomena (e.g., "aggression" versus "attraction" versus "relationships") and in efforts to segregate artificial phenomena as higher or lower ("social" versus "biological") based solely on inherent characteristics. By comparison, the Galilean mode of thought eschews classifications based on inherent properties. Instead, the focus is on the functional interdependence of an object/event and the immediate context or field surrounding it.

The second theme is equally relevant to the construct of self-monitoring. If causation is to be found in the functional interdependence of persons and context, then an "active ingredient" is needed. Lewin insists that the critical link between persons and contexts is the immediate phenomenology of an individual perceiver (see Lewin, 1935, pp. 33, 242). If other variables like personality and social structure exert any effect at all, their effect occurs primarily through their impact on the individual's phenomenology. Remote experiences like those discussed by Freud (e.g., childhood disruptions in maternal attachment) do not directly cause social behavior. Remote experiences are not causal, other than to leave tiny residues that may affect the perceiver's interpretation of events and the perceiver's immediate phenomenology (Lewin, 1935, pp. 53-54; see Kahneman & Miller, 1986). Lewin likens the impact of earlier life events on an individual's current behavior to the gravitational impact of the stars on individuals on the earth—conceptually possible, but, practically, infinitesimally small.

The third theme involves psychic structure, and is relevant to recent discussions about the structure of self-monitoring (Briggs & Cheek, 1986; Hoyle & Lennox, 1991; Hoyle & Sowards, in press; West & Finch, in press). The structure that generates phenomenology is built in memory of the context of events belonging to the same motivational process. An individual's phenomenology—whether two psychological events are linked—is determined by whether the events are embedded within the same or different motivational processes. Thus social behavior is determined by the phenomenology of an immediate context, actively generated by the self not from the intensity or duration of cues, but from the belongingness of events to the same total motivational process (Lewin, 1935, p. 55; see also Vallacher & Wegner, 1985, p. 27).

These three themes, taken together, should make Lewinian social psychology an unfriendly place for persons interested in either personality or social development (Jones, 1985, p. 52). Lewin clearly prefers an analysis of the immediate situation to a historical analysis (see the discussion of whether the floor of an attic is sufficiently strong to carry a weight, Lewin, 1951, pp. 48-49). Lewin believes that historical approaches like those of Freud that seek causation from an individual's life history are less productive in the long run than his approach.

From a social-cognitive developmental perspective, however, it is interesting that Lewin speculates that, within a person's cognitive structure, there may be regions or "modules" that vary in their degree of coherence. That is, the mind forms a general unity with no "higher" or "lower" elements, but some structures are less well organized than are others. There may also be relatively segregated energetic systems. Lewin (1935) notes that recognizing this possibility is "an exceedingly important condition of a more penetrating psychological research" (p. 57; but see Hoyle & Sowards, in press). The topic he specifically thinks will benefit from a modularized analysis is what we would now call social-cognitive development: "The formation of definite psychical systems is related in part to the ontogenetic development of the mind. It therefore shows, as does that development, a specifically historical component" (Lewin, 1935, p. 58).

Value of a Lewinian Analysis of Self-Monitoring

Tracing the subtleties of Lewin's thinking on social development, or more generally, the intellectual genealogy of ideas in personality and social psychology, can be a meaningless exercise. What does it matter whether we link the self-monitoring construct to James and Goffman rather than to Lewin? One answer to this question involves construct validity. Constructs gain their meaning from the relations that they are assumed, purported, or hypothesized to have, both with other hypothetical constructs "horizontally" (Goldberg, 1993) and with more concrete operationalizations "vertically" (Cook & Campbell, 1979; Feigl, 1970; Graziano, 1984, 1987; Houts, Cook, & Shadish, 1986; McGuire, 1983).

More specifically, an intellectual genealogy helps establish the family of constructs toward which discriminatory validation should be directed and how construct validity in general should proceed (see Briggs & Cheek, 1986, for a discussion of the intellectual genealogies of several constructs relevant to the self). It helps separate variables that are plausibly causal from those that are presumed spurious, and implicitly defines contexts relevant for eliciting effects (McGuire, 1983). Like a theory, it can also blind us to important historical, temporal, and contextual dependencies (Greenwald, Pratkanis, Lieppe, & Baumgardner, 1986; Houts et al., 1986).

Some of the best known critics of the self-monitoring construct may have been too quick to accept Snyder's Jamesian genealogy in building their criticisms (e.g., Briggs & Cheek, 1986, p. 113). Had the critics looked past the claimed genealogy toward Lewin's ideas, they might have recognized the need for a more interpersonal, motive-based analysis of self-monitoring, and a corresponding critique. Existing critiques seem to miss the larger point: Self-monitoring is a Galilean process, not an Aristotelian disposition.

Given Lewin's general orientation and influence on the intellectual Zeitgeist, then, we can see the "force lines" steering theory and research in social psychology toward the topic of the self. The Lewinian self is a Galilean process, not an Aristotelian disposition. It is flexible and responsive to variations in situations, as they are construed by the self (Markus, 1977; Vallacher & Wegner, 1985). The Lewinian self should be manifest more commonly in person X situation interactions, not in person main effects. In our analysis, self-monitoring clearly fits the requirements for a Lewinian self. The primary focus is on common motivational ("strategic") processes, not dispositions per se, that link seemingly different classes of adult social behavior. The link is mediated through social perception of the immediate situation (Snyder, 1987; Snyder & Cantor, 1980). From the perspective of the Lewinian themes that dominate contemporary social psychology, issues involving a biogenetic basis (Gangestad & Simpson, 1993), precise mathematic-statistical specification (Hoyle & Lennox, 1991), or factorial structure, per se (Briggs & Cheek, 1986), are largely Aristotelian tangents.

THE DEVELOPMENT OF SELF-MONITORING

With this background, we now examine the concept of self-monitoring (Snyder, 1974, 1987; Snyder & Gangestad, 1986) as a tool for probing personality and social development. Even in Snyder's earliest presentations, the dynamics of self-monitoring have a Lewinian, historical cast. The motivation underlying the individual difference is linked to concerns for social appropriateness within a specific, immediate context. Furthermore, even in his earliest theorizing, Snyder (1974) speculates that some individuals may have learned that their affective experiences and expressions are somehow socially inappropriate or lacking. To compensate, these individuals will monitor (i.e., observe and attempt to control) their own self-presentation and expressive behavior. These are high self-monitoring individuals. On the other hand, some persons have not learned a concern for appropriateness of their self-presentation, and do not have "such well-developed self-monitoring skills" (p. 527). These are low self-monitoring individuals. Relative to the high self-monitoring individuals, they appear to be monitoring their own self-presentation less, but may be monitoring their own attitudes and affective states more.

Snyder (1974) originally presented self-monitoring as a unidimensional construct, with lower and higher levels. He seemed to define a low self-monitoring person by default; the low self-monitor lacks the skills and motivation that the high self-monitor possesses. In later explications, however, Snyder (1979) moves to a two-prototype model. These prototypes may be conceptualized in terms of two coequal, and possibly developmentally coequal, strategic/motivational processes that influence the interpretation of the immediate situation. The prototypical high self-monitoring individual appears to be asking the strategic question "What does the situation want me to be and how can I be that person?" In comparison to the high self-monitoring person, the low self-monitoring person generates expressive behavior from his or her own affective states and attitudes; lows express it as they feel it. The strategic question for the low self-monitoring person is "Who am I and how can I be me in this situation?"

Snyder's shift away from a unidimensional-level model to a prototype model has important theoretical implications, both formally and substantively. First, the prototype system allows room for the operation of multiple, "configured" motives, and implies that differences in self-monitoring may represent multidimensional configurations or syndromes (Goldberg, 1993). The motive system underlying behavior in high self-monitoring persons may not be the same as, or even collinear with, the motive system underlying behavior in low self-monitoring persons. We may have modules, or in Lewin's terms, differences in patterns of local organization within psychical structure.

Second, the prototype model meshes better with subsequent research. Virtually all of the larger-sample empirical analyses of self-monitoring find at least three factors underlying self-monitoring (Briggs & Cheek suggest the factor labels extraversion, other directedness, and acting; see also Gabrenya & Arkin, 1980; Hoyle & Lennox, 1991; Penner & Wymer, 1983; West & Finch, in press; for an alternative view, see Gangestad & Snyder, 1985).

Third, and potentially most important for our purposes, a prototype approach facilitates a process-oriented, truly developmental analysis. The earlier, unidimensional approach implies that low self-monitoring is essentially the absence of high self-monitoring. As critics of Piaget's theory have noted, without extensive "preprogramming" through genetics, there is something miraculous about cognitive structures that develop from nothingness. Furthermore, the unidimensional approach essentially equates low self-monitoring with lower levels of development. The prototype approach gives low self-monitoring a developmentally coequal status. It implies, however, that a developmental analysis may require tracking several "modules" simultaneously.

Emotions and the Development of Self-Monitoring

Three different ways of conceptualizing the development of self-monitoring share the assumptions that

- Self-monitoring differences are closely linked to the development of emotions and motivational systems.
- The process is truly developmental in that changes in behavior and cognition are induced by changes in underlying structure ("centrality structure," as in Connell & Furman, 1984), and are not just relatively peripheral changes in behavior induced by simple learning.
- The structural representation is presumed to be a latent variable, with different phenotypic indicators at different developmental levels (e.g., Eder, 1987; Graziano, Leone, Musser, & Lautenschlager, 1987; Graziano & Ward, 1992).

First, we briefly discuss a quasi-orthodox, Waddingtonian conceptualization that the development of self-monitoring is induced primarily by ontogenic processes in an individual person. The developmental change occurs within a single, structural representation of the world (Bonner, 1958; Flavell, 1972; Mandler, 1983; Waddington, 1962). Second, we criticize this approach and consider a second option, an interactive, interpersonal developmental model that focuses on emotional self-regulation through observation and

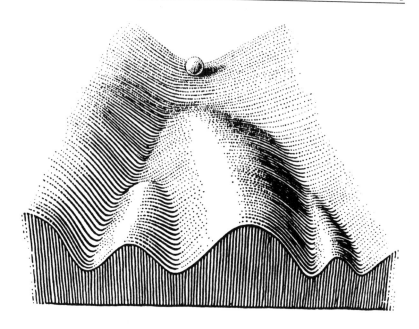

Figure 10.1. Waddington's Epigenetic Landscape
SOURCE: C. H. Waddington, *The Strategy of the Genes: A Discussion of Some Aspects of Theoretical Biology* (1957), London: George Allen & Unwin (Ruskin House).

social learning, with special attention to emotional self-regulation during social exchanges. Third, we reconsider the idea of a single structural representation common to all social and personality development, and discuss the notion of multiple, dedicated modules, or special subsystems.

Self-Monitoring as the Development of a Single Structure

The developmental geneticist Waddington (1962) offers a metaphor and visual representation for describing development in his "epigenetic landscape" (see also Bonner, 1958). Here we adapt it to describe links among emotion/motivational systems, self-monitoring, and social development. In Figure 10.1, the ball represents the individual, uniquely configured at birth with a characteristic emotional core and predispositions. The individual

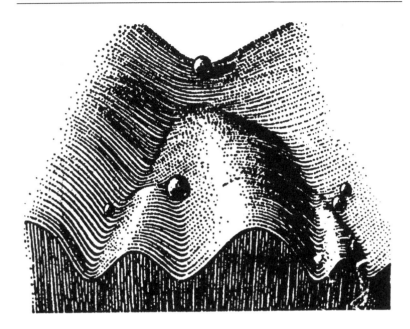

Figure 10.2. Lewinized Epigenetic Landscape
SOURCE: Adapted by the authors from Figure 10.1 by Waddington (1957).

moves down the landscape, but due to his or her unique emotional "spin," may be more likely to roll one way or another.

Channels or "creodes" differ in depth, which for Waddington represent the extent to which genes buffer the individual from displacement by environmental forces. A wide valley implies a developmental pathway that is not well buffered, and permits environmental forces to displace the phenotype.

This metaphor has been criticized for being vague, incomplete, and potentially misleading. It is. The Waddington ball operates like a socially isolated, windowless Leibnitzian monad. Environments are sources of disruption in preprogrammed development. Even the contours of the landscape are determined by the individual genotype, with the ball's relative position representing the value of the developing phenotype. The ball's size or shape does not change.

We can salvage this individual, temperament-based approach to development by adding interactive, interpersonal elements. We can "Lewinize" the landscape for a better metaphor of social and personality development (Figure 10.2). First, we make the landscape social. Within our new metaphor, the hills may be regarded as age-related life tasks or transitions. We allow "mud" to accumulate around the ball as it moves down the landscape past the life tasks, leaving residues of experience. The core ball may remain beneath the mud, but we allow the structure to be transformed. Another social element is added by placing other people (balls of different sizes and locations) on the landscape. The balls retain their own unique "spin," but they are able to observe what happens to some (but not all) of the other balls as they move down the landscape. Some channels may be completely blocked because other balls are blocking the entrance (e.g., older brothers or sisters, an abusive teacher), so default channels need to be available.

To Lewinize Waddington's landscape more fully, we would probably need to allow individual balls to perceive hills and valleys differently; the phenomenology of the sizes of hills and valleys should affect choices and willingness to enter particular valleys. We would also need mechanisms for social influences to allow balls to couple together in their trajectories, and to separate selectively.

Using this new landscape, let us offer some conjectures about the development of self-monitoring. First, beneath the mud of social-cognitive differences are emotional-motivational, temperamental predispositions toward self-monitoring. One characteristic emotional disposition that may be important both to the kinds of valleys into which an individual rolls and to the development of self-monitoring is emotional self-control. Persons temperamentally disposed toward high emotional reactivity and low self-control probably have socialization experiences systematically different from their less emotional peers (Rothbart, 1988, 1989). Our hypothesis linking emotionality to self-monitoring is derived in part from data suggesting that high self-monitoring college students report that they are more responsive to emotion-related experiences than low self-monitoring college students (Snyder & Monson, 1975, Study 2). Our hypothesis is also derived from extending Lewin's idea that motive systems are the organizing force in phenomenology.

Self-Monitoring and the Socialization of Emotion: Correlational Studies

Until recently, few researchers considered the links among socialization practices, temperament, and emotional self-regulation. Theory and research has emphasized the cognitive underpinnings of the development of emotional self-control (e.g., Kopp, 1989; Mischel & Mischel, 1983). More recently, theorists have recognized that socialization and cognitive approaches are not necessarily incompatible with temperament approaches (Halverson & Wampler, in press; Rothbart, 1988, 1989).

Eisenberg, Fabes, Schaller, Carlo, and Miller (1991) report data that are relevant to these hypotheses as part of a larger study of socialization of emotional responding. These authors collected data from third graders and their parents. They found that parental reports of encouraging children to change or control their negative feelings were associated with high self-monitoring in both boys and girls. In addition, they found that mothers and fathers have different effects on the self-monitoring tendencies in sons and daughters. For girls, high self-monitoring was positively associated with paternal restrictiveness in regard to the display of potentially hurtful emotions. Mothers high in personal distress, defined as experiencing self-oriented feelings of personal anxiety and unease in tense interpersonal settings, had daughters who were low in self-monitoring. In contrast, paternal sympathy was positively related to boys' self-monitoring.

There are several interpretations of these data. One is that parents who differentially socialize their children to control negative emotional expression and to be accommodating to other people may also be differentially socializing individual differences in self-monitoring. By emphasizing the need to accommodate to others and to be accepted, parents may be stimulating the development of structure in children to be responsive to norms, especially those for avoiding hurt feelings or doing harm. This interpretation is consistent with research demonstrating that high self-monitoring college students change their behavior more in response to normative information about helping others than do low self-monitoring students (e.g., White & Gerstein, 1987).

Musser and her colleagues Browne, Helling, Hines, and Yu present research relevant to these hypotheses. Musser and Browne (1991) first examined the relations among self-monitoring and family variables in first-, third-, and fifth-grade children and their parents. Self-monitoring was measured using the Graziano et al. (1987) scale, and was correlated with the number of children in the family (.40), and with the number of older siblings in the family (.28). There were no significant correlations with either of their parents' self-monitoring or extraversion scores. More interesting, perhaps, is the relatively high stability of self-monitoring scores across a 15-month period.

The stability was high for both girls (.62) and boys (.48); even for first graders, the 15-month stability was .50.

Helling, Yu, and Hines (1991) asked mothers of high and low self-monitoring children, as measured by the Graziano et al. (1987) scale, how they would respond to conflicts involving their child. Mothers of high self-monitoring children attributed equal responsibility to both children involved in a conflict, whereas mothers of low self-monitoring children placed more responsibility on their own child. Mothers of high self-monitoring children appeared to be more flexible across situations. For example, they expected their child to be less responsible when interacting with an older child. In contrast, mothers of low self-monitoring children expected their children to assume responsibility for conflict regardless of the age of the partner.

The Helling et al. (1991) study raises interesting questions about the direction of effect. The "direction of effect" in socialization in the case of self-monitoring (at least of blame for conflict) may not be from parent to child (but see Eisenberg et al., 1991). If a child's self-monitoring level is not related to that of his or her parents (Musser & Browne, 1991), then the child's level of self-monitoring may be eliciting differential socialization from parents.

If self-monitoring structure in children is stimulated in part by characteristics of the child, then it becomes important to identify those characteristics. Parents may be alert to individual differences in their children's emotionality and their implications for social interaction (e.g., interpersonal conflict). Parents who socialize the motivation to accommodate to others may invest more time in their more emotional children, encouraging them to be other directed and to acquire role-taking skills relevant to social accommodation. In this approach, the skills associated with self-monitoring are developmentally subsequent to earlier, parent-recognized motives and emotions.

Another approach involves emotionality and "unreliable" parental training. High self-monitoring persons may have been temperamentally more emotional as children, but over the course of development have learned from interaction with certain classes of adults and peers that emotional reactivity can have negative repercussions. Some parents may be intolerant of emotional expression in children, and encourage them to control its expression. Other parents may deny the validity of their children's reports of certain emotion ("That doesn't really hurt"). One consequence of this "unreliability" in the socialization of emotion is that for some children, internal, emotional reactions lose their value as reliable guides to overt action. When a high self-monitoring person needs to choose a course of action, he or she may not regard internal cues as sufficiently reliable or valuable to be guides.

Regardless of parental motivation, we need a proximal mechanism within the individual child to explain self-monitoring differences. In the case of persons who ultimately become high self-monitoring adults, these persons may have developed a system to disengage the link between affect and overt action as children. The "circuit breaker" system is self-monitoring; it is inserted into the circuitry linking emotional reactivity to overt behavior. When an emotion-relevant situation arises, high self-monitoring persons may become aware of situational cues, especially those relevant to "appropriateness." The self-monitoring system may lie dormant most of the time, but it can be tripped by specific situational cues (e.g., presence of persons in certain social categories). In this analysis, high self-monitoring individuals are no less emotional as a result of developing the circuit breaker; they are merely less direct in their responsiveness to emotional events. The ball remains beneath the mud.

Graziano, Danheiser, and Halverson (1989) probe the idea that early temperament differences in emotional self-control might be related to the development of self-monitoring. These authors used Eder's (1987) self-monitoring scale for preschool children, completed by the children's teachers. Through factor analysis, Eder identifies separate factors she labels "acting" and "flexibility" within the larger self-monitoring construct. Teachers also completed temperament ratings of the children (Buss & Plomin, 1984). In addition, a subsample was measured for motor activity during free play across 5 noncontiguous days, using mechanical activity recorders (Halverson & Post-Gordon, 1984). Nearly all classifications of children include activity as a basic factor (Zuckerman, Kuhlman, Joireman, Teta, & Kraft, 1993); theorists have implicated motor activity as a major target for cognitive control (e.g., Luria, 1976); and activity differences are related empirically to the development of self-regulation (Halverson & Wampler, in press). Ratings were taken late in the term, so that teachers had extensive contact with the children ($N = 41$) before rating them.

Teacher-assessed temperament dimensions were related to self-monitoring. Self-monitoring was positively related to activity ($r = .76$), and sociability (.61), but negatively related to shyness (–.54). Teacher-rated activity was related in turn to the Buss and Plomin (1984) dimensions of sociability (.63), shyness (–.63), and to the Eder factors of acting (.81) and flexibility (.52). Activity was not related to age or sex. There was no relation between self-monitoring and emotionality (.03), age (.26), or sex (.02).

Self-regulation is a complex construct (e.g., Luria, 1976), and it is unlikely that a single individual difference like self-monitoring would explain all or even much of it. Nonetheless, the pattern of intercorrelations among self-monitoring and early temperament variables suggests that future research should explore the links between the development of self-regulation and interpersonal interaction. Given the adult literature (e.g., Briggs & Cheek, 1986), we might expect self-monitoring to be related to sociability and (inversely) to shyness; it is, at least in the teachers' ratings. The link to teacher ratings of activity would not have been anticipated based on the adult studies.

Regarding the lack of evidence linking emotionality to self-monitoring, the Graziano et al. (1989) data are not necessarily fatal to our hypothesis. The items used to assess emotionality on the Buss and Plomin (1984) measure focus on negative emotionality (e.g., "Child gets upset easily," "Child reacts intensely when upset"). The Buss and Plomin measure may reflect individual differences in the observable failure of self-regulation. That is, the processes of negative emotional self-regulation may have already begun to develop in 3-, 4-, and 5-year-olds (but see Kopp, 1989), and the Buss and Plomin measures may be showing us children who are developmentally delayed in some way. Furthermore, the original Graziano et al. (1989) conceptualization of emotionality had a static, "off-the-shelf" Aristotelian quality; it was not situated in context.

Self-Monitoring and the Socialization of Emotion:
The Mistaken Gift Studies

One way to observe emotional processes is to generate a situation likely to provoke emotions and to observe differences in emotional displays. These differences in emotional displays are probably related to important aspects of social development; children in all cultures are expected to learn socially defined norms for emotional displays, and the acquisition of these display rules is an important part of the self-regulation of emotion (Ekman & Friesen, 1984; Kahneman & Miller, 1986; Saarni, 1985). High self-monitoring children may be especially likely to adjust their emotional displays in situations that elicit emotions.

A situation ideal for probing this hypothesis involves the giving and receiving of gifts (Graziano, 1984). Gift exchange appears to be universal in human societies (Harris, 1968), and children often receive gifts from friends and relatives. It is not unreasonable for children to have positive expectations about gifts: Most gifts are attractive to them. More important, from a theoretical level, is that processes associated with social exchanges and gift giving have been implicated as parts of evolution-based, specialized cognitive modules (Cosmides & Tooby, 1992; but see Graziano, 1984).

From the perspective of the child receiving a gift, what happens when the gift is not attractive? In this situation, it is likely that the child experiences feelings of frustration and negative affect. In the prototypic gift-giving situation for children, however, the child is under the scrutiny of an adult, who wants to see displays of positive affect and gratitude. The result is a conflict between the demand for a positive affective display and the internal negative affect (Cole, 1986; Saarni, 1984, 1985). Gift exchanges may represent for children a special developmental experience; this may be the first time children learn to generate public behavior that is inconsistent with private feeling states (see Goodnow, 1987, "Plans that evoke approval and disapproval"; Graziano, 1984). Gift giving may have a fundamentally different phenomenology for children high and low in self-monitoring.

Ward (1990) invited third-grade students to perform a toy-rating task, followed by a book-rating task. In compensation, each child was given a wrapped package containing a desirable gift (one of the toys the child had assigned a high rating). The child was then asked to come back for another book-rating task. After the child had rated the second set of books, another wrapped prize was given. At this point the child usually unwrapped the prize immediately, to discover that it was the toy he or she had ranked last. (The second gift was a "dud.") Using a procedure adapted from Cole (1986), the experimenters maintained a neutral expression for 20 seconds, so as not to influence the child's response after the child opened the present. The experimenter then noticed the "mistake," and produced a more appropriate gift. Videocameras placed unobtrusively across the room recorded each child's displays of emotion, which were coded by persons blind to the child's personality scores and experimental conditions.

Prior to any experimental manipulations, children completed a computerized, self-paced version of the Junior Self-Monitoring scale (Graziano et al., 1987), and for purposes of discriminatory validity, age-appropriate measures of extraversion and locus of control. These scores were then correlated with ratings of positive affect, happiness, interest, negative affect, disgust, surprise, disappointment, anger, and fear within each episode of gift giving.

The gift-exchange situation seems well suited for studying children's attempts to control their emotional displays. For example, children displayed more positive affect, happiness, and interest following the mistaken gift than following the attractive gift. At the same time, negative emotions of anger and fear increased after the disappointing gift, suggesting that attempts to mask negative emotions are not easy for all children. As expected, low self-monitoring children showed more surprise when receiving the mistaken gift than did high self-monitoring children. Self-monitoring effects remained significant even when individual differences in extraversion were removed through partial correlation. On the other hand, there was no evidence that high self-monitoring children displayed more positive affect, or less negative affect, in the face of a disappointing gift relative to low self-monitoring children.

SELF-MONITORING AND DISTRIBUTED
PROCESSOR MODELS OF SOCIAL DEVELOPMENT

Self-monitoring does not always behave like a good Aristotelian personality attribute. It is probably composed of more than one underlying factor. Sometimes self-monitoring differences do not appear where theory says they should (e.g., Ward, 1990). Individual differences in self-monitoring do seem to be stable across time, however, both in adults (Snyder, 1987) and in children (Musser & Browne, 1991). When we consider self-monitoring as a Galilean process, we can see patterns anticipated by Lewin (1935); these patterns are compatible with other ideas within the current social psychology zeitgeist.

Nonetheless, we may need a new way to conceptualize self-monitoring and its development. Rather than considering self-monitoring as a single latent variable, single structural representation, or single set of strategic tendencies with a single coherent developmental pattern, we might consider self-monitoring as a loosely federated "distributed processor system" (Laboratory of Comparative Human Cognition, 1983). More precisely, we can conceptualize self-monitoring as differences in levels of connectedness among separate subschemas and modules.

Two figures adapted from the Laboratory of Comparative Human Cognition (1983) will help illustrate. In Figure 10.3, we see a "central processor" model, a traditional generic model of cognition and personality. In this model, events operate on a central cognitive machinery (e.g., IQ, conceptual level, cognitive style), which in turn guides performance on the range of tasks the individual encounters. This central processor interprets all experiences. In this system, the same head that solves math problems also solves

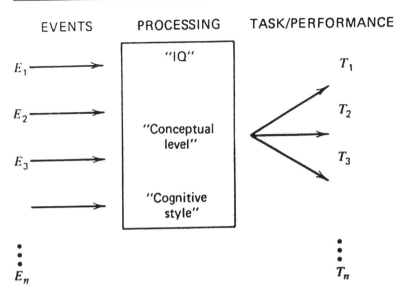

Figure 10.3. Central Processor Model
SOURCE: Laboratory of Comparative Human Cognition (1983). Copyright © by John Wiley & Sons, Inc.
Reprinted by permission.

problems of social relations; a concrete operational child is concrete in solving math problems and in solving interpersonal problems. In development, the central processor is assumed to evolve as a single faculty. The Waddington ball rolls as a single entity.

The well-known concept of "horizontal decalage" in cognitive development was introduced in part to explain discrepancies in performance on structurally similar tasks, and has been described as a "safety valve" for saving stage theory models of development. The assumption is that discrepancies in performance are not attributable to a lack of competence in the central processor, but to some peripheral problem like information-processing loads of one task relative to another. But as critics have noted, horizontal decalage is a description, not an explanation, of a phenomenon. Mandler (1983) records that in many areas of thinking, there may be no generalizable competence, but "only hard won principles wrested anew from each domain as it is explored" (p. 475).

An alternative way of conceptualizing cognitive representations is through a distributed processor model (Figure 10.4). In this model, we do not assume

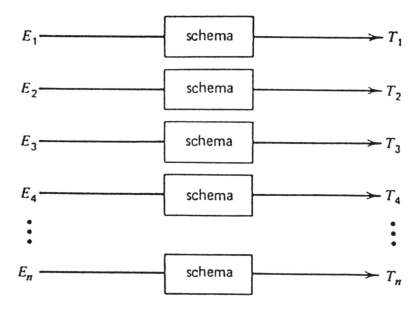

Figure 10.4. Distributed Processor Model
SOURCE: Laboratory of Comparative Human Cognition (1983). Copyright © 1983 by John Wiley & Sons, Inc. Reprinted by permission.

that events are all processed through a single central processor. The human mind may include a number of functionally distinct, cognitive adaptive specializations. These units may operate in a generally concerted way, but in certain contexts may perform their specific work relatively independently of each other, just as the heart pumps blood and the liver detoxifies poisons (Tooby & Cosmides, 1990). Interestingly, these dedicated cognitive modules may not interconnect in certain contexts. For example, if there were separate modules for controlling the public expression of negative affect, and others for regulating attitude-behavior consistency, then situational cues could selectively elicit processes in one subsystem without eliciting processes in the other. (See Scholnick & Friedman, 1987, for similar issues relevant to the analysis of the development of planning.) In this approach, the head that solves math problems will not necessarily show the same competence in dealing with math and interpersonal conflict.

Costanzo (1991) suggests that modularity may characterize social and personality development in ways similar to that described for cognitive development. His model shows definite Lewinian themes. Costanzo suggests that two separate systems, or localized energetic areas, underlie social cognition and its development. A "generative system" (System 1) involves acquired principles of reasoning about the social and moral world. It constructs the meaning of social action by deploying attention. A "conservative system" (System 2) is responsive to the specific content of social action, and contains the residues of socialization. This system drives automatic processing, reflected in encoding biases, and valuative reasoning. System 1 is concerned with discontinuities and distinctive qualities of situations, whereas System 2 is concerned with the continuity of the self and identity. Put simplistically, System 2 deals with important matters, as determined by socialization. When cues from the situation are novel or do not encroach on personally important themes, System 2 allows System 1 the luxury of treating the material rationally.

This model is still new, but Costanzo (1991) uses it to generate some provocative hypotheses. Memory processes for important (System 2) behaviors and stimuli may operate on different principles than memory for unimportant (System 1) stimuli. System 2 may operate "preemptively," monitoring context for important cues. The actual construction of context may be as much a matter of monitoring importance of items as of monitoring frequencies (but see Graziano, 1987, pp. 284-291; Kahneman & Miller, 1986).

One major issue associated with distributed processing models is patterns of communication and coordination among separate modules. If there are dedicated modules, how do the outcomes of their analyses influence the operation of other modules? Two elements are important, and both are potentially relevant to the development of self-monitoring. First, some executive schema must be involved in directing connections among modules. In Costanzo's (1991) model, System 2 serves this function, in addition to being a dedicated module. Individual differences in the way this executive operates could influence the level of communication among modules (see the Selfridge and Neisser, 1960, "pandemonium model"). For example, a weaker executive might direct fewer communications across modules.

The second element involves how differences in operation of the executive schema might occur. Part of the answer probably lies in patterns of socialization (Costanzo, 1991; Eisenberg et al., 1991; Goodnow, 1987; Laboratory of Comparative Human Cognition, 1983). When socialization agents combine certain tasks or juxtapose tasks as part of a larger activity (e.g., selling grain or rugs, memorizing religious texts), communication across these juxtaposed schema should be more frequent or more efficient (Kahneman &

Miller, 1986). It is especially interesting to see the examples used by the Laboratory of Comparative Human Cognition (1983) to illustrate cultural socialization differences; its focus is on cognitive processes such as memory and quantitative skills, but the prototypic example involves some form of training for social exchange.

There are several implications of this line of thinking for the development of self-monitoring. First, self-monitoring differences may be related to differences in the degree to which dedicated modules "shake hands" with each other. Low self-monitoring persons may exhibit greater cross-situational consistency because communication across dedicated modules is more complete. Phrased differently, high self-monitoring individuals may exhibit greater cross-situational variability than low self-monitoring individuals in part because the cognitive representations of the former are more distributed than those of the latter (but see Wymer & Penner, 1985).

Second, if the general pattern of cognitive development is toward progressively improving communication across schemas (Vygotsky, 1962, p. 33), then a reasonable question is what processes block cross-schema communication in some persons? Part of the answer probably lies in ways that socialization agents juxtapose tasks and events. If children are socialized to read and memorize primarily for purposes of religious education, then we might expect closer links between cognitive skills and religious thinking for persons in these cultures than in other, more secular cultures. That is, elements may be unified through a common action identification (Vallacher & Wegner, 1985). Similarly, if socializing agents link emotional self-control to an altruistic motive system (e.g., concerns about hurting the feelings of others, as in Eisenberg et al., 1991), then we might expect communication between emotional control and altruistic motivation systems. If, however, socializing agents link emotional control primarily to self-protective motives (e.g., the Spartan boy and the stolen fox) then communication between emotional self-control and altruism might be negligible. Another, related answer might lie in the socialization of motivational systems, particularly in the priority assigned to motivational systems by socialization agents (Eisenberg et al., 1991; Goodnow, 1987).

Third, patterns in social adjustment may be related to self-monitoring and its development. Snyder (1987) notes that there is no evidence that personal problems are more common in high or low self-monitoring persons, or that one type is more susceptible to pathological conditions. We should not expect simple, cross-context, main effect relations from a Lewinian self. Yet, social adjustment differences may be the result of communication (or its lack) in distributed processing systems (see Colvin's, 1993, three conceptualizations of adjustment, pp. 862-863). If we assume that self-monitoring develops from an emotional substrate, then self-monitoring may be related to the kinds of events that precipitate personal distress (see Snyder, 1987, p. 115), the intensity and duration of emotional distress, and the ways of coping with distress once it occurs. In addition, self-monitoring may be related to how emotional distress is expressed and to whom it is conveyed (but see Shaffer et al., 1982).

Graziano and Ward (1992) asked teachers and counselors to evaluate the adjustment of sixth- and seventh-grade adolescents. There was moderately good agreement between teachers and counselors ($r = .44$) about the adjustment of students; students' self-reported self-monitoring was not related to teacher or counselor ratings of adjustment. There is, however, another way to consider adjustment data. It was possible to cross-classify students in a 2 × 2 matrix, with teacher ratings (well adjusted, not well adjusted) crossed with counselor ratings (well adjusted, not well adjusted). Due to high teacher-counselor agreement, the cells with the largest frequencies involve teacher-counselor agreement (both rate student as well adjusted; both rate student as not well adjusted). More interesting, however, are the students on which the teachers and counselors disagree (e.g., teacher rates as adjusted, but counselor rates as not well adjusted). Some students may have two different modules for dealing with teachers and counselors; these may generate different behaviors in the presence of the two different adults. It would be valuable to identify such "controversial" students. Graziano and Ward found that these controversial students were higher in self-monitoring (and extraversion) than the students on whom the teachers and counselors agreed.

One explanation for these data is that high self-monitoring adolescents have different strategies, and possibly separate processing modules, for dealing with different classes of persons. As a consequence, they may have different "stories" to tell different people about their emotional experiences. We need not assume that high self-monitoring persons are manipulative in their disparate stories. Their motivation may derive from concerns about "appropriateness" in the presence of persons in different social categories. It may be difficult for other people to evaluate high self-monitoring persons who appear to be doing very different things in different situations (Vallacher & Wegner, 1985; but see Snyder, 1974, Arbitrary Emotion Study). Using a converging, multimethod study, Colvin (1993) demonstrates that some people are systematically judged more accurately than others, and that "judgability" is positively correlated with adjustment. This relation holds even when partial correlations are controlled for favorability and commonness of the target's individual differences.

Social adjustment is a complex, multifaced phenomenon; it is unlikely that one individual difference like self-monitoring will explain most of the variability. Nonetheless, if self-monitoring is conceptualized as one social-cognitive manifestation of a distributed processing system and if it develops from an emotional substrate, then it might be profitable to probe the aspects of adjustment that are related to communication (or its lack) across modules.

DIRECTIONS FOR FUTURE RESEARCH

The material discussed in this chapter is highly speculative, and is painted with a very broad brush. In the absence of a solid empirical base on the development of self-monitoring, this is not unreasonable. Nonetheless, future theory and research must address important issues. First, there is a great need to reconsider the basic nature of self-monitoring as a Galilean process, and not dismiss it prematurely because it does not always behave like a good Aristotelian disposition (Snyder, 1987, pp. 201-208; but see Briggs & Cheek, 1986).

Second, it may be profitable to reconsider self-monitoring processes in terms of social-cognitive development through its links to emotional self-regulation. Self-monitoring differences in adults may emerge from temperament differences in children's emotionality, which are differentially socialized. Some important steps in understanding socialization of emotional self-control have been taken by Eisenberg et al. (1991). Self-monitoring in children is related to parental efforts to have children inhibit hurtful emotions. This suggests that self-monitoring may develop as a consequence of parental efforts to socialize prosocial behavior (White & Gerstein, 1987), and may be a form of agreeableness (Graziano & Eisenberg, in press).

Third, it is not clear at this point precisely how emotions operate as modules or are differentially socialized as modules. The usual "central processor," one-head-does-it-all approach to social-cognitive developmental is probably not useful. We need to consider the development of self-monitoring in terms of distributed-schema models of cognition that have dedicated modules. We need theoretical specification of modules and motives (Costanzo, 1991; Markus & Cross, 1990). A modularized approach suggests that processes like "self-regulation" or "adjustment" probably do not operate in a monolithic, omnibus way across all content domains. Consequently, self-monitoring may be related to self-regulation in some domains but not in others. Relative to their peers, high self-monitoring children may appear to be better self-regulators in some activities (e.g., emotional expressivity), but worse in others.

Another view of cognitive modules comes from theorists interested in human evolution (Buss, in press; Buss & Schmitt, 1993; Cosmides & Tooby, 1992). These theorists suggest that humans have evolved dedicated, but context-sensitive, modules organized around social exchange (but see Graziano, 1984). It is interesting is this regard that high self-monitoring college students appear to be more sensitive to subtleties in social exchange than low self-monitoring college students (Danheiser & Graziano, 1982). Socialization surrounding social exchanges may be critical for the development of self-monitoring differences (but see Graziano, 1984, 1987), and personality development more generally (Graziano & Eisenberg, in press).

Fourth, if self-monitoring differences are linked to motivation organized around social exchanges, then it might be interesting to probe the link between self-monitoring and the phenomenology of social exchanges. More specifically, it might be profitable to relate self-monitoring differences to self-reports of what individuals say they are doing (i.e., action identification) during social exchanges (Vallacher & Wegner, 1985). Social exchanges may have different fundamental characters for high and low self-monitoring persons. For example, low self-monitoring children may perceive themselves as bartering to obtain a needed commodity through social exchange, whereas high self-monitoring children may perceive themselves as engaging in a social exchange, with the specific commodity itself a secondary consideration (e.g., Graziano, Brody, & Bernstein, 1980). If these speculations are valid, then low self-monitoring children may be less willing to negotiate or to make adjustments in exchanges across commodity classes (Foa & Foa, 1974), or to make adjustments based on extra-exchange considerations (e.g., status or power of exchange partner) relative to high self-monitoring children (Graziano, 1984, 1987). High self-monitoring children may engage in more extra-exchange relationship maintenance activities during social exchanges than low self-monitoring children. At this time, there are no studies to support (or refute) such speculations.

Finally, it may be profitable to reconsider the intellectual genealogy of self-monitoring and to return to Lewin's (1935) themes about personality and social development. Self-monitoring offers us a potentially useful tool for understanding the development of the phenomenal self and its role in the active transformation of situations.

REFERENCES

Bonner, J. T. (1958). *The evolution of development.* Cambridge, UK: Cambridge University Press.

Briggs, S., & Cheek, J. (1986). The role of factor analysis in the development and evaluation of personality scales. *Journal of Personality, 54,* 106-148.

Buss, A. H., & Plomin, R. (1984). *A temperament theory of personality development* (2nd ed.). New York: John Wiley.

Buss, D. M. (in press). Evolutionary psychology: A new paradigm for psychological science. *Psychological Inquiry.*

Buss, D. M., & Schmitt, D. P. (1993). Sexual strategies theory: An evolutionary perspective on human mating. *Psychological Review, 100,* 204-232.

Chomsky, N. (1980). *Rules and representations.* New York: Columbia University Press.

Cole, P. M. (1986). Children's spontaneous control of facial expression. *Child Development, 57,* 1309-1321.

Colvin, C. R. (1993). "Judgable" people: Personality, behavior, and competing explanations. *Journal of Personality and Social Psychology, 64,* 861-873.

Connell, J. P., & Furman, W. C. (1984). The study of transitions: Conceptual and methodological issues. In R. N. Emde & R. J. Harmon (Eds.), *Continuities and discontinuities in development* (pp. 153-173). New York: Plenum.

Cook, T. D., & Campbell, D. T. (1979). *Quasi-experimentation: Design and analysis issues for filed settings.* Chicago: Rand McNally.

Cosmides, L., & Tooby, J. (1992). Cognitive adaptations for social exchange. In J. H. Barkow, L. Cosmides, & J. Tooby (Eds.), *The adapted mind: Evolutionary psychology and the generation of culture* (pp. 163-228). New York: Oxford University Press.

Costanzo, P. R. (1991). Morals, mothers, and memories: The social context of developing social cognition. In R. Cohen & R. Siegel (Eds.), *Context and development* (pp. 91-132). Hillsdale, NJ: Erlbaum.

Danheiser, P. R., & Graziano, W. G. (1982). Self-monitoring and cooperation as a self-presentational strategy. *Journal of Personality and Social Psychology, 42,* 497-505.

Eder, R. (1987). *Uncovering young children's psychological selves: Individual and developmental differences.* Unpublished manuscript.

Eisenberg, N., Fabes, R., Schaller, M., Carlo, G., & Miller, P. A. (1991). The relation of parental characteristics and practices to children's vicarious emotional responding. *Child Development, 62,* 1393-1408.

Ekman, P., & Friesen, W. V. (1984). *Unmasking the face.* Palo Alto, CA: Consulting Psychologist Press.

Elliott, G. C. (1979). Some effects of deception on planning and reaction to self-presentation. *Journal of Personality and Social Psychology, 37,* 1282-1292.

Feigl, H. (1970). The "orthodox" view of theories: Remarks in defense as well as critique. In M. Radner & S. Winokur (Eds.), *Minnesota studies in the philosophy of science: Analyses of theories & methods of physics & psychology* (pp. 3-16). Minneapolis: University of Minnesota Press.

Flavell, J. H. (1972). An analysis of cognitive-developmental sequences. *Genetic Psychology Monographs, 86,* 279-350.

Foa, U. G., & Foa, E. B. (1974). *Societal structures of the mind.* Springfield, IL: Charles C Thomas.

Gabrenya, W. K., Jr., & Arkin, R. M. (1980). Factor structure and factor correlates of the self-monitoring scale. *Personality & Social Psychology Bulletin, 6,* 13-22.

Gangestad, S. W., & Simpson, J. A. (1993). Development of a scale measuring genetic variation related to expressive control. *Journal of Personality, 61,* 133-158.

Gangestad, S., & Snyder, M. (1985)."To carve nature at its joints": On the existence of discrete classes in personality. *Psychological Review, 92,* 317-349.

Goldberg, L. R. (1993). The structure of personality traits: Vertical and horizontal aspects. In D. C. Funder, R. D. Parke, C. Tomlinson-Keasey, & K. Widaman (Eds.), *Studying lives through time: Personality & development* (pp. 169-188). Washington, DC: American Psychological Association.

Goodnow, J. J. (1987). Social aspects of planning. In S. L. Friedman, E. K. Scholnick, & R. R. Cocking (Eds.), *Blueprints for thinking: The role of planning in cognitive development* (pp. 179-201). Cambridge, UK: Cambridge University Press.

Graziano, W. G. (1984). A developmental approach to social exchange processes. In J. C. Masters & K. Yarkin-Levin (Eds.), *Boundary areas in social and developmental psychology* (pp. 161-193). New York: Academic Press.

Graziano, W. G. (1987). Lost in thought at the choice point: Cognition, context, and equity. In J. C. Masters & W. P. Smith (Eds.), *Social comparison, social justice and relative deprivation: Theoretical, empirical, and policy perspectives* (pp. 265-294). Hillsdale, NJ: Erlbaum.

Graziano, W. G., Brody, G., & Bernstein, S. (1980). Effects of information about future interaction and peer's motivation on peer reward allocation. *Developmental Psychology, 16,* 475-482.

Graziano, W. G., Danheiser, P. R., & Halverson, C. F. (1989, August). *Temperament, self-monitoring, and activity level in preschool children.* Paper presented at the Annual Meeting of the American Psychological Association, New Orleans, LA.

Graziano, W. G., & Eisenberg, N. H. (in press). Agreeableness: A dimension of personality. In R. Hogan, J. Johnson, & S. Briggs (Eds.), *Handbook of personality psychology.* San Diego: Academic Press.

Graziano, W. G., Leone, C., Musser, L. M., & Lautenschlager, G. J. (1987). Self-monitoring in children: A differential approach to social development. *Developmental Psychology, 23,* 571-576.

Graziano, W. G., & Ward, D. (1992). Probing the big five in adolescence: Personality and adjustment during a developmental transition. *Journal of Personality, 60,* 425-435.

Greenwald, A. G., Pratkanis, A. R., Lieppe, M. R., & Baumgardner, M. H. (1986). Under what conditions does theory obstruct research progress? *Psychological Review, 93,* 216-229.

Halverson, C., & Post-Gordon, J. C. (1984). The measurement of open-field activity in preschool children. In E. Pollitt & P. Amante (Eds.), *Protein intake and activity* (pp. 185-206). New York: Alan Liss.

Halverson, C., & Wampler, K. (in press). Family influences on personality development. In R. Hogan, J. Johnson, & S. Briggs (Eds.), *Handbook of personality psychology*. Orlando, FL: Academic Press.

Harris, M. (1968). *The rise of anthropological theory: A history of theories of culture*. New York: Crowell.

Helling, M. K., Yu, H. W., & Hines, F. (1991, April). *Choices in parenting strategies: A link to self-monitoring*. Paper presented at the biennial meeting of the Society for Research in Child Development, Seattle, WA.

Houts, A. C., Cook, T. D., & Shadish, W. R. (1986). The person-situation debate: A critical multiplist perspective. *Journal of Personality, 54*, 52-105.

Hoyle, R. H., & Lennox, R. D. (1991). Latent structure of self-monitoring. *Multivariate Behavioral Research, 26*, 511-540.

Hoyle, R. H., & Sowards, B. A. (in press). Self-monitoring and the regulation of social experience: A control-process model. *Journal of Social & Clinical Psychology*.

Ickes, W., Layden, M. A., & Barnes, R. D. (1978). Objective self-awareness and individuation: An empirical link. *Journal of Personality, 46*, 146-141.

Jones, E. E. (1985). Major developments in social psychology during the past five decades. In G. Lindzey & E. Aronson (Eds.), *Handbook of social psychology: Vol. 1. Theory and method* (pp. 47-108). New York: Random House.

Kahneman, D., & Miller, D. T. (1986). Norm theory: Comparing reality to its alternatives. *Psychological Review, 93*, 136-153.

Kopp, C. (1989). Regulation of distress and negative emotions: A developmental view. *Developmental Psychology, 25*, 343-354.

Laboratory of Comparative Human Cognition. (1983). Culture and cognitive development. In P. H. Mussen (Ed.), *Handbook of child psychology: Vol. 1* (4th ed., pp. 295-356). New York: John Wiley.

Lewin, K. (1935). *A dynamic theory of personality* (D. K. Adams & K. E. Zener, Trans.). New York: McGraw-Hill.

Lewin, K. (1951). *Field theory in social science* (D. Cartwright, Ed.). New York: Harper & Row.

Luria, A. R. (1976). *Cognitive development: Its cultural and social foundations*. Cambridge, MA: Harvard University Press.

Mandler, J. (1983). Representation. In P. Mussen (Ed.), *Handbook of child psychology: Vol. 3. Cognitive development* (4th ed., pp. 420-494). New York: John Wiley.

Markus, H. (1977). Self-schemata and processing information about the self. *Journal of Personality and Social Psychology, 35*, 63-78.

Markus, H., & Cross, S. (1990). The interpersonal self. In L. Pervin (Ed.), *Handbook of personality: Theory and research* (pp. 576-608). New York: Guilford.

McGuire, W. J. (1983). A contextualist theory of knowledge: Its implications for innovation and reform in psychological research. In L. Berkowitz (Ed.), *Advances in experimental social psychology: Vol. 16* (pp. 2-48). Orlando, FL: Academic Press.

Mischel, H. N., & Mischel, W. (1983).The development of children's knowledge about self-control strategies. *Child Development, 54*, 603-619.

Musser, L. M., & Browne, B. (1991). Self-monitoring in middle childhood: Personality and social correlates. *Developmental Psychology, 27*, 994-999.

Patnoe, S. (1988). *A narrative history of experimental social psychology.* New York: Springer-Verlag.

Paulhus, D. (1982). Individual differences, self-presentation, and cognitive dissonance: Their concurrent operation in forced compliance. *Journal of Personality and Social Psychology, 43,* 838-852.

Penner, L., & Wymer, W. E. (1983). The moderator variable approach to behavioral predictability: Some of the variables some of the time. *Journal of Research in Personality, 37,* 339-353.

Rothbart, M. K. (1988). Temperament and the development of inhibited approach. *Child Development, 59,* 1241-1250.

Rothbart, M. K. (1989). Biological processes in temperament. In G. Kohnstamm, J. Bates, & M. K. Rothbart (Eds.), *Handbook of temperament in childhood.* Sussex, UK: Wiley.

Saarni, C. (1984). An observational study of children's attempts to monitor their expressive behavior. *Child Development, 55,* 1504-1513.

Saarni, C. (1985). Indirect processes of affect socialization. In M. Lewis & C. Saarni (Eds.), *The socialization of emotions* (pp. 187-212). New York: Plenum.

Scholnick, E. K., & Friedman, S. L. (1987). The planning construct in the psychological literature. In S. Friedman, E. K. Scholnick, & R. R. Cocking (Eds.), *Blueprints for thinking: The role of planning in cognitive development* (pp. 33-38). Cambridge, UK: Cambridge University Press.

Selfridge, O. G., & Neisser, U. (1960). Pattern recognition by machine. *Scientific American, 203,* 60-68.

Shaffer, D. R., Smith, J., & Tomarelli, M. M. (1982). Self-monitoring as a determinant of self-disclosure reciprocity during the acquaintance process. *Journal of Personality and Social Psychology, 43,* 163-175.

Snyder, M. (1974). The self-monitoring of expressive behavior. *Journal of Personality and Social Psychology, 30,* 526-537.

Snyder, M. (1979). Self-monitoring processes. In L. Berkowitz (Ed.), *Advances in experimental social psychology: Vol. 12* (pp. 86-128). New York: Academic Press.

Snyder, M. (1987). *Public appearances, private realities: The psychology of self monitoring.* New York: Freeman.

Snyder, M., & Cantor, N. (1980). Thinking about ourselves and others: Self-monitoring and social knowledge. *Journal of Personality and Social Psychology, 39,* 222-234.

Snyder, M., & Gangestad, S. (1986). On the nature of self-monitoring: Matters of assessment, matters of validity. *Journal of Personality and Social Psychology, 51,* 125-134.

Snyder, M., & Monson, T. C. (1975). Persons, situations, and the control of social behavior. *Journal of Personality and Social Psychology, 32,* 637-644.

Tooby, J., & Cosmides, L. (1990). On the universality of human nature and the uniqueness of the individual: The role of genetics and adaptation. *Journal of Personality, 58,* 17-67.

Tooby, J., & Cosmides, L. (1992). The psychological foundations of culture. In J. H. Barkow, L. Cosmides, & J. Tooby (Eds.), *The adapted mind: Evolutionary psychology and the generation of culture* (pp. 19-136). New York: Oxford University Press.

Vallacher, R., & Wegner, D. (1985). *A theory of action identification.* Hillsdale, NJ: Erlbaum.

Vygotsky, L. S. (1962). *Language and thought.* Cambridge: MIT Press.

Waddington, C. H. (1962). *New patterns in genetics and development.* New York: Columbia University Press.

Ward, D. W. (1990). *Regulation of emotional expression and self-monitoring in children.* Unpublished master's thesis, University of Georgia.

West, S. G., & Finch, J. F. (in press). Measurement and analysis issues in the investigation of personality structure. In R. Hogan, J. Johnson, & S. Briggs (Eds.), *Handbook of personality psychology.* Orlando, FL: Academic Press.

White, M. J., & Gerstein, L. H. (1987). Helping: The influence of anticipated social sanctions and self-monitoring. *Journal of Personality, 55,* 41-54.

Wymer, W. E., & Penner, L. A. (1985). Moderator variables and different types of predictability: Do you have a match? *Journal of Personality and Social Psychology, 49,* 1002-1015.

Zuckerman, M., Kuhlman, D. M., Joireman, J., Teta, P., & Kraft, M. (1993). A comparison of three structural models of personality: The big three, the big five, and the alternative five. *Journal of Personality and Social Psychology, 65,* 757-768.

11

A Control Theory
Approach to Social Development

WILLIAM J. FROMING
RICHARD P. MOSER
PAULA MYCHACK
WILLIAM NASBY

William J. Froming is the Nancy Black Cozzens Professor of Psychology at the Pacific Graduate School of Psychology in Palo Alto, CA. His work has focused on the public and private aspects of the self and how these aspects develop. His current work is aimed at understanding how interpersonal behavior can be understood using the regulatory concepts of control theory and how males and females may regulate different aspects of the interpersonal domain.

Richard P. Moser is an advanced graduate student at the Pacific Graduate School of Psychology in Palo Alto, CA, working on a Ph.D. in clinical psychology. His research interests include the development of self-regulation, gender socialization, and the affective context of the family. Upon graduation, he hopes to work with adolescents and families and teach.

Paula Mychack is a doctoral candidate in clinical psychology at the Pacific Graduate School of Psychology in Palo Alto, CA. Her research interests include child and adult neuropsychology, with particular interest in emotional development.

William Nasby is the Newman Family Chair in Psychology at the Pacific Graduate School of Psychology in Palo Alto, CA. He received a Ph.D. from the Department of Psychology and Social Relations at Harvard University. His major research interests are in the area of cognitive approaches to personality processes, particularly the impact of mood states on social cognition and the relations between self-consciousness and schematic articulation of the self.

Prior to the late 1960s, psychological explanations of social development were based on a model that made a number of (implicit or explicit) assumptions: Causes and effects were distinct and separable; causes operated in a unidirectional fashion; and causes resided in the parents and effects resided in the child (e.g., traditional learning approaches). Bell's (1968) seminal article broke with the prior literature in arguing that the child was the source of many socialization practices in the family. In Bell's view, the child possesses a limited number of biological predispositions that dictate his or her needs and a limited response repertoire with which to meet them. This situation requires that the caretaker adjust his or her behavior to meet the needs of the child at least as much, if not more, than the reverse. This perspective added a second causal arrow, in the opposite direction, to the existing social development models.

More recently, models that take a systems approach to understanding human behavior have been developed. These approaches incorporate feedback about prior behavior that then partly guide future behavior. Such models add a further complication when discussing the direction of causal relationships, because now the effects of an organism's prior behavior can be the causes of future behavior. In developmental psychology, Bowlby (1969) was the first to develop a systems model using control theory. He argues that attachment behavior is best thought of as a control system operating internally to regulate behavior, thereby maintaining the child at some comfortable distance with respect to the attachment figure. He discusses the idea of both mother and child regulating their attachment behavior around some optimal level of physical proximity. Bell (Bell, 1971; Bell & Chapman, 1986) has also been at the forefront in delineating a control theory model. His model views the parent and child as forming a (second-order) system in which each member regulates his or her own and the other member's behavior. Using this regulatory process, the two parties reach some acceptable (that is not to imply desirable) framework within which the dyad functions.

We adopt the control theory perspective in this chapter. Further, we argue that the characteristics of the interregulatory process influence the development of the intra- or self-regulatory system. Current efforts in developmental psychology to conceptualize self-regulation (e.g., Eisenberg & Fabes, 1992; Ford & Lerner, 1992; Kopp, 1982), while alluding to the possible interpersonal origins of such mechanisms, have focused primarily on understanding how the internal functions of self-regulation are organized. We believe, as does Bowlby (1969, 1982), that control theory provides a theoretical framework powerful enough to handle both interpersonal and intrapersonal regulation. Developmental psychologists are moving in a similar direction. For example, Bretherton (1985) and Main, Kaplan, and Cassidy (1985), picking up on a theme of Bowlby's (1969, 1982), now view the attachment process as giving rise to mental models of the self and relationships, which, in turn, influence later interpersonal relationships. This type of thinking makes the bridges we hope to construct in this chapter—between developmental psychology and personality/social psychology—easier to build.

In personality/social psychology, thinking based on control theory ideas (e.g., negative feedback mechanisms) has increased greatly in the last 15 years. Negative feedback approaches have their origins in engineering and mathematics. The earliest known models date to the ancient Greeks (Richardson, 1992). However, recent treatments generally trace their roots to Wiener's (1948) *Cybernetics*. Carver and Scheier's (1981) control theory model of self-regulation, which builds on Power's (1973) work, has been the recent impetus to this kind of thinking; it has been applied to a wide range of topics (e.g., depression; Hyland, 1987). Although Carver and Scheier do not apply control theory to the interregulatory process, their model (and associated empirical findings) of self-regulation demonstrates the importance of several mechanisms. In addition to incorporating negative feedback (i.e., discrepancy reducing) loops into an account of adult self-regulation, they discuss how a hierarchical control system functions, something that others (e.g., Bell & Chapman, 1986; Bretherton, 1985) recognize as important but do not develop in any detail. Further, Carver and Scheier (1981) demonstrate the importance of self-attention for activating the self-regulatory process; the role of outcome expectancies in accounting for persistence in goal striving; and disengagement (physical or mental) as the result of negative outcome expectancies for goal attainment. These processes are extremely difficult to measure in infants, so it is understandable that such constructs have not received attention in the developmental literature. However, we believe it is important to draw on such notions as we extend the control theory model to a new problem: social development.

To do so, we have taken Carver and Scheier's (1981) basic self-regulatory model and assume, as they do, that a person is in one of two attentional states—self-focused or environmentally focused. Their work concerns the regulatory process the person engages in when self-focused (i.e., self-regulation). We develop the arguments for when the individual is attending to the environment and attempting to regulate the behavior of another person within it. The dyad is the unit of analysis, as each member is periodically self- and other-regulating. Because our interest is social development, the dyad is a parent and child. Before introducing these ideas, we first review current thinking on the problem.

STATEMENT OF PROBLEM

The central issue for social development is how to conceptualize the pressures acting on the individual to satisfy its needs, versus satisfying the needs of the social environment (not implying that the child's needs and those of the caretaker are always in conflict). Social psychologists have a long history of studying this balancing act, dating back to the classic conformity studies of Sherif (1935) and Asch (1956). The early studies, showing the influence of behavioristic thinking, tended to be external, functional, and descriptive (e.g., what size of group produces maximal conformity). The last 20 years have seen a shift in social psychology toward the study of the self and its employment as a psychological mediator of many effects (e.g., self-presentation, self-monitoring). This has led to the localizing of the individual/group question within the individual; group pressure needs to be perceived (at some level) by the individual to have an impact. In the self-attention literature, this distinction is referred to as the public self versus the private self. Given the nondevelopmental nature of the personality/social literature, little attention has been devoted to which (if either) self is acquired first. The general assumption is that both selves are developed and can be accessed in the normal adult. The self that is accessed and, therefore, operative, depends on which situational factors are salient.

Carver and Scheier (1981, 1987) argue for the importance of the public/private distinction with respect to self-regulation. The private self refers to the internal, unobservable aspects of the self (e.g., thoughts and feelings), whereas the public self refers to the external, observable aspects of the self (e.g., one's public impression). The position of these authors is that the public/private distinction is useful, but only at one level (the principle level) in their control hierarchy. Self-schemata are one example of a principle level control mechanism. Nasby (1989) shows the presence of both private and public self-schemata in adults. (For a contrasting view of the public/private distinction, see Wicklund & Gollwitzer, 1987.)

Most developmentalists adopt some form of public/private distinction. In the developmental literature the issue is usually cast as pitting external factors versus internal factors. Cialdini, Baumann, and Kenrick (1981), in the prosocial behavior domain, advocate a sequential view, wherein awareness of social norms precedes private acceptance and the time frame is measured in years. Kopp's (1982) view of the development of self-regulation also emphasizes the shift from external to internal sources of regulation, tracing a pattern wherein the infant initially reacts to the environment and later intentionally acts on the environment. Kopp sees self-regulation being achieved by 36+ months. Thus she also sees the development of self-regulation in external-to-internal terms, though the behaviors of interest to her as well as her time frame are much different than those of Cialdini et al. (1981). Kochanska (1993) employs an approach similar to Kopp's (1982) in her account of the development of conscience, with the child moving from compliance to external demands to the internalization of those demands.

Although we believe that Carver and Scheier's and the various developmental positions have merit, we argue that the public/private distinction is important throughout development and is a central mechanism by which social development occurs. Before developing our arguments, we will ground the discussion in the terminology and concepts of control theory. Because the majority of work in control theory has been in the context of self-regulation, we draw almost exclusively from that literature to illustrate what we mean.

THE CONTROL THEORY MODEL

To speak as if there is a single model on which all control theorists agree would be to neglect important differences among various authors. For now, however, the disagreements are less important than communicating the central concepts. Therefore, we focus on the elements shared by most models (for an overview of self-regulatory models, see Karoly, 1993).

The basic regulatory unit in control theory is the negative feedback loop. The feedback loop uses a standard as a guide to goal-directed behavior. The individual compares current behavior to the relevant standard by a "comparator," which serves a regulating function. When behavior is found to be within acceptable limits by the comparator, no corrective action need be taken. When behavior falls outside acceptable limits, an error signal is produced that alerts the organism to the discrepancy. The existence of a discrepancy generally triggers behavioral adjustments so as to reduce (one's perception of) the amount of discrepancy between the behavior and the standard. Because the feedback produces behavior that reduces discrepancies, it is called a negative feedback loop. Other people or events may intervene and reduce the discrepancy between current behavior and the standard for an individual, thereby making any corrective action unnecessary on his or her part (e.g., a boy is intercepted by his mother as he approaches a busy street before a passerby has time to act).

Building on this central notion, the origins of the specific reference values (i.e., standards) can be explained by positing that control loops are arranged hierarchically in increasing order of abstraction. The loops receive an input signal either from the environment (in the case of the superordinate loop) or from a superordinate loop (in the case of subordinate loops), which they then compare to their respective reference values. Input signals are always being monitored. In the case of no discrepancy between the current state and the reference value, nothing is done (i.e., current behavior is allowed to continue). When a discrepancy is detected, a signal indicating the presence of a discrepancy is transmitted. This signal sets/resets the reference criterion of the immediately subordinate loop, which, in turn, processes the signal to check for a discrepancy. This process is repeated until no discrepancy is found. Such a system is able to identify where in the system the discrepancy lies, and therefore where corrective action must take place. It is also able to link together (within one system) behaviors that range from the very concrete to the very abstract. (for more detail, see Carver & Scheier, 1981; Powers, 1973).

An example might be helpful in illustrating the hierarchical ideas. We argue elsewhere (Froming, Nasby, & McManus, 1994), along with Carver and Scheier (1981), that self-schemata (i.e., abstract representations of the self) can be thought of as standards in the control hierarchy (see Markus, 1977, for a further explanation of the self-schema notion). Self-schemata as standards are thought to exist at one of the highest levels of control, the principle level of control. Consider two individuals. Person 1 has a self-schema that, in part, consists of being a helpful person. Person 2 does not have the helpfulness component in her self-schema. According to control theory, in a context where help is needed (e.g., a foreign couple appears lost), the person with a helpfulness self-schema will be motivated to help. He sees himself as one who helps those in need (i.e., he possesses a specific standard) and not to help when there is a helping opportunity produces a discrepancy between the self-standard and the behavior. Person 1 is therefore motivated to help and thereby reduce the discrepancy. Person 2, lacking a prosocial self-schema, will experience no such discrepancy and, therefore, not offer to help.

Now, consider the hierarchical nature of the control system. Once a discrepancy is detected, behavior to reduce the discrepancy is needed. For example, Person 1 notices a couple looking around with confused looks on their faces and pointing in opposite directions on a downtown street corner. The presence of a (self) standard (i.e., I am the kind of person who helps people in need) and a discrepancy (i.e., these people need help and I am not helping) means that effective action must be taken to reduce the discrepancy. This is accomplished as one moves lower in the hierarchy. Entering the next lower level of control, the individual examines the situation for possible options. This is referred to as the program level of control and is characterized by "if-then" kinds of thinking (Carver & Scheier, 1981). For example, "If they are lost, then I'll provide directions. If they do not speak English, then I will find someone who speaks their language to provide directions. Or, because it is easier, if they have a paper and pencil, I'll draw a map." These possible strategies are assessed for their ability to meet the standard that derives from a higher level (e.g., why one should help strangers who are lost), but now the question is a matter of how to help, a less abstract proposition). Once a particular strategy is chosen, the component behaviors must be organized. This requires moving down one more level in the control hierarchy. (Powers [1973] calls this the relationship level, which is followed by the [lower] sequence level. Carver and Scheier [1981] think these two labels should be reversed.) If the chosen action is to draw a map, the individual must now decide the best map to draw (e.g., the shorter but more complicated route or the longer but easier route). The choice will be consistent with the original discrepancy and its reduction at the principle level, but now the choice of routes is meeting some lower-level standard (e.g., the simplest solution). When this decision is made, the next lower level is called upon. The necessary components, that is, the physical medium (paper and pencil), the required movements (arm and hand), the map's characteristics (orientation and level of detail), and the chosen plan (movement from present location to desired location) must be identified and organized vis-à-vis each other before commencing the map drawing act. Once the desired action sequence is organized, it must be executed (note that so far, no overt action has taken place—the hierarchy operates on information, not on the environment, at all but the lowest level). The pencil must be brought to the place on the paper where the map will begin. The chosen starting point on the piece of paper now represents the standard against which "behavior" at this level is compared. To get the pencil to the starting point, the individual must first be able to identify the pencil and the paper successfully (sensation level). Finally, the pencil must be grasped with the fingers and moved with the hand and arm through appropriate muscle commands so as to draw the map (intensity level). At last, the tourists have their map.

The point of this example is to show how the control hierarchy is thought to operate. In the execution of goal-oriented behaviors, higher loops "behave" by providing standards for lower-level loops until the lowest-level loop acts on the environment. The impact of the executed behavior is then perceived by the individual, and the success of the behavior in reducing the original discrepancy is assessed. If the discrepancy is reduced so as to fall within acceptable limits, then no further action need be taken. If the discrepancy continues to exist, the individual will continue to engage in the discrepancy-reducing behavior (as long as his or her outcome expectancies are positive). In the above example, we assumed that the highest level of control the individual was capable of was the principle level of control, and that this level was driving the behavior. This is not necessarily the case. Lower levels in the hierarchy can be accessed through other means and be temporarily in control for a period of time. An individual could simply trace over a pre-existing map, thereby drawing the map but operating from a lower level in the control hierarchy. At whatever level the control hierarchy is entered, the lower levels function in the manner described.

In discussing the hierarchy, we are making the whole action sequence appear very deliberate. When new behavior sequences are being acquired or old levels of control are being (re)organized in new ways, this may well be the case. As such, there may be "if-then" thinking at several levels of the hierarchy, although control theorists have not addressed the issue in any detail. For well-learned sequences, the levels of the hierarchy are thought to act simultaneously (not sequentially).

Developmentally, the hierarchy is organized in terms of the order in which the levels are acquired. The infant must first acquire the sensory motor skills to locate visually (in our example above) a pencil (or more appropriately, any desired object, e.g., a crayon), reach for it, and grasp it (Kopp, 1982). This process involves low-level control systems where a standard defines success (e.g., extending your arm, opening your fingers and picking up the object); feedback is important to reduce and correct initial errors. In the Powers (1973) hierarchy, the lowest-level control loop is called the intensity level, and would be the muscle tension used to grasp the object. With further development, the child comes to form a more abstract sensory motor concept of "graspable" objects, the pencil/crayon being one of the things that fits into the class of objects that get grasped (but not smiled at). This is the sensation level in the hierarchy. Because only the ends of the pencil/crayon can be used to write, simply grasping the object in any fashion is not adequate; a certain configuration (the next level of the hierarchy) of hand to pencil/crayon must be acquired. This configuration is different than the "hand to mouth" configuration. The acquisition process continues until, years later, the very abstract levels dictate that the (now) pencil should be picked up to draw a map for lost tourists, thereby reducing discrepancies at those higher levels.

Several other qualifiers are important to the model. First, expectancies are critical because an organism will not continue to attempt matching to standard *ad infinitum.* Carver and Scheier (1981) show that when expectancies for success are negative (e.g., My sense of direction is so poor that I am unable to draw a map), subjects disengage from pursuing the original goal, either literally or mentally. Second, the process of self-regulation appears (at least at higher levels) to require self-focused attention for it to be activated. Again, Carver and Scheier (1990b) argue that when the organism is not self-attentive, the mechanisms of the self-regulatory process are not regulating behavior to the same extent as when the organism is in a state of self-attention. Finally, we assume that the importance (to the individual) of the dimension(s) being monitored influence the likelihood of corrective action. Given finite resources and the existence of discrepancies in several domains, not all discrepancies can be responded to equally or, perhaps, adequately. Under these circumstances, the most important dimensions are expected to be the focus of corrective action, with less critical needs being put on hold until resources are sufficient for them to be attended to (Carver & Scheier, 1990). (We are not addressing how one arrives at the judgment as to what is important. We are simply trying to point out that not all discrepancies can be addressed simultaneously.)

In summary, the control theory perspective is built around the idea of negative feedback loops arranged hierarchically. Compared to some developmental theories (e.g., stage theories), control theory is a more fluid and flexible model in which control can reside at any level within the system at any point in time. It also is clearer in specifying the linkages from cognition to overt behavior. Finally, it is able to incorporate state factors into the operation of the system. Attentional mechanisms are critical for engaging the self-regulatory process, and persistence in goal pursuit is controlled by expectancies of success. (Although our focus so far has been to describe the basic constructs of control theory, we do not want to leave the reader with the impression that control theory does not address emotion. We take up this issue later.) With this model in mind, we will attempt to extend these notions into the interactive situation of a dyad.

THE GENERAL MODEL

Self- Versus Other-Regulation

Self-attention is an important factor in engaging the self-regulatory process. When attention is not self-focused, we assume that it is environmentally focused. This dichotomy has been at the root of the self-awareness literature since it was first proposed by Duval and Wicklund (1972). Up until that time, the self-focus part of the process had not been adequately conceptualized or operationalized. Utilizing Duval and Wicklund's proposal, research in the last 20 years has focused on the "self." Much has been learned about the process of self-regulation. We concentrate here on the environmental focus component and apply what we have learned about self-regulation to regulating the environment. Because we are interested in the social environment, the environment of concern is the dyadic "other." (At the same time, we do not mean to imply that regulation of the environment is independent of regulation of the self. Regulation of the environment is likely an indirect means of regulating the self, and thus all behavior is self-regulatory. For now we simply employ the self versus other regulatory terminology as an expository device.)

We believe that the same basic mechanisms that are proposed to underlie self-regulation underlie environmental regulation. Cognitive psychologists discuss how information is represented internally and how categories are formed (Fiske & Taylor, 1984; Matlin, 1983). Most agree that, as information gets processed, at least two qualities exist. First, cognitive categories have central or prototypic representatives that define the categories. (How this representation is arrived at is a source of controversy; Fiske & Taylor, 1984.) Second, new objects are assessed for their fit to the categories. We effectively have a categorical standard and a comparison process that detects the discrepancy between the standard and the object being analyzed. For our purposes, the category and the object can be concrete (e.g., "can this thing be eaten?") or abstract (e.g., "how should I interpret his remarks?"). In the social domain, work with the semantic differential (Osgood, Suci, & Tannebaum, 1957) documents that evaluation is the predominant response in assessing new stimuli and, reasoning backwards, a standard can be presumed to exist against which stimuli are compared. Assuming the observed stimulus is something we perceive to be (at least potentially) influenceable by our actions, and the stimulus is of sufficient importance to merit our efforts to engage in a regulatory process, we will attempt to influence or (partly) regulate the stimulus. In the context of social development, both the parent and child clearly fulfill these requirements; thus we see them engaging in a mutually regulating relationship.

A few developmentalists have proposed mechanisms that fall along the lines of our current thinking. Bell and Chapman (1986) write in detail about this type of regulation (i.e., regulation of the environment) in the context of the parent and child dyad. In their view, both members of the dyad have upper and lower limits of tolerance regarding the other's behavior (i.e., acceptable limits on deviations from the respective reference values), and each member acts to bring the dyad back into a comfortable state of equilibrium. In principle this can be accomplished by regulating the other member of the dyad or by regulating the self (though the child's capacity to do this effectively is more limited and, in the current context, this issue is of secondary importance).

On a more general level, Kopp (1982, 1989) discusses the development of self-regulation within the context of the parent-child dyad, viewing the parent as a "facilitator" of the child's development. Although Kopp discusses the cognitive skills necessary for the infant to engage in the stages of development preceding (and including) self-regulation, her discussion of the interactive process is on a very general level. Stern (1985) suggests that the caregiver is the "self-regulating other" for the infant in the first 6 months of life, insomuch as the infant is with another who regulates the infant's own self-experiences (primarily affective experiences). Youniss (1980) argues that individuals are always embedded in social systems in which they must accept some degree of regulation from others while simultaneously exercising influence on others. Finally, Maccoby (1992) discusses the concept of coregulation (which we discuss in more detail below). Thus the view that the parent-child relationship is a coregulating system is gaining acceptance, particularly during the last 10 years.

Regulation Within a Parent-Child Dyad

Employing control theory as a conceptual tool, we can now examine what happens in the parent-child dyad during socialization. We assume that the parent already possesses standards that are important in the regulation of his or her own behavior. The child, although possessing standards at lower levels of abstraction, lacks higher-level standards with which to self-regulate. Therefore the parent needs to transmit the standards to the child. For this process to be successful, we believe that a presentation of standards needs to exist at the appropriate level of abstraction by the adult, accompanied by proper feedback, so that the child can successfully acquire both the standards and the necessary (self-generated) feedback. The transmission of standards is accomplished by the adult functioning as an external regulatory mechanism: being attentive to the child's behavior; having a relevant standard; possessing the capacity to detect discrepancies from the standard; and providing corrective feedback to the child when a discrepancy arises or confirmation when the child is successful. In addition, the process must take place within an appropriate emotional climate for it to be successful. The standards and feedback conveyed through this interpersonal process are what the child will come to adopt in his or her self-regulatory processes. We discuss this process by first examining factors that influence the parent and then by looking at the role of the child.

PARENTAL FACTORS

Attentional Availability

Each member of the pair is capable of both self-regulation and other regulation (though the adult clearly has more levels of the control hierarchy at his or her disposal). The success of the interchange between adult and child first requires that each member of the dyad has attentional capacity available to devote to the enterprise. In the case of the parent, this situation cannot be considered a given. Parents who are struggling with their own self-regulation may have little time available to devote to the socialization process. For some parents, this inability to attend may be because they work long hours to generate sufficient income to live on. Working this hard may help meet the lower-level needs of the child (e.g., food and housing) but leave little time for addressing the higher-level needs because the parent is too exhausted to engage the child meaningfully. Other parents may work such long hours to succeed (due to the higher-level standards of their own self-schema) that they have little time left for the needs of the child. A third case may be where the parent is physically, but not attentionally, present. Self-absorbed or substance-abusing parents are functionally unavailable to engage in the regulatory process. Beyond their availability, parents faced with any of the problems described above are likely to set an emotional tone that is not conducive to the inculcation of standards. Home environments that are characterized by stress, tension, or fear are not conducive to the acquisition of new knowledge (Baumrind, 1989; Darling & Steinberg, 1993). From the opposite perspective, Dix (1991) discusses how positive and empathic emotions not only motivate attunement to children, but also facilitate responsiveness to the child's wants and needs.

Selection of Standards

If the parent is attentionally available to the child, the domains in which the parent will choose to regulate the child are likely to derive from the parent's own socialization. The parent's socialization history has presumably provided the parent with values that he or she considers important, and are therefore likely to serve as the focus of the socialization process. These parental standards may derive from the way in which the parent was socialized or, perhaps, in reaction to the way the parent was socialized. The "template" from which the parent is operating is tied to experiences he or she has had; thus we might expect some standards to show transgenerational transmission patterns within families; these patterns will show differences between families (Ricks, 1985).

Once the parent seeks to engage in the other-regulation process in a particular domain, he or she is faced with identifying where in the control hierarchy the child is currently operating so that the appropriate standard can be used to shape behavior. Although the topic of parental beliefs about children's capacities has started to receive some attention in developmental psychology, most of the work is in the area of intelligence, with relatively little work in the social behavior domain. It is our assumption that there are individual differences in parental ability to gauge the child's current capacities correctly. Some parents may underestimate the child's capacities, and thus not present the child with standards that promote growth. Other parents may overestimate the child's capacities and choose standards that are well beyond the child's capacities and thereby produce needless frustration as the child attempts to master (currently) impossible goals. Maccoby (1992) discusses the Vgotskian concept of "scaffolding," which involves the way parents arrange situations and event sequences so that the demand of a situation will be within the "zone of proximal development" for the child. Along with the Skinnerian concept of shaping, it captures the idea of successive approximations that parents engage in to raise the competence of the child in manageable steps.

Identifying the child's place in a control hierarchy is further complicated by the many meanings behaviors can have. A particular behavior may be perceived as belonging to one of a number of possible hierarchies. For example, if Pat is found dissecting a grasshopper, is Pat displaying a healthy curiosity in trying to understand living organisms, or is this behavior a harbinger of future aggressive tendencies? How Pat's parents interpret the meaning of this behavior will determine whether they encourage or discourage this act. This topic has been addressed by Vallacher and Wegner (1985) in terms of how an individual interprets his or her own behavior and thereby forms an identity. We believe it is important to study the same question from the perspective of an observer (i.e., a parent) making inferences about a child's behavior and what the observer believes the behavior means for the child's developing identity.

If a parent considers the regulation of the child in a given domain to be important and is able to identify accurately the child's place in the appropriate control hierarchy, there is still another issue to consider. Within a given level, the standard around which the regulatory mechanism will operate can vary in level of difficulty. The achievement motivation literature (Atkinson, 1964) teaches us about the importance of individual differences in the difficulty level of goals people set for themselves in the self-regulatory process. Some people choose exceedingly difficult goals, whereas others set very easy goals. Optimal goal achievement appears to be a function of setting moderately challenging goals that maximize achievement while minimizing failure. We assume that this model applies equally well to the process of setting goals for the child in the other-regulatory process.

The Nature of Feedback Provided by the Parent

With the parent and child engaged in the regulatory process and the standard chosen on the part of the parent, the nature of the feedback is the next aspect to focus on. Three characteristics are central. One is the parent's ability to detect deviations from chosen standards. This is partly a function of the parent's monitoring of the child's behavior and partly a function of the parent's knowledge base and beliefs in the relevant domain (i.e., what a parent believes to constitute a deviation). If a parent believes that a normal adolescent will go through times of rebellion, the occurrence of such behaviors does not necessarily require a response on the part of the parent. If rebellion is seen as the first sign of the adolescent's ultimate demise, then corrective feedback is deemed appropriate.

Assuming the presence of a perceived deviation from desired standards, some parents may have a very narrow tolerance level. In control theory terminology, the parental comparator is very sensitive to errors. This sensitivity to errors leads to continual intervention on the part of the parent. This can be both exhausting for the parent and intrusive for the child. The thermostat that is set to detect small variations in temperature will have the air conditioner/furnace continually turning on and off as it keeps the temperature in a narrow range. In a similar fashion, the parent who is (overly) sensitive to the child's deviations from the standard will be constantly monitoring the child and correcting the child's deviations. To the extent this level of intervention is unnecessary, it can produce deleterious effects. Lepper (1983) discusses the use of superfluous extrinsic constraints on children's behavior and the consequences. Borrowing from attribution theory, he argues that when pressure on the child is superfluous, the child will comply to the parent's standard but will attribute this compliance to the external pressure. In our view, this would facilitate the development of a public self, but not a private self. In contrast, more subtle parental control techniques will result in internalization of standards because the child will attribute compliant behavior to personal dispositions. At the other end of the continuum is the parent who requires large deviations before intervening. The outside observer may see such children as wild and unruly, because most behaviors are tolerated with little or no intervention on the part of the parent.

If the parent detects a deviation and decides to intervene, the nature of the intervention is important. As Baumrind (1989) has found, communication with the child about the nature of the transgression and the reasoning behind it leads to successful self-regulation. In this case, the parent has the child's long-term interests in mind, can empathize with the child, and may realize that the transgression was not committed intentionally but out of ignorance. Helping the child reframe the behavior in a new way can lead to effective self-regulation in the future. However, the parent may simply be acting out of his or her own interest, in which case suppression of the unacceptable behavior can be the goal. The intervention will then likely not involve anything more than simple unqualified power assertion. Although effective for immediate behavioral control, such assertion appears to undermine children's progress toward becoming independently prosocial and self-regulating (Lepper, 1983; Maccoby & Martin, 1983).

The effectiveness of parental feedback in regulating the child's behavior also must be gauged over time by the parent. Some new behaviors will not be acquired quickly, nor will many unacceptable behaviors be extinguished quickly. Thus the issue is how best to deliver feedback and how to know when to change strategies if the current approach is not successful in regulating the child's behavior. Initial strategies are likely to be based on some of the factors discussed above, as well as methods of regulation the parent was exposed to during socialization. Following Carver and Scheier's (1981) lead in the self-regulation literature, we expect unsuccessful regulation of the child to interrupt the parent's actions, leading him or her to consider the likelihood that the current strategy will be successful, continue with the current strategy if the parent's expectancies are sufficiently high, or switch to an alternative strategy if expectancies are negative. Finding successful strategies requires the parent to be both psychologically minded, so as to understand what is likely to work, and flexible, in order to find strategies that work.

It should be noted that parents can also choose a new level of standard for the regulatory process. If the parent decides that the child, for whatever reason, is unlikely to be able to use the initial standard as the basis for self-regulation, the parent may decrease (or increase) the level of the standard.

Although the parent is trying to regulate the child, the adult's temperamental characteristics are also important. The inability to regulate the child's behavior successfully can lead to frustration and/or anger. Perhaps this is due to the lack of psychological mindedness, or cognitive inflexibility, on the part of the parent, or to a low frustration tolerance. Dix (1991) found that negative emotions can lead to parenting that is hypersensitive, avoidant, punitive, overly controlling, and focused on the self rather than on the child's concerns. (He says that parental emotions, perhaps more than any other single variable, reflect the health of parent-child relationships.) We believe that negative emotions like anger and frustration will interfere with the higher, more abstract levels of other regulation as these emotions assume functional control of the parent's behavior (Carver & Scheier, 1981; Frijda, 1986). The parent is then more likely to resort to lower-level regulation such as getting the child to perform the desired behavior with threats, physical punishment, or bribery. Regulation is accomplished, but not in a way that facilitates the development of higher levels of self-regulation. Instead, the child is likely to abstain from certain behaviors when the parent is around but engage in them when they are not detectable (Lepper, 1983).

A second temperamental dimension on the part of the parent is also relevant. For the anxious or emotionally reactive parent, small deviations from standards on the child's part may be cause for alarm. Such an internal reaction may lead the parent to respond to very small deviations on the part of the child and to be constantly intervening. The result may be to transmit a style of self-regulation that involves (overly) strict adherence to standards by the child.

Characteristics of the Process

Although we have tried to articulate the nuances of the other regulatory process from the parental perspective, we also need to think more broadly about the process over time. Higgins (1989) addresses the issue in his discussion of self-other contingency knowledge. He points out that this knowledge base (the extraction of standards from the regulatory process) is strengthened by a number of factors. The first element is frequency. As the process is repeated again and again, the knowledge is better learned. Consistency, the second aspect, allows the child to experience the same standard and feedback over time, thereby strengthening his or her understanding. Consistency appears to be related to the degree to which the parent is committed to the parental role. Increasingly, researchers are finding that some parents are more fully committed to their parenting role than others, and that the degree of commitment may be even more important than the style with which that commitment is expressed (Maccoby, 1992). The third factor is clarity. Because behavioral interchanges can be fraught with many meanings, the more the parent can highlight the critical issue and bring the child's attention to it, the more likely the child is to attend to the relevant aspects of the situation. Higgins's fourth factor, significance, is already presumed in our discussion, as we have been focusing on the parent-child relationship. Given the overall significance of this relationship, a parent often communicates the significance of a particular standard through affective intensity. Maccoby and Martin (1983) hypothesize that parents' own affective reactions, rather than the cognitive content of their communications, may have the greatest impact on their children's affective reactions, particularly in early childhood. For example, Zahn-Waxler, Radke-Yarrow, and King (1979) found, with 2-year-olds, that the degree of affective intensity accompanying the mothers' verbal reactions to the children's distress-producing behavior, rather than solely the use of explanations per se, influenced the amount of sympathetic arousal and helpful action the children displayed over other people's distress. In all of these points, the central issue is how to facilitate the child's extraction of standards that can then be used in the self-regulatory process.

CHILD FACTORS

Turning to the other half of the dyad, the infant/child must be able to engage in the dyadic process for it to work. First we focus on the infant/child as the receiver of regulatory signals from the parent. Then we consider the infant/child's role as an initiator in the dyad.

If the regulatory process between parent and child is essential, we would expect to find the neonate possessing the necessary skills to engage in the process (at least in some rudimentary fashion). This appears to be the case. Newborns have both the reflexes and the psychological readiness that equip them for the rapid establishment of interactive behavior patterns with parents. One of the best examples of this is the direction of each partner's visual attention during interaction, that is, mutual gazing. As Maccoby and Martin (1983) discuss, studies of mutual gazing have shown that one person's gaze attracts the other person's eyes and initiates a mutuality (reciprocity) that then spreads to other behaviors (e.g., vocalizing, touching).

The neonate attends to the parent like few other stimuli and can respond to the parent's facial displays (e.g., sticking out his or her tongue) almost from birth (Meltzoff & Moore, 1977), showing acute sensitivity to signals from the primary socializing agent. Indeed, studies in social referencing have repeatedly shown that infants as young as 10 months can make deliberate and specific use of another person's judgment to form their own appraisal of a situation (Emde, 1992). Thus biological and social elements interact on the part of both parties from the beginning of the parent-child relationship, allowing the parent and child to engage in the interregulatory process.

A second form of evidence we should expect is the individual differences in infants and children. If the basic interactive mechanisms have been evolutionarily selected for, then we should expect some variation on these dimensions (to give the evolutionary selection process flexibility). These various dimensions, aspects of temperament, have received considerable interest in the last 20 years. Although there is no clear consensus as to the exact number, we choose several to illustrate how we believe these dimensions can add to our understanding of the socialization process. Before discussing them, we introduce the idea that, from our perspective, aspects of temperament are themselves (low-level) control mechanisms. They can be viewed as defining "comfort" standards for the individual. Deviations in either direction from these standards may produce discomfort that then motivates the individual to engage in regulation of the environment in order to return the individual to the desired state. Sociability is an aspect of temperament with a very strong biological component (Buss & Plomin, 1984). We see this as a measure of the child's predisposition to orient to the parent-child dyad and other social situations where social regulation might occur. Although all children orient to their parents, by necessity if for no other reason, some thrive on social interaction while others simply tolerate it (e.g., Schaffer & Emerson, 1964). The more sociable the child, the more attentive he or she will be to the parent and the more the feedback will be meaningful. Other things being equal, we expect the dyadic process to be more successful with a more sociable child because the less sociable child will be harder to engage in the basic process. At the same time, the child who is predominantly socially (and externally) oriented may not consolidate the information into his or her private self and, thereby, not evolve more abstract standards to use for self-regulation. Extremes of sociability (in either direction) are likely to produce deleterious results.

N. Eisenberg (personal communication, 1994) suggests an alternative view of sociability wherein the parent-child dyad, perhaps because of its centrality to the socialization process, should be less likely to show much in the way of individual differences in sociability. She argues that it is with other people (i.e., nonparents) that differences in sociability will emerge and lead to differences in dyadic interactions. We find the point to be an interesting one that deserves empirical attention. In any case, the fact that sociability is so essential that it has been selected for in evolution strengthens the argument that the infant is born prepared to interregulate.

A second aspect of temperament, emotionality, is a dimension that captures both the threshold and the intensity of an individual's reactions to positive and negative stimuli (Buss & Plomin, 1984; Eisenberg & Fabes, 1992). Emotionality is important as a moderator of the child's responsiveness to feedback. Although it is relevant to all dyadic interactions, we focus on parental feedback. As Kochanska (1993) discusses, the sensitivity of the child is an important factor in the development of self-regulatory mechanisms. We see this as operating in at least two ways. The first is in terms of the general emotional climate, or parenting style (Darling & Steinberg, 1993), in which the parent-child dyad functions. As studies have repeatedly shown (for reviews see, e.g., Baumrind, 1989; Dix, 1991; Maccoby & Martin, 1983), the emotional tone of the family is the background against which specific socialization takes place. A child prone to distress is more likely to have a hard time focusing in on the specifics of the dyadic process because of excess arousal. In addition, the arousal may interfere with the child's ability to engage in the necessary cognitive work to be able to abstract the relevant standards. The affectively unresponsive child may not respond to appropriate emotional cues in the dyad that are sources of important information. The second role that emotionality plays may directly alter the dyadic process. The emotionally responsive child may require little feedback in the dyadic interaction because the arousal component is readily activated. A light rebuke may be so salient that additional feedback is not needed. However, the same child is more easily overwhelmed and distressed, which can produce negative side effects. Kochanska (1993) concurs with this idea in stating that children who have low thresholds for anxiety will develop conscience with parents who use subtle disciplinary techniques, but may become overwhelmed with parents who use more powerful forms of control. In contrast, the nonresponsive child may require many repetitions and the parent may or may not have the patience for such repetition (a potential problem for the consistency factor).

Other aspects of temperament also have been discussed in the literature (e.g., Kochanska, 1993). Given the diversity of viewpoints among researchers on the definition and number of temperaments (see Goldsmith et al., 1987) we are not able to explore the topic in the detail it deserves. The point we wish to make is that several of the major temperamental dimensions are directly relevant to the child's successful participation in the dyadic regulatory process. These dimensions are all the child has to start the process. It is our belief that problems that are severe enough to interfere with the interregulatory process will hinder the acquisition of the lower levels of the control hierarchy. This will leave the child with more to overcome as he or she attempts to acquire higher-level standards. To the extent the interregulatory process is unsuccessful, we expect the child to manifest problems in self-regulation. An analysis, albeit post hoc, of self-regulatory problems should provide information as to the problems encountered in the earlier self-other regulatory dyad.

HOW THE SYSTEM FUNCTIONS

So far we have focused on each member of the dyad while holding the other member constant. Obviously the process is a dynamic one. At a given moment each member of the dyad can be in a state of self-directed attention or other-directed attention. The regulatory process engaged in (self versus other) will depend on the direction of attention. We believe all combinations are possible. An important question then is what controls the attentional focus in the dyad?

It has always been assumed (e.g., Duval & Wicklund, 1972) that attention shifts back and forth between the self and the environment rapidly and repeatedly in the course of normal events. What controls this process is not well known. It is our assumption that conscious attention is a problem-solving mechanism. Duval and Wicklund (1972) assume that, when attention is self-focused, a discrepancy between one's ideal self and one's real self is the focus of attention (Higgins, 1989). The goal is then to reduce the discrepancy (i.e., fix the problem). The models of self-regulation proposed since then have focused on the presence of discrepancies between standards and actual behavior to examine the self-regulatory mechanisms in action. Extrapolating from this, we might hypothesize that when problems arise in the dyadic context, attention will flow to the likely source of the problem. In the parent-child situation, this might be assumed (perhaps incorrectly) by the participants to be the child. Indeed, (at least) young children typically see their parents as all knowing and all powerful and, in terms of a control hierarchy, parents have attained a higher level of functioning and presumably are operating from a higher level in the hierarchy. That leaves the child receiving feedback based on a set of concepts he or she does not fully understand (which may be interpreted by the child as a problem with him or her). We are suggesting that the regulatory interchange between parent and child is biased in favor of the parent focusing on the child and therefore doing more other-regulating, and the child focusing on the self and thus self-regulating (or attempting to). In addition, the type of regulation is likely to be different because the adult has access to higher-order, intentional regulatory mechanisms, whereas the child is limited to lower-level regulating. The parent will be seen as more knowing and powerful and, when a problem arises, the source of the problem is likely to be localized in the child.

Once the regulatory mechanisms are engaged, the standards employed by each member are likely to differ. According to control theory, when the child is self-focused he or she will function at the highest level he or she is capable of or at a lower level if it is functionally superordinate at that point in time. The adult who is regulating the child's behavior (i.e., is other-focused) can employ a wider range of standards because he or she can interpret the current situation at higher levels of abstraction than the child. If the current situation makes low-level demands, the child's self-regulatory behavior may be judged as adequate by the adult and no intervention is needed. In control theory terms, the standard the adult judges to be appropriate for the given context is being met by the child, and no discrepancy exists. Therefore, no action need be taken to bring the child's behavior in line with the standard. This situation corresponds to Maccoby's (1984) coregulation concept. She suggests that coregulation occurs during middle childhood, at which time parents continue to exercise general supervisory control while children begin to exercise moment-to-moment self-regulation. We view this as the parent operating at a higher level of abstraction in his or her control hierarchy vis-à-vis the child. With the child having mastered lower levels of control, the parent need no longer intervene on those levels (as long as things are proceeding smoothly). This allows the parent to give the child more freedom (i.e., for the parent to be less intrusive) while, at the same time, to monitor progress toward more abstract goals (e.g., the child becoming a caring person). When the situation makes demands beyond the child's current capabilities, the child's self-regulatory skills will be inadequate. At this point, the adult's expectancies are likely to play a role much as they do in Carver and Scheier's model of self-regulation. If the parent judges the child to be incapable of self-regulation in the given context, the adult may remove the child from that context and place him or her in a more appropriate setting. Alternatively, if the parent believes that the child may be able to handle the situation (i.e., has somewhat favorable expectancies), he or she may try to teach the child how to cope with the situation. This intervention may be in one of two forms. It may represent a redeployment of self-regulatory skills the child already possesses, or the parent may attempt to employ a standard slightly beyond the child's current capabilities. The child is then given feedback so as to meet the parental standard. However, the child's capacity to enact the behavior is limited to the times when external guidance is present because, as of yet, the child does not have the necessary cognitive skills (Kopp, 1982) to adopt the standard for self-regulation purposes.

THE ROLE OF EMOTION IN THE REGULATORY PROCESS

We have made suggestions as to how emotion may play a part in the regulatory process. Although we are not able to address the role of emotion in any detail here, we do want to note that the regulatory process has emotional consequences and, likewise, emotions influence the regulatory process. We believe, in particular, that a dyad member's inability to regulate the other's behavior may follow the pattern first outlined by Wortman and Brehm (1975). Initially there is a rise in the attempts to regulate the other's behavior, accompanied by feelings of frustration and hostility. The continued inability to regulate the other's behavior eventually leads to disengagement and emotional distancing. Field et al.'s (1985) work with infants whose mothers suffered from postpartum depression exemplifies this process. The infants initially attempted to engage the mother in social interaction. When this failed, the infant escalated attempts. Continued failure eventually led to disengagement by the infant.

With the failure of the initial attempts to regulate the other's behavior, the initiating individual (be it child or parent) may seek alternative methods of regulation. The negative emotions that arise as a result of the initial failures may interfere with cognitive processing, and thereby lead the individual to resort to lower, more primitive forms of regulation. The child, for example, might start crying (instead of asking) in order to get the adult to respond, and the adult may threaten the child with physical force (instead of reasoning) to obtain compliance. Carver and Scheier (1981) discuss this scenario as one involving an interruption of the usual control system, with functional control being assumed by lower levels of the control hierarchy. Certainly high levels of emotion are incompatible with thoughtful consideration of how best to obtain the cooperation of the other when regulation is the goal. Even moderate levels of emotion have been shown to increase attention directed toward the self (Wood, Saltzberg, & Goldsamt, 1990)—and therefore away from the other member of the dyad. Thus it appears that both intraregulatory and interregulatory control processes are influenced by the onset (and offset) of emotion.

Work is also proceeding on the idea that the goal of the regulatory process may (sometimes) be the regulation of the other person's emotional state rather than behavior (e.g., Kopp, 1989). In this case, the regulatory process can take several forms. It may focus on the source of the problem that led to the emotion (e.g., failure to achieve a particular goal) and help the person strategize about alternatives when the current emotional state is interfering with his or her problem-solving capacities. Alternatively, the regulatory process may focus on the emotion itself. In this case there may be attempts to distract the person from the current negative mood or induce an incompatible positive mood that neutralizes the negative mood. Interest in this area is increasing (Eisenberg & Fabes, 1992; Garber & Dodge, 1991; Kopp, 1989).

The socialization literature (e.g., Darling & Steinberg, 1993) consistently indicates that the emotional tone of the family environment is important for the transmission of parental standards to the child. For example, Baumrind's (1989) "authoritative" parenting style, partly defined by parental warmth and control, is associated with positive outcomes in children (successful self-regulation). Other parental styles are less successful, either because they lack clear standards (Baumrind's "permissive" style) or because of the presence of negative mood in the family environment (Baumrind's "authoritarian" style). In the case of the authoritarian style, the presence of negative mood in the dyadic environment could alter the interregulatory process in either of the two ways outlined above (i.e., emotion interfering with higher level cognitive processing or the regulation of emotion, rather than the learning of appropriate standards, becoming the focus of the dyadic interaction).

Finally, emotion can result from the way in which the regulatory process is functioning. Carver and Scheier (1990a, 1990b; Scheier & Carver, 1988) have begun to consider affect from this perspective, emphasizing the intra-organismic signal functions of affect. More specifically, emotions represent the output of a metamonitoring system that "senses" the perceived rate of progress in the control system that regulates behavior. At this point, Carver and Scheier's work is important primarily because it demonstrates that a control theory perspective can readily incorporate affect.

However, as important as the intraorganismic signal functions of affect may be to the regulation of behavior, there is more to affect that must be considered, especially in the context of socialization and dyadic or inter-systems regulation. For example, many developmentalists, especially those who investigate temperament (e.g., Derryberry & Rothbart, 1984, 1988), emphasize the processes whereby children regulate affect through behavioral and cognitive means. These processes can be understood in terms of control theory. For example, affect can be seen as perceptual input to the negative feedback loop. This input can then be compared to the affective standard. If the perceptual input falls within acceptable levels, nothing need be done. However, input outside acceptable limits triggers corrective action. Under these circumstances, we would expect the affective standards to assume superordinate control, setting the reference criteria of lower-order behavioral and cognitive loops. In this view, affect constitutes one form of perceptual input to the individual, but we see no need to construe it in other than basic control theory terms.

In addition, many theories of emotion (Frijda, 1986; Oatley 1992) have also long recognized the interorganismic signal functions of affect—a class of functions that developmental psychologists (e.g., Bowlby, 1969; Feinman, 1992) have well appreciated. Oatley (1992) argues that, "when communicated between people, emotions have the quality of setting the highest level goal of the interaction to be friendly or hostile, dominant or submissive, and so on" (p. 179). The same communicative function could be no less served in the interactions between a parent and a child.

Ultimately, our approach to socialization must incorporate affect more explicitly and systematically. We anticipate that the extensive theorizing and research that have already considered affective regulation from a developmental perspective (e.g., Eisenberg & Fabes, 1992; Garber & Dodge, 1991; Kopp, 1989) will provide the necessary means to flesh out our preliminary account of dyadic interregulation. The point we wish to make is that emotion is closely linked to the self- and other-regulatory process. Further, we believe that a control theory analysis is a fruitful way to tease apart and articulate what has, up to now, been a number of different phenomena subsumed under the broad heading of "emotion."

RELATED ISSUES AND FUTURE DIRECTIONS

We have covered much ground in this chapter. Primarily we argue for the usefulness of a control theory approach to social development. We realize that many questions remain unanswered. For example, what are the boundary conditions for the regulatory process we have described? Are members of the parent-child dyad ever not engaging in the regulatory process? Although we have suggested some such conditions (e.g., being attentionally unavailable), if one member of the dyad becomes too deviant, the other member's attention may, in fact, be drawn to him or her. Finally, how does control theory relate to other theories of social development? Due to the complexity of these issues, we cannot reasonably address them in this chapter. Our goal has been to show that control theory has the explanatory power to address both the self- and other-regulatory process, thereby shedding new light on social development. If we have been persuasive, then perhaps others will join in as we extend control theory to these related topics.

REFERENCES

Asch, S. E. (1956). Studies of independence and conformity: A minority of one against a unanimous majority. *Psychological Monographs, 70*(9), 416.

Atkinson, J. W. (1964). *An introduction to motivation.* Princeton NJ: Van Nostrand Reinhold.

Baumrind, D. (1989). Rearing competent children. In W. Damon (Ed.), *Child development today and tomorrow* (pp. 349-378). San Francisco: Jossey-Bass.

Bell, R. Q. (1968). A reinterpretation of the direction of effects in studies of socialization. *Psychological Review, 75,* 81-95.

Bell, R. Q. (1971). Stimulus control of parent or caretaker behavior by offspring. *Developmental Psychology, 4,* 63-72.

Bell, R. Q., & Chapman, M. (1986). Child effects in studies using experimental or brief longitudinal approaches to socialization. *Developmental Psychology, 22,* 595-603.

Bowlby, J. (1969). *Attachment and loss: Vol. I. Attachment.* New York: Basic Books.

Bowlby, J. (1982). *Attachment and loss: Vol. I. Attachment* (2nd ed.). New York: Basic Books.

Bretherton, I. (1985). Attachment theory: Retrospect and prospect. In I. Bretherton & E. Walters (Eds.), Growing points in attachment theory and research, *Monographs of the Society for Research in Child Development, 50,* 3-35.

Buss, A. H., & Plomin, R. (1984). *Temperament: Early developing personality traits.* Hillsdale, NJ: Erlbaum.

Carver, C. S., & Scheier, M. F. (1981). *Attention and self regulation: A control theory approach to human behavior.* New York: Springer-Verlag.

Carver, C. S., & Scheier, M. F. (1987). The blind men and the elephant: Selective examination of the public private literature gives rise to a faulty perception. *Journal of Personality, 55*(3), 525-541.

Carver, C. S., & Scheier, M. F. (1990a). Origins and functions of positive and negative affect: A control process view. *Psychological Review, 97,* 19-35.

Carver, C. S., & Scheier, M. F. (1990b). Principles of self regulation: Action and emotion. In E. T. Higgins & R. M. Sorrentino (Eds.), *Handbook of motivation and cognition: Vol. 2* (pp. 3-52). New York: Guilford.

Cialdini, R. B., Baumann, D. J., & Kenrick, D. T. (1981). Insights from sadness: A three step model of the development of altruism as hedonism. *Developmental Review, 1,* 207-223.

Darling, N., & Steinberg, L. (1993). Parenting style as context: An integrative model. *Psychological Bulletin, 113,* 487-496.

Derryberry, D., & Rothbart, M. K. (1984). Emotion, attention, and temperament. In C. E. Izard, J. Kagan, & R. Zajonc (Eds.), *Emotion, cognition, and behavior* (pp. 132-166). New York: Cambridge University Press.

Derryberry, D., & Rothbart, M. K. (1988). Arousal, affect, and attention. *Journal of Personality and Social Psychology, 55,* 958-966.

Dix, T. (1991). The affective organization of parenting: Adaptive and maladaptive processes. *Psychological Bulletin, 110,* 3-25.

Duval, S., & Wicklund, R. A. (1972). *A theory of objective self awareness.* New York: Academic Press.

Eisenberg, N., & Fabes, R. A. (1992). Emotion, regulation, and the development of social competence. In M. S. Clark (Ed.), *Review of personality and social psychology: Vol. 14* (pp. 119-150). Newbury Park, CA: Sage.

Emde, R. N. (1992). Social referencing research: Uncertainty, self, and the search for meaning. In S. Feinman (Ed.), *Social referencing and the social construction of reality in infancy* (pp. 79-94). New York: Plenum.

Feinman, S. (Ed.). (1992). *Social referencing and the social construction of reality in infancy.* New York: Plenum.

Field, T. M., Sandberg, D., Garcia, R., Vega Lahr, N., Goldstein, S., & Guy, L. (1985). Prenatal problems, postpartum depression, and early mother infant interactions. *Developmental Psychology, 12,* 1152-1156.

Fiske, S. T., & Taylor, S. E. (1984). *Social cognition.* New York: Random House.

Ford, D. H., & Lerner, R. M. (1992). *Developmental systems theory: An integrative approach.* Newbury Park, CA: Sage.

Frijda, N. H. (1986). *The emotions.* New York: Cambridge University Press.

Froming, W. J., Nasby, W., & McManus, J. (1994). Prosocial self schemata, self-awareness, and children's prosocial behavior. Manuscript under review.

Garber, J., & Dodge, K. A. (Eds.). (1991). *The development of emotion regulation and dysregulation.* New York: Cambridge University Press.

Goldsmith, H., Buss, A. H., Plomin, R., Rothbart, M. K., Thomas, A., Chess, S., Hinde, R. A., & McCall, R. B. (1987). Roundtable: What is temperament? Four approaches. *Child Development, 58,* 505-529.

Higgins, E. T. (1989). Continuities and discontinuities in self regulatory and self evaluative processes: A developmental theory relating self and affect. *Journal of Personality, 57,* 407-444.

Hyland, M. E. (1987). Control theory interpretation of psychological mechanisms of depression: Comparison and integration of several theories. *Psychological Bulletin, 102,* 109-121.

Karoly, P. (1993). Mechanisms of self regulation: A systems view. *Annual Review of Psychology, 44,* 23-52.

Kochanska, G. (1993). Toward a synthesis of parental socialization and child temperament in early development of conscience. *Child Development, 64,* 325-347.

Kopp, C. B. (1982). Antecedents of self regulation: A developmental perspective. *Developmental Psychology, 18,* 199-214.

Kopp, C. B. (1989). Regulation of distress and negative emotions: A developmental view. *Developmental Psychology, 25,* 343-354.

Lepper, M. R. (1983). Social control processes and the internalization of social values: An attributional perspective. In E. T. Higgins, D. N. Ruble, & W. W. Hartup (Eds.), *Social cognition and social development: A sociocultural perspective* (pp. 294-330). Cambridge, UK: Cambridge University Press.

Maccoby, E. E. (1984). Middle childhood in the context of the family. In W. A. Collins (Ed.), *Development during middle childhood: The years from six to twelve* (pp. 184-239). Washington, DC: National Academy Press.

Maccoby, E. E. (1992). The role of parents in the socialization of children: An historical overview. *Developmental Psychology, 28,* 1006-1017.

Maccoby, E. E., & Martin, J. A. (1983). Socialization in the context of the family: Parent child interaction. In E. M. Hetherington (Ed.), *Mussen manual of child psychology: Vol. 4* (4th ed., pp. 1-102). New York: John Wiley.

Main, M., Kaplan, N., & Cassidy, J. (1985). Security in infancy, childhood, and adulthood: A move to the level of representation. In I. Bretherton & E. Walters (Eds.), Growing points in attachment theory and research, *Monographs of the Society for Research in Child Development, 50,* 66-104.

Markus, H. (1977). Self schemata and processing information about the self. *Journal of Personality and Social Psychology, 35,* 63-78.

Matlin, M. (1983). *Cognition.* New York: CBS College Publishing.

Meltzoff, A. N., & Moore, M. K. (1977). Imitation of facial and manual gestures by human neonates. *Science, 198,* 75-78.

Nasby, W. (1989). Private and public self consciousness and articulation of the self schema. *Journal of Personality and Social Psychology, 56,* 950-957.

Oatley, K. (1992). *Best laid schemes: The psychology of emotions.* New York: Cambridge University Press.

Osgood, C. E., Suci, G. J., & Tannenbaum, P. H. (1957). *The measurement of meaning.* Urbana: University of Illinois Press.

Powers, W. T. (1973). *Behavior: The control of perception.* Chicago: Aldine.

Richardson, G. P. (1992). *Feedback thought in social science and systems theory.* Philadelphia: University of Pennsylvania Press.

Ricks, M. H. (1985). The social transmission of parental behavior: Attachment across generations. In I. Bretherton & E. Walters (Eds.), Growing points in attachment theory and research, *Monographs of the Society for Research in Child Development, 50,* 211-230.

Schaffer, H. R., & Emerson, P. E. (1964). Patterns of response to physical contact in early human development. *Journal of Child Psychology and Psychiatry, 5,* 1-13.

Scheier, M. F., & Carver, C. S. (1988). A model of behavioral self regulation: Translating intention into action. In L. Berkowitz (Ed.), *Advances in experimental social psychology: Vol. 21* (pp. 303-346). New York: Academic Press.

Sherif, M. (1935). A study of some social factors in perception. *Archives of Psychology, 27,* 1-60.

Stern, D. (1985). *The interpersonal world of the infant.* New York: Basic Books.

Vallacher, R. R., & Wegner, D. M. (1985). *A theory of action identification.* Hillsdale, NJ: Erlbaum.

Wicklund, R. A., & Gollwitzer, P. M. (1987). The fallacy of the private public self focus distinction. *Journal of Personality, 55*(3), 491-523.

Wiener, N. (1948). *Cybernetics.* New York: John Wiley.

Wood, J. V., Saltzberg, J. A., & Goldsamt, L. A. (1990). Does affect induce self focused attention? *Journal of Personality and Social Psychology, 58,* 899-908.

Wortman, C. B., & Brehm, J. W. (1975). Responses to uncontrollable outcomes: An integration of reactance theory and the learned helplessness model. In L. Berkowitz (Ed.), *Advances in experimental social psychology: Vol. 8* (pp. 277-336). New York: Academic Press.

Youniss, J. (1980). *Parents and peers in social development: A Sullivan-Piaget perspective.* Chicago: University of Chicago Press.

Zahn-Waxler, C., Radke Yarrow, M., & King, R. A. (1979). Child rearing and children's prosocial initiations toward victims of distress. *Child Development, 50,* 319-330.